Y0-DBX-409

MEMORIES OF A GIANT

EULOGIES IN MEMORY OF

RABBI DR. JOSEPH B. SOLOVEITCHIK *zt"l*

**The
Rabbi Soloveitchik
Library**

Series Editor: Rabbi Jacob J. Schacter

מעיין זכרונות

MEMORIES OF A GIANT

EULOGIES IN MEMORY OF

RABBI DR. JOSEPH B. SOLOVEITCHIK *zt"l*

edited by Michael A. Bierman

The Rabbi
Joseph B. Soloveitchik
Institute

URIM PUBLICATIONS
Jerusalem • New York

Memories of a Giant: Eulogies in Memory of Rabbi Dr. Joseph B. Soloveitchik *zt"l*
Edited by Michael A. Bierman

The Rabbi Soloveitchik Library – Volume 1
Series editor: Rabbi Dr. Jacob J. Schacter

Published with the assistance of the
Jennifer and Scott Tobin Jewish Educational Publication Fund.

A list of original publications and permissions for reproduction of some of these eulogies may be found in the back of this book.

 Printed at Hemed Press, Israel.

First Edition
ISBN 965-7108-50-0

Urim Publications, P.O. Box 52287, Jerusalem 91521 Israel

The Rabbi Joseph B. Soloveitchik Institute
34 Philbrick Road, Brookline MA 02445 U.S.A.
www.rav.org

Lambda Publishers Inc.
3709 13th Avenue Brooklyn, New York 11218 U.S.A.
Tel: 718-972-5449 Fax: 718-972-6307
Email: mh@ejudaica.com

www.UrimPublications.com

דברי חכמים בנחת נשמעים

In tribute to Rabbi Jacob J. Schacter

With profound respect, admiration and gratitude

Debra and David Schiff

❧

Lovingly dedicated to the memory of

Abraham and Sylvia Wintman

אברהם צבי בן יצחק חיים ע״ה, שרה בלומא בת קלמן מרדכי הכהן ע״ה

Dedicated and devoted friends of the Rav

By their children Kenny Wintman and Sandy and Gary Welkes

❧

In honor of our parents

Muriel and Scotty Marcus and Muriel and Bernard Gopin

עד מאה ועשרים שנה

Ellen and Heshy Marcus

❧

In loving memory of our wife, mother and grandmother

Lily Trauring ליבקא בת חיים ע״ה

תנו לה מפרי ידיה ויהללוה בשערים מעשיה

Sharon and Charles Trauring, Audrey and Simi Chavel and Philip Trauring,

Jack and Milton Trauring, Vivian and Larry Creizman

❧

In honor of our parents

Estee and Nysen Mael

יושר הורי זכרה להאחיל

Fishel and Elaine Mael, Audrey and David Mael, Lynn and Joel Mael

Dedicated to the Memory

of

Freda bas Asher *a"h*

My beloved grandmother
She taught me Yiddish so she could share her wonderful stories about life in the *shtetl* and her years of outwitting the Nazis. She thus lovingly taught me to appreciate the mosaic of our Jewish tradition.

and
Ephriam Fishel ben Tzvi Yoel Freschl *z"l*

My beloved Uncle Kurt
who constantly taught our family, by his every act, lessons of *chesed*, *anivut* and *yirat Shamayim.*

Michael Bierman

RABBI DR. JOSEPH B. SOLOVEITCHIK zt"l

1903–1993

The arrival of the Rov over sixty years ago (at the end of 1932) [is to be viewed] as a turning point in the spiritual destiny of American Jewry.... He emerged as the *hakham hamasorah* par excellence. As was the case with previous *hakhmei hamasorah* who appeared at critical moments when people were engulfed by despondency and a sense of futility, the Rov, whose reputation as a youthful prodigy was widespread, emerged on the stage of history and was destined to bring brilliant, beautiful Torah to the twentieth century from his base in Boston and New York. We should not underestimate how the impact of one great *hakham*; one towering scholar – whose grasp of the *masorah* is majestic and magisterial, whose teaching is original and insightful, whose influence is profound and pervasive – is indeed able to change the entire landscape. The Rov was such a *hakham hamasorah*. His decisive contribution was quantitative and qualitative: he disseminated Torah and enhanced *kevod haTorah*. His tireless, vigorous, imaginative teaching, on so many different levels, suffused the *masorah* with charm and fascination, revealed its profundities and thereby buoyed the confidence of so many individuals....

Rabbi Dr. Yitzchak Twersky *zt"l*

CONTENTS

CONTENTS

FOREWORD

There was only one person capable of appropriately eulogizing Rabbi Joseph B. Soloveitchik, and that was Rabbi Soloveitchik himself. In a number of *hespedim* he delivered over the course of some three decades, this master *maspid* modeled for his listeners and readers what a genuine eulogy needs to be.[1] On one occasion he explicitly and dramatically delineated the elements that a eulogy must contain: both emotional and intellectual, "clear understanding" and "emotional impression," "honest true recognition" and "heart-warming feelings."[2] Only Rabbi Soloveitchik would have been able to present in clear and concise language the central elements of his life and personality. But "the Rav" is no longer and we are left to memorialize him by ourselves as best as we can.

This towering figure of the twentieth century, this giant of emotion and intellect, left an indelible impression upon his generation: upon the tens of thousands of students who passed through his Talmud classroom at Yeshiva University; the thousands of rabbis he taught and counseled and personally nurtured for decades; the thousands of graduates of the Maimonides School in Brookline, MA that he founded; the tens of thousands of Jews from all walks of life who thronged to his public lectures and *shiurim* in New York and Boston for over fifty years; the hundreds of leaders of the various communal organizations he graced with his

---

[1] See Marvin Fox, "The Rav as *Maspid*," *Tradition* 30:4 (1996):164-81. In this article, the late Dr. Fox analyzed the Rav's *hespedim* for his uncle, R. Yizhak Zev Soloveitchik, the "Brisker Rav," R. Hayyim Heller, R. Zev Gold, R. Hayyim Ozer Grodzenski, and his *mehutanim,* the Rabbi and Rebbitzen of Talne.

[2] See the beginning of Rav's *hesped* for R. Hayyim Heller delivered in 1960. It was first printed with the title "R. Hayyim Heller *z"l* – Shmuel ha-Katan shel Doreinu," in *Ha-Doar* 40:23 (April 21, 1961): 400-05. It was reprinted as "*Peleitat Sofreihem,*" in Pinchas Peli, ed., *BeSod haYahid ve-haYahad* (Jerusalem, 1976), 255–94 and in *Divrei Hagut veHa'arakhah* (Jerusalem, 1982), 137–62. The phrases in quotes here come from an English translation by Shalom Carmy published in Joseph Epstein, ed., *Shiurei HaRav* (NY, 1974), 7–8; reprinted (Hoboken, 1994), 47.

leadership and advice; and the countless individuals who read and were inspired by his writings and teachings.

The *hespedim* collected in this volume, edited with great care and devotion by Michael Bierman, are not designed to present an objective scholarly academic portrait of the Rav, geared to the closed circle of the scholarly elite. One will not get an objective analysis of the full depth of his scholarly contributions to the worlds of talmudic learning and modern philosophy in all their profundity, but that is not the goal of this volume. Rather; it seeks to portray the Rav to the average thoughtful layperson from the very human and personal perspectives of members of his family as well as devoted disciples. In addition to being a man of deep learning and powerful intellect, Rabbi Soloveitchik is presented here as a man of deep *chesed*, profound personal piety and impeccable integrity. These *hespedim* chronicle the impact not only of a brilliant philosopher and master pedagogue, but of a caring, thoughtful and awe-inspiring teacher and role model. We at the Rabbi Joseph B. Soloveitchik Institute share Mr. Bierman's contention that it is very important for the world to be exposed to this human and personal side of the Rav as well.

Mr. Bierman has undertaken this task with great sensitivity and insight. He has sifted through many eulogies delivered for the Rav in the days and months after his passing and has judiciously selected those which best represent the fullness of the Rav's personality. He pursued his goal, for him a labor of love, with dogged determination, sparing no effort to present his subject in the most meaningful and honest way. As a reflection of the seriousness of this endeavor for Mr. Bierman, from the very beginning he has been in constant touch with learned students of Rabbi Soloveitchik's thought as well as with me, to ensure that he was proceeding in the most appropriate and efficacious manner. In addition, his own introduction to the volume helps the reader better appreciate the scope of Rabbi Soloveitchik's life and accomplishments.

The Rabbi Soloveitchik Institute is pleased to join with Urim Publications in making this book available to all the Rav's students and admirers and to the broader public on the occasion of his tenth *yahrtzeit.* I have no doubt that this volume will be a great contribution to contemporary Jewish life and that the example of the Rav *zt"l*, our beloved and revered *rebbe* and mentor, will serve to challenge and inspire many of us to make our own contributions to Judaism and Jewish life today.

Rabbi Dr. Jacob J. Schacter
Dean
The Rabbi Joseph B. Soloveitchik Institute

PREFACE

Jews have traditionally viewed themselves as disciples of the *gadol hador*, the master teacher and leader of the generation, even though they may never have had personal contact with him. This is likely due to the ripple effect his influence exerts over the entire generation. With this in mind, Rabbi Mayer Twersky observed: "Thus, all of us are the Rav's disciples. His memory deserves to be perpetuated, and we are obligated to eternalize it." It was with that thought in mind, that I boarded one of two buses in Teaneck, NJ very early on *Chol ha-Moed* Pesach, Sunday morning, April 11, 1993. I was bound for Brookline, MA, to pay my final respects to the *gadol hador*, Rabbi Dr. Joseph Dov Halevi Soloveitchik *zt"l*, respectfully referred to as "The Rav."

In the years since the Rav's passing on April 8, 1993, corresponding to 18 Nissan, 5753, I have come to understand and appreciate but a small measure of his greatness. Throughout his life, he was both idealized and simply not understood. This book is designed to introduce Rav Soloveitchik to the majority of people who hereunto have had no exposure to him or his writings. My dilemma was how best to share the Rav's multiple levels of genius. This anthology of eulogies – written primarily by family members and students – is designed as an introduction to the Rav, to his unique contributions to Torah thought, to the many other aspects of wisdom that he bequeathed to us and to future generations, and to his human and personal characteristics.

It is my desire to share the legacy of the Rav as I have come to appreciate it. To say that the Rav was a most complex rabbinic leader is to state the obvious. What distinguished him from all his contemporaries was his mastery of *kol haTorah kulah*, the entire range of Torah and Rabbinics, *Kabbalah* and *Chassidut* at a very young age, his incomparable oratorical skills in several languages, and his vast knowledge of Western philosophy and literature. It was as though the Almighty sent a special *shaliach* endowed with the truly unique talents and abilities necessary to lead American Jewry in the second half of the twentieth century. The Rav was at home in the modern world, and yet was very aware of its vulgarity and pitfalls. He sought to integrate and embrace only those elements of modernity that did not conflict with *halakhah.*

Regrettably, I was not a *talmid* of the Rav. I have, however, always been conscious of the awe with which his students regarded him. He was, after all, a member of the Brisker dynasty, a most learned, and aristocratic-like, family, unparalleled in its influence on the method of Talmud learning pursued in the contemporary yeshiva world. But the Rav represented so much more than just a link with his illustrious past; he was himself a trailblazer in Torah learning and in Western philosophy, and he ultimately developed his own unique style of using the latter to explain and enhance the former.

I want to thank *Hashem Yisborach* for granting me this very special *zechus* to serve as a link in disseminating these *hespedim*, in memory of the Rav, to future generations, thereby keeping alive the Rav's legacy. I am pleased to acknowledge the involvement of those who helped me accomplish the fulfillment of this labor of love. While I am grateful for their help, I assume full responsibility for the introduction, the translations and transcriptions of all the material presented.

Rabbi Leib Tropper, the Rosh Yeshiva of Kol Yaakov, Monsey, NY, was at my side every step of the way, offering *chizuk* and sagely advise. Rabbis Allen Schwartz, Julius Berman and Sam Hartstein graciously opened their files of the Rav and shared their personal reflections of the Rav with me. Rabbi Moshe Gorelick and Dr. Chaim I. Waxman reviewed early versions of the project and my introduction. I owe a debt of appreciation to Rabbi David Stavsky of Columbus, Ohio for providing me with the numerous *hespedim* he received from colleagues in the Rabbinic Council of America. Rabbi Asher Bush of Congregation Ahavas Yisrael of Wesley Hills, NY reviewed the text and provided invaluable assistance in transcribing the *hesped* of Rav Ahron Soloveichik *zt"l*, delivered at the Rav's funeral. Rabbi Aaron Rakeffet-Rothkoff provided critical factual clarification as he reviewed the introduction just prior to its delivery to the publisher. I am very grateful to him for devoting so much of his time to this project while visiting his family in New York. Elie Jacobs and Jay Avilev, both personal friends, doubled as invaluable research assistants in locating hard-to-find background material in America and in Israel respectively.

I extend a most sincere appreciation to Rabbi Dr. Jacob J. Schacter, Dean of the Rabbi Joseph B. Soloveitchik Institute in Brookline, MA. In offering to publish this anthology, Rabbi Schacter sensed its value as the accumulated record of significant *hespedim* of the Rav that might otherwise have been lost to the future. Rabbi Schacter provided a critical review of my introduction and continuously offered encouragement and significant advice on virtually every aspect of this project. His keen editorial eye and demanding high standards enhanced this anthology greatly.

My *Rebbe*, HaRav Yehuda Halevi Tirnauer *shlit"a*, Brooklyn, NY, has been my spiritual guide and mentor for over forty years. I thank him for his *brachah* for the success of this book and his personal encouragement. May Hashem bless him with continued good health and long life.

Lastly, I express gratitude to the members of my dear family who have had to live with my obsession with this project for many years. My wife Carol showed us that with determination and vision our dreams can become a reality. Her own book challenged me to pursue this project. More than any one else, Carol shared my daily frustrations and joy, but never ceased to offer strength and indispensable encouragement. We thank God for our children, Beth and Jonathan, Joshua, and Rena, and our grandson Gavri, and pray that we may be blessed "to see our children and children's children occupied with Torah and *mitzvot*."

Michael A. Bierman

INTRODUCTION

In his *hesped*, Chief Rabbi Jonathan Sacks notes that Rav Soloveitchik's major contribution was to serve as an indispensable transition personality and bridge between the yeshiva world of Lithuania, the American rabbinate and the world of the cosmopolitan Orthodox businessman, attorney and physician of New York, Boston or Denver. Rav Soloveitchik was just as concerned with transmitting the experiential/emotional aspects of *Yahadus* as he was in teaching a *blatt* (folio of) *Gemara.* He would regularly intersperse his *shiurim* and public lectures with stories of his grandfathers, his parents, and everyday occurrences in the life of the simple Jews among whom he lived in Khaslavichy. He told those stories in order to share with his American-born students the warmth and faith of a bygone era. In his 1970 *Teshuvah Drashah*, he said:

> Here I am, sitting in my classroom trying to explain the concepts of *Yom HaKippur* to my students.... From an intellectual point of view, there is much that I can transmit to my students from what I received from my forefathers and mentors about the significance of the day and about the sanctity of the Days of Awe. What I cannot give them, however, are my personal emotional experiences that I have experienced on these days. I cannot lift them into the world of emotion that a Jew has to feel when he says the *Zikhronot* [Remembrance Prayers], when he declares the words, "And the Lord God will sound the *shofar* and march amid the storms of the south" [*Zekhariah* 9:14]. How can I transmit to them the feelings that I felt when I heard my grandfather, Reb Chaim, recite the prayer after the description of the Temple Service with so much emotion and fear: "All this took place when the sanctuary was firmly established. The high priest ministered, his generation watched and rejoiced." You could tangibly feel that at that moment Reb Chaim was in a totally different world, as if he had left Brisk and had been transported back to the Jerusalem

of thousands of years ago. This experience of feeling the emotion of the sanctity of the day is lacking for American Jewry."[1]

The Rav also expressed these thoughts in the context of the *hesped* that he delivered for the Talner Rebbitzen:

> We have two *massorot*, two traditions.... Father teaches the son the discipline of thought as well as discipline of action. Father's tradition is an intellectual-moral one.... What kind of Torah does a mother pass on?.... Most of all I learned from [my mother] that Judaism expresses itself not only in formal compliance with the law but also in a living experience. She taught me that there is a flavor, a scent and warmth to the *mitzvot*. I learned from her the most important thing in life – to feel the presence of the Almighty and the gentle pressure of His hand resting upon my frail shoulders. Without her teachings, which quite often were transmitted to me in silence, I would have grown up a soulless being, dry and insensitive.[2]

In a practical sense, the Rav believed that the *erev* Shabbat home preparations are almost as important as the Shabbat observances themselves. In a *teshuvah drashah* recorded in *On Repentance*,[3] the Rav commented:

> Even in those neighborhoods made up predominantly of religious Jews one can no longer talk of the "sanctity of the Sabbath day." True, there are Jews in America who observe the Sabbath.... But, it is not for the Sabbath that my heart aches, it is for the forgotten "eve of the Sabbath." There are Sabbath-observing Jews in America, but there are not "eve-of-the-Sabbath" Jews who go out to greet the Sabbath with beating hearts and pulsating souls. There are many who observe the

---

[1] Aaron Rakeffet-Rothkoff, *The Rav: The World of Rabbi Joseph B. Soloveitchik*, Vol. 2 (Hoboken, 1999), 175–76.

[2] Rabbi Joseph B. Soloveitchik, "A Tribute to the Rebbitzen of Talne," *Tradition* 17:2 (Spring 1978): 76–77.

[3] Pinchas H. Peli, *On Repentance* (Ramsey, NJ, 1984), 88–89.

> precepts with their hands, with their feet and/or with their mouths – but there are few, indeed, who truly know the meaning of service of the heart.

Yahadus, he taught, was more than abstract concepts and clinical *halakhot*; it was a way of life that had to be appreciated with all one's senses:

> The Rov's modernity was an enthralling, sustained attempt to probe our *masorah* so as to find untapped sources and unperceived dimensions of vitality and vibrancy which make our commitment to Torah more robust and our steady performance of *mitzvos* more resonant. Anyone who listened to the Rov's *derashos,* read his writings from *Ish ha-Halakhah* to *The Lonely Man of Faith*, knows that he unfailingly called attention to the pulsating inner religious life of the individual who is serious about his or her observance of *mitzvos.* Just as the Rambam taught us to speak and to be aware of *mitzvos* of belief and *mitzvos* of morality in addition to *mitzvos* of deeds, the Rov taught us to speak and be mindful of *mitzvos* of experience, emotion, love, attitude and perception. His own comprehensive systematic interpretation of the *masorah* yielded what appears to be a new configuration, with its salient motifs.[4]

Rabbi Menachem Genack put it this way: "For the Rav, it was important to communicate both the logic and the passion of Torah."[5] Rabbi Aharon Lichtenstein offered a similar observation: "His quintessential aspiration was the fusion of spirituality and *lomdut.*"[6]

Some characterized the Rav, by the title of one of his books, as being an *ish hahalakhah* or "halakhic man." This image, however, should not be misconstrued as representing a constricted range of identities or concerns. This halakhic man was very much concerned with the events taking place in the world, and in the neighborhood marketplace. For example, the Rav's

---

[4] Yitzchak Twersky, "Make a Fence Around the Torah," *The Torah U-Madda Journal* 8 (1998–1999): 40.

[5] "My Teacher, My Master," reproduced below.

[6] "The Rav at Jubilee: An Appreciation," reproduced below.

sense of proper conduct caused him to reject those Boston shopkeepers who offered to waive the sales tax for him.[7] He was equally at home in the *beit midrash* as in the halls of government; in the slaughtering house as in the university lecture hall. In any setting, his dynamic personality, intelligence and wisdom assured him of successfully impacting on others.

Rabbi Dr. Norman Lamm, a *talmid* who knew the Rav for over forty-five years, described the Rav's relationship to the general Jewish society as follows:

> The Rav refused to isolate himself in an ivory tower. He sought contact with ordinary Jews – whom he *never* disdained. This practical turn of mind and interest served him well. Thus, the Rav functioned not only as a *Rosh Yeshiva* but also as a *Rav*, as a Rabbi for ordinary Boston *baalebatim*. As such, he was in contact with the realities of American Jewish life, and as a result, his halakhic decisions and communal policies were leavened by an intimate awareness of their lives and loves, their needs and limitations, and aspirations, their strengths and their weaknesses. His *rabbanut* in Boston was the perfect counterpoint for his life as *Rosh Yeshiva* in Manhattan, and protected him from making decisions that were appropriate, perhaps, for the high ideals of a yeshiva but not for *amkha*, for ordinary laymen. He dominated the ivory tower; it did not dominate him.[8]

The Rav's Formative Years

The Rav was uniquely suited to succeed in his life's task. He was born in Pruzhan, Poland on 12 *Adar*, 5663, corresponding to February 27, 1903. His parents were Rabbi Moshe and Pesha Soloveitchik. His maternal grandfather, Rabbi Elijah Feinstein, known as Reb Elya Pruzhiner, was *rav* of the city. The scion of a most illustrious family on both sides of his lineage, the Rav could count outstanding rabbinic personalities, heads of *yeshivot* and community leaders. His *rebbe* in *cheder* was a Lubavitch *chasid*

---

[7] Interview with Leonard Small, retired Brookline merchant, December 24, 2001.

[8] "*Hesped Mar:* A Eulogy for the Rav," reproduced below.

who, unbeknown to his father, was teaching his son and the entire class *Tanya*, the *sefer* of the first Lubavitch Rebbe. The story is told that Rav Moshe's wife complained to the young boy's grandfather, Rav Hayyim Soloveitchik, that he did not know any *Gemara* and did not seem to have a head for such studies. On a visit, Rav Hayyim tested his grandson and saw that, indeed, he understood very little in the *Gemara*. When pressed as to what he did know, the young boy repeated complete pages of *Tanya* from memory. Rav Hayyim then advised that his son, the young boy's father, personally assume total responsibility for the child's studies.

Rabbi Moshe Meiselman, a nephew of the Rav who grew up in Boston and was very close with his uncle, related the following incident which demonstrated the Rav's extraordinary Torah scholarship as a young boy:

> His greatness in Torah was, in truth, extraordinary. The prior generation of *gedolim* and *tovim* considered him as a *gadol baTorah*. In his youth, when he was twelve years old, he wrote *chiddushim* for his grandfather, Reb Hayyim. Reb Hayyim reacted with amazement at this young boy's level of Torah knowledge. The Rav and Reb Hayyim exchanged several letters on a particular *inyan*. Reb Hayyim's style in those letters (and his sense of awe) was as though he was writing to one of the Torah *gedolim* of that time.
>
> I remember once, when we were learning together an *inyan* in the third chapter of *Masekhet Eiruvin*, my uncle shared with me the following episode from his youth. He was once talking in learning with the future Brisker Rav, his uncle Reb Velvel, about the same *inyan* we were studying, when suddenly Reb Hayyim came into the room. He asked them, "What are you learning?" and they told him the discussion. Reb Hayyim thought for a bit and said "Velvele is correct." In other words, the future Brisker Rav was correct in his understanding of the issue, and Reb Hayyim left the room. About five minutes later, he re-entered the room and said "No, Berel is correct." [The Rav's family referred to him as Berel.] A few minutes later, Reb Hayyim entered for the third time to declare, "No, I gave the issue some more thought and the truth is that this discussion represents a famous difference of opinion between the Rambam and the Raivad, and

> both of you are correct." At the time of this incident, Rav Yosef Dov Soloveitchik was only thirteen years old.
>
> At the occasion of the Rav's bar mitzvah, Reb Hayyim gave him a set of Rambam. He inscribed the gift with such lofty words of praise for his grandson's Torah that many of the rabbis of Lithuania would have been thrilled to receive such praise.[9]

The first twenty-two years of the Rav's life were spent almost exclusively in the study of Torah. In his youth, he spent almost his entire day engrossed in learning. He was so singularly devoted to Torah studies that he wrote in a rather sad passage that he had no friends of his age.[10] His constant companion and friend was the Rambam; later, as he got older, Rashi and the sages of the Talmud rounded out his immediate world. The room he slept in at home was his father's study. On a typical day, he would either be learning privately with his father, sitting in on his father's classes with older boys, or catching a few hours sleep. From the age of eight or nine, his only teacher was his father, himself an unusually gifted scholar and a master of the family's unique style of Talmud study. The Brisker method was one of intensive critical analysis, exact classification and precise definition of talmudic terms and concepts, and an almost exclusive emphasis on Rambam's *Mishneh Torah.* In the Rav's late teens, at his mother's insistence, he received the equivalent of a high school education from private tutors, and at the age of twenty-two, he entered the University of Berlin.[11]

It is critical to emphasize that until his late teens, Rav Soloveitchik's entire efforts were directed toward Torah and the absorption of the Polish/Lithuanian Yeshiva world outlook. Growing up in the house of his father, the grandson of two respected community rabbis, the Rav's entire being was absorbed with, and directed toward, Torah and Torah personalities. He was privileged to know intimately his grandfather, the Brisker Rav, Rav Hayyim Soloveitchik, the *dayyan* of Brisk, Rav Simcha

---

[9] R. Moshe Mieselman, from an unpublished *hesped* delivered in Jerusalem, 1993.

[10] A. Rakeffet-Rothkoff, *The Rav*, Vol. 1, 247.

[11] See the memoir written by the Rav's sister, Shulamith Soloveitchik Meiselman, *The Soloveitchik Heritage: A Daughter's Memoir* (Hoboken, 1995), especially pp. 177 and 214.

Zelig, and an entire generation of outstanding Torah personalities, who formed and shaped his Torah identity. He once observed: "After all, I saw the giants of European Torah Jewry before the Holocaust. I discussed talmudic topics with my grandfather, Reb Hayyim Soloveitchik of Brisk. I visited with Reb Chaim Ozer Grodzinski [1863–1940] in Vilna. I debated with Reb Shimon Shkop [1860–1940; Rabbi Shkop was the leading Lithuanian *rosh yeshiva* in that period] concerning the explanation of certain talmudic passages. I spent entire nights with Reb Baruch Ber Leibowitz of Kaminetz [1866–1939, Rabbi Leibowitz was the closest student of Reb Hayyim Soloveitchik] attempting to comprehend difficult rulings in the code of Maimonides."[12] These Torah giants, in turn, delighted in his Torah knowledge and saw in him the genius of his distinguished ancestor, the *Bet Halevi*, Rav Joseph Ber, after whom he was named. He spent a significant amount of time with both his grandfathers, watching them in prayer, in their public role as community rabbis, and in the privacy of their homes. He later spoke and wrote extensively about them, and they remained his lifelong role models.[13]

While a student in Berlin, he conducted himself as the son and heir to a rich, proud and illustrious rabbinic tradition. The implications and ramifications of his personality, molded by the past and directed to the future, later became manifest in the public and influential positions he held at Yeshiva University, in the Boston Jewish community, in the Rabbinical Council of America and in Mizrachi, the Religious Zionists of America.

By the time the Rav journeyed to Berlin, he had completely mastered the entire Talmud. Professor Alexander Altmann, a colleague of his in Berlin, observed that he was a *"mushlam"* or complete.[14] His reputation as a first-rate Torah scholar was already established as he entered adulthood. As for his secular education, we have an autobiographical note that he prepared:

---

[12] A. Rakeffet-Rothkoff, *The Rav*, Vol. 2, 16.

[13] Virtually in all of the Rav's writings, *shiurim* and public lectures he would make reference to his illustrious grandfathers, his parents and the experiences of his childhood. For the extent of the Rav's incredible achievements in Torah study as a teenager, see Haym Soloveitchik, ed., *Iggerot haGrid* (New York, 2001).

[14] Hillel Goldberg, *Between Berlin and Slobodka* (Hoboken, 1989), 93.

> I, Joseph Solowiejczk, was born February 27, 1903, in Pruzna, Poland. In 1922, I graduated the liberal arts "Gymnasium" in Dubno. Thereafter I entered in 1924 the Free Polish University in Warsaw where I spent three terms studying political science. In 1926 I came to Berlin and entered the Friedrich Wilhelm University. I passed the examination for the supplementary subjects at the German Institute for Studies by Foreigners and was then given full matriculation at the University.[15]

Although the Rav studied Western philosophy, literature and critical historical inquiry – including the writings of Immanuel Kant and Soren Kierkegaard – and wrote a dissertation on Herman Cohen's epistemology – he left Berlin, after six years, with his ideology and religious convictions intact. Rabbi Dr. Walter Wurzburger *z"l* offered the following observation on the Rav's "conflicted experience" while in Berlin:

> Reminiscing about his student days, the Rav once remarked to me: "You have no idea how enormously difficult it was for me to move from the world of R. Hayyim to that of Berlin University. Even my children cannot appreciate it, because they already found a paved road. But my generation was challenged to become pioneers…." It was out of this tension that Rav Soloveitchik developed a formula which enabled him to encounter the value system of modernity while remaining fully committed to traditional halakhic methodology."[16]

While a student at the University of Berlin, the Rav hardly slackened from his Torah studies.[17] He did not pursue his university studies as an escape from a more confining or antiquated perspective; he was not

---

[15] Manfred Lehman, "On My Mind," *Bnai Brith Messinger* (November 11, 1994), 16; reprinted in Jacob J. Schacter, "Facing the Truths of History," *The Torah U-Madda Journal* 8 (1998–9): 222.

[16] Walter S. Wurzburger, "Rav Joseph B. Soloveitchik as *Posek* of the Post-Modern Orthodoxy," *Tradition* 29:1 (Fall 1994): 9.

[17] For examples of his involvement in Torah during those years in Berlin, see H. Soloveitchik, *Iggerot haGrid*, 8, 90, 130, 139, 140, 141, 161, 169, 211, 219, 222, 223, 231, 273, 276, 280.

looking to abandon his religious roots but, on the contrary, to defend them in the world of academia. Rav Soloveitchik viewed his engagement with the university world as a positive proactive step in projecting traditional Judaism to a new generation.

Berlin also served as a magnet for other exceptional young men who would, in time, make a lasting mark on twentieth-century world Jewry. There, the Rav befriended Rav Yitzchak Hutner who, quite literally, drifted between Berlin and Rav Kook in Jerusalem until he founded Yeshiva Chaim Berlin in NY: Rav Menachem Mendel Schneersohn who was to become the seventh Lubavitcher Rebbe, Rav Yehiel Yaakov Weinberg who headed the Berlin Rabbinical Seminary, and others.

It was in Berlin, too, that he encountered a unique institute for advanced talmudic scholars, such as himself, under the direction of Rabbi Chaim Heller who combined Lithuanian talmudic learning with modern critical historical scholarship. "Rabbi Heller nurtured not [an] implicit or latent encounter with secular study but explicit and open confrontation. He both fostered and cushioned his students' struggle, impelled cross-cultural research and reflection, and softened their effects."[18] Rabbi Heller served as the Rav's teacher, role model and mentor in navigating the dangerous road from the world of the yeshiva to the world of academia and modernity, without in any way diminishing his *yirat Shamayim* and *ahavat haTorah*. Thus, the Rav was well suited to articulate the quest, the loneliness and the uniqueness of the *ben Torah* adrift, and yet at home in the sea of twentieth-century Western thought. Accordingly, in his *hesped* for the Rav, Rabbi Dr. Norman Lamm was able to offer the following significant observation: "The Rav had no use for the currently popular transcendent parochialism that considers whole areas of human knowledge and creativity as outside the pale."[19]

In 1932, the Rav received his doctorate from the University of Berlin, writing a dissertation entitled "The Epistemology of Pure Thought and the Construction of Being According to Herman Cohen." One year earlier, in 1931, in Vilna he married Tonya Lewit (1904–67), herself the recipient of a doctorate in education from the University of Jena, Germany. There is a

---

[18] H. Goldberg, *Between Berlin and Slobodka*, 93.

[19] "*Hesped Mar*: A Eulogy for the Rav," reproduced below.

tradition that the Rav of Vilna, Rabbi Chaim Ozer Grodzinski, a second cousin of Tonya Lewit,[20] performed the ceremony, though it could not be confirmed.[21]

In 1929, the Rav's father migrated from Warsaw to New York where Reb Moshe became the *Rosh Yeshiva* of the Rabbi Isaac Elchanan Theological Seminary (RIETS). Rav Moshe's wife and children arrived in NY in the early months of 1930. The Rav arrived in the United States in 1932 with his wife and infant daughter, Atarah, to assume a position at the Hebrew Theological College in Skokie, Illinois. However, due to the economic crisis brought on by the Great Depression, the offer was rescinded. Within a few months of his arrival, he became Rav of the Orthodox Jewish community of Boston, the city which remained his home until his death in 1993. On his way to America, the Rav realized that he did not possess a formal written certificate of *semichah*, although, in actuality, he had been "tested" and awarded *semichah* verbally by several European Rabbanim including the famed Rav Avraham D. Kahana Shapiro, the Kovner Rav, and Rav Simcha Zelig Reugur before he left Warsaw for Berlin.[22] In anticipation of future needs, Rabbi Shapiro was more than pleased to provide the formal documentation. In his letter of *semichah,* Rabbi Shapiro wrote: "Happy is the county that will be the home of this great sage. The sages have ordained him to be the true interpreter of all religious problems, and the *halakhah* shall always be decided in accordance with his rulings."[23] The world class leaders of the *yeshiva velt* who arrived in America during and following the Second World War respected the Rav's superior Torah knowledge, and the fact that he was heir to the Brisker heritage. Regardless of any differences they may have had with him, concerning the approach to the role of Western culture in Judaism, there

---

[20] Interview with A. Rakeffet-Rothkoff, August 1, 2002, New York.

[21] See, for example, Eli Mandel, "Rabbi Yosef Dov Soloveitchik *zt"l,*" *The Jewish Homemaker* (September–October, 1993): 26. See also Shlomo Pick, "The Rav: Biography and Bibliography," *Bekhol Derakhekha Daehu* 6 (Winter 1998): 30. However, some members of the Rav's immediate family do not believe this to be the case.

[22] Interview with A. Rakeffet-Rothkoff, January 8, 2002.

[23] Rabbi Shapiro's letter was first published in *HaPardes* 6:7 (October, 1932): 6 on the occasion of the Rav's arrival in America, and reprinted in *Mesorah* 9 (1994): 7.

were always those who were eager to hear the contents of the Rav's Talmud *shiurim* and public lectures.

The American Years – *Rav* and *Rosh Yeshiva*

One of the first issues that demanded the Rav's attention in Boston was the *kashrut* needs of the community, and the disrespectful manner in which the *shochtim* were being treated.[24] The Rav also devoted much time and energy to improving the quality of Jewish education through his involvement in many educational initiatives in Boston. In 1937, almost single-handedly and in the face of much opposition, he founded the Maimonides School, the first day school in New England. For years, Dr. Tonya Soloveitchik served as Chair of the Educational Committee and, with her passing in 1967, their daughter, Dr. Atarah Twersky, assumed that position. To this date, the school is an outstanding one, known for the number of its students continuing their Judaic studies in Israel upon graduation and for its success in achieving high levels of admission to the nation's leading colleges and universities.

In 1935, the Rav sailed to Palestine in support of his candidacy for the position of Ashkenazic Chief Rabbi of Tel Aviv.[25] While in *Eretz Yisrael*, he delivered *shiurim* at several significant yeshivot in Jerusalem, impressing all who heard him.[26] He also met privately with the then Chief Rabbi, Rabbi Avraham Yitzchak Kook. Rav Kook had been a student at the Volozhin Yeshiva at the time that Rav Hayyim lectured there and he sensed that the Rav had inherited his grandfather's intellectual genius.[27] In the end, the position in Tel Aviv was awarded to Rav Moshe Avigdor Amiel of

---

[24] For a description of the Rav's involvement in this arena, see Seth Farber, "Reproach, Recognition and Respect: Rabbi Joseph B. Soloveitchik and Orthodoxy's Mid-Century Attitude Toward Non-Orthodox Denominations," *American Jewish History* 89:2 (June 2001): 193–214.

[25] The Rav's father, Rav Moshe, sent a letter of approbation to the Tel Aviv Rabbinic Search Committee, in support of his son's candidacy. An English translation is printed below in the Appendix.

[26] A. Rakeffet-Rothkoff, *The Rav*, Vol. 1, 37–38.

[27] See above, n. 19.

Antwerp, Belgium,[28] and the Rav returned to America. Never again did he travel to *Eretz Yisrael.*

In addition to the Rav's intense involvement in the twin communal needs of *chinuch* and *kashrut* supervision, he conducted post-*semichah* Talmud classes for young scholars who gathered around him. In 1939, he founded the Heichal Rabbenu Hayyim Halevi for European yeshiva students who were emigrating to the United States. At first, the yeshiva was housed in the Yeshiva Torah Israel building and then moved to its own quarters. His father, Rav Moshe was influential in arranging that this institution serve as a branch of the Rabbi Isaac Elchanan Theological Seminary under the joint guidance of both Rabbi Dr. Bernard Revel, President of the Yeshiva, and the Rav.[29] In December 1941, Rav Moshe Soloveitchik passed away and the Rav succeeded him as *Rosh Yeshiva* of RIETS. For many years, the Rav also simultaneously served as Professor of Jewish Philosophy at the Yeshiva's Bernard Revel Graduate School. The Rav's position as *Rosh Yeshiva* at RIETS gave him the platform to serve as the spiritual mentor of the majority of the American trained Orthodox rabbis from the late 1930s to 1985.

Reflecting on Rav Soloveitchik's significantly singular impact on the character of RIETS, Rabbi Dr. Lamm observed that:

> The one who shaped RIETS and put the stamp of his genius on it was the Rav, Rabbi Joseph B. Soloveitchik *zt"l*, and it is his legacy that must be preserved, expanded, and continued.... But, it must be his *true* legacy. No one-sided distortion of this complex intellectual and spiritual giant should be countenanced. Let it be stated clearly and unequivocally: his attitude to "the wisdom of the nations," to *Torah Umadda*, to the broader Jewish community, was not cavalier; it was *le'khat'chilah*, not *bidiavad.* Any contrary assertion diminishes the *Gestalt* of this unconventional Rosh Yeshiva and *gaon she'bigeonim.* The Rav was an integrated human being whose thinking was complicated and deep, and we should be suspicious of any effort to cut him down to fit the size of our

---

[28] H. Goldberg, 107.

[29] A. Rakeffet-Rothkoff, Vol. 1, 36.

> own minds, minds so much less capacious, less bold, less profound than his. We here stand by the man he was, as the highest instance of our ideals and our aspirations. And the Rav was a man of the broadest vision, intellectually and spiritually; he was not an advocate of lifelong voluntary incarceration in the cave....[30]

Upon arriving in the United States, the Rav was active in the Agudat HaRabbanim, a traditional American rabbinic organization founded in 1902. This organization attempted to unite the East European rabbis who were serving the American Jewish immigrant community. Gradually, the Rav became more active in the Rabbinical Council of America (RCA), which comprised primarily of American-born and trained rabbis. Similarly, the Rav was among the founding members of the Agudat Israel in the United States in 1939. At the second Agudat Israel convention in the United States held in Cincinnati, Ohio in August 1940, Rav Soloveitchik was given the honor of delivering the eulogy for Rav Hayyim Ozer Grodzinski who had died only twelve days earlier.[31] In 1940, the Rav was selected to serve as Chairman of the Agudah's National Executive Committee, and, in August of 1941 – after he had already assumed the position of Rosh Yeshiva of RIETS – was given a seat on its Council of Torah Sages. In the wake of the unthinkable fate that befell European Jewry in the Shoah, the Rav came to see the importance of the State of Israel and became a leading member of the American Mizrachi movement. In an address before the annual Mizrachi Convention, in which he discussed how difficult it was for him to part with his family's tradition and become affiliated with Mizrachi, the Rav observed:

> Regardless, the years of the Hitlerian holocaust, the establishment of the State of Israel, and the accomplishments of the Mizrachi in

---

30 Norman Lamm, "Caves and Enclaves," in *Seventy Faces: Articles of Faith* (Hoboken, 2002), Vol. 2, 168.

31 A. Rakeffet-Rothkoff, *The Silver Era* (Jerusalem, 1981), 168. An excerpt of the Rav's *hesped* given in memory of Rav Hayyim Ozer is recorded in *HaPardes* 14:7 (1941): 5–9.

> the land of Israel, convinced me of the correctness of our movement's path.[32]

Eventually he served as Honorary President of the Religious Zionists of America, and Honorary President of the Mizrachi-Hapoel Mizrachi World Organization.[33]

In 1952, the Rav assumed the chairmanship of the Halakha Commission of the Rabbinical Council of America, and, in that capacity, was able to exert decisive influence and formal authority over American "modern" Orthodoxy. His Commission reviewed and decided upon all important halakhic decisions affecting the growing Americanized Orthodox community. One of the first actions that the Rav took, in his capacity as chairman, was to invite Rabbi Dr. Samuel Belkin, President of Yeshiva University, who had learned at the yeshivot in Mir and Radin and Rabbi Chaim Heller, who was the Rav's former mentor in Berlin, to join him as co-chairs of the Commission.[34] This move was designed to enhance the commission's image and extend its influence. Among other public positions, the Rav served as a member of the Advisory Committee on Humane Methods of Slaughter, established by the United States Secretary of Agriculture. He was also a principal Jewish participant in a National Institute of Mental Health project, undertaken jointly by Harvard University, Loyola and Yeshiva University, to study religious attitudes towards psychological problems.

The Rav's influence continues to be felt through the extraordinary achievements of his children: Dr. Atarah Soloveitchik married to Rabbi Dr. Yitzchak Twersky *z"l*, Dr. Tovah Soloveitchik married to Rabbi Dr. Aharon Lichtenstein, and Rabbi Dr. Haym Soloveitchik. That the Rav was a *gadol ba-Torah* was obvious to those who heard him give a *shiur* or public lecture. What may not have been so clear was his humility and c*hessed.* I

---

[32] Rabbi Joseph B. Soloveitchik, *The Rav Speaks: Five Addresses* (Brooklyn, 2002), 36.

[33] For aspects of the Rav's position on the State of Israel, see Rabbi Joseph B. Soloveitchik, *The Rav Speaks: Five Addresses* (Brooklyn, 2002) and "*Kol Dodi Dofek*: It is the Voice of My Beloved that Knocketh," Lawrence Kaplan trans., in *Theological and Halakhic Reflections on the Holocaust*, Bernhard Rosenberg and Fred Heuman eds. (Hoboken, 1992), 51–117.

[34] Louis Bernstein, *Challenge and Mission* (New York, 1982), 51.

want to share two stories that dramatically portray the Rav's special qualities of sensitivity and caring for others. Rabbi Herbert W. Bomzer wrote:

> I shall never forget the sight of the Rav leading Rav Chaim Heller *zt"l* (in the late 1960s) into a classroom. It was during the summer and the students in the graduate school were informed that Reb Chaim *zt"l* would be giving a *shiur* at 12 noon. Reb Chaim was old and frail and was led by hand by the Rav into the room. Reb Chaim spoke about twenty minutes and it was impossible to hear his words since his voice was very low. When he finished, the Rav said, "I will tell you the *chidush* of the Gaon, Rav Chaim." He then repeated that *chidush* with clarity, which was in itself interesting because it was a first time novel idea and the Rav absorbed it immediately. Seeing how the Rav escorted Reb Chaim like a servant helping a master was an experience in *derech eretz*, and *kavod haRav*, and a living lesson in *Shulchan Aruch*.[35]

The second vignette is described in a *hesped* of the Rav delivered by Rabbi Dr. Yitzchak Twersky, his son-in-law, at a memorial program in Boston. Rabbi Dr. Twersky recalled:

> About 30 years ago there was a man named Yossel, who davened at the Talner *Bais Medrash*. He didn't seem to have any family. He was a simple man, who didn't have much to do with the Rav except occasionally when he would bring him a chicken with a *shayla*. Yossel died on the first day of *Chol haMoed* Pesach. The Rav led *Tehillim*, not only attending his *levayah* but went to the cemetery and shoveled earth on the grave himself. He wanted to do this, even though he was very busy and could ill afford the time, because, he said, this was a rare case of a genuine "*meis mitzvah*." The Rav's students did not have to ask him "*Lamdeinu orchot hechaim*," he was continually doing that.[36]

---

[35] Herbert Bomzer, "The Rav," *Young Israel Viewpoint* (Fall 1993): 18.

[36] This *hesped* can be found on the Internet in the posting by Mike Gerver on Mail.Jewish Mailing List (Vol. 7, no. 72, from June 11, 1993).

For over fifty years, Rabbi Soloveitchik guided the development of Americanized Orthodoxy with his personal synthesis of the Brisker yeshiva world, the pious faith of Chabad Chasidut, and the erudition of the sophisticated University of Berlin philosophy doctoral degree recipient. Through his dual roles as *Rosh Yeshiva* at RIETS and guiding spirit of the Maimonides School in Brookline, he trained rabbis, educators, lay leaders and ordinary folk in his unique blend of humility and majesty, logic and mysticism.

The Rav's unparalleled importance in the revival and preservation of Orthodox Judaism in America is described in the following remarks from Rabbi Dr. Moshe Sokol:

> The years following Rabbi Soloveitchik's arrival at Yeshiva (University) were critical for Orthodoxy in the United States. Large numbers of Jews, immigrants and their children, were abandoning their European roots in Orthodoxy and blending into American society. The great challenge at that point was to create a version of Orthodox Judaism that would remain loyal to tradition, yet show itself capable of responding to the conditions of American modernity. It was Rabbi Soloveitchik, perhaps more than any other individual, who made this possible, thereby contributing immeasurably to the survival and eventual flourishing of Orthodoxy in the United States.
>
> Rabbi Soloveitchik's success in this endeavor was the result of his integration of three interconnected roles – halakhic authority, charismatic teacher and role model; and theologian.... It must be remembered that authority in Orthodox Judaism rests in large measure on mastery of the Talmud and the halakhic codes. It was due precisely to Rabbi Soloveitchik's unmatched credentials in this area that his positive response to modernity proved so influential in Orthodox circles.[37]

It is significant to recognize that the Rav was a *Rosh Yeshiva* that dealt with the existential issues of belief and Godliness in an age of extreme

---

[37] Moshe Sokol, "Joseph B. Soloveitchik (1903–1993)," *American Jewish Year Book 1995* (New York, 1996), 577.

secularism and indifference to such issues. He once said of himself that he was not isolated in the ivory tower of learning, but was fully aware of the issues affecting and challenging the community.[38] He came on the scene at a critical moment in the development of the American Orthodox Jewish community; he provided answers, and, at the very least, reassured the community that their questions, concerns, and, at times, the isolation they felt as God-fearing Jews, were real and shared by others. It was not so much that Orthodoxy was out of touch with twentieth-century society, he taught, but rather that this society had come to redefine man's historical relationship in a way that is out of touch with Torah.

Rabbi Reuven Ziegler writes:

> I believe that the Rav's primary reason for not writing about these subjects (i.e., intellectual challenges to Judaism, such as Biblical criticism, evolution, etc.) was that he simply did not regard them as the most important issues or the main problems facing Judaism in the modern world. The main arena of combat, in his opinion, was the soul, not the mind. We saw that the Rav believed that the God-experience lies at the core of faith, and the role of the intellect is only a *posteriori* – it is both ancillary and subsequent to the faith-experience. Therefore, there is no point in addressing questions of the intellect before one establishes within himself an experiential basis of faith.
>
> Thus, the Rav chose to address primarily issues related to the human existential situation: the possibility of experiencing faith within contemporary society, the relationship between the fundamental attitudes of modernity and religiosity, and the experiential crisis of the contemporary believer. He states clearly at the outset of *The Lonely Man of Faith* that he does not want to deal with the abstract, intellectual side of the problem of faith and reason, but rather with its existential dimension: "Theory is not my concern at the moment. I want instead to focus attention on a human life situation in which the man of faith as an individual concrete being, with his cares and hopes, concerns and needs, joys and sad moments, is entangled…."

---

[38] The Rav said this in a talk given at the RIETS Alumni meeting in 1975.

> Rav Soloveitchik saw his task mainly as helping the modern Jew to understand his tradition, grasp its relevance and appreciate its desired effect upon his attitudes and lifestyle. The Rav's concern, thus, was far more with the crucial question of inner commitment to God rather than the secondary issues of intellectual critique.[39]

Following in the family tradition of not publishing, the Rav left behind only five major philosophical essays, *Halakhic Man*, *The Halakhic Mind*, *The Lonely Man of Faith*, *Kol Dodi Dofek*, and *uVikkashtem miSham*. However, more publications are currently being prepared, based on thousands of tapes and some written manuscripts. The Rav also authorized the release of several lectures and eulogies which appeared in the RCA publication, *Tradition*.[40] These writings, especially the longer ones, reflect the range of the Rav's philosophical and academic background. He employed that knowledge to explore and explain the validity and uniqueness of Judaism to an academically sophisticated and philosophically oriented American audience. His shorter speeches and essays deal with a number of recurring issues such as freedom, holiness, repentance, the laws of prayer and festivals, and spiritual worship.

As an example of the Rav's creative interpretive insight, he provides a new answer to the age-old question: By what right does man offer petitionary prayers to the Almighty, and what purpose do they serve? He writes:

> Prayer in Judaism, unlike the prayer of classical mysticism, is bound up with human needs, wants, drives and urges, which make man suffer. Prayer is the doctrine of human needs. Prayer tells the individual, as well as the community, what his, or its, genuine needs are, what he should, or should not, petition God about…in short, through prayer man finds himself. Prayer

---

[39] Reuven Ziegler, "Introduction to the Philosophy of Rav Soloveitchik," Yeshivat Har Etzion Virtual Beit Midrash (www.haretzion.org), Lecture 20b.

[40] *Tradition* 17:2 (Spring 1978):7–83. That issue of *Tradition* includes the Rav's essays entitled: "The Community," "Majesty and Humility," "Catharsis," "Redemption, Prayer and *Talmud Torah*," and "A Tribute to the Rebbetzin of Talne."

> enlightens man about his needs. It tells man the story of his hidden hopes and expectations. It teaches him how to behold the vision and how to strive in order to realize this vision, when to be satisfied with what one possesses, when to reach out for more. In a word, man finds his need-awareness, himself, in prayer.[41]

The Rav was teaching us that in prayer we are not attempting to manipulate God, but rather come to discover, through dialogue, what our needs truly are.

Rabbi Dr. Moshe Sokol referred to the Rav's writings as follows:

> Indeed it is precisely for this reason that the essays are so powerful. In effect, then, we have multiple installments of the intellectual and spiritual autobiography of one of the most creative and fertile Jewish religious minds of the century.... In many ways, then, he is the paradigm of the contemporary thinker in segmented search of a satisfactory stance towards modernity, self and tradition.[42]

On another occasion, Dr. Sokol observed that:

> Even a cursory review of Rabbi Soloveitchik's major writings underscores the complexity of his religious approach. Throughout his life, Rabbi Soloveitchik struggled with the tension between an affirmation of human autonomy and self-sufficiency on the one hand, and deep feelings of submission before God on the other. Rabbi Soloveitchik strove mightily to live at once in different worlds – the worlds of science and faith, of Brisk and Berlin, the traditional house of Talmud study and the edifice the philosophers built. To his credit, he refused to compromise or adulterate his rigorous conceptions of, and commitments to, these different worlds.

---

[41] R. Joseph B. Soloveitchik, "Redemption, Prayer, *Talmud Torah*," *Tradition* 17:2 (Spring 1978): 65–66.

[42] Moshe Sokol, *"'Ger veToshav Anokhi':* Modernity and Traditionalism in the Life and Thought of Rabbi Joseph B. Soloveitchik," *Tradition* 29:1 (Fall 1994): 33–34.

> As a religious leader, Rabbi Soloveitchik was a heroic figure to countless young Orthodox Jewish intellectuals of his day. His own ongoing, existentially resonant struggles to shape a religious identity astride both tradition and modernity, the sophisticated as well as personal articulation he gave to that quest, and his religious passion and uncompromising rigor in classic Talmud study, mirrored both the aspirations and conflicts of his students and followers, as it gave them erudite voice and often even long-sought resolution.[43]

From time to time, the Rav publicly addressed some of the spiritual and practical halakhic concerns of the contemporary scene. In clearly crafted, well-reasoned and flawlessly articulated papers, he emphatically condemned the practice of mixed seating in synagogues,[44] and he loudly and forcefully opposed participation in ecumenical debates or dialogues (1964).[45] These statements were crucial in delineating the boundaries of Orthodox halakhic practice and communal policy at a critical time (the 1950–1960s) of flux and instability.

The Rav was as equally adamant in his support of interdenominational cooperation over issues of public concern (*klappei chutz*) affecting the entire Jewish community. He strongly supported Religious Zionism and the modern State of Israel, the teaching of *Torah she-be'al peh* to women who were otherwise exposed to the highest levels of secular learning, and the acquisition of secular knowledge. He urged and encouraged members of his family and many of his students to pursue high levels of secular education.

Rabbi Dr. David Shatz offers the following observation regarding the Rav's personal philosophy and rationale for involvement with the modern world, based on the Rav's essay, *The Lonely Man of Faith*:

> [The Rav's] endorsement of culture (and involvement in the secular world) is founded on a principle rooted in *sefer Bereshit*,

---

[43] Ibid., *AJYB*, 1995, 584.

[44] Rabbi Joseph B. Soloveitchik, "On Seating and Sanctification," in *The Sanctity of the Synagogue*, Baruch Litvin ed., (NY, 1959), 109–118.

[45] Rabbi Joseph B. Soloveitchik, "Confrontation," *Tradition* 6:2 (Spring–Summer 1964): 5–29.

> one we might describe as moral. Human beings fulfill their divine charge and actualize their divinely ordained nature only by aggressively striving to improve human existence in concrete, material ways. They must "harness the elemental forces of nature" to conquer disease and to subdue the threats that nature poses to human life and security. Only by doing so do they imitate God's creativity, fulfill the responsibilities imposed by the mandate "*mil'u et ha'aretz vekivshuhah*," and attain dignity.[46]

Furthermore, in a footnote attached to this paragraph, Dr. Shatz points out that the Rav does not limit *"vekivshuhah"* to the development of medicine and technology; economics and politics can likewise "play a vital role in the transformation of human life."

The Rav was unequivocal about his view of some of the halakhic innovations that were designed to make Orthodoxy more in touch with contemporary societal trends. Comparing the approach of "creative *halakhah"* to Korach's rebellion, the Rav stated, "Korach thus posited that any intelligent person could interpret *halakhah* using common sense, that halakhic analysis was an exoteric competence derived from empirical experience."[47] In a 1975 talk before the Rabbinical Council of America, the Rav stated in the clearest language possible that there had to be a line drawn between the desire for societal innovation and what the *halakhah* stands for, because otherwise there would be no limit to redefining and reinterpreting Torah. Although the Rav's position on this matter is complex, the following quote clearly indicates an approach that he was prepared to take publicly:

> The thought should never occur that it is important to cooperate just a little bit with the modern trend or with the secular, modern philosophy. In my opinion, Judaism does not have to apologize either to the modern woman or to the modern representatives of religious subjectivism. There is no need for apology, we should have pride in our *masorah*, in our heritage. And of course, certainly

---

46 David Shatz, "The Rav's Philosophical Legacy," reproduced below.

47 Rabbi Joseph B. Soloveitchik, "The First Rebellion Against Torah Authority," in Joseph Epstein ed., *Shiurei HaRav* (Hoboken, 1994), 104.

> it goes without saying, one must not try to compromise with these cultural trends, and one must not try to gear the halakhic norm to the transient ways of a neurotic society, which is what our society is. A thought, *kabbolas ol malchus shamayim,* which is an identical act with *talmud Torah*, requires of us to revere and to love and to admire the words of the *chachmei hamasorah*, be they *Tannaim*, be they *Amoraim*, be they *Rishonim.*[48]

As the Rav so clearly stated, *kabbolas ol malchut shamayim* requires of us to suspend our thinking and accept Torah and *mesorah* as it is, not as we would necessarily like to redesign it. He rhetorically proposed to his rabbinic audience, "Let me ask you a question – *Ribbono shel Olam* – God Almighty, if you should start modifying and reassessing the *chazakos* upon which a multitude of *halakhos* rest, you will destroy the very foundations of *Yahadus.* So, instead of philosophizing, let us rather light a match and set fire to the *beis Yisrael*, and get rid of our problems."[49]

The specifics of Rabbi Soloveitchik's involvement in many important issues of the second half of the twentieth century are discussed and analyzed in several of the eulogies and reflections included in this anthology.

There is a story told of a group of people who stood blindfolded around a huge animal: Each of them examined the animal by touching a different part of its body, and accordingly tried to define the elephant based only on the small area with which they came into contact. Similarly, although these eulogies and memories were written by men who knew the Rav over a span of time, each perceived only one or a few facets of the Rav. Rabbi Dr. Yitzchak Twersky wrote, "It is necessary to identify his unique features, not '*gadol hador*' but '*yachid hador.*'" Those who write eulogies don't have the vocabulary to describe him, so they distort his image, reducing it to images they can understand."[50] The distortion of the Rav's image, with few exceptions, is certainly not intentional. I would prefer to see it as individuals confronted by his multi-faceted strengths, coming away with

---

48 See above, n. 38.

49 Ibid.

50 See above, n. 36.

different perceptions of the very complex personality that constituted the Rav.

Our Sages have an expression that "words that emanate from the heart enter the heart," sincere words of reflection and praise are clearly discernable and make the most impact. The memories, stories and eulogies that comprise this anthology were written and delivered from the saddened and broken hearts of those who were closest to the Rav. The Rav was known as a master *maspid* and in the course of some of those talks he left instructions on the art of developing a eulogy: "The *maspid* must cause the sounds of agony to be heard and tears to flow as he makes his audience aware of their loss. At the same time, he must serve as a pedagogue, using calm reason to teach the people the full significance of the personality whom he eulogizes."[51] I believe that many of the *hespedim* printed here meet this standard.

The reflections gathered in this anthology are representative of many more which reflect an outpouring of love, respect and appreciation for Rav Soloveitchik. [52] They also serve to educate us about the Rav's teachings, his philosophy and his incomparable display of *chessed.* His disciples have learned well from the master *maspid* to draw us into the images and memories of their *rebbe.* Taken together, these essays portray the Rav as *rebbe*, talmudist, *Rosh Yeshiva*, *gadol hador*, *zeide*, humanist, philosopher, halakhist, and social critic. No doubt Rav Soloveitchik filled all of these roles and so many more: he was truly greater than the sum of his parts.

Above all, Rav Soloveitchik is to be remembered as he saw himself, as a "*melamed*," a *rebbe* or teacher of Torah to *klal Yisroel,* as a vital indispensable link in the chain of *chakhmei hamesorah.* That he was one of *gedolei yisrael* is indisputable, and therein lies the strength of his singular personality. His uniqueness was in his ability to share of himself, to successfully communicate both the collective and his personal *mesorah* to a generation of

---

[51] Rabbi Joseph B. Soloveitchik, "*Peleitat Sofreihem,*" in *Divrei Hagut veHa'arakhah* (Jerusalem, 1982) 139.

[52] The *hespedim* included here were presented at memorial gatherings in Baltimore, Boca Raton, Boston, Denver, Jerusalem, Efrat, London, Los Angeles, St. Louis, Monsey, New York, and Pittsburgh. Some of them have already appeared in print (see the end of the book for a list of sources and credits), but all have been lightly edited to help maintain the sylistic consistency of this volume.

native-born American men and women. As a *melamed,* he trained and left an impact on over 2,000 rabbis in his RIETS classroom, on the thousands to whom he taught Talmud and *Chumash* in Manhattan for over thirty years at the Moriah synagogue, on those who attended his weekly Saturday night lectures and Sunday morning Talmud *shiurim* at the Maimonides School, and, of course, on those who were part of the audience in his eagerly anticipated annual *Teshuvah* and *Yahrtzeit shiurim.* Many of the eulogies presented refer to him as the *melamed* par excellence.

Rabbi Herschel Schachter, the Rosh Kollel of RIETS, offered the following observation at a *Yahrtzeit* gathering for the Rav on *Chol ha-Moed* Pesach 2001 in Englewood, NJ. He said:

> In Europe, when a *gadol* passed, they would erect a huge monument at the cemetery listing the titles of his books so he would be remembered for a long time. But among the Rav's *talmidim*, his Torah will never be forgotten, because the Rav said something on every facet of Jewish life: on *Shacharit*, *Minchah*, *Ma'ariv*, *Neilah*, *Mussaf*, *Rosh Chodesh*, *Hallel*, Rosh Hashanah, Yom Kippur, the *Chagim*, *Sefirat haOmer*, Tisha b'Av, etc.

He thus influenced two generations not only with his classroom and public lectures, but by the sheer breadth of the topics he addressed. The Rav left indelible impressions on the psyche of countless individuals who were touched by him and his Torah.

Only three years after the Rav's *petirah*, Rabbi Stanley Boylan introduced his article on the Rav by noting: "Because there is already a new generation 'who did not know Joseph,' who were never exposed first-hand to the Rav's brilliance and *gadlut*, such an account is all the more timely."[53] As we approach the tenth *yahrtzeit* of Rav Soloveitchik, this collection of memories is even more timely. It is meant to serve as a vehicle to introduce both young and old to the many facets of the Rav's life and legacy, and to demystify the memory and teachings of Rav Soloveitchik. It is hoped that some will be motivated to read the Rav's essays and books available in

---

[53] Stanley Boylan, "Learning With The Rav: Learning From the Rav," *Tradition* 30:4 (Spring 1996): 131.

English and Hebrew and thus become acquainted with the intellectual and spiritual mind of the most creative and fertile Jewish thinker of our time.[54]

May the beloved memory of HaRav Yoseph Dov Halevi Soloveitchik, his Torah and intellectual legacy, truly be a blessing for us all. And may he be a *melitz yosher* on behalf of *Klal Yisrael* and hasten the coming of the final *geulah*.

---

[54] For comprehensive bibliographies of Rabbi Soloveitchik's works, see Zanvel E. Klein, "*Benei Yosef Dovrim*: Rabbi Joseph B. Soloveitchik *z"l*: A Bibliography," *The Torah U-Madda Journal* 4 (1993): 84–133; Eli Turkel, "Partial Bibliography of works by and about Rabbi Joseph B. Soloveitchik *zt"l*," listed through the website www.tau.ac.il.

THE FAMILY REMEMBERS

A *HESPED*

RABBI AHRON SOLOVEICHIK *zt"l*[*]

The *Gemara* says (*Sukkah* 46b): "Chezkiah said in the name of R. Yirmiah, who said in the name of Aramia, who said in the same of Reb Shimon ben Yochi: 'I took notice of the fact that the superior beings are very few. In our day, if the superior beings add up to a thousand persons, I, Reb Shimon ben Yochi, together with my son, R. Eliezer, am among them. If the superior Jews are a hundred in total, then I and my son are among them. If the superior Jews add up only to ten, then I and my son are among them. If the superior beings total only two, then I and my son, Eliezer, are the two.'"

What is the meaning of this mysterious saying? It doesn't *chas veshalom* speak of *ga'avah*. Reb Shimon ben Yochi and his son, Eliezer, were hidden in a cave for seven years. They were hidden not only from the Roman authorities but even from their own brethren. No one knew of their greatness. No one knew what they were involved in for seven years without seeing the light of the sun. They were engaged in writing the *Zohar*, light. What kind of light? Spiritual light, light that would reflect and refract and defract upon the entire Jewish people and indirectly upon the whole world.

Whenever I think of my brother, Reb Yoshe Ber *zichrono levrachah*, I cannot help but think of my father, Reb Moshe, *zichrono levrachah*, because my brother, Reb Yoshe Ber, and my father, Reb Moshe, had one *neshamah*, one soul, one mind, one heart. When they were *mechadeish chidushei Torah*, they were *mechadeish* together. I don't know of any parallel in the history of *gedolei Yisrael*. The only one I can think of is Reb Akiva Eiger and his son Reb Shlomo Eiger. These two also, when they were *mechadeish chidushei Torah*, it wasn't in a monologue, it was a dialogue. You see that in the writings of the *chudishim* of Reb Akiva Eiger, he constantly mentions "my

---

[*] A copy of this *hesped* was reviewed by Rav Moshe Soloveichik, the eldest son of Rav Ahron *zt"l*, in advance of publication. He wanted to make sure that his father's words were not misunderstood and, as a result, we have added some footnotes written by him for clarification.

son, Reb Shlomo" and in the writings of Reb Shlomo Eiger, he constantly refers to "*avi mori*, Reb Akiva Eiger." But there's one difference. Reb Shlomo Eiger and Reb Akiva Eiger had one *neshamah*, one mind, one heart, but they were not hidden in a cave. Reb Yoshe Ber and Reb Moshe were hidden in a cave, hidden from everybody, hidden even from their own *talmidim*, the thousands of *talmidim* they had. Reb Moshe and Reb Yoshe Ber were *rashei yeshiva* in Yeshivas Rabbenu Yitzhak Elchanan from 1929 until 1993, but the two of them were not really revealed. They tried to hide, and not reveal their Torah. When people say that there is a tradition in Brisk not to publish Torah, it's true. But what is it? It's not that there simply is a tradition in Brisk not to publish Torah. The tradition is grounded in the fact that they felt that the *Zohar* cannot be revealed the moment it is reflected. It has to go through a process, a threefold process, known in physics as reflection, refraction and defraction.

What is reflection? Reflection, by definition – whether in connection with waves of light or waves of sound – means that the body emits waves that bounce back to the place from which they were generated.

Reb Hayyim Brisker, as well as his father, the *Beis Halevi*, and his grandfather, Reb Itzele, had a relatively simple task: to reflect the Torah that was given at Sinai in all the corners of the earth. When my father, Reb Moshe, came to America in 1929, he faced a more difficult task. Reflection could not have been enough. Reflection is possible when there is one medium. In Volozhin and in Brisk, there was one medium through which the rays of the light of Torah were able to penetrate. There was no need to have recourse through the process of refraction, which means the bending of the rays. When the rays of the sun have to change their direction from one medium to another, from the medium of pure air to the medium of water or rain, there is a bending of the rays but no breaking off of the rays. But sometimes, when the rays of the sun have to penetrate into an opaque body, even bending is not enough.

Then there is a law of nature that the rays of the sun have to manipulate, to penetrate, by breaking off into the spectrum of colors. This is the phenomenon of the rainbow, "*Es kashti nasati be'anan*" that was the covenant. Every covenant was coupled with the symbol of the rainbow. What was the symbol that expressed the covenant between the *Ribono Shel*

Olam and the entire human race? It was the rainbow. When does a rainbow appear? When it stops raining. There is a flood, it keeps on pouring, there is no sun and then, all of a sudden, the sun comes out. At that point, the sun not only is required to change its medium, but it has to manipulate to break off into its numerous and multifarious components called the spectrum of colors.

This is what we say in the *Avodah*, "For the sight of the sun is the sight of the *kohein gadol*." The *kohein gadol* was the spiritual leader of *Klal Yisroel* and, indirectly, of all humanity. He was *mispallel* for rain, for the economy, and for the spiritual life of all the Jewish people. How did he do it? He had to resort to this spectrum of colors. You have to preport into the numerous and multifarious rays.

When my father, Reb Moshe, came to the United States, he had to change the medium. In Reb Hayyim's days, in the *Beis Halevi*'s days, in the *Netziv*'s days, in R. Elya Pruzhiner's days, in R. Itzele Volozhiner's days, in R. Hayyim Volozhiner's days, the way to shed light was, relatively speaking, a very simple one. All you had to do was to explain the *inyanim*, the elements of the Torah. But when Reb Moshe came to the United States, he had to penetrate into students who were living in a different medium (in America), in a medium of Torah and *chochmas haOlam*. It wasn't easy for my father, Reb Moshe, to explain the[1] concept of *shtoros*, concepts of *akirah* and *hanachah*. My father used to tell me, "When I give a *shiur* on *rov vechazakah*, it is simple, I don't have to explain it ten times. But when I give a *shiur* on *akirah tzorech hanachah*, on *shtoros* (*eidim hachasumin al hashtar kemi shenechkera eidusan bibeis din*), that an ordinary piece of paper testifies everything (as the *Gemara* in *Kesuvos* brings down), there I have to explain it several times and I have to prepare how to explain it because the[2] students[3] in Yeshivas Rabbenu Yitzchak Elchanan, who were raised in a different medium, cannot grasp the concepts of *shtoros*, of *akirah tzorech hanachah*. They can grasp concepts of *rov vechazakah* and *sfek sfeika*. Those are very

---

[1] Halakhic.

[2] American.

[3] Of that time.

simple things, every judge can understand that. But not so the[4] concept *shtoros*, of contracts.

When my brother, Reb Yoshe Ber, became *Rosh Yeshiva* in Yeshivas Rabbenu Yitzchak Elchanan in 1941, he had an even bigger challenge, to transmit the Torah to opaque students. I'm not, *chas veshalom*, criticizing them. They were opaque because they were raised in an[5] environment[6] that was hostile to Torah. He had to resort to giving lectures in Jewish philosophy, in *Chovos haLevavos,* in *Moreh Nevuchim*, in the *Kuzari.* That was a most difficult challenge but he fulfilled that function of defraction, of breaking off the rays of the Torah into its numerous components, gloriously and successfully.

I would like to mention certain *pesukim* in *Parshas Vayeisehev* that are very relevant to my brother, Reb Yoshe Ber. In *Bereishis* (37:3), the Torah says "And Israel loved Joseph more than all his sons because he was a *ben zekunim.*" What is the *peshat*, the meaning, of the phrase "*ben zekunim*?" There are two explanations: One is that he was the son who was born at the old age of Yaakov Avinu. The other explanation is that he was a very wise, smart son, in the sense of *"ein zaken ela mi shekanah chochmah"* referring to the fact that Yosef haZaddik received the entire Torah that Yaakov learned at the *beis midrash* of Shem and Ever. In order to symbolize Yaakov's preference for Yosef, he made for him a "*kesones pasim*," a coat of many colors, a striped shirt. When his brothers saw that Yaakov, their father, loved Yosef more than any one of them, "*Vayisni'u oso.*" In all the English translations, this phrase is translated to mean "they hated him." But this is a very inaccurate translation. Even "they disliked him" is incorrect. In my opinion, *"vayisni'u oso"* means "they resented him." *Chas veshalom*, they did not hate him, God forbid. They did not dislike him, *chas veshalam*, but they resented him. They loved him and wanted Yosef to be one of them, but they felt that he was superior to them. Not because they didn't have that potential. They had the same potential as Yosef did, but Yosef tried all the time to galvanize the potential while they didn't. And so, they were jealous. Jealousy is not grounded in hatred although sometimes it is

[4] Halakhic.

[5] American.

[6] Of those years.

conducive to hatred. Jealousy is grounded in not being ready to do what the other person does. The other person does his utmost to utilize his potential and they don't. They resented him so much that they couldn't even talk peacefully with him.

Yosef was a dreamer, "and he dreamt a dream and told it to his brothers." This time, he didn't tell the dream to his father Yaakov. The second dream, he told his father. Yosef dreamt two dreams. In one dream, he dreamt that all the brothers were standing in the field and they were binding sheaves and he was also binding his sheaves. Then, all of a sudden, their sheaves started to encircle and walk around his sheaf, and then they bowed down to it. This was one dream. The second dream was more involved; it was a more glorious dream, a more spiritual dream. The sun and the moon symbolized Yaakov and Leah and the eleven stars symbolized the brothers of Yosef, who were are all bowing down to him. It was a very strange dream. He related this dream to his father Yaakov, and Yaakov rebuked him although Yaakov felt that Yosef was conveying something important to him, that this was no ordinary dream. Yaakov realized that this was a prophetic dream that was destined to be fulfilled. So Yosef's brothers resented him even more and their dislike grew. The Torah says, "His father scolded him, and said to him, 'What is this dream that you have dreamt! Are we to come – I and your mother and your brothers – to bow down to you to the ground?' And his brothers were jealous of him, but his father kept the matter in mind."

What did this dream symbolize? Yaakov Avinu was also a dreamer. The Torah says *(Parshas Vayeitzei)* that he dreamt of a ladder sent out from the earth with its rungs reaching into the heavens. Yosef haZaddik dreamed two dreams, but those two dreams were really two component dreams of Yaakov's one dream. Yaakov lived at a time when everyone he mingled with, before his appearance in Charan, was convinced of the heritage of Abraham and Isaac. So one dream was enough. He had to dream of a ladder which rested on the earth and reached into the Heavens. But Yosef dreamt of the day when he will go to pagan Egypt and will become its Prime Minister. Could he talk to them about "a ladder that rested on the earth and reached into the Heavens?" If he would, they would consider him crazy. They had no concept of the Heavens. They only had a concept of the earth. So he had to divide his father Yaakov's dream into two dreams.

Reb Hayyim himself was criticized by many *gedolim* who recognized that his Torah is the truth of Torah, *amitah shel Torah*, but nonetheless criticized him by calling him "*der chemiker*," the chemist. Reb Hayyim also discovered that there are two *halakhos*, two *dinim*, while they felt that there is always only one *din*, only one *halakhah*. Therefore they resented him. The brothers of Yosef also resented him because he dreamt two dreams. In the days of Yosef, in the pagan world of Egypt – where everything, even the birds, absorbed pagan melodies – Yosef had to dream two dreams.

The same problem was with my brother, Reb Yoshe Ber. It's not his fault. I'm not criticizing any *ben Torah* and any *Rosh Yeshiva*, but the *rashei yeshiva* who toiled in America alienated themselves from Reb Yoshe Ber. Why? What did Reb Yoshe Ber do? He gave *shiurim* in *Halakhah* for five hours, something that no other *Rosh Yeshiva* ever did. Surely there was nothing wrong with that. But he also gave lectures in philosophy, in *Chovos haLevavos*, in the *Kuzari*, in the *Moreh Nevuchem*, and that they could not do. They could not do it because they did not know how to break the rays of the Torah into its various hues and colors. So they resented him to the extent that they published some of the *chidushei Torah* that they heard and liked and enjoyed and realized shed light on certain *sugyos* in *Shas*, in the name of Reb Hayyim, not even in the name of my father *zt"l*.

I'm not criticizing them. If I had been among them, I probably would have behaved the same way. *Al tadin es chavercha ad shetagi'a limekomo.* But let me quote certain *pesukim* from the *brachah* that Yaakov Avinu bestowed upon Yosef in *Parshes Vayechi*: "May you be a fruitful bough by the well whose branches flow over the well, the archers." Who are the archers? They are not the Egyptians but Yosef's own brothers to whom he was so close. They were the archers who sincerely, *leshem Shamayim*, cast arrows against Yosef. The archers fiercely attacked him, shot at him and hated him, but his bow was his strength. The arms of his strength were made to suffer, from the hands of the Almighty God of Yaakov from there, and with the Shepherd, the Stone of Yisrael, by the God of your father, who shall help thee and by the Almighty who shall bless thee. With the blessings of

Heaven from above, the blessings of the deep that crouching beneath, the blessings of the breasts and the womb (*Bereshit* 49:24–5).

Yosef was endowed with all the genes that he inherited from his father, Yaakov and from his mother, Rachael, together with the milk that he, as a child, sucked from the breasts of his mother. He also sucked concepts of *kedushah*, concepts of *chessed* and, of course, the brothers of Yosef resented that.

This was also true of my brother, Reb Yosef Ber. The *Ribbono Shel Olam* blessed him with all the genes of his father, Reb Moshe, and his grandfather, Reb Hayyim, and his great ancestor, the *Beis Halevi*, the Netziv and Reb Hayyim Volozhiner. He was also blessed with all the genes of my mother *z"l*, of Reb Elya Pruzhiner. That is why he was *zocheh* to become the *rosh* of our *mispachah*. It is not that the other brothers were not able to do so, but that the other brothers did not try to galvanize the qualities that they inherited from their parents, while my brother, Yosef, did.

I would like to conclude with two statements, I beg each and every one of you not to misunderstand; I don't want, and I don't mean, to single out any child of my brother, Reb Yoshe Ber. They are all the same, but everybody has his destiny, just as Yosef had the tragic but fortunate destiny, as the *Ribbono Shel Olam* said to Yaakov Avinu, "Yosef, your son, will put his hand on your eyes before you die." That is a *zechus* that not everybody can have. I was not *zocheh* to it. I was *meshamesh* my father but I was not *zocheh* that I should put my hands on the eyes of my father *zt"l* fifty-two years ago. Reb Yoshe Ber, my brother, was *zocheh* and he was there with my father in the last few moments of his life. My father woke up and had to say the *Birchos haShachar*. He said to my brother, "Berel, I beseech of you, I beg you, I must say the *Birchos haShachar* but I have no strength, so you say them. Pour water over my hands and say them and I will answer '*Amen*.'" So my brother did it. He filled up a cup with water, poured it over my father's hands, wiped my father's hands and said all of the *Birchos haShachar*. Then my father said to him, "Berel, I want to say to you two things: Firstly that you have fulfilled the *pasuk* of "Yosef, your son, will put his hand on your eyes before you die." And secondly, I want to say the *pasuk*: "*Semach Zevulun bitzeisecha ve-Yissachar be'ohalecha*," Zevulun will rejoice when you go out and Yissachar in your tent. And than he closed his eyes. He was referring to the *Midrash Rabbah* that "*Semach Zevulun bitzeisecha* means when you leave this world for the next world." And so now I am saying to Reb Yoshe Ber, "*Semach Zevulun bitzeischa* – from this world to the next world," and "*Yissachar bi'ohalecha.*"

But I want to single out two children, Reb Yitzhak Twersky and Atarah Twersky. They were *zocheh* to that *zechus* to take care of their father, Reb Yosef Ber, in the last days of his life. Yesterday I walked over to Atarah's house and I stayed there two-and-a-half hours. I think the entire house was saying *Tehillim* and I was *patur* because I am an *onen*, and the *mes* was lying before us. Atarah was not saying *Tehillim* either, but every half-hour I saw her get up and bend her face, and take a good look at my brother as he was lying on the floor, the *tallis* covering him up. She looked at her father, whose eyes she was not able to see then, with so much love and affection. I am seventy-five years old. Soon I will be seventy-six years old but I never saw that. I've seen many mothers looking at their deceased children with love and affection, but I never saw, in my life, a daughter looking with so much affection at her father who was lying on the floor, covered with a *talis*. Then I felt a certain jealousy toward Atarah and toward Reb Yitzchak, that they were *zocheh* to this tragic and unfortunate *zechus*.

And secondly, I want to mention one more thing, something that my brother mentioned in his *hesped* fifty-two years ago for my father, in 1940. He said that when Reb Hayyim Volozhiner passed away, his son, Reb Itzele, who filled his place at the Yeshiva in Volozhin, said to the *talmidim* there (at that time Volozhin had very few *talmidim*; I don't think it had a hundred *talmidim*): "*Talmidim* of Volozhin: The *Midrash Eichah* tells us that when the *beis hamikdash* was destroyed and was in flames, the *pirchei kehunah*, the young *benei Torah* in the *beis hamikdash*, went to its roof and threw up the keys. And they said to the *Ribbono Shel Olam*, 'We do not need these keys any more. Please take them.' And then a figurative hand came out from Heaven and grabbed the keys." Reb Itzele Volozhin continued, "You think that it was to the credit of the *pirchei kehunah* that they did this? *Chas veshalom*, it was in criticism of the *pirchei kehunah*. That was the biggest blunder that they could ever have done. If they hadn't thrown the keys into the fire, then, in short time, with the required effort, they would have been able to rebuild the *beis hamikdash*."

Don't repeat that blunder. I'm telling you now, not only to those who are assembled here, but to all *benei Torah* in the United States and Canada and in Israel. Don't repeat that mistake, don't throw the keys of the *beis ha-mikdash me'at* of Yeshivas Rabbenu Yitzchak Elchanan where *mishpachas Brisk* has been influencing lives of *benei Torah* since 1929. Don't throw away the keys into the fire.[7] Keep the keys and rebuild[8] the gates of the *beis ha-mikdash me'at* of Yeshivas Rabbenu Yitzchak Elchanan.[9]

[7] That was ignited with the passing of Rav Yosef Ber *zt"l*.

[8] Again.

[9] In the manner that they were rebuilt in Volozhin after the passing of Reb Hayyim Volozhiner *zt"l* and the way that the gates were rebuilt at the Yeshivas Rabbenu Yitzchak Elchanan after the passing of Rav Moshe Soloveitchik *zt"l*.

THE RAV AT JUBILEE: AN APPRECIATION

Rabbi Dr. Aharon Lichtenstein

Any account, testimonial or critical, of the significance of a major spiritual figure must refer to two intersecting axes: the vertical and the horizontal. On the one hand, he is to be perceived within his own field, as a laborer in its vineyards – relating in part to current peers, but as a link in a historical chain, to be measured primarily against predecessors and successors. On the other hand, he is to be regarded within the ambience of his broader contemporary milieu, with which he interacts and upon which he presumably impacts.

This point is particularly salient with respect to *moreinu verabbeinu,* the Rav *zt"l*, inasmuch as this dichotomy dovetails with a second distinction, pertinent to the Rav generally, and to his first major work, *Ish haHalakhah*, particularly. The Rav always had, of course, a penchant for positing antitheses and antinomies; and one of these – classically rooted in *Hazal* and *rishonim*, and constituting a major crux of general religious thought – was the relation of *talmud* and *ma'aseh.* Throughout *Ish haHalakhah*, a dual at times, even an ambivalent attitude, obtains with respect to the issue. At one juncture, we read:

> And when many halakhic concepts do not correspond with the phenomena of the real world, halakhic man is not at all distressed. His deepest desire is not the realization of the *Halakhah* but rather the ideal construction which was given to him from Sinai and this ideal construction exists forever.

Indeed, disengagement is idealized, even with reference to Torah activity proper, so that abstinence from *pesak* is not just reluctantly countenanced but virtually celebrated:

> The foundation of foundations and the pillar of halakhic thought is not the practical ruling but the determination of the theoretical *Halakhah.* Therefore, many of the greatest halakhic men avoided,

> and still avoid, serving in rabbinical posts. They rather join themselves to the group of those who are reluctant to render practical decisions.... The theoretical *Halakhah*, not the practical decision, the ideal creation, not the empirical one, represent the longing of halakhic man.[1]

This formulation is fully consistent with the Volozhin tradition's emphasis upon *Torah lishmah,* on the one hand, and with an ardent interest in the abstruse abstractions of neo-Kantian metaphysics and epistemology, on the other. Yet, elsewhere, a very different chord is struck. At one point, *talmud* and *ma'ase* are defined, objectively, as twin coordinates of halakhic existence:

> If a Jew lives in accordance with the *Halakhah* (and a life in accordance with the *Halakhah* means, first, the comprehension of the *Halakhah per se*, and, second, correlating the ideal *Halakhah* and the real world – the act of realization of the *Halakhah*), then he shall find redemption.[2]

Indeed, at one point, realization seems to be regarded as the ultimate telos, to which instrumental study is possibly subordinate:

> Halakhic man does not long for a transcendent world, for "supernal" levels of a pure, pristine existence, for was not the ideal world – halakhic man's deepest desire, his darling child –

---

[1] *Halakhic Man,* p. 23. With respect to the substance of this specific passage, several points may be noted: 1) The examples subsequently cited all refer to modes of dealing with deviant phenomena, whose failure to materialize – so that the relevant *halakhot* can be applied – is obviously not to be lamented. It does not follow from this, however, that a *talmid hakham* may be equally apathetic about the fate of positive or even ideal elements. 2) Abstinence from *pesak* out of *yirat hora'ah* may not reflect indifference to implementation but, rather, responsible concern about it, and hence, anxiety over possible error. 3) The statement about the reluctance of *gedolim* to enter the lists of *pesak* probably requires some qualification. It is true of some venues, nineteenth century Lithuania, out of whose tradition the Rav sprang, possibly being a case in point, but, as historical generalization, strikes me as somewhat sweeping.

[2] Ibid., p. 38.

> created only for the purpose of being actualized in our real world?[3]
>
> At the subjective plane, similarly, practical implementation is described as a desideratum of Halakhic man – perhaps, as *the* desideratum: "Halakhic man implements the Torah without any compromises or concessions, for precisely such implementation, such actualization is his ultimate desire, his fondest dream."[4]

This antithesis – ultimately, I believe, unresolved in the essay – is reflected in the Rav's life as well. As he and his father *zt"l* spent days and long winter nights by the hearth of the Khaslavitch *bet hamidrash,* poring over the niceties of *hatfasah bishvua* or of *holakhat haketoret beYom haKippurim,* could any flight of the imagination have led either to envision him as battling, in later years, for the welfare of as yet ununionized *shohetim,* scraping to meet weekly Maimonides School salary deadlines, or regularly addressing RCA or Mizrachi conventions? Yet, both aspects, the contemplative and the active, engaged the Rav throughout; and each, as well as their interaction, must be discussed in any survey of his achievement.

Between the distinctions I have posited, there is, to be sure, no correspondence. There is, however, a measure of correlation – the world of *ma'aseh* being viewed primarily with reference to the contemporary, while that of *talmud* looks before and after. Beginning, then, with the vertical axis, we focus initially upon the Rav's place within the historical continuum of *hakhmei hamesorah.* His role in this capacity is itself dual, spanning the realms of *halakhah* and *mahshavah* respectively. I believe that his position with respect to both differs markedly, however. Any objective description of the Rav as a *gadol* in the world of "learning" begins perforce by referring to his place within the Brisker tradition – begins, that is, by positing that in this sphere, he has not so much innovated a course as pursued one. The element of *hiddush* – as measured, say, against the achievement of the Rav's

---

[3] Ibid., p. 30.

[4] Ibid., p. 79.

grandfather, Reb Haym, or of a *Rabbeinu Tam* – is, therefore, in a meaningful sense, constricted.

This is, of course, stated without the slightest trace of deprecation. By definition, genuine methodological innovation in any field is unusual – all the more so in the Torah world, so oriented to *mesorah*; and it would be singularly rare for a person reared, like the Rav, in a highly self-conscious and articulate tradition, at a stage at which one could yet meet its founder. Moreover, excessively frequent sharp methodological shifts are, from an overall perspective, not only unlikely but undesirable, the value of novelty being very much a function of its historical context. Surely, however, such radical originality is not the litmus test of intellectual greatness, within the Torah world or elsewhere. Does anyone challenge the credentials of Rash of Sens or Rashba simply because they trod in the footsteps of Ri or Ramban, respectively?

If the Rav did not found a tradition, he certainly proved himself – within the parameters of the Brisker mode in which he was reared – a remarkable *me-haddesh*. Over the years, the Rav's creative powers awed *talmidim* repeatedly and, more than any other factor, charged the atmosphere of so many *shiurim*. The fusion of imagination and precision, of energized sweep and rigorous discipline, continually resolved cruces and informed insights. At its most electric, however, it enlarged the bound of halakhic empire by enriching its lexicon with fresh concepts. Ideas such as the *safek* of *tarti desatri* – doubt resulting from unresolved tension of conflicting elements rather than lack of knowledge – or of *mitzvot* whose *kiyyum* is inwardly experiential, although their implementation entails a normatively mandated physical act, may perhaps be retrospectively traced to some inchoate precedents. Unquestionably, however, as developed concepts, they bear the Rav's stamp, and it was he who implanted them within the Torah world.

Moreover, his creative energies ranged far afield. He was instrumental in significantly extending the scope of *lomdut,* particularly with respect to many areas of *Orah Hayyim*. What the Rav said of Reb Haym – that he had transmuted the *siddur* from the preserve of *shamashim* and *ba'alei batim* into the domain of *talmidei hakhamim* – was even truer of himself.

And yet, at bottom, the Rav's achievement in the realm of *halakhah*, remarkable as it was, bore fruit within a familiar field, one Reb Haym had tilled and sown; and he acknowledged this readily and gratefully. The situation is quite different with respect to the sphere of *mahshavah*. The areas of experience explored, the mode and level of inquiry, the resources employed, the problems formulated, above all, the ideas and emotions expressed – these indeed, constitute, conjunctively, a new departure. As regards *halakhah*, the Rav's achievement had, at least, analogues within the panoply of his peers – especially among those who moved within a common orbit and, hence, paralleled some of his *hiddushim*. None, however, even remotely approached the range and depth, the subtlety and complexity, of his *mahshavah*. And it was truly his – neither an extension nor an expansion of an existing defined tradition, but genuine innovation. After one has peeled away some of the homiletic component, for which there was ample precedent, so much of his work – and, particularly, the entire constellation – remains remarkably original, as regards both form and substance. Raw material he, of course, mined from many sources; but he was, in no sense, eclectic, and the product bore the imprint of his innermost thought and being. If there have been recent significantly comparable antecedents in the Torah world, I am unaware of them. Only Rav Kook, with whose views the Rav agreed in certain areas, but from which he diverged sharply in others, provides any basis for comparison; and both his primary concerns and his philosophic focus were very different. With regard to some aspects of the Rav's work, there were, of course, analogues in general culture, and this is obviously of interest to students of his thought or to intellectual historians at large. However, for *benei Torah*, in quest of spiritual direction, this fact does little to alter our perception of the uniqueness of the Rav's total *hashkafah* and experience.

His contribution was particularly significant at the interface of his two primary interests – in his attempt to formulate and enunciate a philosophy of *halakhah*. The attempt is not, of course, novel; but its undertaking by a *gadol* of the first rank, endowed with a rigorous philosophic training, is – at least, in the modern period – most striking. In approaching the issue, the Rav evidenced traces of both rationalism and fideism – and yet, in the spirit of *na'aseh venishma*, transcended both. While seeking, in a sense, to interpret *halakhah* in terms of general categories, he had little propensity for *ta'amei hamitzvot* in the tradition of, say, the *Sefer haHinukh* or Rav Samson Raphael Hirsch. For one thing, he eschewed the recourse to utilitarian considerations, if not the outright apologetics, which often typify this tradition. Rather, he persistently stressed that while the halakhic regimen is, as the Torah describes it, ultimately, *letov lakh,* its short – and intermediate – term message is that of demand and sacrifice. Beyond this, however, he had no predilection for explaining – much less, explaining away – the nitty-gritty of minutiae, and manifested no sense of responsibility to do so. He preferred, instead, broader vistas, addressing himself to overarching concerns, delineating underlying assumptions and ultimate goals, positing values and direction, defining the nature and thrust of *halakhah* as a normative order. In doing so, he sought – in the spirit of a much-cherished analogy to modern science – to focus upon the "what" rather than the "why." He insisted upon rigorous analysis of a *halakhah*, in its own legal terms, as a prerequisite to philosophizing about it; and he differentiated, radically, between rationale as extraneous to a *mitsvah* and that which may be of its woof and warp.

The enterprise is, admittedly, at times, delicately balanced. The Rav was vehement in rejecting the intrusion of subjective pseudophilosophic explanations as an instrument of interpreting objective halakhic material. And yet, with respect to *mitzvot* whose halakhic essence itself bears moral or theological import – tefilla is a prime examplethe Rav's own *hiddushim* clearly reflect his philosophic orientation. He insisted, vigorously, upon the autonomy of *halakhah*, regarding as quasi-heretical attempts to ascribe its content to historical, sociological, or psychological factors. And yet, the very notion of a "philosophy of *halakhah*" entails, by definition, viewing – although not, of course, judging – *devar Hashem* through the prism of universal categories. Moreover, the use of detail – to which recourse may be had to buttress a thesis but which can be neutralized, fideistically, as technical and inscrutable when inconsonant with it – opens up the charge of selectivity.

These issues are legitimate concerns, and certainly need to be addressed in any serious analysis of the Rav's work. And yet, delicate or not, balance there is. The fundamental difference between a philosophic orientation which is grounded upon *halakhah* and that which is imposed upon it, is clear. Even if, as applied to borderline cases, the distinction is nice, it is, nevertheless, conceptually sharp. Fine though the line may be at times, the Rav regarded it as a Rubicon. Unless mandated by the raw halakhic data proper, he was consistently wary of sacrificing formal to teleological considerations. Whether with respect to *bein adam laMakom or bein adam lahavero,* he rejected, categorically, inclinations to substitute contextual for normative thinking – unless, again, there was built-in flexibility within the halakhic base. Hence, he enriched our Torah world with a philosophic perception which is both authentic and insightful. The Rav's was an authoritative voice, elucidating the substance of *halakhah*, in all its ramifications, on the one hand, and relating it to general axiological and human concerns, whether personal or collective, on the other. In so doing, he broke fresh ground and put us all very much in his debt.

Sheer novelty or even singularity apart, what, in the Rav's thought and expression, has so powerfully gripped us? In part, of course, the force of his charismatic personality – especially as we have, at times, been alternately overwhelmed and enchanted by it, in the course of mesmerizing *derashot* and stimulating *shiurim*. Ultimately, however, his hold upon us has been far more substantive. W.B. Yeats once commented that a person writes rhetoric about his struggles with others and poetry about his struggles with himself. As an orator, the Rav had no peer in the Torah world. But it is the poet in him which has so touched and enthralled us. He has opened for us new vistas of spiritual experience, vistas within which the drama of human existence, in the form of confrontation with oneself, the cosmos, and, above all, the *Ribbono Shel Olam* – all within the context of halakhic existence in its most rigorous Brisker formulation – is charged with hitherto unperceived force and meaning. It is not as if we had engaged in the quest of *uVikkashtem Misham* and had faltered. We had simply never thought in those categories. It is not as if we had felt tremulous anxiety as lonely men and women, but in a minor chord. Mired in the pursuit of mundane daily concerns of faith, most of us had simply never confronted that reality. The Rav did. What we have missed, he experienced – in terms of the dichotomy so cherished by him – at both ends of the scale: *gadlut hamohin*, the depth and force of a powerful mind mastering its environment and impacting upon it, and that of *katnut hamohin*, the simplicity of the child – not as the epitome of intuited holistic existence idealized by the Romantics, but as the archetype of a helpless humble spirit groping towards his Father and seeking solace in Him and through Him.

Something of that experience he, through various channels, communicated to us; and, in so doing, he has sensitized us to the need for a fuller dimension of our own *avodat Hashem*. Flashes of what he saw and showed both engage and haunt us; chords of what he heard and said resonate in our ears; strains of what he felt palpitate in our hearts. Beyond detail, however, we have been gripped and stirred by *demut diyukno shel rabbeinu* – magisterial but sensitive, winsome and yet, ultimately, inscrutable – and his spiritual odyssey. At home, we have hanging one picture of the Rav with an engaging smile on his face; another of him, bent over pensively, with a somber, almost brooding expression. In looking at the latter, I am frequently reminded of Wordsworth's portrayal of the statue "Of Newton with his prism and silent face,/ The marble index of a mind for ever/ Voyaging through strange seas of thought, alone." Only not just a mind but a soul, not just thought but experience, and, above all, not marble, but a passionate human spirit.

From the realm of *talmud*, broadly conceived, we move to that of *ma'aseh*. Some of the Rav's activity in this sphere might be perceived as *askanut* – quasi-political, in a sense, and yet of genuine spiritual import. Two instances immediately spring to mind. The first is his stand vis-a-vis the Conservative and Reform movements. Hearing some current dilettantes, one might get the impression that the most eloquent and vigorous statement the Rav made with respect to the non-Orthodox was his protracted silence about the Synagogue Council of America. But those who remember the 50s accurately know better. Who issued the radical *pesak* that if one had to choose between forgoing *tekiat shofar* and hearing it in attendance at a mixed temple, he should opt for the former? Who, in the public mind, gave Orthodoxy intellectual respectability and credibility in its confrontation with other movements? To whom did *metukanim shebahem*, right-wing Conservative rabbis seeking to stem the tide of tinkering with *halakhah* – whether with respect to gentile wine or women being called up to the Torah – turn for guidance? Of course, the Rav knew, as we ought to know, that many, rabbis and laymen both, in deviationist movements, are genuine *mevakshei Hashem,* sincerely seeking the *Ribbono Shel Olam* within the context of *yahadut* as they perceive it; and to these, he accorded both respect and understanding. But, as a custodian of tradition, he was, in thwarting institutionalized revisionism, adamantly unwavering. One can truly apply to him Ramban's encomium, in his letter to the Northern French *rabbanim*, of Rambam: *Mi hika hatseddukim asher hayu bagiborim bosim, mi natan habaytusim leshusim, halo haRav z"l ki Hashem imo.*"[5]

The second instance concerns interfaith, rather than intra-communal, relations, although it, too, had internal ramifications as well. I refer, of course, to the Rav's adamant stand against Jewish Christian theological dialogue. Concerned – in the wake of Catholic overtures encouraged by the thaw in anti-Semitism mandated by the Second Vatican Council – that the sense of the singularity and uniqueness of *Kenesset Yisrael* might become jaded, both within and without the Jewish world, the Rav fought vigorously against incipient ecumenism. He, and only he, had both the stature and the courage to restrain those who, whether *leshem Shamayim or* otherwise (the prospect of having one's picture with the Pope appear on the front page of the *New York Times* is no mean temptation), sought the warm embrace of our erstwhile contemners; and the policy he enunciated – assent to dialogue about moral or social issues but rejection of discussions of faith and dogma – has stood the Orthodox community in good stead.

In retrospect, some may feel that the Rav's anxiety about missionary impulses and possible mass apostasy was exaggerated. Be that as it may, however, the episode – and it was more than that – boldly manifested the Rav's engagement in communal affairs and the leadership he exercised in that capacity.

Even in the realm of *ma'aseh,* however, sociopolitical activity was not the Rav's forte. His primary practical role was realized, rather, through the interface of *talmud* and *ma'asseh* – through teaching, which Aquinas aptly defined as the ideal fusion of the active and the contemplative life. This interaction probably lies at the heart of the Gemara's discussion, as understood by Rashi, about the comparative merits of *talmud* and *ma'aseh.*

---

[5] *Kitvei HaRamban* (Jerusalem 5746), 1:341.

Resolving an apparent contradiction about their respective priority, the *Gemara* concludes: "*Lo kashya, hahi lemigmar, ha leagmurei.*" Rashi explains: "*Lemigmar leatsmo, ma'aseh adif, aval leagmurei leaharinei adif mima'aseh.*"[6] Presumably, the intent is not simply that teaching is more meritorious, qua *talmud*, than *ma'aseh,* but rather that, in effect, it incorporates both, in the spirit of *Hazal*'s formulation: *"Torah lilamdah, zo hi Torah shel hesed; shelo lilamdah, zo hi Torah she'einah shel hesed."*[7]

As regards the Rav, then, his primary practical contribution was as *moreinu verabbeinu,* our master teacher. And this, in two respects: First, of course, in the narrow sense of exposition, explication and instruction. He often – albeit, at times, with a note of conveniently feigned self-deprecation – described himself as a *melamed*; and that he was without peer. His capacity for formulating pivotal questions, with an eye to the relation between principle and detail; his sheer pedagogic skill, in stimulating curiosity and insight; above all, his fertile and suggestive solutions – these continually left their imprint upon students, over the span of half a century.

He addressed himself to this task with conscious dedication, dictated, in part, by his professional responsibilities as a *rav ha'ir* or as a *rosh yeshiva*, but driven, far beyond what those duties required, by the impetus of mission, that pervasive sense of *shelihut* of which he often spoke, so fervently and so eloquently. This was, obviously, primarily manifested in the course of regular *shiurim*, whose sheer scope is strikingly impressive; but it is also impinged upon his *harbatsat Torah* as a whole. It largely influenced, for instance, the choice of topics for the *Yahrtseit shiurim*, so heavily tilted toward *Orah Hayyim*, and almost wholly devoid of more abstruse areas such as *Kodashim*, which had been his father's forte and in a sense, his own first love. I vividly recall how one year, several decades back, he began to prepare a *Yahrtseit shiur* to deal with *kinyan hatser*, but then dropped the idea out of concern that the infrastructure might not be sufficiently familiar to many in the audience. In a similar vein, when, in later years, his interest in publication intensified, he was firm in encouraging the assignment of

---

6 *Baba Kama* 17a; Rashi, *s.v. lemigmar.*

7 *Sukka* 49b.

primacy to writings which would best serve the general Torah public, rather than to those which were geared to his indigenous "*lomdische*" constituency.

In the Rav's thought and experience, his role as *moreinu verabbeinu* went in tandem with a second role, that of *meturgeman.* He once remarked to me that, basically, it is the function of *marbitsei Torah,* in each generation, to render its content into the language and categories of their contemporaries; and there is no question that this facet was an integral component of any self-portrait he limned. That rendering was, of course, interpretation rather than mere translation, and very much in the spirit of the *Gemara* in *Kiddushin*: "*Tanei, Rabi Yehudah omer, 'Hametargem pasuk ketzurato, harei zeh badai, vehamosif alav, harei zeh meharef umegadef, ela mai Targum – Targum didan.*"[8]

As a halakhic entity, *Targum didan* is related to an area much developed by the Rav, *keriat haTorah.* Explicating a *pasuk* in *Nehemiah*, describing Torah reading upon the return from exile, the *Gemara* explains:

> *Amar Rav Hananel amar Rav, "Mai dikhtiv, 'Vayikre'u basefer beTorat haElokim me-forash vesom sekhel vayavinu bamikra'? 'Vayikre'u basefer beTorat haElokim,' ze Mikra, 'Meforash,' ze Targum, 'Vesom sekhel,' eilu hapesukim, 'Vayavinu bamikra,' ze pisuk te'amim, veamrei la, elu hamesorot."*[9]

In this connection, the Rav repeatedly developed a distinction between the *keriah* of mid-week or *minhah* on Shabbat – primarily geared to maintaining continual contact with Torah as a vivifying force – and that of Shabbat morning, intended to provide not only inspiration but instruction and direction. Hence, he contended that *targum* was confined to the latter, as a vehicle for the realization of public *talmud Torah,* for which an intermediary interpreter could be pivotal, in line with the prescription of an oft-quoted *Yerushalmi*:

---

[8] *Kiddushin* 49a.

[9] *Nedarim* 37b.

> *Keshem shenitenah al yedei sirsur, kakh anu tserikhin linhog ba al – yedei sirsur. A'al Rabi Yehuda bar Pazi ve – avda she'eilah, 'Anokhi omed ben Hashem u'veineikem ba'eit hahi lehagid lakem et devar Hashem.*[10]

The Rav was central to our weekday and Shabbat *keriah* both as our link to the *mesorah* – infusing us with the substance of Torah, on the one hand – and through creative explication, halakhic and philosophic, relating it to the realities of the modern world, on the other. This dual integrated function of *rav meturgeman* is a difficult and delicate enterprise. Interpret too literally, and you run the risk of ossification and obscurantism – *harei zeh badai;* range too far afield, and you raise the specter of blasphemous deviation – *harei zeh meharef umegadef.* Only *Targum didan*, traditional creative exposition, in the hands of a thoroughly responsible and richly innovative master, hits the mark. And we are all deeply in the Rav's debt for having embarked on this undertaking.

The Rav's dual role as spiritual mentor was, for him, a source of immense gratification. However, it was also, perhaps inevitably, a cause of considerable frustration. That frustration centered, primarily, on the sense that the full thrust of his total *keriah-targum* was often not sufficiently apprehended or appreciated; that, by some, parts of his Torah were indeed being digested and disseminated, but other essential ingredients were being relatively disregarded, if not distorted. In a moment of striking candor, when my colleague, Rav Yehuda Amital, first visited these shores, over twenty years ago, the Rav commented to him: "You know, I have devoted *talmidim* – very devoted *talmidim.* If I were to announce a *shiur* at two o'clock in the morning, they would come *en bloc.* And yet, deep in their hearts, they think I'm an *apikoros.*" The remark was laced with characteristic humor and confined, presumably, to a select group. Nevertheless, it gave vent to a genuine, if painful, sentiment.

The ideological fault aside, he often felt – and this, with respect to a far broader group – that even among his *talmidim*, some of his primary spiritual concerns were not so much rejected as ignored; indeed, that spirituality itself was being neglected. He was, like Rambam, persistently perturbed by religious vulgarization, practical or conceptual, and by shallow ritualization,

---

[10] *Yerushalmi, Megilla* 4:1.

of either the "modern" or the "*frum*" strain; and the tension between the subjective and the objective, between action, thought and experience, was a major lifelong concern. The sense that he was only partially successful in imparting that concern gnawed at him, and impelled efforts to redress the imbalance; but these, too, were only partly successful.

After his wife's death in 1967, he initiated intensive *shiurim* for *talmidim* who would come to Brookline to learn during the summer. One day (*ca.* 1969–70), he stunned the group by announcing that, inasmuch as he found them spiritually desiccated, he would now, in addition to the regular *shiurim* on the *massekhet*, learn the *Likutei Torah* of the *Ba'al haTanya* with them; and he started, the following day, with the section on *Ani ledodi vedodi li*. "But," he confided to me subsequently, "it didn't really help."

The most forceful expression of this sentiment is to be found in a brief essay which I regard as the single best introduction to the Rav's thought – all the more so, as it bears the stamp of total genuineness, having been conceived and composed during and shortly after his bout with cancer in the winter of 1959–60. After lamenting that the current Torah world has produced aspiring *talmidei hakhamim* who are intellectually assertive but experientially deficient, he goes on to assign part of the blame to himself:

> Therefore, I hereby announce that I am able to identify one of those responsible for the present situation – and that is I myself. I have not fulfilled my obligation as a *moreh derekh vehora'ah* in Israel. I lacked the spiritual energies which a teacher and rabbi needs, or I lacked the necessary will, and did not dedicate everything I had to my goal. While I have succeeded, to a great or small degree, as a teacher and guide in the area of "*gadlut hamohin*" – my students have received much Torah from me, and their intellectual stature has been strengthened and increased during the years they have spent around me – I have not seen much success in my efforts in the experiential area. I was not able to live together with them, to cleave to them and to transfer to them from the warmth of my soul. My words, it seems, have not kindled the *shalhevet y-ah* in sensitive hearts. I have sinned as a *marbits Torah shebalev*, which has

> been given over in a fashion which has been *mema'et haDemut* to the point *of katnut hamohin.* Blame me for the mistake.[11]

That, too, is part of the Rav's legacy. Not just spellbinding *shiurim*, magnificent *derashot,* and electrifying *hiddushim*, but the candid recognition of failure – failure which is transcended by its very acknowledgement. In his own personal vein, so aristocratic and yet so democratic, he has imbued us with a sense of both the frailty of majesty and the majesty of frailty. He has transmitted to us not only *Torat Moshe Avdi*, but the Midrashic image of Moshe Rabbeinu constructing and then dismantling the *mishkan* daily during *shivat yemei hamilu'im* – whose import the Rav interpreted as the fusion of radical, almost Sisyphean frustration, with ultimate hope. He has initiated us, far from the admiring crowd, into the anguished quest – unlike Plotinus, he did not necessarily experience it as a flight (as either ascent or escape) – of the alone for the Alone. He has left us not only with memories of packed audiences, dazzled by his multi-faceted powers, but the riveting sense of the message of the *Mishna*, so humbling and yet so inspiring: "*Minayin she'afilu ehad sheyoshev ve'osek baTorah, sheHakadosh Barukh Hu kove'a lo sakhar? Shene'emar, 'Yeshev badad veyidom ki natal alav.*'"[12]

The Rav repeatedly referred to this *Mishnah* when expatiating upon the experiential character of *talmud Torah*; the meeting envisioned by it may be regarded as the epitome of the Rav's *talmud* and *ma'aseh* combined. His quintessential aspiration was the fusion of spirituality and *lomdut.* We, who come after, cannot retrospectively imagine the past half-century without him. Prospectively, as dwarfs on a giant's shoulders, we feel charged to persist, impelled by his spirit, in the implementation of his goals – to learn, to teach, to realize. To the best of our abilities, we are called and we are pledged to continue, in the *bet hamidrash* and in the community, his multi-faceted enterprise – *lehagdil Torah u'leha'adirah.*

---

[11] "*Al Ahavat haTorah uGe'ulat Nefesh haDor,*" in *Besod haYahid vehaYahad* (Jerusalem, 1976).

[12] *Avot* 3:2.

MY GRANDFATHER HAS LEFT ME*

RABBI MOSHE LICHTENSTEIN

How can a grandson eulogize his grandfather? How dare he assume such a task? Will not fear and awe overtake him? Would it not be preferable to wrap himself in the silence of sorrow and the solace of tears? Can he really hope to accurately portray the departed persona or faithfully describe his personality? The eulogy must be a full and accurate description of the deceased, his personality and acts, the wonderful and unique within him. But the grandson could observe the great creative powers of his beloved grandfather only through the blurry vision of childhood, the veil of youth cast upon his eyes throughout the period of his elder's zenith. Yet, when the grandson matured and ripened, ready to receive his grandfather's bounty, it was too late, for by then the elderly figure had already begun to withdraw, slowly receding from younger generation. The grandson could see the present, but he passed. Though a glimpse of the towering stature was still discernible, and although retrospection is a form of vision, can it possibly compare to direct contact with the power and intensity of fully active years?

Furthermore, how can a grandson attempt to eulogize a grandfather who was a supreme master of Torah, a figure who expressed his great

---

* This *hesped* originally appeared in Hebrew in *Alon Shevut-Bogrim,* the alumni journal of Yeshivat Har Etzion, on the occasion of the Rav's first *Yahrtseit.*

Though urged by friends to publish an English translation, and wanting to do the utmost to honor and respect the memory of my grandfather and rebbi, I nevertheless have certain misgivings which I have not been able to completely overcome. First, it would appear from the *Gemara* in *Yevamot* [79a; see also *Ketubot* 103b and *Yore De'ah* 394:2] that a *hesped* should be performed only within the first twelve months of the *petirah*, as the original indeed was. Second, though the formal halakhic problem can be overcome – since it should be understood to refer to an oral *hesped* as part of the process of grief and mourning – the underlying emotional truth that the period of a grieving obsession with the departed should not exceed twelve months (no matter how great or how close) retains its validity.

Thus, my involvement with the English version lacked the sense of immediacy and directness which accompanied the writing of the Hebrew original, which was a cathartic outpouring of a grieving soul struggling to comprehend and express its sense of loss. Despite these misgivings, which I feel a need to share with readers, it was decided to proceed and publish this *hesped* in the hope that it may strike a chord in some hearts and serve as reminder of he who was amongst us and is no longer here.

personality through force of intellect and breadth of vision, as he attempted to penetrate the mysterious and the deep. Who can gather the strength to describe a grandfather who defined the art of eulogy as follows: "It is the duty of the eulogist to present a full, comprehensive description of the greatness of the departed, in reasoned tranquil categories, to stress all the mysterious wonder interwoven in the concrete personal reality.... The eulogist is an excellent educator, the agent of the cool quiet intellect, and also an artist representing the irrational, absurd experience.... The eulogist explains and interprets, illustrates and creates."[1] Can a grandson rush in, fearless of where he treads, to comply with these rigorous criteria, which have been imposed by his own grandfather, the greatest eulogist of the generation? Even if his inferior intellect supports him in this endeavor, will he be able to control his emotions in the face of his great loss? As soon as he begins to describe his grandfather, powerful feelings will overwhelm him as he remembers their warm and loving relationship and recollects fond memories of the many beautiful hours which they spent together. Moreover, were all these emotions to be controlled, the struggling grandson will, nevertheless, be overcome by a sense of disappointment and guilt for the Torah that he lost and the wisdom, which he missed.

However, in spite of all this, how can one not eulogize and lament a grandfather such as the Rav *zt"l, a* genius of *halakhah* and a giant of spirit, a figure belonging to the select group of the Sages of our Tradition (*Hakhmei haMesorah*)? Both natural human feeling and the halakhic obligations regarding human dignity (*kevod haberiot*) and the honor of Torah (*kevod haTorah*) require me to set forth upon this endeavor. And though I may be unable to fulfill the task of faithfully portraying his image, the *Mishnah* in *Pirkei Avot* has already taught us that a person may not shy away from his charge, even though it is unexpected of him to complete it.

I

The *Gemara* in *Baba Batra* (59a) relates: "A pipe which drains water to the yard of one's neighbor and the owner of the roof tries to stop it up, the owner of the yard can prevent him.... Rav Oshaya said he has the right to prevent him; Rav Hama said he does not have the right to prevent him.

---

1 "*Peleitat Sofereihem*," in *Divrei Hagut veHa'arakhah* (Yerushalayim, 1981), 139.

They went and asked Rav Bisa, who said he has the right to prevent him. Rami bar Hama said of him 'The threefold cord is not readily broken' – this is Rav Oshaya, the son of Rav Hama, the son of Rav Bisa." The *Tosafot* remark: "There were many such that they and their fathers and their fathers' fathers were outstanding scholars, yet this is not said of them; here, however, all three saw each other."

Thus, it was not merely the fact that three generations of the same family achieved Torah scholarship that so impressed Rami bar Hama, nor was his exclamation due to the uniqueness of this phenomenon. After all, there have been many such families. Rami bar Hama felt that he was witnessing something extraordinary. Rav Oshaya was not merely a member of the group of sages who were fortunate enough to be the sons and grandsons of learned scholars; it was rather that he embodied a special combination that contained the treasures and traditions of former generations. Old and new were integrated within him. His threefold cord wove together his father's Torah learning, fully absorbed and comprehended, with his own great native forces of innovation and creativity. In his youth, he learned Torah with his father and grandfather and debated with them weighty halakhic issues; delving into difficult passages together, he acquired their mode of learning as a lasting possession. Returning as an adult to these same *sugyot*, he was able to pour new content into them as result of the personal method which he had developed and perfected over the years. The unique strength of the threefold cord is not due to its additional thickness, but to its complexity; each thread adds a new dimension to the cord. Thus, he who builds his personality and learning by combining his native powers and individual approach with those of his fathers can attain a singular level that is not to be found in those who rely solely on their own powers or depend on those of their forebears.

It is the way of the world that a son takes over from his father. One generation passes on the tradition to its successor: "Instead of your ancestors will be your children; you will appoint them princes throughout the land" (Psalms 45:17). A child receives instruction from his father, a student from his teacher. Thus, the torch of traditional learning and scholarship is passed on from generation to generation. The passage in

Isaiah (59:21), which the *Gemara* in *Baba Metsia* (85a) interprets as referring to Torah, describes and emphasizes this process: "And this shall be My covenant with them, said the Lord. My spirit which is upon you, and the words which I have placed in your mouth, shall not be absent from your mouth, nor from the mouth of your children, nor from the mouth of your children's children – said the Lord – from now throughout all time." No premium can be placed upon the centrality or importance of this transmission, about which God entered into a covenantal relationship with us. Studying with and teaching one's children are the foundation of our tradition, and thus, Torah remains rooted within families. *Tosafot* inform us that there have been many learned families throughout the course of our history. A succession of three generations, a grandfather, father and grandson, all Torah scholars, is an extremely important but not a particularly rare phenomenon and does not justify an exclamation of wonder. Generations may differ or they may resemble one another; what is common to them, though, is that each member is rooted within the Torah world of his time. Whether he applies and continues his learning method as he was trained, or develops a different approach, each participant is an additional link in the chain of tradition, a continuation of the previous generation. "Perets begot Hetsron, Hetsron begot Ram, Ram begot Aminadav, Aminadav begot Nahshon, Nahshon begot...." Generations come and go, but tradition remains forever.

Sometimes, though, instead of the usual thread attached to the previous one at its tip – the son taking the place of the father – a unique threefold cord presents itself. A person who carries both his own talents and those of the preceding generations appears. Not only his capacities, but also those of his ancestors are evident in him. Three generations are combined within one individual. The forces of the past and present ferment within him. He succeeds in breaking the barrier of the present as he weaves together elements of the past's mighty heritage with his own innovations. He does not merely reconstruct the past, nor does he simply cling to his ancestors' Torah. Although every fiber in the layers of his personality is capable of standing on its own, his unique power is created by the integration of all three elements in a single persona. When confronted with a Rav who uses the achievements of the past to create a new method and approach, who is able to draw from the past and impress a new stamp upon it, all shall rejoice and proclaim: "The threefold cord is not readily broken."

Rav Oshaya was such a man. When Rami bar Hama came to the *bet midrash* and found Rav Oshaya ruling – in opposition to his father's opinion – that the owner of the yard has the right to prevent the pipe from being stopped up, he sent for the opinion of Rav Bisa, the grandfather. Rav Bisa determined that the pipe cannot be stopped up unilaterally. This caused Rami bar Hama to wonder: if this is his grandfather's opinion, what is Rav Oshaya adding? Why doesn't he simply cite Rav Bisa's ruling? Does the addition of extra names add any weight to the ruling? He carefully reexamined the issue and understood; Rav Oshaya was not merely repeating his elder's opinion, he was expressing an independent view. A new perspective was being brought to the question. Though his conclusion was identical to his predecessor's, the rationale behind it reflected his own particular approach. Thus, the old and the new were combined to form a new method.

My grandfather, the Rav, was also such a figure. He, too, was an illustrious grandson, an outstanding product of his family's Brisker school. His mastery of the rigorous analytical method and innovative approach of the "Brisker *derekh*" was complete. A full-fledged member of the inner circle of Reb Hayyim's children and grandchildren, he acquired the Brisker way of learning at a very young age. While yet a young boy whose wisdom far exceeded his years, he sent his *hiddushei Torah* to Reb Hayyim himself, who proudly exhibited them to others. When he grew older, he engaged in an active correspondence with his uncle Reb Velvel, the Brisker Rav. But the supreme influence upon him in the formative learning years was, of course, the constant, uninterrupted years of study with his father, Reb Moshe Soloveitchik, as they sat together day and night, clarifying most of the difficult passages in the Talmud. This marvelous relationship between father and son, linked together in heart and soul, which began in a tiny Byelorussian *shtetl* and remained constant until the day of Reb Moshe's death in New York, created a Torah giant proficient and creative in the ways of his ancestors.

Though the Rav was born in Lithuania, he died in the United States; though commencing his studies in Chaslavitch, he ended them in Boston.

Though clearly a Brisker scion, he was an independent personality who stood by himself, uniquely different from all who preceded him. A threefold cord interweaving the past and the present, the old and the new, Berlin with Brisk, Boston with Volozhin – such a figure was my grandfather, the Rav.

II

The Rav was a multi-faceted individual. A great scholar in many fields, he was a master of *halakhah* and *aggadah*, learning and philosophy exoteric and esoteric wisdom. However, attempting to delineate his persona and to describe his spiritual world, we must emphasize the world of Torah study and *halakhah* as its prime mover. If there was one feature imprinted upon the depths of his soul, if there was a single primordial experience for the Rav – it was the study of *Torah lishmah.* If I had to describe my grandfather in two words, they would undoubtedly be "Halakhic Man." He regarded himself as a teacher surrounded by students engaging in *Torah lishmah*, a Rav instructing his congregants in the details of halakhic *sugyot* as they all joined together to form the community of tradition. His self-image was neither that of the philosopher, communal leader, or author, even though all these were part of his personality and achievements.

Before the holidays, he would bless his students that they should be able to experience the *kedushat hayom* through the study of its *halakhot.* It was Torah study that supported him during the difficult years in the aftermath of his wife's death, enabling his bleeding soul to find some repose. The enormous energy that he poured into teaching and disseminating Torah protected and preserved him; it may be said of this period that "the Torah of duress is what stood by me." A particularly striking instance of how deeply ingrained Torah was in the Rav's personality is worth relating. In the immediate aftermath of surgery, when medication loosened the grip of his stern, conscious self-control and his inner self freely expressed itself, a series of solutions to difficult Rambams poured out! The qualities of Halakhic Man, so brilliantly depicted in his great essay, were firmly imprinted upon the depths of his soul.

Let us begin, therefore, with a description of his halakhic enterprise. The rigorous Brisker approach of strict analysis and clarification of concepts, well known throughout the modern Torah world, was masterfully continued and developed by the Rav. All areas of *halakhah* were illuminated by his penetrating analysis. Issue after issue, from the beginning of the *Shas* to its end, were examined, taught, and interpreted.

Actually, he was not alone in this endeavor. Reb Hayyim's method – itself a combination of elements long existing in the world of *halakhah* with the vigor and vitality of the new tools of systematic analysis and criticism – was securing for itself a central role in the Lithuanian Torah world. Although surrounded by only a handful of close students throughout most of his teaching career, Reb Hayyim's approach rapidly won over the hearts of the learning public. Despite encountering initial opposition on the part of the senior *rabbanim*, within a generation his method reigned supreme in the Lithuanian *yeshivot*. All those familiar with the works of the so-called "*Roshei Yeshivas* generation" are well acquainted with the Brisker influence. Thus, the Rav was a partner in an enterprise that many others were also participating in. Some of the *hiddushei Torah* which he wrote as a youth and declined to publish, as befitting an authentic member of Brisk, were subsequently published by others who had independently arrived at similar conclusions. Nevertheless, he was superb in this endeavor, producing Torah of the highest quality. An understanding of Reb Hayyim's method and its characteristics will enable us to explain and demonstrate the Rav's achievements in this respect.

There are many ways to approach the methodology developed by the Rav's grandfather, Reb Hayyim Soloveitchik of Brisk, and it is certainly not our intention here to provide a comprehensive analysis. However, if we limit ourselves to a single point, the core of the method consists in shifting the center of interest from the intent and goal of the halakhic ruling to its actual manifestation in practical terms *(nafka mina)*. It is not a hidden rationale or biblical intention (*ta'ama di-kra*) that provides the point of origin for the discussion, but the phenomenon in and of itself. The student places his interest in the fruit of the tree rather than its roots. Thus, unsubstantiated hypotheses relating to hidden matters are eliminated and scholars are prevented from speculating about unverifiable issues which cannot be judged by concrete halakhic phenomena. Torah study is, therefore, placed upon firm ground and criticism established as the cornerstone of the learning activity. Purely speculative hypotheses (*sevarot*) are subordinated, as reasoning is required to account for halakhic manifestations in actual practice. Principles are not accepted unless they grow directly and organically out of the details in the *Gemara* and Rambam and are capable of being criticized by them. Disagreement among the *rishonim* must be explained, and if a theoretical distinction is suggested, it must provide a practical manifestation that illustrates the difference. There should be no phenomenon without an explanation and no explanation without a phenomenal expression.

This principle is obviously analogous to the scientific revolution of the early seventeenth century. Here, as there, there is a shift of interest from the "why" to the "what" and "how," from the final cause to the effective cause. In the same manner that the change in scientific outlook led to far-reaching achievements, so, too, did the new critical approach of Reb Hayyim do so in the sphere of Torah study. The Brisker revolution is the Copernican revolution of the halakhic world.

Part of this process is the increased emphasis placed upon Rambam by the followers of Brisk. As long as Torah study focused upon the supposed theoretical reasoning underlying a Talmudic passage, a gap existed between the Talmudic commentators *ad locum* and the *Mishneh Torah*, which is essentially a book of applied *halakhah*. Thus, a commentator would ordinarily devote his time and effort to the study of other commentaries dealing with the same text, while a *posek* of practical *halakhah* would deal with the relevant halakhic literature, each remaining within his specific field. (This is obviously a generalization and is not meant to be absolute.) However, as soon as the interpretation of the Talmudic passage itself becomes dependent upon its practical implications, it is imperative to systematically examine the various practical conclusions which may be derived from it. This, of course, is where the *Mishneh Torah* enters the picture, for it is the monumental review of the conclusions which have developed out of the Talmudic passages, and, therefore, ideally suited for Reb Hayyim's purposes.

To be totally clear and to prevent any misunderstandings, I would like to point out that the emphasis upon the halakhic conclusions of the *sugya* is not meant to arrive at any conclusions regarding practical behavior, but is a purely interpretive enterprise. Therefore, the interest is not necessarily in the final conclusions, but in the halakhic manifestations throughout all stages of the discussion. The aim of the Brisker approach is the conceptual formulation, not the prescription of behavior, and in this, too, it resembles the scientific attempt to derive abstract laws and concepts from concrete phenomena. However, the abstraction and conceptualization must be sought through the practical manifestations dictated by the Talmudic passage and subject to their criticism. Therefore, the method is equally applicable in all areas of the Talmud – *Kodashim* and *Taharot* as well as *Mo'ed* and *Nashim*. This, according to Reb Hayyim's method, is the real meaning of *"le'asukei shemateta a'li dehilkheta"*: the interpretation of the *sugya* based upon its halakhic implications, regardless of our actual ruling regarding practice.

This approach, which is the foundation of Reb Hayyim's method, and which gives it its unique quality, also poses a danger. If we focus on the "what" rather than the "why," we have remained faithful to the facts and have been careful not to proceed beyond what is warranted. However, focusing upon the pure structural logic within a *sugyah* without examining the plausibility of the conclusions, erecting a halakhic paradigm based upon the concrete details regardless of whether it is reasonable or not, is as serious a defect as pure speculation detached from the details. Both the "speculative fallacy" and the "logical fallacy" must be avoided. The "what" must also withstand the criticism of the "why." Even though two separate alternatives can function as two facets of a halakhic investigation (*hakirah*), explaining differences of opinion and enhancing various details, they cannot be accepted if there is no rationale behind them which is reasonable in the context of their topic. The relationship between these two factors must be a mutual one, each engaging and critical of the other element. The point of contact between these two elements is where the problematic aspect of the Brisker approach is exposed. The heavy emphasis placed upon the analytical element may easily undermine the delicate balance between the two factors, since any investigation which postulates two sides to a question and demonstrates their practical implications can be accepted without any further ado.

It is this very point of encounter which enables us, it seems, to comprehend the unique quality of the Rav's learning (aside, of course, from his natural intellectual ability). Indeed, many followed Reb Hayyim's footsteps and attained important achievements. However, even the most capable of his disciples were not always able to avoid the "logical fallacy." Radical formulations which were logically possible but opposed to any reasonable standard of plain halakhic thinking were adopted on occasion, creating conclusions which were highly implausible, even though valid if judged by *a priori* logic alone. Others, who were not satisfied with merely explaining the phenomena, abandoned Reb Hayyim's method altogether and lost the critical anchor of the concrete halakhic expression (*nafka mina*).

The Rav avoided both extremes. Fundamentally faithful to his grandfather's method, his ideas were subjected to the critical control of the actual halakhic case. He was careful not to rashly charge into areas where he could not exercise such control. Nonetheless, he took care to examine the results of his inquiry into the actual halakhic manifestation in the light of simple logic. When one of his students mentioned a well known (and seemingly self evident) *hakirah* to him, the Rav's response was, "I have no idea what the second option could possibly mean." I vividly remember this tension dramatically expressing itself the first day I was in his *shiur*. We were learning the issues of *gezeilah* in the ninth chapter of *Bava Kama* that year. The first *shiur* began with the following statement by the Rav: "There is a well-known inquiry into the nature of the obligation to return stolen property. I don't like it since it is obvious to me that one of the possibilities should be rejected; however, what can I do, it is clear that both sides are represented in a debate between the *Ba'al haMa'or* and Ramban" [*Sanhedrin* 72a]. Personal logic and common sense must have their say, but if the evidence in the sources indicate otherwise, the evidence must be accepted.

What should be emphasized, moreover, is that the Brisker method was not, for the Rav, an acquired technique or a scholarly method which he received from his mentors. His natural thought patterns were forged out of analytic understanding. His initial reading of a *sugyah* was an analytic one; intrinsically, he read the passage in such a manner. The prism through which he viewed all issues was an analytic one, exposing the conceptual structure of the text as a matter of course. Thus, his manner of learning was not the application of a technique or the utilization of acquired tools, which may be occasionally employed and occasionally forgotten, accepted at times and neglected at others. His learning was not founded upon sudden flashes of insight or based upon an intuitive reasoning as fleeting as it is sudden. The Rav's Torah was based upon the rock-solid foundation of an internalized systematic thought process, steady and sure, analytic and innovative. Therefore, the Rav's leaning did not distinguish between greater or lesser issues, minor or major *sugyot*; whatever he studied was subject to his scholarly critique and intellectual discipline. Brief and minor issues were analyzed in the same manner as weighty, intricate and well-known passages, since the same inner logic applies to them all. Great or small, weighty or trivial, all matters were treated equally.

It is worth noting in this context that the Rav's scholarly net was spread over all areas of Torah learning. I do not mean to claim that he devoted a great amount of time and energy to relatively neglected halakhic sources such as the *Yerushalmi* or the *Sifrei* or that he had a phenomenal memory, but rather that he trained his scholarly eye even upon sources which are not generally considered deserving of halakhic attention. Thus, he gleaned pearl after pearl from the *siddur*, *kinot*, and *piyyutim* and interwove them into his halakhic presentations. My memory still retains, in all its vividness and freshness, the wonderful *shiur* which he gave upon the structure of *tefilat musaf* of the *shalosh regalim,* weaving together the relevant *sugyot,* passages from the *siddur, keriat haTorah* and *Sefer haMitzvot.* The *Yahrtseit shiur* on the issue of *mehikat haShem* (which was later published in *Shiurim leZekher Abba Mari)* ended with a fundamental distinction *(hiluk)* between two aspects of *yud he* as a *shem,* which was based, in part, upon a *diyyuk* in *Targum Onkelos.* With his sharp eye, the Rav was able to identify and transform such non-halakhic material, utilizing it for his purposes time after time.

The systematic thought that analytically penetrated everything it took in – great or small, classic or unconventional sources – is what gave the Rav's learning its authority and force. However, a systematic critical ability was not the only quality that characterized his Torah. The Rav was also blessed with an abundance of creative and innovative powers. These burst forth from the depths of his personality, forming a fountain of learning creativity, flowing along the lively new paths of Torah through which their creator channeled them. What he claimed about Halakhic Man – "[he] received the Torah from Sinai not as a simple recipient, but as a creator of worlds"[2] he was able to achieve in his own person, and what he added there, that "the power of innovation is the basis of tradition," can be seen as an accurate description of his own endeavor, a Torah which is original and innovative, yet deeply rooted in the continuity of tradition.

Thus, the Rav remained firmly rooted in the family tradition of Brisker learning, through his adherence to the mutually controlling relationship between cause and effect, concrete phenomena and analytic conceptualization. The additional quality which he added as a third thread to the existing cord of tradition was an involvement in halakhic areas which unite cause and effect into a single learning unity. The establishment of areas and issues which entwine the two together, in contrast to the usual Brisker opposition between cause and effect, is what characterized his unique contribution.

Addressing issues of halakhic import whose primary motive is to be found in the religious experience, he was able to combine his analytic Brisker approach with his philosophical powers, as he interwove the religious rationale with the concrete details to create a unified halakhic entity. The greater the link between *halakhah* and *aggadah*, the more he felt at home in that area. Thus, he laid new foundations in areas such as *berakhot, avelut, keriat haTorah, gerut, tefillah, mo'adim, kiddush hahodesh,* and many others. Totally new concepts were created in this manner. This trend can be clearly discerned in some of the opening passages of the book of *hiddushei Torah* which he co-authored with his father, Reb Moshe *zt"l,* while still a youth. This combination would fully blossom later in the *shiurim* which the Rav would deliver on these topics as part of his teaching routine, and attain its most outstanding expression in the *yahrtseit shiurim* which he would deliver in memory of his father. Anyone perusing the two volumes of his book, *Shiurim leZekher Abba Mari*, will clearly see what achievements were realized in these areas and how unique he was in this, both in contrast to his Brisker predecessors and his contemporary colleagues.

Nonetheless, it is important to reiterate that this development did not entail an abandonment of the basic Brisker method, neither in terms of his

---

[2] *Halakhic Man*, L. Kaplan trans. (Philadelphia, 1983), 81.

self-image nor in actual substance. Development and innovation are found here, but not a renunciation or disclaim of the fundamental system. This is the secret of the threefold cord.

III

The Rav's halakhic achievement, his bright white threefold cord, was accompanied by an additional strand of *tekhelet*, the colored thread whose associations remove man from his personal world and garment to contemplate the sea, skies and Heaven, reaching up to the Heavenly throne itself. The personal *tekhelet* which my grandfather affixed to his halakhic *lavan* was a philosophical and experiential acceptance of the natural physical world in which man was placed by God, as well as an involvement with man's complex relationship towards this world as he strives to present himself before his Creator. The majesty and greatness of a dignified human existence accompanied with the proper sense of humility and respect, an ongoing dialogue between man and the Almighty (and between the covenantal community of Israel and its Divine companion), the place of man within a technological society, these and similar dilemmas all appear in his writings. Such were the topics which the Rav dealt with and wrote about, and such were the issues which he experienced in his inner being.

The interweaving of both strands, the blue thread of philosophical enquiry with the white one of Torah scholarship combined to create a special personality and philosophical approach. Since a eulogy is not the place to deal with the specifics of my grandfather's philosophical outlook, we will confine ourselves here to the essence and aims of his approach. The linchpin of the system is to be found in the synthesis of *halakhah* and philosophy and the Jewish and general worlds which serve both to establish the topics of consideration and as source material for the actual discussions. It is this unique combination which gives the Rav's teachings their vitality and force. The mastery which the Rav achieved in both *halakhah* and Jewish philosophy is itself a notable phenomenon, worthy of mention in an evaluation of his works. Anyone who wants to form a complete impression of the Rav's achievement and versatility must take into account his occupation with such diverse sources as the teachings of

Habad (which included *shiurim* which he gave on *Likkutei Torah)* and his epistemological, metaphysical work, *Halakhic Mind.*

However, it must be made clear that it is not the coincidental presence of halakhic and philosophic profundity within a single personality which we are discussing, but rather the fusion of the two into an integrated Torah perspective. Rav Soloveitchik is not a halakhic *gadol*, unaware of the dilemmas of general culture, nor a religiously observant philosopher; he is a master of both fields who is able to illuminate both of them with the light of his Torah. An artificial division between the rabbinic and philosophical element within his personality is inconceivable. The two are mutually compatible and complementary. The dilemmas and acts of the God-fearing Jew receive, in the Rav's world, assistance and enhancement from general knowledge, if used with the proper care and attention, while the Torah has within it the capacity to solve questions of pure philosophical interest.

Thus, the Rav portrays Halakhic Man as imposing his Torah upon the natural world which he encounters:

> When halakhic man approaches reality, he comes with his Torah, given to him from Sinai, in hand. He addresses the world by means of fixed statutes and firm principles. An entire corpus of precepts and laws guides him along the path leading to Being.[3]

Halakhic Man addresses not only uniquely Jewish questions or those of interest to a general religious philosophy, but also tackles issues of philosophical import such as epistemology, the status of nature, and other similar topics. All are reviewed and examined, since the answers to these general perplexities can be found in the Torah which God presented to man at Sinai. Not only were "righteous laws and religious messages handed down to Israel, but also Divine wisdom which reveals and interprets the

---

[3] Ibid., p. 19. The concluding word, "*havayah*," translated by Kaplan as "existence," has been switched to "Being." This is a key word in the text, as our remarks below indicate, whose significance is in establishing that halakhic man treats Being itself, ontologically as well as experientially, as subject to the halakhic discipline. The same difference of interpretation also dictated changing "*misdakek*" in the second sentence of the quote from "orient" to "address." These changes seem to indicate differing readings of the quoted text which are basic to one of the important aspects of *Halakhic Man*. The issue certainly deserves attention and requires a more lengthy discussion; this, however, is not the occasion.

world of experience to humankind: "...the path leading to Being." The treasury of Torah and *mitzvot* contains within it remedies for epistemological and ontological problems. The Rav does not merely utilize general wisdom to harness its information for the purposes of Torah, as the medieval Jewish philosophers did; rather, he attempts to fuse the two in a manner that allows each to illuminate the other. Though the rabbis have taught us that wisdom, if not Torah, is to be found amongst the nations, wisdom itself cannot satisfy its own needs without the assistance of the Torah. This very issue was addressed by the Rav at the conclusion of *Halakhic Mind*, where he wrote the following:

> To this end there is only a single source from which a Jewish philosophical *Weltanschauung* could emerge; the objective order – the Halakhah.... Problems of freedom, causality, God-Man relationship, creation and nihility would be illuminated by halakhic principles. A new light could be shed on our apprehension of reality. Out of the sources of Halakhah, a new world view awaits formulation.[4]

This aspect of the Rav's philosophical enterprise, that which may be called from "Volozhin to Berlin," is a distinctive feature of the Rav's philosophy, not to be found amongst his contemporaries. For though this approach to the relationship between Judaism and general philosophy was also attempted by other Jewish thinkers in the early twentieth century,[5] these figures did not belong to the world of the *bet hamidrash,* while the Torah scholars, even those who were aware of developments within the general world, did not see the Torah as providing solutions to philosophical problems.

There is, of course, another aspect – the purely religious one. Metaphysical and ontological issues were not the only ones which concerned the Rav. His primary interest was the existential state of the religious individual in the modern world. Actually, his involvement with philosophical concepts was mainly due to their significance for the religious

---

[4] *Halakhic Mind* (New York, 1986), 101–02.

[5] See M. Schwartz, *Hagut Yehudit Nokhah haTarbut haKelalit* (Tel Aviv, 1976), 9–11.

experience. His writings – *Halakhic Man*, *"U-Vikkashtem miSham," The Lonely Man of Faith,* and others – are the cry of the believing individual searching for existential meaning as he approaches his Creator in all his loneliness, greatness, pettiness and confusion. These essays reflect and express man's quest for experiential meaning and a living faith within this world, and, unlike *Halakhic Mind,* are not limited to a search for ontological recognition. Thus, the Rav makes the following existential claim in *The Lonely Man of Faith:*

> The trouble with all rational demonstrations of the existence of God, with which the history of philosophy abounds, consists in their being exactly what they were meant to be by those who formulated them: abstract logical demonstrations divorced from the living primal experiences in which these demonstrations are rooted. For instance, the cosmic experience was transformed into a cosmological proof, the ontic experience into an ontological proof, et cetera....
>
> Maimonides' term *leyda (Yesodei haTorah* 1:1) transcends the bounds of the abstract *logos* and passes over into the realm of the boundless intimate and impassioned experience where postulate and deduction, discursive knowledge and intuitive thinking, conception and perception, subject and object, are one. Only in paragraph five [of *Yesodei haTorah* ch. I], after the aboriginal experience of God had been established by him as a firm reality, does he introduce the Aristotelian cosmological proof of the unmoved mover.[6]

This is the essence of the approach that he advocates to the sensitive individual in his quest for a spiritual dimension within the material world.

In sum, the Rav's philosophy weaves together the approaches of Scientific Man and Religious Man with that of Halakhic Man to provide existential experience and significance to religious life. Halakhic Man, who is also the man of faith, is nourished by the achievements of others in clarifying and elucidating issues of concern to him, while those others are able to receive satisfaction from the halakhic Torah of our sages. To grasp

---

[6] *The Lonely Man of Faith* (New York, 1992), 51–52.

the scope of this phenomenon within the Rav's writings and to appreciate its breadth and depth, one has to go no further than the footnotes which accompany *Halakhic Man*. There, summoned by the author, one can meet, side-by-side, famous *rabbanim* and German professors, Rambam and William James, *Minhat Hinukh* and I.L. Peretz, along with many other such figures. In the Rav's world, it is possible to use such diverse sources and create a single, coherent, Torah-true whole from them. Lest anyone mislead himself and think that this was an intellectual posture detached from the fiber of his soul, I must emphatically state that this was not so. Many a time did he preach to my brothers and myself, from the depths of a grandfather's loving concern, the importance of acquiring general and scientific knowledge.

Other aspects of the Rav's achievement, such as his use of Kabbalah and Habad *Hassidut,* his extraordinary ability to explain such esoteric issues in a plain and lucid manner, his electrifying rhetorical power and masterful *derashot,* all require the space and emotional tranquility which I lack here. Therefore, rather than dwell on these aspects, I will relate to the reader a personal experience which left a lasting impression upon me. The last summer that I had the privilege of learning with my grandfather, we studied Ramban's commentary on *BeMidbar.* It was an awesome experience. Under his steady and sure guidance, we set out to tackle all the issues which Ramban presented to us. Wherever the winding paths of Ramban's multifaceted curiosity took us, there we followed. If it was a halakhic discussion of an issue such as *yayin nesekh* or *tumat met,* we dealt with it. When a purely interpretive or linguistic question came up, there we were, ready to examine it with the proper tools. Whenever Ramban scaled the heights of a philosophical issue, we were able to follow in his footsteps. And when the commentary approached the Torah from the perspective of the *derekh ha'emet* ["the true path," *i.e.,* a Kabbalistic approach], my grandfather explained it clearly and lucidly. Suddenly, Ramban's cryptic hints were transformed into language and concepts accessible to all. I was convinced at the time that Ramban must have known that centuries later there would arise amongst the Torah scholars a man capable of fully appreciating his work, and that to this person, and his peers over the ages, he directed his monumental enterprise. The entire time that we sat learning together, I could not but help feel a silent ongoing dialogue of hidden love between Ramban and the Rav, leaping over the distance of time and place that separated them but by accident. Those who enjoyed the privilege of participating in the *Yarhei Kallah* in the summers or hearing him on many other occasions surely know what I am talking about. All that I can manage to say in conclusion is that my grandfather, the Rav, has left us, and we cannot even study Ramban on our own!

IV

A transitional figure, the Rav embraced a variety of worlds and periods. Born in a tiny *shtetl* in eastern Europe into a world in which the majority of the Jews were faithful to religious tradition and that had not yet been exposed to the innovations of modern science and technology, he passed through many communities and countries during his lifetime. After spending time in Jewish Warsaw and Vilna as a youth, he lived for a few years in Berlin before settling down, on the other side of the Atlantic, in Boston and New York. Most of his life was spent in places where only a handful of the local Jews remained committed to Torah. The dilemmas and struggles of the believer in the modern world were, as mentioned above, topics which he dealt with in his writings. However, as a source of inspiration and guidance for his contemporaries, the Rav's own person and way of life were no less important than his explicit teachings. A modern man he was, and it was in the modern world that he lived. The Rav led an active life of *Torah lishmah* within the surrounding general world in which he lived, without ensconcing himself or attempting to escape from it into a sheltered environment. He was well acquainted with American society, thoroughly familiar with its language and culture. People confused by the skepticism and relativism of modern philosophy saw him as a figure certain in his faith and convictions even after being exposed to philosophical analysis and scientific theories. For the younger generation, who was so wonderfully attached to him, the Rav was not only a link with a world that had passed, but also a living example and a prototype of vigorously intensive Torah study by a person who related to the world in which they lived. While many other *rabbanim* represented a choice between the world of the past and that of the present, between America and Eastern Europe, the Rav was able to serve as a guide to the path of Torah study integrated into an existence in the present.

Part of this power came from his deep inner conviction on this issue. Thus he thundered forth, in the midst of the years of horror, boldly and confidently:

> I, too, who have just now witnessed the old in all its splendid grandeur, view the new, peeking forth and, rising...and the spirit shall yet rest upon Israel's community, who rides the firmament and subdues the earth, and it shall be prophetic. Westward, beyond the great ocean, in a new land of freedom and opportunity, Israel will be successful, multiplying and rapidly expanding; between tall and mighty walls, in the shadow of skyscraping towers, the laws of personal status will be fervently discussed, as will the halakhot of *kodshim* and *taharot;* there, on the banks of the Hudson, the Torah of Rabban Gamliel and his associates will be transmitted....[7]

If all this now seems self-evident in 1995, this is the best testimony to the success of the Rav's enterprise. Fifty years ago, in the America of the forties, matters were not so simple; not even *rabbanim.* were sure that Torah could be established in the *"treife medinah."*

In the eulogy for his close friend, Rav Chaim Heller, the Rav developed the idea of *"peleitat sofereihem"* – "remnant" scholarly figures, such as Rav Chaim Heller – who live with us in the present but really belong to a past, vanished world. The Rav describes this phenomenon at length and elaborates upon its importance as a vital link in the chain of tradition. His remarks are as fitting for he who said them as for he for whom they were said. However, I must add that the "remnant" scholars and the link they establish with the past are of little help if there are no contemporary scholars to provide elementary leadership and guidance in the present. The past alone is meaningless if it lacks the support and Torah of the present. If

---

7 Published in a supplement to the *HaPardes* journal on the occasion of Reb Moshe Soloveitchik's third *Yahrseit* (i.e., *Shevat* 5704 or Jan. 1944). The title page relates that the published material (a *shiur* and a *derashah*) was originally delivered by the Rav in June 1943. The quoted passage appears on pp. 19–20. The translation is mine.

the Torah leadership is firmly rooted in the modern milieu and aware of current trends in society, and therefore able to penetrate the hearts of the people, then there is beauty and grandeur in the unique link to tradition that the past-oriented souls amongst us are able to provide. Without the Torah scholars of the current generation, the remnants of the previous one are out of touch with their time and place and cannot relate to the concerns of their contemporaries. The basic work is that done by the leadership of the new generation; Though the Rav's personality contained flashes of his past in another world, he essentially belonged to the world within which he lived. His involvement in the American scene was that of a person who felt at home with it. Even the seemingly minor issue of language may serve to illustrate this point. Many outstanding Torah figures who arrived on American shores did not master the language of the country they lived in, thus detracting greatly from their ability to understand and influence the local youth. This, of course, is untrue of the Rav. He spoke and wrote a fluent and articulate English despite having learned the language as a mature adult. When the need arose to teach in English, he made the transition from his mother tongue to an adopted language with ease. This provided him with an opportunity, unavailable to many of his peers, to reach out to a large audience, scholars as well as laymen, Jews as well as non-Jews. Though this is a practical example, the essence of the issue which it represents runs much deeper.

The Rav was a very modest person. His concern for the people and his attachment to them brought him to serve as a shul and school rabbi, a position which he undertook with the fullest spiritual and emotional involvement rather than remaining within the confines of the *bet midrash.* He lived amongst his people and loved them. Anyone who wanted to know the Rav fully had to see him at home, within his community, in Boston. There, he and the members of the community developed a warm relationship of mutual love and care as the *gadol hador* was transformed into the local rabbi, relaxed and at home amongst his *ba'alei batim.*

The Rav's Torah was a *Torat Hesed.* The first steps he undertook in his Boston *rabbanut* were accompanied by a harsh and bitter struggle, involving vicious personal attacks and *malshinut* against him, due to his insistence on improving the work conditions of the abused *shohatim,* mistreated to such a degree that they were compelled to start walking to work late *Shabbat* afternoon.[8] He extended his sympathy and compassion towards both the small and the great, willingly giving of his time to plain people as to famous leaders. If he browbeat his *talmidim,* it was out of the depths of his attachment to Torah and his concern for developing their learning skills and knowledge. Many other examples could easily be added to these to illustrate his modest and unassuming ways, as well as the *hesed* which accompanied his teaching and leadership.

V

A eulogy, even after twelve months, is meant to describe the figure of the departed and his personality, in order to heighten our awareness of the loss and to enhance our sense of his absence. Neither analysis nor evaluation are the primary aim of the eulogy; its purpose is strengthening the sense of personal involvement and loss for both he who delivers it and for the audience to whom it is addressed. Let me conclude my presentation with a more personal tone. May the reader forgive me if, henceforth, clear reasoning surrenders to a feeling heart.

The intellect has the power to criticize itself. It examines whether love has outdone itself or if claims and issues have been misrepresented. It will do the utmost to remain within the realm of the universal, where all are equal. The public sphere is strictly separated from the private one. One must remain discreet and not display his feelings to the outer world. Not so the heart; its grief bursts forth and pours out. Nothing can stand in its path as it rushes to express its feelings. It recognizes no boundaries and will not rest until it has proclaimed to all its aching sense of loss and grief. It ventures forth into the public square and shouts; it does not restrain itself, though it knows well that there is nothing novel or unique in its loss. A commotion of confused and overwhelming emotion explodes from within the depths of the soul as it struggles with its loss.

Until now, the intellect has expressed itself; now my heart must have its say. Throughout this eulogy I have spoken of "the Rav" and referred to "my grandfather." Neither is how I knew him, though. For me, he was simply *"Zeide."* "The Rav" is certainly a title of honor and respect; "my

---

[8] Cf. *Halakhic Man*, p. 95.

grandfather" is an appropriate and proper description. Yet, how poor is the emotional attachment of these phrases in contrast to that plain, simple word, *"Zeide."* No title of honor can approach the emotional power of such awesome words as *"Zeide"* or *"Sabbah."* I know and respect, value and appreciate the bitter grief displayed by his *talmidim* from the depths of their aching hearts and the sense of loss that pervaded the general public. What can I do, though, if my heart insists on violating propriety and cries out: "I've lost my *Zeide,* Not only a Rav and a great figure, but also my own loving grandfather!" He was with us, and now he is not.

To be sure, I learned with him; I heard his *shiurim* and listened to his Torah. However, we did not only learn together, *we* lived and experienced together. Not only halakhic discussions, but also the pain and joy which we shared together united us. In his own way, true to his personality traits, he knew how to express the intense love and care of a grandfather to his grandchildren. The opinion of Rashbam (*Baba Batra* 128a) that an ancestor cannot testify against his offspring, no matter how great the generational distance, was one of his favorite quotations. During the Lebanon war, when I was serving in *Tsahal,* he contacted one of the heads of the Israeli government, a person who respected Torah and *rabbanim,* and requested that his voice be heard; not as a Rav or communal leader, but as a grandfather. Like Yosef *haTsadik,* he had the privilege of seeing great-grandchildren. When his first great-grandson was born, he added his smiling color photograph to those of his solemn forebears that adorned his study. There, on the walls of the study, the past encountered the present and the former grandson and current sage became the proud grandfather of the future

The time has come for the grieving grandson to conclude. He began with a description of the great *niftar* as a grandson to his forebears and ended by portraying him as a grandfather to his offspring. Between these two poles of his life, the Rav studied and taught, experienced and led an intense life of Torah and *mitzvot.* Thousands were his students in *halakhah,* many more in *aggadah*; they heard his teachings and were captivated. More than has been depicted here was found in him. At times he hid himself from us and retired into the innermost recesses of his soul; on other occasions he presented a smiling face to us. The Rav hinted at his secrets but did not reveal them.

The Ark has been seized and removed to the heavens. Our teacher has left us and departed to his place in the world of absolute good. We remain with the blessing of the great light of his Torah which dwells amongst us, continuously burning in our hearts and *batei midrash.* A beacon from the Western Diaspora, it links with those lit by *Hakhmei Yisrael* in previous eras, illuminating our heritage from Sinai throughout time. We shall continue to follow his guiding light, to participate in his Torah and preserve it. We will preserve it by comprehension and enjoyment, development and expansion, debate and argument. His teachings are his memorial. He continues to live among us. We are inspired by he who was with us, we weep bitterly over his loss, and conclude with a prayer that the Torah shall not be absent from his children and his children's children, his *talmidim* and *talmidei talmidim,* now and forever.

The Rav speaking in the late 1940s. (courtesy of Yeshiva University)

The Vaad Hasemichah from the late 1940s through the early 1950s at Yeshivat Rabbenu Yitzchak Elchanan. (L to R) Rabbi Moshe Shatzkes *zt"l*, the Lomza Rav; the Rav; Rabbi Chaim Heller *zt"l;* Dr. Samuel Belkin *zt"l*, President of Yeshiva University, 1943–1976.
Rabbi Heller did not always participate in the group.
(courtesy of Yeshiva University)

Rabbi Dovid Lifschitz *zt"l* and the Rav.
(courtesy of Yeshiva University)

First Chinuch Atzmai dinner, January, 1956.
(L. to R.) The Rav *zt"l*, Rabbi Aaron Kotler *zt"l*, Mr. Irving Bunim *z"l*.
(courtesy of Torah Schools for Israel)

The Rav saying *shiur* in the 1960s. (courtesy of Yeshiva University)

Wedding of Professor and Mrs. Chaim Waxman, June, 1962.
(L. to R.) Rabbi Moshe Feinstein *zt"l,* the Rav *zt"l,* Dr. Haym Soloveitchik (back to camera), Rabbi Yitzchak Isaac Small, Rabbi Nosson Kamenetsky, Dr. Samuel Belkin *z"tl,* Rabbi Dovid Lifschitz *zt"l* (the bride's father), Rabbi Eugene Geller.
(courtesy of Professor and Mrs. Chaim I. Waxman)

The Rav delivering a public lecture at Yeshiva University in the early 1970s.
(courtesy of Yeshiva University)

ישיבת רבנו יצחק אלחנן

אוי לנו כי נפלה עטרת ראשנו!

הספד מר

לע"נ של מורנו ורבנו
רבן של כל בית ישראל
מרן הגאון האדיר
ר' יוסף דוב הלוי סולובייצ'יק זצ"ל
יום ראשון ד' אייר תשנ"ג אחת עשרה לפנה"צ
בישיבתנו הקדושה באולם למפורט

HESPED MAR

IN MEMORY OF THE RAV

MARAN HAGAON
HARAV JOSEPH DOV HALEVI SOLOVEITCHIK zt"l
THE TEACHER OF ALL ISRAEL

SUNDAY, APRIL 25, 1993, 11 AM

YESHIVA UNIVERSITY
NATHAN LAMPORT AUDITORIUM
AMSTERDAM AVE & 186th ST
NEW YORK CITY

The invitation to the public gathering in memory of the Rav held at Yeshiva University, New York, on Sunday, April 25, 1993. (courtesy of Michael Bierman)

The *matzevot* of Rabbi and Mrs. Soloveitchik, West Roxbury, MA. (courtesy of Elie Sabo)

TALMIDIM AND COMMUNITY LEADERS REMEMBER THE RAV

DEDICATION OF THE SPECIAL ISSUE OF *TRADITION*

RABBI JULIUS BERMAN

It is the evening of the third of *Shevat,* the *yahrtzeit* of the Rav's father, Rav Moshe *zt"l,* and we are in Lamport Auditorium at Yeshiva University awaiting the arrival of the Rav to deliver his annual *Yahrtzit Shiur.* Some of us have been sitting for a few hours, having come early to obtain seats as close as possible to the Rav. The auditorium is now packed and overflowing. Suddenly, as if an electric current has run through the room, the entire audience, as one, rises: the Rav has arrived!

Sitting in front, we do not immediately see the Rav, for he enters from the rear, and must traverse the entire length of auditorium to reach us. Everyone is standing, blocking our view; yet the feeling of his presence pervades the room. Finally, the Rav emerges from the crowd, walking briskly, manuscript in hand, steps onto the stage and sits down behind an empty table to begin the *shiur.*

Then the journey starts. The Rav, usually focusing on one or more *halakhot* of the Rambam, ticks off one question after another that reflect obvious difficulties in the *Halakhah* at least they are obvious after the Rav sets them out in his clear, lucid and inimitable manner of exposition. Then, after developing each of his questions – superlative pedagogue that he is – he reviews in summary form all of them, to assure that we understand what the problems are that will now be clarified.

That phase of the *shiur* concluded, the Rav goes on to develop a concept – the *hiddush* of the *shiur* – traversing a plethora of passages in the Talmud, commentaries (mostly *Rishonim), Midrashim,* and others. We watch, listen, and many of us avidly write notes, trying to keep up with the Rav's rapid-fire delivery as he lays out the *hiddush,* brick by brick by brick, reconciling all the varied and seemingly contradictory texts.

Now that the foundation has been set and the text reconciliation completed, the Rav returns to the original series of questions. Each is repeated, and then almost summarily disposed of through application of the *hiddush,* one after the other, after the other. It is more than two hours later and the circuit has been completed; the first portion of the *shiur* is concluded.

The Rav now turns to the *agaddic* portion of the *shiur,* usually with a prefatory, albeit rhetorical, question – *"Ir vilt nach"?* "Do you want more?" The audience responds with a resounding "yes" as the Rav, embarks on another two hour *tour de force,* in his beautiful poetic Yiddish. We sit there entranced, swallowing every word. It is much more difficult now to take notes. In this portion of the *shiur,* we are overwhelmed, not only by the ideas and concepts being presented, but also by the beauty of the language, the choice and combination of words and phrases, the sheer poetry of the presentation, the masterful delivery and, of course, of course, the absolute brilliance of the speaker. We sit entranced; the *shiur* is entering the fifth hour. Finally, it is over. It takes us a while to return to reality, but, perforce, we have no choice.

It was an unforgettable experience, one that we will carry with us the rest of our lives. We will relate this special privilege we lived through to our children and grandchildren, but we must acknowledge how ill equipped we are to convey the feeling, the mood – indeed, the exhilaration – we felt at the time.

And all that is now history!

There are various customs surrounding the timing of setting up and unveiling the monument over a grave. In Jerusalem, the custom is to set the monument immediately after *shi'vah;* in many other places, the custom is to wait until after the first *yahrtzeit.*

Rav Akiva Eiger explained the latter custom by pointing out that there is a generally accepted psychological phenomenon that the memory of a departed one fades after twelve months, so the monument is not needed as a remembrance until that point in time.

From time to time, the Rav would point out during an annual *Yartzeit Shiur* that, contrary to this psychological principle, as the years had gone by, his longing for his father had not diminished; indeed, it had increased. What he would have given to have fifteen minutes with his father to discuss some of the critical issues facing him!

What we would give to have fifteen minutes with the Rav, *mori verabbi zt"l!* But all we have now are our memories.... We hope to hold on to those memories a bit longer, sharing them with those who were not privileged to learn with him directly, reminding those of us whose lives were directly shaped by him of our debt and gratitude.

Yehei zikhro barukh.

RABBI SOLOVEITCHIK REMEMBERED

RABBI DR. LOUIS BERNSTEIN *z"l*

Once again, for the last time, we planned our *Chol Hamoed* trip to Boston. For years, Yisrael Friedman, the Mizrachi Executive Director, and I would happily travel to visit the Rav and spend relaxed and enjoyable hours with him in the Twersky home, where he resided. This last time, the *Chol Hamoed* plans were darkened by the ache of the last farewell.

The stab of pain was even sharper when we realized the Rav had passed away on the same date as his friend, Rabbi Shmuel Belkin, the second President of Yeshiva University. Together they built the greatest Torah citadel in America. There was the Rav, standing before us on that day staring at the wooden coffin, eulogizing him in the huge Lamport Auditorium as only he and no other could. Shortly afterwards, when his own *talmid*, Rabbi Norman Lamm, became Yeshiva's third president, the Rav was instrumental in rescuing Yeshiva from insolvency.

It is too early to properly evaluate the Rav, and greater people than I will surely do so as the years pass. His stature will surely be greater then. In this hurried appraisal, we can only write from the heart and record recollections still fresh in the mind before time embellishes and polishes them.

For years, the Rav was chairman of the Halakha Commission of the Rabbinical Council of America. It was his consistent support of the position that kept the Rabbinical Council and the Orthodox Union within the Synagogue Council of America, despite heavy pressure from the Agudat HaRabonim.

The Rav was a master teacher. On more than one occasion, he referred to himself as a *melamed*. His intellectual world embraced every aspect of Jewish knowledge and thought as well as a vast range of secular knowledge. Rabbi Dr. Bernard Rosensweig points out that he raised the Brisk form of analysis to unprecedented levels with the discipline of academia.

As a *Rosh Yeshiva*, he was totally committed to his students. This commitment was reciprocated with love, admiration and devotion. Rabbi Jacob Rabinowitz points out that at his zenith, the Rav would give more *shiurim* in a week than most *roshei yeshiva* give in a month. There would be three *shiurim* given at Yeshiva University to rabbinical students, two in Boston to the Harvard intelligentsia, and another at Moriah in New York to synagogue laymen.

In addition, there was the hour in Maimonides School, in between *Mincha* and *Maariv* on Saturday afternoon, "Ask the Rabbi." The Rav would field all and any questions directed to him and respond fully and directly.

As one who teaches the written law, my admiration for his expounding of a verse with Rashi is boundless. I am still enthralled by having studied with him the first chapter in Genesis with the Ramban's commentary. That single chapter took up an entire semester.

And with that load, the Rav delivered the annual *yahrtzeit shiurim* and the annual *teshuvah drashot*, carefully and painstakingly prepared and written out in script. There is no other comparable intellectual event in American and Jewish life today. The thousands who attended came from every walk of life. The Rav's rare intellectual brilliance was matched with an outstanding oratorical ability. He was equally fluent in English, Yiddish, and Hebrew.

Others have, and will, write much of the Rav's halakhic brilliance. The *ish hahalakhah* was indeed peerless in his knowledge and scholarship. This aspect of the Rav tends to obscure his deep piety and faith.

Rabbi Dr. Walter Wurzburger, one of the Rav's close disciples and an outstanding philosopher, surprised me when he told me, "I may have forgotten some of his *shiurim*, but I shall never forget the saying of *Hallel* at the *seder* in the Rav's home on Passover."

I knew the Rav best as a man of great courage and principle. When he first came to the United States, he was a star at the Agudath Israel conventions. World events, the tragic history of the Jewish people, must have turned him into a committed religious Zionist that he was. He never wavered in that conviction. His masterful piece, *Kol Dodi Dofek,* remains the outstanding exposition of Jewish history, written with the insight of a prophet of yore.

His commitment to Israel, religious Zionism, and to the Mizrachi movement, never for one minute took precedence over his commitment to justice and what was right. Just after the war in Lebanon, I received a call from the Rav. In the most direct terms, he asked me to call Dr. Joseph

Burg and Zevulun Hammer, who were then members of Israel's government, and tell them in no uncertain terms that he would resign from the Mizrachi if they did not vote for the commission to investigate the Sabra and Shatilla massacres. I have never quoted the Rav, so I asked him specifically for permission to do so. "Yes" was the unequivocal response. There is every reason to believe his words had the necessary effect.

As two-time president of the Rabbinical Council, I always consulted with him, even to ask his permission to stand for public office. He stood by me during my first term as President of the Rabbinical Council, during the controversy of the "who is a Jew" issue. There was even an unprecedented attempt to censure a RCA President, which could have led to impeachment. When controversy swirled ten years later, when I invited the President of the Rabbinical Assembly to an RCA convention after speaking at the Conservative Rabbis' convention, he let it be known that I had first asked him how to respond to the initial invitation.

It was the Rav who single-handedly prevented the Jewish community from entering into a theological dialogue with Christianity. To this day, there is no one in the Jewish community, let alone among Orthodox Jews, who knows and understands Christian theology as well as he did.

It was his responsum in the early 1950s that permitted the establishment at Yeshiva University, of the military draft of rabbis for chaplains. The wisdom of that approach became apparent almost two decades later in the legislative struggle to preserve *yeshivot* in America while Congress was considering eliminating the theological deferment.

And then, there was his brilliant defense of techniques of *shechitah* at a time when the humane societies had actually succeeded in restricting it. He also spelled out the guidelines for prayers on special occasions such as the 300th anniversary of American Jewry.

Now this story can, and should be, told. When the Rabbinical Council *siddur* was first published, the translation was heavily criticized. The Rav assiduously avoided public controversy. I was rushed to his Boston home by the late Rabbi Israel Klavan, where the Rav dictated to me a lengthy Responsa which appeared in the *Hadoar* under another name.

It was an unforgettable experience. During that session, the Rav received a call from an intermediary of Israeli leadership offering him the

Chief Rabbinate of Israel. I never had the audacity to ask why he didn't accept the offer, but I do know that we are all the beneficiaries of his remaining in America, even Israel itself.

Basically a shy man, the Rav engendered the love and support of his students and disciples. "I never impose my views on anyone." He didn't have to. The thousands whose lives he enriched appreciated his wisdom.

The Rav was a wonderful family man. His stories of his father and grandfather made us feel that we were walking with them in Brisk and in European *yeshivot.* His relationship with his wife was especially moving and touching. The love and respect of his daughters, his sons-in-law, and son, particularly in the Twersky home where the Rav resided, were exemplary manifestations of *kibbud av.*

Whenever I visited Chief Rabbi Abraham Shapira of Israel, he would ask about the Rav. The first, and I believe the only, time they met, at Yeshiva University, the Rav embraced him. I asked the Chief Rabbi why he kissed the Rav. His response was, "The Rav is a walking *Sefer Torah.*" I told him I had difficulty coming to grips with why so saintly an individual could be suffering in such a terrible way.

Rabbi Shapira responded, "There comes a time when an individual has fulfilled all the *mitzvot* he was destined to, and taught all the Torah that he was to teach. But the generation still needed him."

That need now looms even larger. We can only be comforted by the thought that we had the rare privilege of basking in his radiance. This *lonely man of faith* will continue to ennoble and enrich our lives, the lives of our descendents, and our congregations until the coming of the Messiah, soon, and in our time.

ONE STUDENT'S MEMORIAL TO HIS *REBBE*

RABBI JEFFREY BIENENFELD

The Boston sky was dreary and overcast on the Sunday of April 11th as hundreds of mourners accompanied the coffin of Rabbi Joseph B. Soloveitchik to its final resting place in Roxbury, Mass. Hours earlier, over 2,000 people crowded into the Maimonides Day School in Brookline where Rabbi Soloveitchik was eulogized by his brother, Rabbi Ahron Soloveichik of Chicago. Rabbi Joseph Soloveitchik's reputation was such that had the funeral taken place on a day other than the Eve of a Festival, the assembled would have numbered in the tens of thousands.

Who was this man whom some have described as "one of the preeminent Torah personalities of this generation," as the "unchallenged leader of mainstream Orthodoxy" who earned the respect and admiration of all elements in Judaism? Who was this rabbi whose spiritual persona captured the minds and souls of multitudes and made him unique among the rabbinic giants of this and previous generations? Indeed, what accounted for the veneration and awe in which his thousands of disciples and the Jewish community at large held him?

Rav Soloveitchik was born in Pruzhan, Poland on February 27, 1903. The oldest of five children, Rav Soloveitchik was gifted with a rabbinic heritage whose ancestors included some of the most eminent rabbinic luminaries of the eighteenth and nineteenth centuries.

Until his late teens, Rav Soloveitchik studied almost exclusively with his father, Rav Moshe *zt"l,* who bequeathed to his son a method of Talmudic study known as the *Brisker derekh*. The Rav's grandfather, Rav Hayyim Brisker *zt"l* founded this approach to the world of the Talmud. It consisted of a rigorous analysis of the Talmudic text along with a painstaking conceptualization of the oftentimes conflicting legal principles involved, all of which invariably yielded profound insights into the complexities of Jewish law and practice. Revolutionary in its day, the incisive sophistication of the *Brisker derekh* was quickly mastered by Rav Hayyim's grandson, and soon, all of Torah literature was studied under its disciplined and exacting rules.

Rabbi Soloveitchik entered the University of Berlin to pursue his education in a wide range of secular subjects. Physics, mathematics, languages and philosophy were studied, ultimately culminating in his Ph.D. degree in the Philosophy of the Neo-Kantian philosopher, Hermann Cohen. During his six years in Berlin, however, his intensive study of Torah never ceased. While often seen in the university library, once back in his apartment, Rav Soloveitchik's attention was exclusively devoted to his Torah studies. During the Rav's years at the University of Berlin, there were other future rabbinic leaders who shared each others' company and friendship. Among them were: Rav Menachem Schneerson *zt"l,* the Lubavitcher Rebbe, and Rav Yitzchak Hutner *zt"l,* the founder of Yeshivat Chaim Berlin in Brooklyn.

In 1931, Rav Soloveitchik married Tonya Lewit, herself a recipient of a Ph.D. degree in education, and together with their first child, immigrated to America in 1932 to accept the post of Chief Rabbi of Boston. While occasionally lecturing at Harvard and MIT, Rav Soloveitchik's primary vocation was the study and teaching of Torah. In 1937, he founded the Maimonides School, the first Hebrew Day School in New England. Starting a *yeshiva* in the 1930s, especially outside the New York area, was a pioneering effort, one that, with the help of his wife, proved both successful and rewarding. During his early years in Boston, Rav Soloveitchik also established a *kollel* to meet the needs of students, who were already quite advanced in their study of the Talmud and post-Talmudic literature.

In 1941, after his father's passing, Rav Soloveitchik assumed his father's distinguished position as the *Rosh Yeshiva* of the Rabbi Isaac Elchanan Theological Seminary of Yeshiva University. It was here, in the hallowed halls of the Yeshiva, that Rav Soloveitchik taught Talmud and Codes (Jewish law) for over forty years.

From the outset, it was evident that Rav Soloveitchik's sheer genius, erudition and brilliance were simply unprecedented. It had been hundreds of years since the emergence of a rabbinic personality, whose knowledge was as profound and vast as was Rav Soloveitchik's. During these years, the

Rav, as he became affectionately known to all, ordained over 2,000 rabbis. Many more students passed through his classrooms and thousands of Jews came to listen to his weekly *shiurim* (Torah lectures) at Congregation Moriah in Manhattan. On special occasions (e.g. the *Yarzheit* anniversary of his father's death), the Rav delivered learned discourses in Jewish law that attracted thousands. Often lasting for three to four hours, the audience was transfixed by the Rav's brilliant explication of some of the Talmud's most challenging debates. These public lectures became among the major religious and academic events of the year for American Orthodoxy, the entire Jewish community and then some.

In 1959, the Rav declined an invitation to succeed Rabbi Isaac Herzog, the Chief Rabbi of Israel, who had just died. His remaining in America, however, did not detract from the immeasurable impact he was to have upon the many leaders of world Jewry, both rabbinic and lay, who would visit with him periodically in his Washington Heights apartment. Rav Soloveitchik's typical weekly schedule would see him arrive in New York from his Boston home on Monday or Tuesday, give his regular mid-week *shiurim*, meet with an array of community leaders, lecture at Moriah, and then return to Boston on Thursday or Friday for the extended Shabbos weekend.

Rav Soloveitchik's growing prominence eventually made him the acknowledged *posek*, rabbinic decisor, for the thousands of rabbis of the Rabbinical Council of America, Orthodoxy's largest rabbinic organization. In the Religious Zionists of America (RZA), the Rav played a leading role in articulating a religious approach to Zionism, which both endorsed the State of Israel and advocated its continued material and spiritual growth.

Inevitably, such positions of enlightened, charismatic leadership and authority extended the Rav's influence and teachings to Jewish communities throughout North America and overseas. Young rabbis were inspired to courageously meet the challenges of modernity and win back generations who had all but given up on living an observant Jewish lifestyle in America. Furthermore, Jewish leaders in all walks of life were moved to make considerable financial investments in a wide range of Jewish educational and organizational initiatives that served to reestablish Orthodoxy as a powerful force in American Jewish life. That Rav

Soloveitchik's role was a major factor in the reshaping and resurgence of this religious vibrancy and dynamism remains undisputed. Both the policy and agenda of Orthodox Judaism was, in large measure, inspired and directed by the teachings and counsel of the Rav.

Unfortunately, family tradition made Rav Soloveitchik reluctant to publish. The Rav's teachings were transmitted primarily through the spoken word. Nonetheless, over the years, some articles and essays began to appear in publications such as *Halakhic Man*, *The Halakhic Mind*, *The Lonely Man of Faith*, "Confrontation," "Majesty and Humility," "Catharsis." These works quickly became classics in Jewish philosophy and Biblical exegesis. More recently, small selections of the Rav's halakhic oeuvre have also slowly seen their way into print, much to the joy of the Torah scholarly community. The remaining manuscripts and tapes of lectures and classes are presently unpublished. Together with Rav Soloveitchik's vast oral teachings, this voluminous written legacy comprises a Torah scholarship of colossal proportions, one that will continue to instruct and inspire generations to come.

To properly assess the singular genius of the Rav is a task that must be approached with much hesitation. His prodigious talents in both the Torah and secular worlds only begin to portray his intellectual virtuosity. And the Rav's genius, daunting as it was, simply cannot convey the charm and magnanimity of Rav Soloveitchik's moral and ethical personality. For both, you had to be there. And for the many who were, their rather humbling responsibility is to attempt to tell the story, incomplete and imperfect though it may be, of a great sage whose wisdom in mind and soul transformed their lives forever.

Rav Soloveitchik's remarkable uniqueness can perhaps best be understood by describing the range of his genius in a series of impressions, perhaps subjective, but in shared consensus with countless others.

Rav Soloveitchik was a master of the entirety of Torah literature. His knowledge of the text was titanic both in breadth and depth. And yet, his intimacy with the Bible and Talmud went beyond the exacting scholarship of interpretation and analysis. He knew its soul and essence, it was his home. Employing the *Brisker derekh*, the Rav would boldly advance upon the text, exposing ambiguities, and resolving contradictions with sweeping conceptualizations of the Talmudic discussions. Intellectual honesty reigned in his classes as he would often solicit critical comments and never wished to impose his view upon his students.

Listening to the Rav's halakhic discourses, you often felt transported back in time. The ancient debates came alive and, as his son, Rabbi Haym Soloveitchik put it, reality and truth seemed more present in the classroom than outside: beyond the *shiur*, all else appeared insignificant.

The stunning creativity and originality of the Rav's *shiurim* not only made the Talmudic text intellectually exciting but spiritually invigorating as well. It also enabled Rav Soloveitchik to display his genius in an other arena, in the realm of *pesak*, the rendering of rabbinic judgements on contemporary issues. The Rav reflected not only the traditional considerations in making such decisions, but his broad, in-depth grasp of the *mesorah* (rabbinic transmission) opened new and innovative ways of sensitively and forthrightly dealing with the problems at hand. Uncompromising in his allegiance to the *halakhah*, his decisions always demonstrated the inherent cogency and compassion of the halakhic system. In fact, the very popularity and respect accorded to the word *"halakhah"* is in no small measure due to Rav Soloveitchik's uncommon ability to rehabilitate this concept and make it religiously and intellectually compelling to the twentieth-century mind.

Rav Soloveitchik was probably most unique among his contemporary rabbinic peers in his attitude toward secular knowledge. He embraced it without fear or apology. The supremacy of Torah was such that under its sacred umbrella, the sciences and humanities could find a proper dwelling. As "handmaidens" to Torah scholarship, these studies not only provided important insights and information, but broadened the perspective of the Torah scholar in his attempt to understand and grapple with the vexing issues of his generation. Rav Soloveitchik's erudition in this arena was simply unmatched; no body of secular knowledge was foreign to him. He moved easily between these two worlds because, for him, Torah had the capacity to critically assess all of secular wisdom and assimilate that which it judged to be true and enduring. He therefore would unhesitatingly call upon the resources of secular thought when they underscored his message, "thus apotheosizing the secular into the sacred."

There was an additional dimension to the Rav's greatness. Beyond his technical proficiencies, he displayed an incomparable ethical genius as well. Rav Soloveitchik had an unerring knack in identifying man's most pressing existential concerns and provided a broad spiritual-ethical framework in which these dilemmas could be confronted. He did so with a theology thoroughly rooted in the legalistic minutiae of the halakhic system. In his famous discourses, he would distill from the complexities of the *halakhah* commanding ethical norms and moral themes. He showed how the halakhic system addressed itself not only to man's mind but also to his troubled heart and alienated soul as well. The psychology embedded within *halakhah* knew the human condition quite well and thus offered up truths and insights to help modern man cope with the paradoxes and mysteries of his life. To some, it was the angst of the "lonely man of faith;" to others, it was the courageous affirmation of the infinite worth of the "anonymous man." He spoke of death and mourning and the powerful dialectical surges of the spirit that buffeted about man's restless soul. He plumbed the meaning of prayer and spoke movingly about the ennobling experience of repentance.

Indeed, to hear the Rav's lectures resonate with such contemporary meaning was both comforting and challenging. Seated among the many listeners, you felt the very personal bonding that can only be experienced when a speaker connects with your innermost feelings. Such empathy with the human condition enabled Rav Soloveitchik to display an enormous generosity in both spirit and deed to the many who came to him for counsel and help. His tone was wise and sure, his gestures filled with compassion and understanding. His unpretentious demeanor and unaffected modesty only added to his luminous personality.

Finally, Rav Soloveitchik was blessed with dazzling oratory skills. His rhetorical prowess was such that you were captive to his words almost immediately. Whether it was the cadence of his prose, the evocative power of his formulations, his witty digressions, the eloquence of his language, or his tender confessions, you were inexorably drawn to his speech. And while the world of Torah scholarship can boast of a profusion of great intellects, what is altogether rare is someone with the combined gifts of articulation and communication. Indeed, Rav Soloveitchik was the consummate platform teacher who, no matter the audience, meticulously prepared for each lecture and yet delivered its contents spontaneously and with an unconcealed love for his subject. To be in his presence was to apprehend both grandeur and humility, the experience was awesome and unforgettable.

According to the *halakhah*, the death of one's rebbe is to be treated almost on par with the death of a parent. Such is the timeless and enduring impact a rebbe has upon his students. Rav Soloveitchik was one such rebbe. His majestic oratory is now stilled, his astonishing, multi-faceted genius is gone, and his sagacity of mind and soul is no more. How fortunate were we to be his students, how overwhelming a task it will be to transmit this noble and rich legacy to a future generation.

May the beloved memory of HaRav Yoseph Dov HaLevi Soloveitchik be a blessing for us all.

A TRIBUTE TO THE RAV

RABBI HERSHEL BILLET

HaRav Yosef Dov Halevi Soloveitchik was affectionately and respectfully called "the Rav" by his students. The Rav cast a giant shadow over Orthodox Jewish life in America which he actively led for more than half a century. I wish to focus on but one aspect of the Rav's greatness, which, from my perspective, is the image of the Rav that is fixed in my memory.

The Rav always used to call himself a *melamed*, a teacher. I have never met a man of his standing who was more dedicated to spending time in the classroom teaching Torah. In my years at Yeshiva University, the Rav gave a *shiur* to his students at the Yeshiva three times a week and in the Moriah synagogue once a week. All of this was in addition to all the teaching he did in Boston over the weekend. Add to this list special public lectures and summer *shiurim* in Boston for seven days a week in July and August. In a sense, teaching was a part of the family tradition. His father Rav Moshe, his grandfathers Rav Hayyim and Rav Eliyahu of Pruzhan, his great-grandfather, Rav Yosef Dov, his other relatives, Rav Naftali Tzvi Yehuda Berlin and Rav Chaim of Volozhin, were all teachers. The traditions of the Volozhin Yeshiva were an integral part of him. Yet, I always had the feeling that the Rav took the best of all of the previous generations, and he became the *melamed* par excellence. His classroom was an exciting place to spend several hours. One felt transported back in time as the Rav directed us from *Eretz Yisrael* to Bavel to Sefarad and Ashkenaz, to Poland and Lithuania. The dialogue of the centuries, all the way back to *Har Sinai*, was presented with tenacity, reverence, lucidity, and simplicity. As much as the Rav demanded of his students, he demanded far more of himself.

COMMITMENT TO TORAH STUDY

The Rabbis tell us that we have to work hard in our pursuit of Torah. The Rav was a master at fulfilling this *mitzvah*. I remember once learning *Perek*

Chezkas HaBatim; we came across a difficult Rabbenu Tam on the subject of *rochlim*, traveling salesmen. and the Rav made us check all of the cross references and the *Sefer HaYashar*. He gave *shiur* for five consecutive days, trying to grasp the principle of Rabbenu Tam. We were all relieved when we finally continued to the next piece of *Gemara*. About six weeks later, the Rav walked into *shiur* on a Tuesday and declared much to our surprise, "I have a new explanation of Rabbenu Tam on *rochlim*." We, who had long ago ceased to be bothered by that Rabbenu Tam, saw that the Rav could not rest until he fully understood the subject. In fact, he often used to say about difficult topics, "it bothers my mind." This is but one of many illustrations of the Rav's commitment to Torah study.

There were times when the Rav expressed his frustrations about the lack of dedication from his *talmidim*. He was always trying to encourage the students to rise to his level. Once he came into *shiur* at the beginning of the week and declared that we would finish the *perek* in *Eiruvin* that week. On Thursday, the last day of *shiur* in New York that week, he delivered *shiur* for almost eight hours without a break. Finally, shortly before sunset, he explained that when he began *shiur* that week, he had declared that we would finish the *perek*. Neither he nor any of the students said "*bli neder*." Hence it was a vow that we all accepted. After eight hours of *shiur* on Thursday, the end of the *perek* was barely in sight. The Rav suggested that we seek three rabbis who were not party to this vow and that they form a *bais din* before sunset to do *hataras nedarim*. Only after the procedure was completed did he dismiss the *shiur*. You can be sure that from then on we were always careful to amend the Rav's weekly goals with utterances of *bli neder*.

Compassionate Teacher

The Rav never used the *shiur* for polemics, speeches, or digressions about other people. He never said a bad word about any one. The *shiur* time was sacred for Torah study only. The Rav had little patience for impertinent questions that showed a lack of preparation. Yet, when there was a weak student in the class, the Rav was always gentle.

Once, a young assistant rabbi, who was attending the *shiur* for the first time, asked the Rav where a certain city mentioned in the Talmud was located. The veterans of the *shiur* were certain that the Rav would be annoyed at having his train of thought broken by such a question. The Rav stroked his beard, appeared to consider the question seriously, and finally replied, "Somewhere in Babylonia, I think."

There were times when the Rav would reprimand the students for poor preparation, inadequate commitment or inappropriate questions. He once explained that, when his father taught him he expected perfection. He felt that, it was likewise his responsibility to transmit it to us.

Generosity with Torah

The Rav often criticized his students for being too selfish. He said that we only learn for ourselves and that was an undesirable trait. He wanted us to learn with dedication and share generously as well with others.

The Rav's love of Torah study translated itself in his support of other Torah institutions. At the request of Rav Aharon Kotler *zt"l*, the Rav worked hard for Chinuch Atzmai. He spoke at their dinner in honor of Rav Aharon. When Rav Aharon took ill, the Rav personally raised funds for Lakewood Yeshiva. He sent a letter on his personal stationary on behalf of Yeshiva Torah Vodaas when they had financial problems. He worked tirelessly to see to it that Maimonides School in Boston always met its payroll on time.

There is so much more to tell and to say about the Rav. There is so much that I do not know about him. But, I hope that this brief description depicts the Rav as a great teacher of Torah who inspired *bnai Torah* to recognize and love what he called "the primacy of Torah and *Halakhah*" with *mentchlichkeit.*

HESPED FOR THE RAV

RABBI YOSEF BLAU

The Rav was so beyond us that I, like so many of his students, am only able to relate to parts of his multi-faceted genius. Incapable of saying a full *hesped*, I will speak about those aspects of the Rav that I understand.

Circumstances allowed me to know the Rav in different capacities and gain some insights. I had the unusual opportunity to attend the Rav's *shiurim* in two different eras. First, as a student from 1957 to 1965, and then as *mashgiach* in the *beit midrash* of Yeshiva University between 1977 and December 1984, until the Rav stopped coming into New York. Second, during the years 1965–1967, I had the privilege to work for the Rav at the Maimonides School, which also gave me many opportunities for private conversation.

The Rav frequently spoke on different aspects of the laws and customs of *aveilut*, mourning. Among his observations was the inherent conflict in simultaneously being an *aveil* and experiencing the joys of *yom tov*. There is an obvious contradiction and conflict of emotions between *simchat haregel* (rejoicing on the *yom tov*) and *aveilut*. The contradiction is not between the formal halakhic manifestations of *simchat haregel* and the rituals of mourning. As a mourner, one is permitted to eat a meat meal and drink wine. Only during the period of *aninut*, after the death of the relative and before burial, is there a prohibition on meat and wine.

The Rav explained that the conflict is not in halakhic behavior, but appears on a more fundamental level. It reflects the essential difference between the *kiyum shebileiv* of *simchat haregel*, the internal experience of joy on *yom tov* – which derives from the concept that the Jew on *yom tov* stands *lifnei Hashem* (before God) – and the *kiyum shebileiv*, the internal manifestation, the sense of a broken heart, of mourning that goes beyond rituals and prohibitions. Being in a state of mourning is to be distant from God and prevents one from becoming close to Him. Losing our *rebbe*, the one who brought us closer to *Hashem*, is creating a distancing between the *Shechinah* and us.

I entered the *shiur* after Pesach, when the Rav was teaching the portion of *Masechet Moed Katan* which deals with *aveilut*. Rabbi Chanoch Henoch Fishman *zt"l* – who was a *rosh yeshiva* in RIETS and had been part of the select group in the Mir Yeshiva in Europe which was selected to study with Rav Velvel *zt"l* (the Rav's uncle) in Brisk – was the *rebbe* who was in charge of the night *seder* in the *beit midrash*. He and I had the following agreement: I would repeat for him the Rav's *shiur* on *aveilut* and he would tell me what he had learned from Rav Velvel on the same issues. The two approaches were remarkably similar yet they often reached different conclusions. The Rav added a significant dimension to the Torah of Rav Hayyim, the Rav's grandfather. He not only absorbed and represented the Brisker intellectual method of halakhic analysis, but personally displayed a sensitive religious personality which moved beyond analysis of outward halakhic behavior and delved into the inner nature of religious life. He applied Brisker methodology to analyze the core of one's inner life.

During 5727 (1966–1967), the Rav lost his mother, brother and wife within a few months. I was working at Maimonides, and during his *shivah* for his wife, I would go back and forth between the Rav's house and the school, bringing students to be *menachem* the Rav.

One afternoon, I arrived when Rav Yitzchak Hutner, *Rosh Yeshiva* of Yeshivas Rabbeinu Chaim Berlin, and Rav Mordechai Pinchas Teitz, Rav of Elizabeth New Jersey and dean of its Jewish Educational Center, were there. The Rav said to them that he found it difficult to comprehend that after completing the *shloshim* for his mother, who lived into her late eighties, he remained obligated to mourn until the completion of twelve months. Now he is an *aveil* for his wife with whom he had chosen to share his life, and his mourning period would be only *shivah* and *shloshim*. Sharpening his question, he contrasted the loss by a parent of a child, a devastating tragedy – in which mourning ends with *shloshim* – with a child's loss of a parent which is natural and yet *halakhah* requires him to mourn for *yud beis chodesh*, twelve months.

Rav Hutner answered that the passing of a parent also represents a loss in the chain that extends back to Mount Sinai. Rav Teitz gave two explanations: The *mitzvah* of *kibud av va'eim*, honoring ones parents, continues even after their passing and creates the additional time of mourning. Additionally, father and mother are the only halakhic relationships that cannot be duplicated.

The Rav then gave his answer, which reflected a remarkable psychological insight. It is precisely the fact that the parent, a generation older, normally passes away before the child that creates an additional need for mourning. Over the years, the relationship of dependency that the child has to the parent reduces and, if the parent lives a long life, may even reverse itself. The sense of loss is diminished by the infirmity of the aged parent. In order to force the child to reflect back on his total relationship with his parent, including his early years, and acknowledge the enormity of the debt owed to both father and mother, *halakhah* requires this extended period of mourning. When a parent loses a child, there is no need for *halakhah* to tell him to mourn. It is a natural response. Rather, what is needed is a process that ends, enabling one to go beyond mourning, return to functioning, and tend to the other family members. This story illustrates the Rav's profound understanding of human emotions while seeing them in halakhic terms.

An addendum to this story occurred fifteen years later when I drove the Rav to Lakewood New Jersey, to pay a *shivah* call to Rav Schneur Kotler who had lost a son. Parenthetically, the house had a large window facing the street. When we arrived, the drapes were open and when Rav Schneur saw the Rav enter, he rose as a sign of respect. This uncommon gesture is not required from a mourner. For the next two hours, they discussed the laws and customs of *aveilut* and the Rav did not mention that insight which he had said years before. Driving back to New York, I reminded him of the discussion in Brookline and the answer he had given. In typical fashion, he dismissed his own insight as *drush*, mere homiletics. This time, he said that parents, in different ways, are teachers of their children as well as physical parents and thus there is a double *aveilut.* This constant rethinking of even his most famous *chiddushim* was a fundamental expression of the Rav's conception of Torah study. He was not interested in repeating what he had said the last time that he learned the material. Learning to the Rav meant a fresh analysis and often produced a completely different interpretation.

One time in *shiur,* the Rav explained a difficult Rambam. One of the old-timers pointed out that this Rambam had been the source of a recorded written dispute between the Rav and the *Chazon Ish*. [Editor's note: the Rav was not yet twenty years old at the time of that debate.] This time, the Rav was interpreting the Rambam in accordance with the view of the *Chazon Ish* decades earlier. The Rav replied, "but now, this is how I understand this Rambam." What he had written earlier was irrelevant.

The Rav did not restrict his *shiurim* to those *Massechtot* traditionally studied in Lithuanian *yeshivot*. He gave *shiurim* on all of *Shas*. This was not merely an exercise in erudition. The Rav was making an important point. He was concerned that American Jewry, the first generation given the opportunity to gain an intensive secular education and to enter the professions, saw the world of secular knowledge as profound knowledge and the world of Torah as mere customs and ceremonies. This was especially true in areas not associated in the past with serious Talmud study. However, no one who heard a *shiur* from the Rav on the *tefillot* of Rosh Hashanah or Yom Hakippurim could possibly observe those days as customs. His students who also attended graduate schools never found a graduate seminar as intellectually demanding as his *shiur*. After leaving the Rav's *shiur*, one was not intimidated by criticism from any secular scholar.

In the earlier years, the Rav was intolerant of unprepared *talmidim*. He saw it as intellectual laziness and was not interested in those who came to see a show. The *talmidim* were partners in the profound *chidushim* that were being developed; in reality, they were very junior partners, but partners nevertheless.

When my wife became educational director at a yeshiva high school for girls, she and I met with the Rav to discuss the education to be provided to the students. When she asked about teaching Torah *shebe'al peh* (Talmud) to women, the Rav replied that the reasoning used by the Chafetz Chaim sixty years earlier, to justify teaching *Torah shebichtav* (Bible) to women exposed to Polish primary schools, requires teaching Talmud to American women who receive a university education. To the Rav, there could be no high-level study of Jewish texts that did not include Talmud. At the same meeting, they discussed the pursuit of higher education and preparing for a career in terms of its effect on traditional life. He felt that a woman's family role should be taught but that she also had the right for self-realization. The contradiction was to be resolved by the student herself.

In general, the Rav gave his students the tools, set them on the way and then trusted them to maturely make life decisions. One of his students completed both *semichah* and law school and went to the Rav to ask him for guidance. He emerged disappointed because the Rav would not make the choice for him. Only later did the student appreciate the importance of his taking responsibility for his life.

The Rav's attitude towards Israel is an instance where he broke with his family's position. His uncle, the Brisker Rav, did not recognize the state because there was no halakhic category into which a secular Jewish state fits. But the Rav felt that there is nothing which cannot fit into a halakhic category. He also felt that God speaks through history as well as in halakhic terms. The Rav transferred his allegiance from Agudath Yisrael to Mizrachi because, through history, God had ruled in favor of the religious Zionism. His religious Zionism, however, was not proto-Messianic. Immediately after the Six Day War, an Israeli had spoken of the lives risked to secure the old city of Jerusalem and the *kotel*. The Rav's response was that protecting the *kotel* does not justify the loss of a single Jewish soldier. Jewish rule over territory was important but not an absolute value.

At a time when external expressions of *kavod haTorah* are continually stressed, the behavior of the Rav reflected a very different approach. Once, the late *rosh yeshiva* of Kerem B'Yavneh, Rav Goldvicht, visited Yeshiva University. The Rav invited him to give a *shiur* and join him for lunch. They walked to the cafeteria where the Rav took two trays and stood at the back of the line and waited for his turn. Then he sat down at a table where some students were sitting and he did not ask them to move. The Rav never demanded formal expressions of *kavod haTorah*; he always held the door for others and answered the phone himself. Still, we were in awe of him.

My first introduction to the Rav was in my first year at Yeshiva College. I was not yet in his *shiur*. The Rav had asked his students if they had any complaints. One student said that the Rav was not around enough for the boys to talk to him. So the Rav began to come into the *beit midrash* on Tuesday nights after his *shiur* at the Moriah synagogue. One such night, he discussed a *sugyah* in *Gittin* and asked his *talmidim* to find a specific Rashi that reflected an unusual perspective on the topic. The Rashi was in a different *massechta* that I happened to be studying. No one in the *shiur* seemed to know the answer. I had the *Gemara* in my hands but when I stood up to answer, no words came out of my mouth. All I could do was put the *Gemara* down in front of the Rav, and point to the appropriate Rashi. The Rav said, "correct" and went on. All of us shared this tremendous awe of the Rav which emerged naturally.

The next step, after the goal of learning the art of Torah study was met, was ethical development. The Rav's view was that the non-observant Jew would not be impressed with Shabbat observance or *kashrut*, but if he saw that an observant Jew lived on a higher ethical plane, then he could be reached. Rav Hayyim defined the role of a Rav as one who does *chesed* for the community. Both Rav Hayyim and the Rav were great *ba'alei chesed.*

The Rav demonstrated his unique *chesed* to my family. Just before we left Brookline, my wife gave birth to a son. The *brit* was on Shabbat and we asked the Rav to be the *sandek*. It was the year that he suffered three family losses and was still depressed. On Thursday night the Rav knocked on our apartment door. He apologized and said that he did not think his presence would add to our *simchah* and was going to Cape Cod to be with to his children for Shabbat. He gave us a generous check as a present for the child. My wife wanted us to save the check, but I thought that was not what the Rav would have wanted. I thought that he would respond that he was not a Chassidic rebbe. In the midst of his pain, he walked up two flights to our apartment to give our newly-born son a present.

The Rav's generosity extended to those who criticized him and those who were jealous of him. He even raised money for their causes and institutions. Recently, I was approached by someone who was upset that a prominent *rosh yeshiva* pointedly did not attend the Rav's funeral or any memorial program for him. This person felt that in protest, he should not participate in a fundraising campaign for that *rosh yeshiva*'s institution. I assured him that the Rav would have wanted him to support the yeshiva.

I was recently told this revealing vignette: One evening the Rav was looking for an early minyan for *Maariv* as he had a *yahrtzeit.* One of the boys he approached was newly observant and clearly had no idea who the Rav was. The boy told the Rav that his rabbi had said that it was too early to *daven.* The Rav did not mention who he was and simply replied that it is alright, "I think we can *daven* now." The boy was adamant that it was too early and only agreed on condition that the Rav promised that he would repeat *kriyat shma.*

There are many experts on the Rambam, who study the *Mishneh Torah* and have no idea that the *Moreh Nevuchim* exists. There are also philosophers who study the *Moreh Nevuchim* and ignore the *Mishneh Torah.* Similarly, among the disciples of the Rav, there are those who understand his *chidushei Torah* but are not interested in his philosophy, and experts on his philosophy who do not understand his *chidushei Torah.* The Rav was a shy person who seldom initiated conversations. People spoke with him about their interests and he responded accordingly. We all benefited from our exposure to the Rav, each in terms of our interests and abilities. Hopefully, we will not confuse our portion with the whole Rav.

MEMORIES OF A GIANT

RABBI KENNETH BRANDER

Twice a day, once in the morning and once in the evening, we are mandated to recite the *Kriyat Shema*, a prayer which encapsulates the responsibilities of the covenantal relationship between ourselves and God.

Misheyakir bein techelet lelavan. The morning *Shema* may be recited when one is able to discern between the blue of *techelet* and white. The morning existentially represents the times in life which are bountiful, when the challenges facing the Jew arise not from pogroms or persecution, but, rather, from power and wealth. The mandate to recite the *Shema* in the morning reminds us that despite the glitz of Madison Avenue, the environment of acceptance and material affluence, our lifestyle must be driven by the norms and mores, which resonate throughout the Torah.

The *Shema* is then recited again at night. In the face of the difficulties and darkness of our personal and communal existence, the *Shema* symbolizes the unwavering commitment of the Jew to Torah.

In addition to the three biblical passages of the *Shema*, there is one phrase which is not found throughout the Torah, *Baruch shem kevod malchuto le'olem va'ed*, Blessed is the name of God, His kingdom reigns forever. The Talmud in *Pesachim* explains that the addition of this phrase to the *keriyat Shema* prayer reenacts a dialogue between Yaakov and his sons. Yaakov was troubled on his death-bed. His father, Yitzchak, and grandfather, Avraham, each had a child who defied the covenantal relationship. Yaakov was afraid that, perhaps like his father and grandfather, one or more of his children were not truly committed to the ideals of monotheism. Immediately, the children of Yaakov turned to him and recited the verse: *Shema Yisrael*, listen our father *Yisrael* (Yaakov), we are all committed to the ideals you taught us, the ideals which celebrate the lives of Avraham and Yitzchak. *Ado-no-y Elokeinu Ado-no-y Echad*, the Lord is amongst us, and He is one with us. With relief and joy, Yaakov turned to his children, the tribes of Israel, and stated, *Baruch shem kevod malchuto le'olam va'ed.*

If the purpose of adding this additional passage is to emphasize the dialogue between Yaakov and his sons, Rabbi Soloveitchik asked, why is it condensed into a monologue? Let there be an exchange between the *chazan* and the congregation, one reenacting the character of Yaakov and the other assuming the role of his children, the twelve tribes. Why is this prize dialogue reenacted as a monologue? The Rav explains that there is an important purpose for the exchange to be transformed into a monologue. The *Shema* asks every Jew to play two critical roles in guaranteeing the future of Judaism.

First is the role of Yaakov's children articulated in the biblical phrase stated to their father, *Shema Yisrael.* We must recommit ourselves to become students of the tradition, children of the *mesorah.* We are introduced to the *mesorah* through a plethora of experiences, *musar avicha* and *torat imecha.* The sounds, sights and smells that waft through the home every Erev Shabbat and Yom Tov, the informal dialogues and formal instruction from our parents and teachers, are all components in the curriculum that makes us students of the *mesorah.* As students of the *mesorah*, we must carry ourselves in a fashion consistent with its ideals. In the process, we affirm, like the children of Yaakov – not as much to God but to past generations – *shema Yisrael.* Our effort as students of the *mesorah* guarantees the immortality of generations past.

However, after making the commitment to be students of the *mesorah*, we are also asked to assume a second role on the covenantal stage, that of Yaakov, the teacher of the *mesorah.* To truly guarantee the future of Judaism, we must share its message with others. We, acting as teachers of the *mesorah*, utter the words *Baruch shem kevod*, for teaching guarantees the eternity of Judaism. Thus the dialogue is experienced as a monologue for it is our responsibility to play both roles on the stage of Jewish continuity.

No family, since the time of Rashi, has had so many great Torah scholars as the Soloveitchik family. It is a family that redefined the style and approach to Talmud study. The Rav was a product of that environment. He was a true student of the *mesorah* learning from his father, Rav Moshe, and mother, Pesha Feinstein, as well as his revered grandfather, Rav Hayyim. His life celebrated the statement of Yaakov's sons, that of *shema Yisrael.* As with Yaakov's sons, the Rav's brilliance allowed him to internalize the rich traditions of his family. However, the greatness and the legacy of the Rav are not limited to his responsibility as a student of the *mesorah*. He lived the character of Yaakov, and was the quintessential teacher of our generation. As Rav Moshe Feinstein was fond of saying, the Rav was the *melamed* of our time. The Rav was at home in any *sugyah* in *shas*, in any issue of *halakhah*, or any idea in philosophy. He used his knowledge to teach us the full spectrum of Torah, and every *shiur* introduced us to another color in the tapestry of Torah. His clarity, charisma, excitement and intellectual integrity made the daily *shiur* exciting and a gathering place for all different types of people. Young *Semichah* students and veteran *rashei yeshiva* hung onto every word. Talmudic scholars came from every *yeshiva* in the world to sit in the room with the master. His philosophy of Judaism may have often been articulated with verbiage found in Kant, Hegel, Kiergegaard, or Cohen but it was predicated on the ideals of the Rambam and Ramban and the traditions of his family. There is no community in the world, which has not been touched by the Rav, his students, or his writings.

I do not have the capacity or ability to expound on the Rav's greatness in learning. However, there are a few observations which I would like to share. First, when the Rav presented an argument between various schools of thought in the Talmud or among *Rishonim*, you felt as if the personalities being discussed were present in the room. It was in the Rav's *shiur* that many of us felt that we met Rashi, Rabbenu Tam, Rav Alfas and the Ramban. It was there that we became closely acquainted with the personality, language and demeanor of the Rav's good friend, the Rambam. Second, a cornerstone of the *shiur* was a demand for intellectual integrity. In *shiur*, the analysis of any concept was an expedition for the truth. What counted in any *shiur* discussion was not the age of the student, or the amount of years a student had spent in *shiur* or the student's family name. What counted was the truth. There were times in which a thesis of a veteran scholar was dismissed and the suggestion of the youngest adopted with respect. I will never forget the time that the Rav responded to several questions at the end of a two and a half hour *shiur*, of which the bulk was spent on the presentation of a specific idea. Each question was answered by the Rav in a very clear and precise way. Yet when the *shiur* was over, the Rav asked me to call over one of the boys, who had asked a certain question. The Rav told him "you were right and I was wrong. Tomorrow we will restudy the topic based on the question you raised."

The Rav loved teaching. I remember one time when we were informed that for the Rav's health, the *shiur* had to be limited to two hours. The Rav agreed to this and so on the first day of this medically imposed limit, I drew signs to be placed on his *Gemara* to indicate how much time he had left. Since I sat next to the Rav in *shiur*, I simply slid the paper on his *Gemara* after an hour, another one after an hour and a half, and a third after two hours. The first day, it worked like a charm. Everybody in *shiur* was surprised. The next day, the situation was quite different. After presenting the two-hour sign, the Rav continued to teach. I found myself in quite a quandary. How does a twenty-year old deal with the fact that the *gadol hador* is not following the medically prescribed time limit? All eyes in *shiur* were on me to see how this dilemma would unfold. After an additional forty-five minutes, I stood and announced that *shiur* was over. The Rav turned to me for a moment, and then to the *shiur*, and said, "Even the Satan does not have as good of an assistant as I do." The boys laughed and class was over. After *shiur*, I was silent on the walk back to the apartment in Morgenstern Hall. Once in the apartment, and after eating a very quiet lunch together, the Rav asked what was wrong? I explained to him that I was not acting on my own accord, just following instructions and that, personally, I would have enjoyed listening to the *shiur* longer. The Rav responded that in the mornings before the *shiur* he was often in pain, in the afternoons after *shiur* he was often in pain, but when delivering *shiur* he was pain-free. How correct he was. During the years that I was a *shamash* of the Rav, the mornings were often difficult, and after *shiur* was again difficult, but during *shiur* the Rav was vibrant, enthused and pain-free. He would often enter *shiur* with blurred sight yet he would read the *Gemara*, Rambam and Rashi as if his sight was unimpaired. The next day in *shiur*, I was not going to remind the Rav when to stop. However, an hour and a half into the *shiur,* the Rav turned to me and asked me how much more time he had left.

The Rav had a reputation of being tough in *shiur*. The demands he made on his *talmidim* were due to his love for them and his commitment to be the best possible *melamed*. However, outside of *shiur,* his demeanor was welcoming, gentle and one of concern. I remember the many times that a person left the Rav's apartment comforted, either because the Rav had a solution to his problem or simply because he had listened so intently. Additionally, when the Rav heard of a problem that a fellow human being had, whether it was Menachem Begin or a simple Jew sent by his/her rabbi, the Rav was so empathetic that he experienced the pain felt by the other, to the extent that the pain and anguish of the visiting person was visible on the Rav's frail face and body. It would now be harder for him to walk, to sleep or to eat. It was like reliving the story of Moshe and the battle of *Amalek*. The Torah informs us that Moshe sat on rocks when Aharon and Chur propped up his hands enabling the *Bnei Yisrael* to triumph in their first war. Immediately, Rashi asks, why was Moshe sitting on rocks? Were there not pillows available for him to sit on, allowing this elderly leader some comfort? Rashi explains that since the Jewish people were in pain, Moshe was in pain and refused any creature comforts, preferring to sit on a pile of rocks. That was the Rav! He truly felt the pain of others, happy when he could halakhically solve their dilemma, pained when he could not, sleepless when he needed to marshal his halakhic arsenal to help another human being.

I will never forget the camaraderie the Rav shared with Rav Moshe Feinstein, Rav Ruderman and the Lubavitcher Rebbe. Every time a new *sefer* came out from Chabad, the Rebbe would send two *shlichim* to the apartment. Many, if not all, were inscribed with a lovely note from the Rebbe. Rav Moshe, Rav Ruderman and the Rav would call each other before every *chag*. I always remember the various times that the Rav, before a *chag*, would ask me to call Rav Moshe's home so that they could extend wishes to each other. On Ta'anit Esther 1986, when Rav Moshe was *niftar,* the Rav was not feeling very well. His family was concerned and asked that he not be informed of the *petirah* of his friend. We obliged. The next morning, *The New York Times* normally delivered to the apartment was somehow "not received." The radio in the apartment, from which the Rav listened to the news, "was broken." We thought we had done a great job of shielding the Rav from the news of the *petirah*, thus avoiding any additional compromise to his frail health.

During that time, I rarely spent the afternoons in the Rav's apartment since I was learning in *Kollel*. However, the week prior to Pesach, as the Rav was leaving to the airport, he requested that I be called out of the *bet midrash* to drive him there. I immediately obliged. As I was driving down the Grand Central Parkway to the Eastern Airlines shuttle, the Rav asked me why I did not inform him that Rav Moshe had passed away. My response was one of silence and disbelief. After several tense moments, I explained that this was done at the request of his family, out of concern for his health. I then turned to him and asked how did he find out. His response was the following: "Every *chag*, either I call Rav Moshe or he calls me. This Pesach it was his turn to call me. There can only be one reason why he did not call…"

I would like to conclude with an idea communicated by Rav Ahron Soloveichik about his brother. When the *beit hamikdash* was burning, the *pirchei kehunah* went to the rooftop and surrendered its keys by throwing them up to Heaven. Rav Ahron explained that this was not an act of greatness but one of cowardice. Even when the *beit hamikdash* was burning, no one had the right to surrender. It was that surrender which doomed the Jewish people to a long and difficult *galut*. Over the past fifty years, many have had the *zechut* of being the students of the Rav. For us, as a community, he defined our mission and our public posture. His passing is not a time to surrender or abandon his calling but to recommit ourselves to be both students and teachers of his tradition. We recommit ourselves to embrace a Torah not shaped by modernity but a modernity shaped by Torah.

May *Hakadosh Baruch Hu* strengthen us and give us the capacity to move from being students of the *mesorah*, students of *Moreinu veRabbeinu* haRav Yosef Dov Halevi Solovietchik, to teachers of his *mesorah*. *Yehi Zichro Baruch.*

MEMORIES OF MY *REBBE*, THE RAV

RABBI ABBA BRONSPIGEL

I would just like to share the memories that I have of my *rebbe*, and I have many fond memories of him. I was a *talmid* in his class for many years. I was quite close to him for many years. I used to go into his apartment very often in the *yeshiva*. Let me begin by telling you of my first meeting with him and my last meeting with him.

My first meeting was in 1957 when I entered his class and we were learning *masechet Sanhedrin*. Until today, I'll never forget that *shiur*; basically I can say over the essence of that *shiur* without any preparation. Not because I have such a great memory or I'm so smart, but simply the impact of that *shiur* was so great that I could not forget it. I still remember that he began with the first Rashi in *Sanhedrin*, which provides a definition of a *gazlan*. Rav Soloveitchik begin to scrutinize every word of Rashi; he asked some very strong questions on what Rashi says and then for the next two hours or so, I sat spellbound listening to his brilliant *chidush* that answered that Rashi. He introduced a *machloket* between Rambam and Raavad, he developed a certain principle in *halakhah*, and after he was finished, not only was every word of Rashi accounted for, but had Rashi said anything else, *that* would have been the difficulty!

As I said, until this very day, I remember that *shiur*. At that *shiur*, I immediately learned three things. I realized: 1) I am sitting at the feet of a master and I will be introduced to a new *derech halimud*, to a *lomdus* that I was not accustomed to until then. I was amazed at the *koach hachidush*, the brilliant *chidushim* that occur to such a great man; 2) the *koach hazbarah*, the clarity of mind, with which the Rav was able to take the most intricate complex topics and explain them in simple terms that was comprehensible to every one; 3) I realized I was developing a new *derech halimud*, to account for every word in Rashi, for every word in Tosafos and for every Rambam, and if we were not prepared for the *shiur*, then God forbid!

My last meeting with the Rav was a different meeting altogether. It happened three and a half years ago, and at that time the Rav was ill. I traveled to Boston together with his son. When we came to his daughter's home (where he had been living for some years), the Rav did not recognize me. Haym tried to remind him who I was, "you know this is…." But not only did he not recognize me, I don't think that he was aware that I even was in his presence. I stood there for at least an hour, I don't remember how long. Why would I stay an hour in such a situation? Because a most unusual thing happened. The whole time, the Rav was sitting on a chair looking down toward the floor, and he was speaking to himself.

All that I heard was him quoting one Rambam after another, all the Rambams dealing with *kodashim,* with *korbanos.* He simply quoted Rambam after Rambam, it went on and on. Then he paused and began quoting some *Gemaras*, one *Gemara* after the other, with the exact language of the *Gemara.* Then he paused again, and in the middle he delivered what I think was a *mussar drashah*, about *shimiras hamitzvos.* The whole thing was in Yiddish. He kept saying that *yiddin* have to be good *yiddin*, honest *yiddin*, frummer *yiddin*, observing and upholding the *mitzvot* and so forth. And then he went back to his Rambams, and I was totally amazed. Here you have a person who was ill, and all you heard from him throughout that period was *Gemaras*, Rambams, *poskim* and Rashis.

This story really tells it all; it best describes who the Rav really was. The Rav basically lived Torah all his life. And at the end of his life, that is all that came out, Torah, Torah and more Torah. And to me this was the most amazing experience I've had. *Chazal* tell us that you can discern a person by observing how he handles three facets of his daily affairs: his money, his anger and his drinking. This is exactly the same concept, you see how a person when he is not aware of his surroundings and you listen to what comes out of him. And when you see that Torah comes out from such a person, you realize that he lived a life of Torah all his life.

A second point that I would like to emphasize about the Rav is the term that he used very often in class, "intellectual honesty." Actually, the biggest insult the Rav could give to anyone was, "you are intellectually dishonest." If he called on you and you were unprepared, or you did not know the Rambam, then look out, he would get angry because he was very demanding of us. He very often would say a *shiur* one day, and come in the next and say, "I erred yesterday, my approach was wrong, and we have to develop a new approach." The Rav was not afraid to say "I made a mistake," he was intellectually honest. Because of his intellectual honesty, the Rav was also not a politician and unfortunately *rabbanim*, even great *rabbanim*, very often get involved in politics. The Rav, because of his great honesty, had no political ambitions. (He didn't even know what to do with it.) It is true that certain organizations tried to draw him into certain things and at times he had to defend them, but he himself remained above them. He was not a *ba'al machlokes*, and he was not a politician. In our days, it is a very important thing to emphasize.

I already mentioned the Rav's *beki'us* in the Rambam. Those who learned by him will remember that there was not a day that he would not go over the Rambam in every page of *Gemara*. We always had to carry a *Gemara* and a Rambam; as a matter of fact, very often he began with the Rambam. I was told an interesting story about his expertise in the Rambam. He was known as a *gadol* already in Europe. The *gedolai hador*, like Reb Chaim Ozer and others, held him in very high regard when he was a young man. This story was told by Rav Kagan *zt"l*, the principal at Yeshiva RJJ. He was a little older than the Rav, and he told the following story in his *yeshiva*:

When he was a young man coming back from *yeshiva* on a vacation, he would frequently stop in Khaslavichy and spend time "talking Torah" with Reb Moshe, the Rav's father. One time, as they were in a heated discussion, they differed on what the Rambam had written. So Rabbi Kagan said, "let's get a copy of the Rambam and we'll look it up." Reb Moshe said, "That won't be necessary," and called over his son Berel (the Rav) who was not yet bar mitzvah, and asked him to recite the words of the Rambam. And, on the spot, the Rav who was under bar mitzvah age quoted the Rambam verbatim. The Rav was an expert in the entire Rambam. The Rav parenthetically once mentioned to us that Reb Hayyim's expertise in the Rambam was most unusual. Not only did he know every word of the Rambam by heart, but he knew every word that comes before it and after it. Very often, Reb Hayyim developed an insight based just on the location of a word in the Rambam. If the Rambam wrote a certain word following another word, that in itself taught Reb Hayyim an important principle. Reb

Hayyim possessed not only an expertise in simply reciting the Rambam; It was an expertise together with *havanah*, insight.

Now let me discuss a little bit about the piety of the Rav. Unfortunately many people think that the Rav was a *meikil* in *dinim*, took the lenient position on matters of *halakhah*. This is absolutely not true. Like all Brisker, he had *chumros* and he had *kulos*, all based on his *shitos*. I would like to emphasize that the Rav never told us what we should do. He never told us what he does either. I remember distinctly that it was around Pesach time and some of the *talmidim* wanted to know what was the *shiur* for a *kazayis* and for a *revi'is*. The Rav was not into these things, and when someone asked him, "Rebbe, what do you do?" He told him "it's none of your business." Now, he didn't say this to be rude. Actually there is greatness here. He did not want his *minhagim* to be imposed on others. He knew that if he would say, "I do such and such," most likely the *talmid* would want to follow suit. He used to say very often, "Do what your father did." This takes greatness for, you know, very often a rav, a *rosh yeshiva* wants his *talmidim* to follow in his ways.

We never knew *minhagei haRav*. Certain things we knew because they were done publicly, but his basic *hanhagah* we never knew. He always hid it from us. This was characteristic not only of the Rav but of the entire Brisker *mishpachah*. The Brisker Rav was like this, Reb Hayyim Brisker was like this. They knew that their *minhagim* were not for *klal Yisroel*, they had their own *shitos*. They were *gedolei Yisroel*, and they knew what they were doing. They had their own *shitos* and they did not want others to follow them.

I will mention something about the Rav that is well known to everyone in the Brookline community. On *motzei Shabbos*, most people wait at most 72 minutes for *yetzias Shabbos*. The Rav used to wait at least an hour and a half and in the summer time at least 2 hours. How many people wait so long *motzei Shabbos*? The following story was told to me last night, by Rav Drillman, a *talmid* of the Rav, and a rosh yeshiva at RIETS.: The Rav once walked past a light switch on Shabbos and accidentally his arm switched off the light. And you know what happened? He fainted! This is true Brisker *eimas hadin*. Those of you who are acquainted with Brisker *yirat shamayim,* this is a real Brisker *yirat shamayim*. An *aveirah* was committed, it was even less than a *shogeg* (I don't know the exact halakhic category that it falls under), but when the Rav realized that there was an act of desecrating the Shabbat done inadvertently by his movements, he actually fainted. Ask yourselves, how many *rabbanim* have you seen who inadvertently did an *aveirah* (after all, we are only human), and afterwards fainted? The Rav fainted, and this shows tremendous piety on the part of the Rav.

Let me also tell you about the *chesed* of the Rav, that I know personally. For instance, there was a certain very fine *talmid* in the Rav's class who was quite poor. There was once an occasion when he needed a large amount of money, thousands of dollars. He did not tell his *rebbe*, the Rav, about it. But one of his good friends knew about it and that *chaver* apparently must have mentioned it to the Rav. A few days later, the Rav simply walked over to him and handed him the thousands of dollars that he needed. No one knew about it. I know it from the *chaver* of this fellow. The Rav raised tremendous amounts of money for his uncle, the Brisker Rav, for the Brisker Yeshiva in Jerusalem, and later on for his cousin, his namesake, Rav Berel Soloveitchik *zt"l*. This was all done quietly; people generally did not know about it. I know for a fact that he helped raise money for other *yeshivos*, *yeshivos* where his name was criticized or was not spoken of well, and he knew it. But it didn't make a difference. I even know that some of the leaders of the Neturei Karta in Jerusalem used to come to him, and he helped them. He once told me, "Even though I do not agree with the Neturei Karta, the *emes* is that they do some good things. If not for them who knows where we would be?" Even though he and the Neturei Karta were at extremes, when it came to help another *yid*, it did not make a difference to him. It didn't even make a difference to him that some of these people were not only critical of him, but even more than critical. This is true *chesed*. The Rav did many favors for various organizations, not only monetarily but in other ways as well.

The Rav was also a great gentleman. As you know, there were certain *machlokisim*, *machlokos lesheim Shamayim,* but I would like to emphasize the following to you: The Rav respected and admired all the *gedolim* of his time. He told this to us and you were able to see it. Especially Rav Aaron Kotler, Rav Moshe Feinstein and Rav Henkin. Those three I knew about personally. And, to my knowledge, they had an equal amount of respect for him. There was a *machlokes lesheim Shamayim* about secular studies, but the mutual, personal respect was there. The Rav was consulted by great *rabbanim* and great *rashei yeshiva*, and by thousands of *talmidim*, about the most difficult problems that they were facing.

If I should want to discuss the *gadlus* of the Rav, if you were to ask me, "Who was the Rav?" the best way I could describe him to you was that the Rav was many things. It is true that the Rav was very educated and learned in many different areas, But basically the Rav sat and learned Torah all his life. Whatever he did aside from learning Torah came to him coincidentally. I came into his apartment many times and I never saw him studying anything else but Torah. I have asked other *talmidim* who are quite close to him, and who had keys to his apartment, and they also told me the very same thing. So, even though the Rav had vast knowledge, still the essence of the Rav was that he sat and learned Torah his entire life.

The Rav instilled in us a tremendous *ahavas haTorah,* a love for the Torah. All his *talmidim* know this. It is not just about setting aside a fixed time to study Torah, but actually to love to learn, to enjoy learning. The Rav very often spoke about the joy of learning. In defining the *brachah* of *talmud Torah*, he used to repeat the famous *Eglei Tal* that *Torah lishmah* means when you learn *besimchah*, when you enjoy that which you learn. You were able to see how he enjoyed learning, and especially if a *talmid* of his said a good *sevarah.* Very often, a student would say something good and his rebbe would knock him down. But the Rav was not like this, unless the student was wrong. But if you said something correct, then the best compliment he could give you was "not bad." That meant that you were very good. I still remember once, around Shavuot time, the Rav gave a *dvar Torah* at a *bris* of one of his grandchildren, one of the Lichtenstein children, in the Yeshiva, and he gave a *dvar Torah* at the *seudah* about the conflict between Rashi and Rabbenu Tam on *parshiot hatefillin.* And than he went into *drush*, (the Rav was a tremendous *darshan*). I remember that on that Shavuot, my desire to learn intensified and it remained with me for a long time. Just listening to his *shiur* was a great inspiration to learn more.

When it comes to his *drush,* I shall describe it to you, to those who never experienced it. The Rav used to give a *yahrtzeit shiur* for his father on the third of Shevat, when thousands of *yiddin* used to come, including great *rabbanim and rashei yeshiva.* It used to be a four-hour experience, two hours of *halakhah* and two on *aggadah.* The Rav used to begin either with a difficult Rambam or a difficult *Gemara,* ask four, five, six questions, then introduce a new *Gemara,* develop a certain principle, and then show how all the questions automatically fall away with this one principle.

If I should want to remember the Rav, there are three main points I would highlight: 1) His *ahavas haTorah*; 2) His dedication to *halakhah*, to the process of *halakhah*, to examine and understand a *din* and not to do things automatically; 3) His commitment to *mesorah.* The Rav followed the Brisker *derekh.* He always continuously used to say, "This I heard from my father, in the name of my *zeideh.*" This was true even when he told stories, and the Rav was a wonderful storyteller. Sometimes in *shiur*, he would tell us stories, but especially on Motzei Shabbos in Boston. I never heard him in that setting, but they used to say that he was very entertaining by bringing in stories of the previous generation. He used to say that by listening to these stories you have a direct link to the previous generation. The Rav himself was one of the links to the previous generation. So if I would want to remember my *rebbe*, whatever I know I learned from him. My *ahavas haTorah* comes from him. If I am dedicated to keeping the *halakhah*, to keeping the *mitzvos*, he gave me the foundation. Finally, I feel like I am at least part of the *mesorah.* Torah cannot just be picked up on the street: it is not in the air. You have to have a *mesorah* for the Torah, otherwise who knows what you get involved in. When an individual makes up his own *chidushim* which is not based on any *mesorah*, you very often stray off the road.

We, the *talmidim* of the Rav, lost a very great rebbe, *Klal Yisroel* lost a *gadol beTorah*, one of the *gedolei hador*, and we will of course always remember him.

Yehi zichro baruch. May his memory always be for a blessing.

A THREE-PART TRIBUTE

RABBI SHALOM CARMY

What I Couldn't Learn Elsewhere

Bereft of the Rav's influence, I would almost certainly have turned my back forever on organized religion. I became a *baal teshuvah*, to a significant degree, through study with the Rav's *talmid muvhak*, my revered teacher R. Aharon Lichtenstein, and by hearing the Rav's public *shiurim* and reading his work.

What did I learn from the Rav that I could not learn anywhere else? Conventional religion tends to edit reality, to soft-pedal existential conflict, to make the ugly aspects of reality disappear behind a rosy glow. More than any other Jewish thinker, the Rav's memorable and sometimes brutal honesty taught us what both conventional piety and fashionable liberalism seemed intent to conceal: that religion is no escape from conflict, but the ultimate encounter with reality. Facing reality, for the Rav, meant striving to penetrate the meaning of Torah and the challenges of human existence, not distracting oneself from these tasks by cultivating doubts about the reality. The Rav radiated a quiet, unyielding, persistent confidence in the truth of Torah. He emancipated us from the burden and the temptation of becoming intellectual Marranos, anxious to curry favor with the regnant academic, cultural and social powers that be.

He once translated the Talmudic query *"tzippita liyeshuah"* as "Did you suffer with dignity?" Beginning in 1976, I had the privilege of spending many hours in the Rav's apartment, where I saw other things I could not have learnt without *shimmush*. I recall, for example, helping him light the Hanukkah menorah, two of us holding him upright because standing unaided and extending his arm were no longer possible simultaneously. He enunciated each word, the *berakhot* and *hanerot hallalu*, distinctly and attentively. How wonderful it was – that concentrated eye-on-*mitzvah* look! This was reality, not mere *frumkeit;* this was the kind of reality that can be described only in the words of *Tehillim* (119) that we recited last week at the *levayah*. The Rav faced the ravages of illness and insult with dignity.

Another face of the Rav's quest is not much in evidence in *Halakhic Man*, with its exaltation of intellectual assurance; nor does it play a major role in the "existential" Rav, where the *mimaamakim* themes take the foreground. On almost every occasion that I was privileged to consult the Rav on matters that touched upon life, whenever his attention settled on the real-life ramifications of his guidance, he invariably reminded me to act and to speak "with dignity and humility, as befits a *ben Torah*." Such advice appears obvious to the point of triviality, but what immense reserves of self-knowledge and commitment are required to take it seriously!

Who is Authority?

"Authority has vanished from the modern world," begins one of the most influential essays in contemporary political philosophy. Along with the other revisions of the Rav's *zt"l* biography perpetrated in the past several weeks has come a yearning for the days when he presumably exercised authority over YU. In that golden era, we are assured, YU had a *Rosh Yeshiva* in the classic mold, who spoke for all, and whose dictates were uniformly and unquestioningly obeyed by all. This story diverges from the reality I perceived, and contradicts the way the Rav wanted to be perceived. I hope the three episodes recounted here help you understand how he guided students on a variety of public matters. They may also shed an indirect light on other facets of his character.

During the early 1970s many students at YU considered the war in Vietnam a misfortune, rife with halakhic and moral problems, and advocated its termination as quickly as possible. Various shades of this view were articulated by R. Ahron Soloveichik and by R. Aharon Lichtenstein. Apparently I attracted the Rav's attention by arguing the position in *Hamevaser*. And so, one bright afternoon in the cafeteria, the Rav parked his tray at my table and, without preamble, launched into a monologue on the political situation.

The Rav was a hawk on Vietnam. Worldwide Communism, he held, was monolithic: its triumph anywhere endangered freedom everywhere, much as a falling domino topples the whole row. But, he acknowledged, skillfully dissecting both sides of the debate, you might reject the domino theory, and in that case you really ought to oppose the Administration's policy. Don't be afraid to do it. Above all don't be paralyzed by the fear that Nixon would avenge himself on American Jews by punishing Israel: such timidity was the curse of the "slavish personality" despised by Nietzsche.

Because the Rav was able to participate in our thinking, though he considered us mistaken, the subsequent anti-war movement at Yeshiva could confidently and proudly call on the Rav's advice when questions arose about proper goals and tactics. As Prof. Gurock observes, events that shattered the covenant between students and their mentors at most universities, brought YU students closer to the ideals of the institution. In large part this was because the Rav gained our respect and admiration the old-fashioned way: by the force of his intellect and the moral impact of the respect with which he responded to us.

Years before, YCSC [Yeshiva College Student Council] had invited Lord Caradon, British ambassador to the UN, to speak at Yeshiva. A petition was circulated by students who objected to something in his past (I no longer recall exactly what). The diplomat got wind of it and hastened to withdraw. The Rav heard about the affair and scheduled a talk in Rubin Shul.

For two hours the Rav went on about the religious experience, which is unique and incommunicable. It is therefore unreasonable to expect non-Jews to fully understand our relationship to Eretz Yisrael. Hence we are wrong to interpret every disagreement with our beliefs as an expression of enmity. What about Lord Caradon? A *rebbi* cannot impose his views, said our teacher: he can only create the frame of reference within which the talmid finds his own way... The student body, needless to say, was now eager to hear the Rav's "suggestions," and the "misunderstanding" with the British statesman was cleared up according to his wishes.

Not every anecdote has a happy ending. In the 1980s a militant politician from Israel visited the States to hawk his wares. The Rav regarded this man's selective citation of Jewish sources as a distortion of Torah and a potential *chillul haShem*. He told people close to him that the individual should not be given a platform. Quite a few Rabbanim risked unpleasantness with their congregants because they accepted their *rebbi*'s concern.

Not surprisingly, there were students who desired the controversial speaker's presence in our midst. Some, when they learned of the Rav's displeasure, proceeded to cast aspersions on his Zionism. When the charismatic speaker ascended the rostrum of Rubin Shul, he allowed himself remarks about the Rav's religious authenticity that would have been inconceivable in a "real" Yeshiva. Academic freedom was served; students were entitled to their own mistakes.

In the modern world, some dismiss authority as no more than rational persuasion, and regard the authority as no more than a better informed equal. Others assimilate authority to the use of force, and adore the inveighing bully. But a great teacher, like a father, is respected and heeded because of who he is, not only because of what he knows. Like a father, however, his authority is founded on spiritual recognition, not merely on his ability to play the galleries or his aptitude at intimidation.

When the occasion warranted, in confronting political and institutional powers, the Rav could stiffen his rhetoric and throw his weight around. He was not afraid to provoke an Israeli cabinet crisis when a *trefah* kitchen was to be installed on an Israeli ship. He was just as adamant in demanding that the Israeli government convene an official inquiry into the Sabra and Shatilla massacres a decade ago. In dealing with students, however, he was not a shrewd political operator, but a concerned rebbe and a committed educator. I hope and pray that his example continues to make Yeshiva University different from other *yeshivot* as it surely must be different from other universities.

In the Incessant Battle

Every day is a good day for *teshuvah*. Yet there is a day that is not like any other. On that day weeks of contemplation and self-examination course through the arteries of our spirit. Among the lengthening shadows of

Neilah twilight we see our lives as they were meant to be. If only Yom Kippur did not come to an end, the vision would never flee; it would remain perpetually before our eyes, and culminate in reality. And so as we turn, each to his dinner and his common weekday world, we wonder and we pray: may some residue of the uncommon day, stamped upon our souls, leave us changed forever.

Every day is a good day for *hakkarat hatov*. Yet there are days that are not like all the others. Such is this day, the thirtieth since our teacher was taken from this world. For the past month he has not been absent from our thoughts. Nearly every exchange, whether the subject was Torah or worldly matters, has offered an excuse to utter his name and bring his words to our lips. We have undertaken special learning commitments in his memory – we who knew him well (or more precisely, aspects of him), and you who barely knew him, or knew him not at all – and our shared experience has mingled recollection with regret and inspiration with desire.

We all know that the Rav *zt"l* charted a new path in *mahshavah*. It is no more possible to survey here the central *sugyot* in Jewish thought that his reflection transformed than it would be to give an inventory of the numerous *halakhot* whose depths he plumbed and put into words, or the myriad of difficult passages whose intricacies he conquered. Let me set down three essential insights and attitudes that underlie the Rav's *derekh* in Jewish philosophy. Without these keys we cannot begin to enter into our inheritance.

II

1) Philosophy of religion is first and foremost the philosophy of religious realities. For a variety of reasons most incisively explored in *The Halakhic Mind*, the religious realities of Judaism are centrally, and objectively, located in the *Halakhah*.

The religious realities of Judaism are manifest, not only in the performance of the *Halakhah*, but also in its study. A full experiential involvement with *mitzvot* is impossible without understanding their meaning and significance, whence the necessity of learning.

The Rav deemed our time propitious for the intellectual quest. In his own words:

> [T]he young American generation... is not totally engrossed in the pragmatic, utilitarian outlook... To the degree that average people in our society attain higher levels of knowledge and general intelligence, we cannot imbue them with a Jewish standpoint that relies primarily on sentiment and ceremony.

If R. Kook witnessed the alienation of Jews from traditional religious commitment and decided that his generation needed exposure to a comprehensive Jewish philosophy deriving from the sources of Kabbalah, the Rav offered a simpler, more startling solution: renew the covenant with the exoteric sources that confront directly our concrete experience. And despite the currently fashionable anti-intellectualism, the Rav is right: no contemporary religious commitment can long stand without an abiding cognitive element.

2) The quest of which the Rav so ardently speaks is to be pursued not only through the "revelational consciousness" (*havayah gilluyit*), through God's encounter with man, i.e. through Torah. It is complemented by the "natural consciousness" (*havayah tiv'it*), the search for God initiated by man, the yearning to understand the mystery of the external world and the mystery of human consciousness and culture, the mystery of being and the nature of religious experience (as distinguished from the confrontation initiated by God). Man is created in the image of his Creator, and the expression of human creativity through the quest for theoretical and practical mastery of the external world and the world within constitute a fulfillment of the nature given to us by God. Every advance in our scientific and cultural endeavors, says the Rav, brings with it a deepening of our religious awareness as well.

Though the Rav heartily endorses the search for God via the natural consciousness, he knows its inadequacy: the heavens speak the glory of God; but a personal relation with God is attainable only through revelation. He also knows the inevitable threat of moral and intellectual anarchy when religion relies on the all too human results of human investigation and culture. But the untruth of a one-sided approach does not diminish his affirmation of man's dual nature: as the active searcher for God and as the passive recipient of Divine revelation.

Please note that the principle outlined above is not to be identified with a specific liberal arts curriculum. The Rav himself devoted a great deal of attention to the discipline of epistemology and its relation to contemporary philosophy of science. More important for most of us is his paradigmatic citation of European authors like Kierkegaard, Tolstoy and Scheler to illuminate the spiritual dimensions of human existence. And surely I am grateful for the example he gave of the critical use of Western intellectual resources to sharpen the opposition between what Torah teaches and what the culture within which we live presupposes. What is distinctive and fundamental is the honest recognition of the duality in man's intellectual life and the significance of both moments: the confrontation initiated by God and the search initiated by man.

3) Because the Jewish philosophy envisioned by the Rav is reconstructive rather than external to religious realities, the Rav is indifferent to the demand that we must abdicate our methodological autonomy and submit to regnant academic doctrines. A letter, dated August 11, 1953, explaining the Rav's objections to proposed RCA involvement in the planned JPS Bible translation, captures something of his attitude:

> After all, we live in an age which admires the expert and which expects him to tell how things are and how they ought to be done. The expert, on the other hand, does not tolerate any opposition; all we ought to do is listen to him and swallow his ideas. I am not ready to swallow the ideas of the modern expert and scholar on our Tanakh....
>
> I noticed in your letter that you are a bit disturbed about the probability of being left out. Let me tell you that this attitude of fear is responsible for many commissions and omissions, compromises and fallacies on our part which have contributed greatly to the prevailing confusion within the Jewish community and to the loss of our self-esteem, our experience of ourselves as independent entities committed to a unique philosophy and way of life.

III

What about the Rav's lasting impact on the intellectual world of Jewish philosophy? The scholars, with their unerring instinct for the arid and trivial, busily plan research programs and conferences. The popularizers, the politicians, the polemicists, with their unfailing affinity for the superficial and the half-true, bravely try to make him do, and purvey many anecdotes. Right wing ideologists blithely erase the "inconvenient" record of his philosophical corpus; their counterparts on the left pay their respects while appearing to ignore the *lomdut* as well.

So what becomes of you and me, looking back on an unforgettable month, and hoping that something of it clings to our souls and leaves us changed forever? What shall we take with us, this sunny and bittersweet morning in a season of lengthening days, as each of us prepares for his kind of summer, and contemplates his notion of life without school?

Every day is a good day for *hakarat hatov.* And every day is a good day to tackle a difficult Rambam, to attempt a closer relationship with the Ramban on *Humash*, to confront seriously some aspect of the human condition, and, yes, even to engage in a modicum of self-examination. We, the *mishpahah halomedet* of Yeshiva University, have been allowed to share, directly and indirectly, in the legacy of a remarkable individual. In the incessant battle between truth and falsehood, between the real and the fake, his voice will always haunt us, a powerful ally, a calm and persistent advocate.

We are blessed beyond our desert, as a community and as individuals. How much we – you and I – have to be grateful for will depend, in large measure, on our spiritual integrity and intellectual courage. With prayers for God's help, let us resolve to be worthy of our good fortune.

"WHEREVER YOU FIND HIS GREATNESS, THERE YOU WILL FIND HIS HUMILITY"

RABBI ZEVULUN CHARLOP

The Talmud (*Megillah* 31a) records a teaching of Rabbi Yochanan which has been incorporated into the *Motzei Shabbat tefillah* of *Veyitein Lecha* and has become part of the everyday idiom of the Jew: "*Bemakom she'atah motzei gedulato, sham atah motzei anvatanuto*," Wherever you find the greatness of the Holy One, Blessed be He, there you will find His humility. In exceptional instances, this surpassing concept has been applied also to very special and holy figures who adorn our history although, of course, not in the same sweepingly complete and unblemished way. Moshe Rabbeinu is never expressly denominated, in the Torah in any event, as a wise man or a good man, although these attributes, no less than any other quality, have surely stamped his essence as the rebbe *par excellence* of the Jewish people. Nonetheless, what is proclaimed, uniquely and above all, is his humility. "And the man, Moses, is the humblest of all men who walked the earth" (*Bamidbar* 12:3). It did not mean that he was obsequious or even diffident. On the contrary. And certainly, once he assumed the mantle of leadership of *Am Yisroel*, he had a sense of who he was, and he could assert himself without the hindrances of false modesty because he had none. This itself indubitably bespeaks an indispensable dimension of *anavah*, of genuine humility.

I think what astonished me beyond all else, when I took on my role at Yeshiva and suddenly was thrust into direct and almost daily contact with the Rav *zt"l* for nearly fifteen years, and for which I was prepared least, was his humility. From the days I was a *talmid* of his, and even before – as Rabbi Soloveitchik, from the earliest moments of my consciousness, was a household name, if not a little bit forbidding – he was intimidating in the classroom, almost ferocious at times.He exuded sheer power in his public persona when he delivered the *yahrzeit shiurim* in memory of his father, Reb Moshe *zt"l*, in his addresses at the Mizrachi, Histadrut HaRabbanim, and Agudat HaRabbanim conventions, and even in glimpses of him in animated conversations with other *gedolim* and with whomever he happened to be speaking. He was formidable.

For me there was an additional and personal cause for awe. I recall something my grandfather, Reb Yaakov Moshe Charlop *zt"l*, told me on my initial visit to *Eretz Yisrael* in the summer of 5709/1949. He questioned me about my education, specifically where was I learning. When I told him "at the Yeshivas Rabbeinu Yitzchak Elchanan," his face lit up, and he exclaimed, "You're a talmid of Reb Yosheh Ber!" I was only a young teenager then, and I had to explain to him that it would be several years before I would begin to hope to be allowed into his *shiur*. With profound disappointment, he said in Yiddish: *"A shod"* – what a loss! And he continued "I heard Rav Soloveitchik when he gave his *shiur* at Yeshivat Mercaz HaRav in 5694/1935. Indeed, I introduced him then." (Rav Kook *zt"l* was lying mortally ill then, several months before his demise, unable to leave his bed.) "I had never heard a *shiur* like his before!"

My grandfather continued, "I would walk for hours to hear his *shiur*." He wasn't referring merely to the Rav's awesome ability to communicate, for which he probably had no equal, but to his originality and the solid clarity of his creative insight into the most complicated and abstruse problems of *halakhah*. Mind you, my grandfather, Reb Yaakov Moshe *zt"l*, was the last *talmid* of Reb Yehoshua Leib Diskin *zt"l*, who had been the Rav of Brisk and the predecessor of the *Bais Halevi*, the Rav's great grandfather who began the Brisker dynasty in that august center of Jewish learning. Rabbi Yehoshua Leib was described as the *gaon hageonim*. It was said that Reb Hayyim Halevi's hands used to shake whenever he uttered the name of Reb Yehoshua Leib. Nonetheless, my grandfather *zt"l* was able to say about the young Reb Yosheh Ber *zt"l*, "I had never heard a *shiur* like his before!" And when, some years later, I finally entered the Rav's *shiur*, I began to sense, although, of course, not nearly in the fullness of his understanding, what my grandfather had meant.

You could hardly imagine that he was among the humblest of men. Indeed, you could have easily come away with an altogether opposite impression. But at the core, his humility was very much part of the abiding truth and charm of the man, *megaleh tefach u'mechaseh tefachayim*. He revealed only a *tefach*, a small measure, of who he was, and it was a splendid *tefach*.

But it is precisely that which he revealed that helped to conceal two *tefachayim* of who he really was. From a distance, you could have hardly imagined him, even remotely, cloaked with that quality otherwise reserved for Hashem Himself, indeed it is clear that he had no self-awareness of this and would not, himself, for a moment, have believed it. With all the pomp and circumstance that surrounded his life, he may have loomed larger in the public eye than any other contemporary Torah figure. Yet, in fact, what we saw, as much as we saw, concealed, in many ways, the biggest part of him. There were countless times and situations which surely illustrated for me this humility. Over and over again, I was amazed by his *anavah*, which was so natural that it could almost be missed. Humility too obvious may not be humility.

I recall having been invited to Cleveland to address a gathering. As the meeting was breaking up, a tall, erect, well-dressed and put-together gentleman, though obviously on in years, came up to me and, having heard of my relationship to the Yeshiva, asked me, "Do you know Rav Soloveitchik?" When I answered in the affirmative, he said to me, "My name is Oliver Altman. I would appreciate it very much if you'd convey to the Rav my regards. I haven't seen him in many years. I knew him well when we were both in Berlin. In fact, we used to attend regularly the same *shiur*." He then gave me the name of the rabbi who gave the *shiur*, who was unknown to me. I knew that the Rav had a very special relationship with the legendary Reb Chaim Heller *zt"l,* whose *beit midrash* in Berlin was a *shem davar* throughout the world and which the Rav used to frequent. So, the unfamiliar name he gave me came as a surprise.

(When I mentioned it later to the Rav, he remembered the rabbi well, and he told me that he was a very big *talmid chacham* and, as best as I can recall, he said, "It may not have been so much what I learned in the *shiur* that was important, but that it helped give me *kevius* in my learning in those turbulent student days." And, the Rav added, "Berlin, then, abounded in *iluyim* and first-rate *talmidei chachamim.* Rabbi Charlop, you just cannot imagine how many potential *geonim* walked the streets of Berlin then," only to be swept away by the irresistible currents that held powerful sway in Germany and, indeed, in the world of that time, and then, of course, later by Hitler *y"s.*)

But what struck me about my conversation with Mr. Altman was his outburst: "You have no idea what the young Rabbi Soloveitchik signified in Berlin then. He was the pride, the ornament, of the Berlin Jewish community, of those who were aware of his being among them. They knew he was the grandson of Reb Hayyim *zt"l* and that, at the same time, he was the *'leibling'* of the academic community at the University of Berlin; yet, all the while, remaining in learning and absolutely singular in his astonishing *hasmadah*, even among the other budding giants of Torah who found temporary refuge in the German capital at that time. There was not a *masmid* like him, and, as young as he was, and with all his genuine deference to the rabbis whose *shiurim* he would attend, he fit into that apt phrase of *Chazal*, '*Gadol miraban shmo*, he was greater than his teachers.'" When I returned to Yeshiva and related this fascinating conversation to the Rav, it took him a little while before he remembered Oliver Altman and differentiated him from the other Altmans whom he knew from those days. And, then, he looked at me unsurely and with genuine embarrassment. He was absolutely flustered, uncomfortable with the picture Mr. Altman drew of him. It was then that he made his remark about the young geniuses who were a dime a dozen in Berlin who could not so easily be shrugged off. He tried to let me know, without saying it expressly, that Altman's memory, kind as it was, was a gross exaggeration, and that there were many like him. But, I was to discover, when I repeated Altman's remarks to other survivors of that period who remembered that time well, and did not have any personal axe to grind, that it was no exaggeration at all.[1]

To have seen the Rav's reaction to this story is to have a glimpse of what *Chazal* meant when they proclaimed, "*Bemakom she'atah motzei gedulato, sham atah motzei anvatanuto.*" With all of his knowledge and wisdom, otherworldliness and worldliness, there was a naivete, an innocence, child-like almost, but altogether endearing.

---

[1] In a letter to Rabbi Rabinowitz of Boston, Rabbi Yosef Yitzchak Schneerson *zt"l*, known as the "previous Rebbe," the father-in-law of the recently deceased Rabbi Menachem Mendel Schneerson *zt"l*, wrote: "Regarding Rabbi Y. Soloveitchik, I know him already for many years. While he was still in Berlin, I was introduced to him by my son-in-law, Rabbi Menachem Mendel Schneerson. My son-in-law told me about his great in-depth fine understanding of Torah and how he studies assiduously. I was very delighted to become close to him." See Rabbi Saul S. Deutsch, *Larger Than Life* (New York, 1995), Vol. 2, 113.

It was during one of our conversations relating to the time the Rav spent in Berlin that I mustered enough courage, or *chutzpah*, as the case may be, to touch on an issue that had been a source of controversy even while he was still alive. With the intention of setting the record straight, and to satisfy my own mystification about the matter, which, for me, was a profound riddle, I asked: "How did you, *rebbe*, the grandson of Reb Hayyim *zt"l*, and who, indeed, was with him in Warsaw during the last days of his life, the son of Reb Moshe *zt"l*, the son of the daughter of Reb Elie Pruzhinoi, leave Poland and go to Berlin, which oozed decadence from its every pore and which, even before Hitler *y"s*, was reckoned then by many as the moral garbage heap of civilization?" He did not seem at all upset by the question or the dramatic cadences which accompanied it, and matter-of-factly answered: "My mother sent me. She felt that to make your mark, even as a Rav, in the new world and a new time, you needed to go to university. She got me tutors in French, German, and (I do not remember what other languages he mentioned), math, and the sciences and sent me off to Berlin." "*Rebbe*," I responded, "I must tell you that I doubt very much if my mother would have taken that risk and sent me off all alone to that forsaken city of lost and tortured souls." He listened to me and, without much emotion, said, "It's a good question." That was all he said. "And, what did Reb Moshe, your father, say?" I continued. "He said nothing!" "Well, *rebbe*," I said, pushing my luck, "didn't you construe that to be acquiescence? "*Shtikah kehoda'ah*," silence is acquiescence. For some reason, a harder look fixed on his face, as if to say, "How can you say that?" I did not pursue the matter. But, then, suddenly, an insight that was simmering within me for some while already, for almost fifteen years, from the time the Rav's mother, Rebbetzin Peshie Soloveitchik *a"h* passed away, came blazingly to mind, and I blurted it out to the Rav:

"*Rebbe*, I shall never forget the fiery *hesped* of your mother by your brother, Reb Ahron Soloveichik *shlita*." Deeply agitated, he shrieked out in Yiddish, "Do you know who my mother was? She kept *chadash*. When Chanukah came, she used to fill the refrigerator with boxes of *matzah*!" (Mind you, this was before the idea of *chadash* in America became fashionable, when the granaries used to store two, three, and even four years' supply of food and there was little fear that any of the new grains were being used. It was years before the giant sales to China and Russia, which emptied the huge silos of this rich and blessed country.) "I also remember '*chadash assur min haTorah*,' that striking metaphor of the Chatam Sofer sounding the alarm against change in our tradition, even when it may not appear, to the untrained eye, to encroach upon *halakhah* at all."

"And," I said to the Rav, "only one who was so scrupulous about *chadash* when nobody else cared could distinguish between which *chadash* is *assur* and which *chadash* is *mutar*. Only one who is uncompromisingly in the thrall of *chadash assur min haTorah* could respond with equal integrity and knowing conviction to '*vehikravtem minchah chadasha laHashem*,' And you shall bring a new offering to Hashem. Only one who knows the unyielding redemptive quality of *chadash assur min haTorah* could be trusted with *vehikravtem minchah chadashah laHashem.* Only your mother, who was so unerringly punctilious about *chadash assur min haTorah* could send *benah bechorah,* her firstborn, to Berlin, unafraid and sure in the knowledge that, in the end, he will know which *chadash* is *assur* and which *chadash* we are permitted, nay bidden, to bring as an offering to Hashem."

Chazal tell us on the *pasuk*, "*Im shamo'a tishme'u*" (*Devarim* 11:13): "*Im shamo'a biyashan, tishmeu bichadash*" (*Sukkah* 46b), if you hearken to the old, you will hear the new as well. That was the clarion call of the Rav who trumpeted the *yashan*, who knew all its tonalities and inflections, very possibly as no one of his time did, and, therefore, was able to distinguish among the new and know which *minchah chadashah* can be offered before Hashem.

It is not easy to know which *chadash* is *assur* and which is *mutar*, indeed, desirable and necessary. It requires a honed sense born out of genuine and profound *yir'at Shamayim* and the highest level of *lomdut*. "*Reishit chochamah yirat Hashem*." This is a very large part of the legacy of the Rav *zt"l* and his challenge to us. *Tehei nishmato tzrurah bitzezror hachaim!*

THE RESERVOIR OF KNOWLEDGE WAS DEEP AND WIDE

RABBI EDWARD DAVIS

It is now twenty years since I was a student in Rav Soloveitchik's *shiur* in Yeshiva University; but it really does not seem as if it was that long ago. My subjective sense of time is influenced by the effect of those years on my life. No one helped shape my outlook on life as did the Rav. In class and out, he embodied the constant struggle to synthesize the holy and secular in this world. And that struggle would be a life-long effort on many fronts. The pages of the Talmud will not solve all your problems, but they will grant you the strength to struggle all the days of your life.

The classroom atmosphere was electric, as each of the sixty students sat on the edge of his seat in a lecture that would last anywhere from two to four hours, concentrating on every word that the Rav said and yet dreading being called on to read. Intense pressure packed the room, and the Rav was usually formal and impatient as he worked through the Talmudic subject matter at hand. He spoke in an academic English with a Yiddish accent, and he had everyone on edge and on his toes.

Whenever he spoke of Shabbat or Yom Tov, he encouraged us to experience the depth of the historical events that are halakhically immersed in these days. The Pesach *Seder* is not a time to reflect and study the Exodus, it was the challenge to re-experience these events at a banquet meal that we were to enjoy as if the Holy Temple were in existence at that very moment in our lives. Tisha B'Av was to be a time of great emotional stirrings within the Jew. We are to truly mourn the Temple's loss and still possess the optimistic hopes of the Mashiach's imminent arrival. The dichotomy of human spirit, between past and future, between the physical and spiritual, between pain and ecstasy, were favorite themes in his lectures. The Rav possessed the unique ability of taking a simple *halakhah* and weaving a total theology and philosophic treatise from its inner, and sometimes hidden, meaning.

One of the most impressive sights was actually not a lecture, but a lull in the Rav's day. He was observing a *Yarzheit.* He would give a masterful special lecture at night, and during the following day, he fasted. He stayed all day in the *beit midrash* teaching *Mishnah* to all who came. Then, we davened *Minchah.* After *Minchah,* we waited for *Ma'ariv,* during which time the Rav sat pensively alone at a table. After all, he had just spent eight hours lecturing. He was not able to rest. Students came over to him and asked him questions from all over the world. One student asked the Rav about a problem he was having in a course in philosophy that he was taking at Columbia University's Graduate school program. Another student asked a question about the Thirty Years War, and the Rav quoted the Treaty of Westphalia as if it were right on the table. The reservoir of knowledge was deep and wide. He answered all comers and challenged them in return.

While the Rav has passed away, his legacy continues. The thousands of his students feel the need to record more of his teachings and to share his thoughts so that we can feel his presence eternally.

THE HALAKHIC *REBBE*

RABBI DR. EMANUEL FELDMAN

It is a scene not likely to be repeated for a long time to come: a large assembly hall with several thousand people in attendance young and old, men and women, learned rabbis and scholars, members of the academic community, Orthodox and non-Orthodox Jews. They listen intently. Tape recorders whir, pencils take rapid notes.

On the podium is a tall, lean, gray-bearded figure delivering a *shiur*/lecture on the fine points of *halakhah* and Jewish thought. His subject is complex and subtle, but he will hold his diverse audience in thrall for two to three hours.

The speaker is Rav Joseph B. Soloveitchik, a *rosh yeshiva* enigmatic yet open, charismatic yet unaffected, distant yet accessible. Born in Poland in 1903, scion of several generations of world-famous Talmudic luminaries, Rav Soloveitchik was one of the preeminent and most intriguing Torah personalities of the twentieth century, a *mitnaged's mitnaged* with a taste for *hasidut,* an analytic philosopher with a gift for the poetic.

When the mysterious resurrection of American Orthodoxy in the twentieth-century is recorded by historians, they will give due recognition to the various great *roshei yeshiva* and Hasidic *rebbeim* who, together, with the newly, arrived immigrant survivors of World War II, brought with them the stubbornness and the vision which were the catalysts for the renewal of Torah in America. The schools they founded, the *yeshivot* they nurtured, the attitude of self-confidence and pride which they, created, the personal examples that they set – all gave birth to the committed corps of Jews who are the vanguard of today's renewed Orthodox Judaism.

At the same time, the historians will have to note a more subtle truth: that it was the unique approach and background of a *rosh yeshiva* like Rav Soloveitchik that provided the intellectual framework that was uniquely suited to present classical Judaism to twentieth century men and women. More than any other religious leader, he was able to demonstrate to a wide audience the intellectual rigor and discipline of *halakhah* as well as the profound world-view inherent in the minutiae of the daily halakhic regimen – a world-view which addresses itself not only to the mind but also to the troubled heart and soul of the lonely modern man.

This demonstration of the universality of Torah, presented with such clarity and passion, also contributed immeasurably to the morale of an Orthodox community which, in mid-century, was being buffeted on all sides and was beset with self-doubt and dispiriting retreats on many fronts.

In particular, he had a major impact on the American trained Orthodox rabbinate. Not all of them studied under him at Yeshivat Rabbeinu Yitzhak Elhanan of Yeshiva University, but they all benefited directly from the spiritual support and inspiration which his teaching provided at a critical juncture in American Jewish history. The undersigned, not a student at Yeshiva University, can directly attest to this. Not only did Rav Soloveitchik help keep at bay those debilitating forces of modernity that threatened to overwhelm and drown the fledgling Orthodox; he was also a major architect of the bridge upon which many marginal Jews were able to return to the tradition.

That he was able to touch the contemporary soul was in great measure due to his recurring themes. The motif of alienation is sounded regularly in his work. We hear of "the dark night of the soul"; the meaning of death and mourning in human life-loneliness (prayer as a dialogue between the lonely Jew and the lonely God); defeat, despair, retreat and anguish; the absurdity of existence without God: the entire lexicon of contemporary existential thought. Whether it be in the moving eulogy for the Talner Rebbetzin or a theoretical excursus into the realm of spiritual authority, the listener is caught up short by the recognition of his own inchoate vexations and anxieties. The message is clear: it is only the saving quality of Torah and *halakhah* which makes it possible for dust-and-ashes man, whose life without God is inherently tragic and whose physical end is in the grave, to reach out confidently to the King of Kings.

Rav Soloveitchik's ability to strike responsive chords within his listeners was in great measure due to his unique gift for language. Whether he spoke in his native Yiddish or in his adopted English, his use of words was at once precise and poetic. His great intellect was expressed in a corresponding gift of articulation and communication. This fusion of rigorous thought and lyrical language is at the heart of Rav Soloveitchik's power, and made him a teacher par excellence, both on the public platform and in the confines of a classroom. In fact, he often described himself not as a philosopher or professor, but as a *rebbe* and a teacher.

In the era of the seven-word-sound-bite-and-on-to-the-next-commercial, the very idea of an audience sitting entranced for several hours at an arcane lecture is astounding. On the lecture platform, he was a study in the use of voice, gesture, inflection, pathos, humor – all done without artifice and guile. Although he crafted his lectures meticulously, rewriting and editing mercilessly his talks were marked by a deep passion, by a spontaneous, incisive wit, by questions to the audience – particularly an audience of rabbis – which were not simply rhetorical, but to which he expected answers from his listeners; by an affect and emotion which did not hesitate to bare his personal life and upbringing. He was a consummate platform teacher.

Perhaps most striking about Rav Soloveitchik was his independent and innovative persona. He once wrote that he had a liking for pioneers, for experimenters, for people who do not follow the crowd. "I have always admired the first ones, the beginners, the originators. Even in my *derashot* I prefer to speak about those who defied public opinion, disregarded mockery and ridicule, and blazed new trails leading men to God."[1]

He was a traditional *rosh yeshiva* with a doctorate in philosophy from the University of Berlin; a brilliant Talmudic authority who was *au courant* with contemporary thought; a preeminent authority on Maimonides who also was familiar with Kant and with Kierkegaard. Deeply religious, he was the classic r*ebbe,* giving regular *shiurim* in Talmud and relentlessly teaching his students the underlying logical core of halakhic discourse. But, perhaps symbolic of the maverick within him, he eschewed the traditional garb of the *rosh yeshiva:* the *kapote* and the black hat or humburg. While constantly upholding the supremacy of Torah learning in all its manifestations, and while emphasizing disciplined, and uncompromising allegiance to halakhic living, he did not hesitate to call up resources of secular thought whenever they could undergird or clarify his message.

---

[1] *Rabbi Joseph H. Lookstein Memorial Volume,* ed. Leo Landman (New York, 1980), 338.

It was because of this attempt to create a symbiosis between the classic world of Torah and the world of contemporary thought that he was occasionally viewed askance by the mainstream world of *yeshivot.* They recognized his formidable genius and scholarship – one great *rosh yeshiva* once told this writer that those who carped at him "do not come close to him in learning and do not understand him at all" but they were skeptical about his attempts to apotheosize the secular into the sacred.

His life was precisely the epitome of the religious pioneers he so admired. Shunning publicity, unconcerned with what others might think of him, authentically, humble before God and man, he blazed new trails in the understanding of every aspect of Torah and in the application of that understanding to the modern world.

Rav Soloveitchik was many things: a *rosh yeshiva,* a *rebbe,* a halakhic decisor, a *ba'al mahshavah,* a philosopher, an orator. In each of these roles he was extraordinary. But over and above all else, he was a genuinely religious personality. For him, Torah and halakha were not abstractions nor platforms for exciting intellectual gymnastics. They were not philosophy or mathematics or physics, all of which he was fond of citing, but all of which were for him merely subjects for study. Torah and *halakhah* were not intellectual subjects, but life itself, the voice through which the soul of Israel speaks, and the prism through which the God of Israel is apprehended.

MY TEACHER, MY MASTER: THE RAV, *ISH YOM KIPPURIM*

RABBI MENACHEM GENACK

Rav Elchonon Wasserman once posed the following question to the Chofetz Chaim: How does one know when a particular period, a *tekufah*, has concluded? How, for example, was it known that the period of the *Tanaim* or the *Amoraim* ended? Did someone enter the *beit midrash*, bang on the *shtender* and announce that the period of the *Tanaim* had come to an end?

The Chofetz Chaim responded that upon the demise of an individual who had surpassed those of his own generation, as well as those of the prior generation, we know that an era has concluded. Such was the case upon the passing of the Gaon of Vilna, said the Chofetz Chaim. And with the passing of Hagaon Rav Yosef Dov Halevi Soloveitchik on the night of the eighteenth of Nissan, an era closed.

The Rav was many things: teacher, theologian and philosopher; but at his core he was a halakhist. The Rav believed that the *halakhah*, the body of Jewish law, is the ultimate prism through which we can glimpse God's mind and his design for mankind and the universe. To the study of Torah, he brought his rigorous, analytical methodology, inculcated in him by his father, who recognized his son's prodigious talents and personally taught him from an early age.

The Brisker methodology has, I believe, a theological root. The Rav would often say that the "why" question as related to Torah study is invalid. We must only ask "what." God's will is self-justifying and beyond human comprehension. We can never pierce the barrier of the *gezerat hakatuv*; what is left to us is to define and understand the given law.

God's essence is hidden behind many veils of transcendence. The existential loneliness that stalked the Rav is inherent in the human condition and to the religious experience, which seeks to know God and to cleave to Him. Alas, that quest is frustrated, in that God is totally other and beyond our reach. We are incarcerated in our finitude. Even the master prophet, Moses, was denied his request to know God. Mortal man can never know God. The drama of the universe remains largely hidden from man and we can only relate to it through the instrumentality of the *halakhah.* This precipitated in the Rav an almost poetic appreciation of the mysterious and a deep sense of humility. In the midst of the swirling forces which William James called "the reality of the unseen," what right does mortal man have to be proud?

The Rav rejected facile speech or the trivialization of profound concepts or relationships. Much in life is hidden, enigmatic. That which is most holy is most concealed. It is in that context that the Rav spoke of the intense relationship between himself and his father, which did not have to be confirmed by a kiss or outward expression of affection, because it was so deep a love. The Talmud tells us that Rav Yochanan referred to his garments as *michubadei* (my dignity). We are dignified, the Rav commented, in that our essence remains hidden, unexposed. That may be why part of *kovod Shabbat* requires that the table which is symbolic of the altar in the Temple be covered.

When I speak of the Rav's humility, I do not mean that he was meek. He set high standards, and woe to the student who asked a foolish or irrelevant question or broke the Rav's trend of thought. Rather, I mean that he had a sense of perspective about our limited capacity and recognition of human frailty, and strove to grasp the full range of possibilities accessible to man, both in relation to understanding a *sugya* as well as matters of the religious spirit.

One summer, the Rav gave some *shiurim* in *Likutei Torah*, a work on the last three books of the Pentateuch composed by Rav Shneur Zalman of Liadi, the famed author of the *Tanya* and founder of Lubavitch Chassidism. He commented that in order to properly appreciate the grandeur of Rosh Hashanah it was important to study *Likutei Torah.* For the Rav, it was important to communicate both the logic and the passion of Torah.

He was enormously generous in his judgment of people, and forgiving almost to a fault. He never held a grudge, even towards people who tried to hurt him grievously. He was an instinctive *ba'al tzedakah* and his munificence knew no ideological constraints. He would remind his students that rabbis are also obligated to give *tzedakah.*

The breadth and depth of the Rav's grasp of Torah in all its diversity – *Tanach*, *Talmud*, *Rishonim*, *Poskim*, *Aggadah*, *Piyut* – was dazzling. Concerning R. Yosef Ibn Megash, the Rambam writes that "his mind was frightening and awesome." So may it be said of the Rav. A mind like the Rav's appears only rarely in each century. His impact on peoples' thinking was powerful and many who heard a single *shiur* were dramatically influenced. Great *lomdim* and laymen alike were captivated by the force of his logic and presentation which left a permanent mark on their future study.

The former Chief Rabbi of Israel, Rabbi Avraham Shapiro, told me that when the Rav came to Israel in 1935, Rav Kook told him to be sure to attend each *shiur* that the Rav delivered, because hearing him was like hearing Rav Hayyim Brisker. When I visited the Ponovitzer Rav in 1967, he told me, ""There is no one like Rav Soloveitchik. He is the greatest *rosh yeshivah* in the world." I cite only two quotes, but there was universal recognition by great Torah scholars that the Rav was singular and unique. In the *semikhah* that the Kovner Rav, Rabbi A.D. Kahana Shapiro, gave to the Rav he wrote: "The *halakhah* should always be decided in accordance with his opinion."

The Rav, who was ascetic by nature, found pleasure and joy only in Torah. Out of his generosity of spirit, and because joy is a shared experience, he had to communicate the majesty of Torah to others. He was a master rebbe, presenting concepts with extraordinary clarity, force and elegance of style and thought. The Rav exercised great discipline in suppressing the torrent of his ideas and limited his exposition to what was necessary for the *talmid* to understand. Material which previously seemed abstruse or even inchoate would be transposed via his *shiur* into an ordered universe with clearly defined categories that, after his exposition, would appear obvious.

He had a total commitment to imparting Torah. On occasion, he would come into the classroom tired and exhausted, but in the process of giving the *shiur* he would become strong, animated and vibrant. Once the *shiur* was over, he collapsed on his desk. He suffered from chronic back pain and always wore a brace. One summer, his back problem flared up, but rather than cancel the *shiur*, he invited his t*almidim* to his room and gave the *shiur* from his bed. He would often say that he was "just a *melamed*," but that wasn't so bad, because even God is called a *melamed*, as stated in the blessing of the Torah.

And this total commitment to teaching Torah was the key to understanding him: it was nothing less than transposing a rational exposition where all logical possibilities were exhausted into an ecstatic religious experience; as if the *Shechinah* itself bent down to hear what was being said.

To the Rav, Rabbi Akiva, Abaye, Rava and the Rambam were not ancient figures, but vital and alive. The Rav would say that until various groups celebrated the 800th anniversary of the Rambam's death, he always thought of the Rambam as a contemporary figure, teacher and friend.

Rabbi Fabian Schonfeld recounts that, as a *talmid* in the Rav's *shiur*, he would on occasion drive him to various appointments. Once he took the Rav to meet a wealthy man on the West Side of Manhattan. While there, the man asked the Rav a *she'elah*. The Rav asked him to bring a Rambam. The man did not move. Again, the Rav said, "bring me a Rambam." Red-faced, the man had to admit that he did not own a Rambam. The Rav looked at him in absolute astonishment and exclaimed, "*Vie lebt a yid ohn a Rambam*?" (How does a Jew live without a Rambam?)

The Rav had a profound, abiding love for the Rambam. During his last years, though debilitated, he would quote entire sections of the Rambam by heart. The story is told of a visit by Rabbi Yehuda Leib Kagan to Rav Moshe Soloveitchik in Khaslavichy (where Rav Moshe was serving as Rabbi). Rav Moshe maintained that Rabbi Kagan had erred in quoting the Rambam. Rabbi Kagan insisted that he was right and suggested that they send Yosef Dov, who was barely bar mitzvah, to fetch the Rambam and confirm the correct reading. Rav Moshe replied that this was not necessary: "My son knows the entire Rambam." And Yosef Dov proceeded to quote the Rambam by heart.

The Rav's extraordinary intellectual and pedagogic talents preserved and expanded the realm of the tradition of Torah and allowed for its expansion in America, thereby allowing an ancient tradition to speak and prosper in a new, otherwise secular and inhospitable environment. The Talmud tells us that a Bedouin once told Rabba Bar Channah that he would take him to the place where heaven and earth embrace and kiss. It was that existential kiss which imbued the Rav with a lifetime sense of responsibility for transmitting the echo of God's word received at Sinai.

The Rav once said that at his father's *Seder*, the Rambam would sit on one side and the Rashba on the other and the Shaagat Aryeh and Rabbi Akiva Eiger were invited guests. Now the Rav has joined them in the Heavenly Yeshiva, in the *yeshiva shel maalah*.

The Rav, *Ish Yom HaKippurim*

Yom Kippur is a day like no other, awesome in its grandeur, enveloped in mystery and intense *kedushah*, as we encounter God, and through the very encounter achieve atonement. *Itzumo shel yom mechaper*. After the catastrophic sin of the golden calf, Moshe, hidden from view, retraced his steps to the top of Sinai to receive on Yom Kippur the second *luchot*, and with them the gift of forgiveness.

The Midrash comments on the verse *"Vayehi erev, vayehi boker yom echad"* – *zeh Yom HaKippurim* (and it was evening, and it was morning, one day – this is Yom Kippur). *Echad* (one) as opposed to *rishon* (first) means that Yom Kippur is unique.

Yom Kippur was very special to the Rav *zt"l* and, in many ways, he personified the sanctity and singularity of that day.

Yom Kippur, though a day of repentance, introspection, even terror, is paradoxically also a day of great joy. The Talmud tells us that Yom Kippur is a *yom tov*, for the Torah was given to the Jewish people on that day. It was decreed that Yom Kippur, as a day of *simchah* (joy), cancels *aveilut* (mourning). What is the source of joy, *simchah*, on this day of fasting and angst? The Rav pointed out that whenever the Torah declares a day of *simchah* it always states *lifnei Hashem,* "before God." Genuine happiness flows from our being before God, in His warm, consoling embrace. Therefore, Yom Kippur, when all humanity stands in judgment before God, generates an obligation of *simchah*, as it states: *Vegilu bire'ada,* "be joyous with trembling."

It is that sense of being in God's presence – which is at once unnerving and comforting – that defined the Rav's sacred persona. Before each Yom

Kippur, the Rav would study in his *shiur* the Yom Kippur service in the *beit hamikdash* – the *avodat hayom.* He said that he had studied the *avodah* so often, and he so identified with it, that if he were a *kohen* in the time of the *mikdash,* and the *kohen gadol* became disabled, he could have stepped in and completed the *avodah.*

Torah study for the Rav was an ecstatic experience because it was a form of *avodah*; like prayer, it transports one into God's presence: *keilu omed baShamayim.* The Rav pointed out that the Rambam in the *Sefer Hamitzvot*, when he defines the Biblical obligation of prayer, stresses that Torah study is included as part of the *mitzvah* of *avodah shebalev.*

Through Torah, finite, limited, frail man – *hayom kan umachar bakever*, "today here, and tomorrow in the grave" – can glimpse the infinite mind of God. As the Rav gave the *shiur*, we felt as if the *Shechinah* herself bent down to hear what was being said.

It was for that reason that whoever heard a *shiur* from the Rav was enormously affected. Just as everyone who was alive at the time remembers where they were when John Kennedy was killed, or when Americans first landed on the moon, so no one will ever forget the first *shiur* they heard from the Rav, even though for the Rav that may have been his thousandth or two thousandth *shiur.*

In many ways he was like the *kohen gadol*, *hakohen hagadol me'eichav*, exalted above all others, carrying the burden of his people like the *kohen gadol*, and he went where no other man could go, alone into *kodesh hakodashim*, created out of the intellectual constructs of his unparalleled genius and religious passion.

He writes in the *Ish haHalakhah* that as a young boy he stood in the courtyard of the *shul* on Yom Kippur in Khaslavitch with his father Rav Moshe, and as the sun was setting and the horizon was ablaze, Rav Moshe turned to his son and said, "This is the most beautiful sunset of the year for it is *mechaper*, it atones for *klal Yisrael* [because atonement comes at the end of the day]." Even nature was interpreted through the penetrating lens of the *halakhah.*

Rabbi Lichtenstein once told that if you ever wanted a favor from the Rav, you should ask him after *Neilah*, because he would be in such a good mood. I once davened with the Rav on Yom Kippur in Boston. You sensed that the Rav, as he said *Selichot*, was reconnected to that first Yom Kippur when the thirteen attributes of mercy were first revealed to Moshe: Hashem, Hashem, *Kel rachum vechanun.*

The Rav's daughter told me that after Yom Kippur the Rav would be in so ecstatic a state, often singing the *nigunim* of *Neilah*, that he would be unable to eat for hours.

Kidmut hakeshet betoch ha'anan. Like the multi-colored splendor of the rainbow, dazzling and inspiring, the reflection of the *Shechinah* herself, this was the image of the *kohen gadol*, of the Rav.

The Rav wrote in one of his articles that his greatest fear was that one day he would be ill and have to eat on Yom Kippur. When the Rav was ill these past seven years, and his powers of recognition and orientation were diminished by disease, he once refused to eat on a particular day, convinced that it was Yom Kippur. And in a sense it was always Yom Kippur for the Rav, as he always stood before Hashem. He was a God-intoxicated individual.

The Rambam writes about the Ri Migash that his mind was frightening. So it was with the Rav, who entered *lifnai velifnim*, into the innermost chambers of Torah: "The King has brought me into his inner chambers."

The Rav said once that Reb Yerucham, the famed *mashgiach* of the Mirrer Yeshiva, told him that Rav Hayyim, the Rav's grandfather, understood the *neshamah* of Torah. So it was with the Rav, whose exquisite *neshamah* was one with the *neshamah* of Torah.

But though the Rav was an aristocrat, by mind and lineage, he was not an elitist. He believed that Torah, in all its rigor and majesty, could permeate any quarter. And he educated generations of not only rabbis, but also doctors, lawyers and businessmen, to become genuine *lomdim.* American Jewry could not survive if ignorant, he believed.

In the Torah we read about *yovel*, the Jubilee year. Rashi states that the etymology of the word *yovel* refers to our obligation to blow *shofar* on Yom Kippur of the *yovel* year, since *yovel* also means *shofar.* The Ramban disagrees and says that *yovel* means to return – deriving from the word *yuval*, to bring back. In the year of *yovel*, all lands that had been sold are returned to their original owners and all Jewish slaves return to freedom. It implies returning to our roots, our unencumbered, pristine source, redeemed and rejuvenated. According to the Ramban, this may be why *yovel* begins on Yom Kippur, as opposed to Rosh Hashanah, because the theme of Yom Kippur is *teshuvah*, return; through atonement we achieve spiritual redemption.

That is why Yom Kippur is the *yom echad*, for its power of atonement flows from our return to our sacred roots, to the *echad.*

It is that theme of Yom Kippur, of *teshuvah*, of return to our glorious tradition, to which the Rav committed his life, to the maintenance of the true *mesorah.*

Vesiftei kohen yishmeru da'at. The Rav always exhorted us to be intellectually honest. He was enormously dignified and principled. Once, the Rav was asked a *she'elah* by a Torah organization that did important *kiruv* work, and represented a constituency close to the Rav. They asked himwhether they could pay some people off the books, since they could not make a go of it – the Rav's immediate reply was, "Then close down."

The Rav would say that he was inspired on Yom Kippur because he remembered the haunting melody of his grandfather Rav Hayyim saying the *avodah*, and it was that emotional experience that he wanted to communicate to his *talmidim* – reason fused with passion. It is not just the words but the melody of the Rav's gracious Torah which is seared in our souls. But *Mishemeit Rebbe batlah kehunah* (when Rabbi Yehudah Hanasi died, the priesthood was canceled). And now we are bereft: "At this time and season, it is revealed and known before You and before the throne of Your glory that we have no leader as in ancient times and no *kohen gadol* to bring an offering."

In our lifetime and in the lifetime of our children and perhaps until the time that the *avodah* will be reinstituted, we are unlikely to see another man with the dimensions of the Rav *zt"l*, the *Ish Yom HaKippurim.*

THE GREAT MUSICIAN TAKES HIS LEAVE

RABBI DR. HILLEL GOLDBERG

A few names come to mind, among them Maimonides, Crescas, Rashbatz – and Rabbi Joseph B. Soloveitchik. Genuine masters of Talmud, they mastered another discipline in Torah, which simultaneously was a common tongue with surrounding civilizations: philosophy. For Rabbi Joseph B. Soloveitchik, "philosophy" had a denotation and a connotation. It denoted the discipline of thought whose basic texts in German, English, Latin and Greek he mastered in their original languages. It connoted something larger: the fields of human knowledge, from medicine to sociology, that located Jews in contemporary civilization. The insatiably inquisitive mind of Rabbi Soloveitchik came to expression through forums beyond his trenchant *shiurim* at Yeshiva University. For example, each Saturday night in Boston he taught Talmud or Tanakh, using the sacred text as a springboard for philosophical observation, personal reminiscence, stories from Eastern Europe, and social commentary.

One night in the late 1960s or early 1970s, he reflected on music. Nothing affected a human being more than music, he said. By happenstance, a person may hear a certain melody at a time of personal difficulty or joy, then let the melody pass from his mind as innocently as it entered. Years, even decades, later, the person may suddenly hear the melody only to be overpowered by the same emotional sadness or joy he experienced the first time. Music is powerful. It does not forget. Emotions are never dead, only dormant. A person's link to his past is never severed. Memory never entirely recedes, and music may summon it. This is what "the Rav" was saying that night.

And now, this great musician is gone. His clefs were the pages of the Talmud. His quarter notes were the letters of the Torah. His melody was the Divine song embedded in the sheet music of Judaism!

His power was the power to summon each Jew's link to his past, to his history, to the Patriarchs and the martyrs, the heroes and the anonymous Jews who lived their lives humbly and then, as he would put it, withdrew from the Covenantal stage. He played his notes, he did. Each letter of the Torah, literally each one, resonated under his searing mental gaze. Uncovered for his listeners and disciples were strands of their own collective memory they did not know they possessed. This great melodist from Brisk, Berlin and Boston sounded the notes of the Torah in a way that one's emotions as a Jew could never die. He cast a spell. He linked Jews to the glorious past and future of the "covenantal community."

Now it is the musician himself, taken from us, who is not to be forgotten. His students are perhaps more completely bereft than other students of Torah who, too, in the past few years have lost towering mentors. What a paradox, Rabbi Soloveitchik! Trained in the critical disciplines of the academy, insistent on independence of thought in his disciples, temperamentally unwilling to impose his views on others, respectful of individual decision, he now leaves a community of rabbis and readers so intimately linked to the memory of *his* Torah teachings, the melody of *his* Torah lessons, that the future seems uncharted and unable to be charted. What a dominating musician he! What a link to the particular genius of his grandfather, the "Brisker method," to the historic encounter of great Torah scholars with the West, to the "anonymous Jew" of the centuries with whom he had so much sympathy, to the Patriarchs and Matriarchs with whom he seemed on such intimate terms. What a link to the Holy One, Blessed be He.

What words do we summon for Rabbi Soloveitchik's uniqueness? *Awe?* His pedagogic clarity, his photographic memory, his encyclopedic mastery of the Talmudic literature, were, taking the word literally, awesome. *Enigma?* Whether distant if articulate in the classroom, whether revelatory if removed in Saturday night lectures – pouring forth personal feelings about his late wife or father or about his own subjectivities (on Hasidism, for example) – he was always a mystery. So revelatory in his teaching, so inaccessible in his being. *Piety?* His palpably communicative and submissive prayer, his exalted recitation of the Passover Haggadah, his exacting observance of the commandments, his fearsome dedication to Torah study, removed from this genius any trace of arrogance. *Controversy?* Precisely his mastery over quarter-, nay, the eighth-, sixteenth- even sixty-fourth notes of the Torah made his progenitors and like-gifted contemporaries wonder:

What draws Rabbi Soloveitchik to the university? Why his attraction to and approval of secular studies? Why his independence from the Torah world that nurtured him? Why? Precisely his ability to sound the strings of tradition truthfully accentuated the controversy.

His legacy is intellectual honesty. He knew that he differed from much of his illustrious family on such matters as secular study, Zionism and the authority of the preeminent Talmudic scholar, and he never cloaked his views, no matter the price in personal relationships. He never shrunk from criticizing non-Orthodox Judaism for its halakhic and theological deviations, despite his desire for Jewish unity; he never shrunk from criticizing interfaith dialogue, notwithstanding his universalist existential understanding. He also did not shrink from critiquing his own following, notably but not exclusively for insufficient action during the Holocaust.

A posthumous word on Rabbi Soloveitchik is datum. Often terrifying in his clarity and definitiveness, often puzzling in his inner enigma and indecision, Rabbi Soloveitchik has attained the irreversible stature and criterion by which generations of Jews fix their masters: *commentary*. With each passing year, more studies, analyses, explications, critiques, and appreciations of Rabbi Soloveitchik's writings appear in journals, Jewish and general, across the world. He has become a fundamental datum of religious experience and philosophy.

His passing, however, leaves a more personal void. He bridged two worlds, but the bridge he embodied – his unique piety and perspective – is not to be reconstructed because the worlds are gone. More salient, he himself – his brilliance and existential suffering, his commanding presence and private loneliness – is gone. What a paradox, Rabbi Soloveitchik! So much gone, irretrievable, even inscrutable. Yet so much sustained, communicated, even indelible. So much sacred music!

PERSONAL GLIMPSES OF THE RAV

ALLEN GOLDSTEIN, MD

For the Rav *zt"l*, whether in *halakhah*, *aggadah*, *drush* or personal relationships, there always seemed to exist two aspects to everything: *din/rachamim, yotzer/borei, zochor/nekeyvah, cheftza/gavra.* My relationship with the Rav was also a dual one.

My initial encounter with the Rav was upon arriving at Yeshiva University as a freshman. After seven years of learning in the Telshe Yeshivah in Cleveland, I had a rather inflated image of my capabilities as a scholar. Rav Mendel Zacks *zt"l* also seemed impressed and I was assigned to the Rav's *shiur.* Needless to say, after the first *shiur,* my self-esteem quickly vanished. My classmates and I rapidly developed acute cases of fear. We all sat in the *shiur* with great trepidation, lest he call on us to read or explain a passage in the *Gemara.* I quickly learned that in the pursuit of intellectual honesty and "truth in learning," nothing can be an impediment. Respect, honor, dignity or esteem became meaningless in the pursuit of the true interpretation. However, with the passage of time, even as we cowered in our seats, we learned to admire the Rav's genius as a *rebbe*, teacher, and, as he used to say, a *"melamed"* par excellence. We listened in awe and reverence as he clarified the most enigmatic and obscure passages.

My favorite and most descriptive episode of the Rav's talent dates back to a *shiur* that lasted for two hours, consisting of a single *Tosafos* of six small lines. It was truly an inspirational and enlightening intellectual trip. By the end of *shiur,* every choice of word, every letter in those six lines "danced and saluted." On the way out, my *chavrusa* turned to me guilelessly and said, "I will bet you *Tosafos* didn't understand that *Tosafos* as well as the Rav does."

It is, however, the other side of my relationship with the Rav that I would like to share with you. After the passing of Rebbetzin Tonya Soloveitchik *a"h*, I was privileged to help care for the Rav's medical needs. I would see him routinely on Tuesday afternoons and on being called.

During these encounters, I began seeing an aspect of this brilliant intellectual giant that he painstakingly hid from the world. The world recognized the Rav as a *gaon* in creativity, in the intellectual challenges to man. They did not realize that he was also a *gaon* in the moral, ethical challenges.

The *Gemara (Yevamot* 79a) states that the nation of Israel is distinguished by three characteristics: *rachmanim* – merciful, *baishanim* – bashful and *gomlei chassadim* – benevolent. During his weekly two-and-a-half day stay in New York, in addition to teaching three lengthy *shiurim* to the students, giving a lengthy *shiur* to *ba'alei batim* at Congregation Moriah in the evening, and occasional lectures in universities and graduate schools, the Rav was continuously badgered and beleaguered by *rashei yeshiva*, students, politicians and organizations seeking an audience for answers to *she'elos*, clarifications of positions, and advice on all number of topics. Nevertheless, no matter how busy he was, he found time each week to visit a wheelchair-bound rabbi, who had been stricken by a neuromuscular disorder.

Every *Erev Yom Tov*, the Rav placed long-distance calls to a number of widowed rebbetzins of *musmachim* who had learned with him. A postcard with the Rav's unique handwriting brought *leShanah Tovah* greetings unfailingly every year. Good Yom Tov wishes by telephone enhanced the *simchas Yom Tov* in our house.

• The Rav spearheaded the creation of an anonymous fund for a widow of one of his students who had been left in a difficult financial position. He also contributed generously from his own pocket. I was astounded when I happened to learn of the vast dollar amounts that the Rav himself distributed to various *yeshivos* and other charities.

• A graduate of Yeshiva University, married with three children, who had never been the Rav's student, lay terminally ill in Mount Sinai Hospital. Upon discovering the gravity of the situation, the Rav asked me to visit him.

• The maid who cleaned the Rav's apartment was retired by Yeshiva University without fanfare. When he became aware of this, he sent one of the boys to buy a cake and a present and himself hosted a farewell party.

• The class was once puzzled when suddenly the lengthy *shiurim* became obviously shortened. The Rav had become aware that a student who had developed a serious hematological disorder would have had to leave before the end of *shiur* to receive his treatments, and discreetly shortened the length of the *shiur.*

• The birth of a son on Shabbos to a *musmach,* with a pulpit in the Midwest, presented a problem which was referred to the Rav. No *mohel* was available for a Shabbos *bris.* The Rav personally arranged a weekend trip for a *mohel* from New York.

A discussion once developed among several of us as to what the Rav's custom was regarding the recitation of the *psukim* and the *Ribono Shel Olam* prayer during *Birkhas Kohanim.* The answer came from a respected rabbi. He related that a congregant of his had been orphaned as a very young child. The boy davened in the Maimonides Shul. During *Birkhas Kohanim,* the Rav would take the young orphan under his own *talis.*

I once had to hospitalize the Rav on an *Erev Shavuos.* My decision to stay with him in the hospital was overridden by him. He opened the Rambam to *Hilchos Yom Tov* (7:17) and insisted that I join my family. A *minyan* was arranged, and the nurses were instructed to attend to the "special patient." After *Yom Tov,* the nurses reported that visitors had been continuously present all day. The nurses were so overwhelmed by this scene, and by the Rav's pleasant conduct, that a gentile nurse exclaimed to me, "I understood that he was a special rabbi, but I didn't know he was the world's greatest rabbi."

One year, on *Shabbos Parshas Vayikra,* our family visited Boston. We davened with the Rav. Following *Minchah,* as was the custom in Maimonides every Shabbos, we all sat around and hurled questions on the *sidrah* at the Rav. The Rav had invited me to sit near him. My son, aged eight, was on my lap. After several beautiful and brilliant explanations by the Rav, my son suddenly called out in a very loud stage whisper: "Daddy, is the Rav smarter than *Hashem*?" The Rav chuckled and flashed him a big smile. The encouragement inspired my son to try to stump the Rav. He asked him "Why is *Vayikra* written with a small *aleph*?" The Rav praised the question and rephrased it for the audience. He explained: "If the purpose of the small *aleph* is to differentiate between Moshe and Bilaam, why did the Torah not do this in *Sh'mos* where V*ayikra el Moshe* first appears?" After again commending my son on the excellence of the query, the Rav proceeded with a beautiful explanation. A large set of Rambam with a poetic handwritten *brachah* on the front leaf of the first volume was a bar mitzvah gift from the Rav to my son which is, of course, a cherished treasure today.

On occasions when he was not feeling well, the Rav stayed in our home. During breakfast one morning, my three-year-old daughter climbed on the Rav's lap, sampled his cottage cheese, and then proceeded to engage in a very serious give-and-take about her favorite doll.

Following the last time the Rav was *Mesader Kiddushin* in New York, I stayed with him near the *chupah* until the dancing crowd cleared the hall. As we were walking out, a little old lady approached the Rav and asked him for his business card. She explained that her granddaughter was about to be married. She was so impressed by the Rav's performance that she would like him to officiate. Politely and gently, he replied that he was soon returning to Boston and would have to decline.

According to the Rav, the prohibition of *lo tesa'ev Mitzri ki ger hoyisa be'artzo* was commanded to Jews to inculcate in us the *midah* of *hakoras hatov*. The theme recurs numerous times in the Torah to establish it as a basic component in the Jewish ethic. Kindnesses to the Soloveitchik family were never forgotten and always repaid in excess. For many months he traveled to the Bronx every Wednesday to visit a *rebbetzin* receiving chemotherapy for a malignancy. Her only tie to the Rav was that her father had done a kindness to Reb Moshe, the Rav's father. When Professor Louis Ginzberg of the Jewish Theological Seminary died, the Rav went to visit the mourning family. They asked if the Rav knew the deceased. He replied that he had met him once. Later, he explained that the meeting occurred when Professor Ginzberg came to pay a *shivah* call after Reb Moshe's *petirah*.

It is well known that Reb Hayyim was *machmir* in *pikuach nefesh*. The Rav extended this position. The father of a student developed a severe post-operative infection that baffled the infectious disease team of a hospital on Long Island. A preeminent specialist from a university hospital, formerly a student of the Rav, refused all calls and invitations to consult on the matter. A personal call from the Rav, including a definition *of pikuach nefesh*, had him at the bedside within two hours.

The Rav amassed a phenomenal wealth of medical information in many areas. When the *rebbetzin* was ill, the Rav was more familiar with medical literature on her condition than many of her attending physicians. At a medical ethics seminar, a noted oncologist was introduced to the Rav. After a lengthy conversation, the doctor commented to me that he thought that he had been speaking to a medical colleague.

When the early signs of Parkinson's appeared, the Rav described his symptoms precisely and clearly to the doctors. They suspected that he had consulted the medical books on the subject. In fact, it was only many years later that the Rav began suspecting that he was suffering from the disease.

The Rambam on *the pasuk "Vayikra lo Kel Elokei Yisrael"* (Gen. 33:20) quotes the *Gemara Megillah* to explain that God called Yaakov *Kel.* The Rav explained: We are commanded (Deut. 13:5) *Vehalakhta b'derachav* – you should walk in his ways. The *Gemara* (*Sotah* 14a) asks: "How can we walk after the *Shechinah*? Is it not a consuming fire?" Rather, it means that one should imitate His ways. This is the meaning of the *pasuk*: If you want to know what are the ways of God, then look at the Yaakovs, the *talmidei chachamim,* and the *Rashei Yeshiva* – they represent God on the earth. The Rav, though well concealed, was such a model.

Reb Velvel Brisker was once asked why the world recognized the Chofetz Chaim as a great *tzaddik* but not as a profound *talmid chacham,* despite his authorship of the monumental halakhic work of the *Mishnah Brurah.* He replied that the Chofetz Chaim prayed daily that God keep his scholarly abilities hidden, and so they were. Why then did he not pray for a similar camouflage of his ethical behavior? The reply was that the Chofetz Chaim was aware of his talmudic abilities – but he was not aware of his *tzidkus.* Similarly, the Rav's ethical behavior was so ingrained that he did not feel it to be extraordinary. Thus, the entire world unanimously acknowledged him as a giant in *talmud Torah* and intellectual creativity. Those of us who had the privilege to get close to him knew him also as a giant in *midos.*

A TITAN AMONG GIANTS

RABBI DR. MOSHE S. GORELIK

It has been pointed out that there are two kinds of texts for study. First of all, there is the written text. It may be a Torah *pasuk*, a talmudic or midrashic passage, or a selection from the works of *machshavah*. They are interpreted and analyzed, and the extracted messages may support an established principle or they may introduce new ideas.

The second kind of text is a person. The person is a paradigm of behavior. His life is valued for the lesson it imparts. *Hassidim*, for example, have a penchant for telling stories about their masters. Storytelling is the engineering instrument for converting abstract theories and philosophic concepts into comprehensible terms. The lives of the great and righteous are living laboratories for the study of moral and religious ideas. The teaching of raw concepts unadorned with story examples fails to impact upon the listeners the fullness of their significance.

With this in mind, I wish to share with you my personal reflections on Maran Harav Yosef Dov Halevi Soloveitchik *zt"l* whose passing last Pesach traumatized thousands, and I do this with profound trepidation and humility. The Rav was a titan among giants. He was a multi-dimensional personality, and a complex one at that. His gaonic stature is virtually unfathomable. To paraphrase a passage in (*Eirchen* 16): "*Temihani im yesh bedor hazeh sheyode'a lehaspid kerau'i,*" who can possibly be competent to define this towering religious personality? However, humility must not impede our effort. We must not remain at a standstill. The more knowledge of the past, the more the present is enriched and the more the future is guaranteed.

First, some basic facts. The Rav was bom in Poland in 1903. He was a grandson of Rabbi Hayyim Brisker *zt"l* and Rabbi Elye Pruzhiner *zt"l*. Until he enrolled at the University of Berlin at the age of 22, the main focus of his studies was the Talmud. Already, at an early age, he attracted the attention of great scholars with his superior mind and prodigious knowledge. While at the University of Berlin, where he earned his Ph.D, he concentrated on mathematics and philosophy.

In 1932, he and his wife emigrated to Boston where he was elected Rav and he remained a resident there until his passing. Within a few years of his arrival, he established the Maimonides School, the first yeshiva of its kind in New England. Upon the passing of his father, Rabbi Moshe Soloveitchik, in 1941, the Rav succeeded him as *Rosh Yeshiva* at Yeshiva University until illness forced him to retire in 1985.

In his combined learning of Talmud and philosophy and other secular subjects, the Rav was probably unmatched. During the twentieth century, he was a legend in his own time. The range of his knowledge of Talmud and *halakhah* as well as general culture, was encyclopedic. His Talmud lectures were exciting dialogues between the *rebbe* and his *talmidim.* The philosophic discourses were effervescent wellsprings of wisdom. His public lectures were special communal events. His orations mesmerized thousands with his brilliant artistic ability to portray concepts and happenings. As he spoke, it seemed as though he beckoned the listener to join him on an adventurous intellectual journey. He loved teaching Torah and communicating ideas.

Now to his legacy. It is a rich legacy, whose lessons, messages and directions leave a lasting value. I believe that as time passes, the intelligent Jew will turn more and more to the study of his writings and tapes. He left us several primary legacies. First, his passion for truth was astounding. He sought truth at all costs. He was precise, letter-perfect and intellectually honest. In class he was often severe, demanding exactitude; he was vigorous and relentless in presenting his case. But when a flaw in his thesis was pointed out to him, he would revise his position.

Some people, *rabbanim* included, were frustrated by what appeared to be the paucity of his *piskei halakhah.* However, he did issue halakhic decisions, especially in one-to-one situations. But, perhaps, it was difficult for him. A man of such gaonic dimensions, superior profundity, with a brilliant analytic and fertile mind, and equally important, with an addiction to precision, would be extremely cautious in issuing public *piskei halakhah. Pesak* is not to be done flippantly. *Pesak* must emerge from the sources and the logic must be impeccable. And I must add that his cautious approach to *pesak* was not due to a lack of patience for small details as some wish to suggest, but because everything had to add up mathematically. No creases in the logical process could remain.

The second legacy is in regard to secular studies. Incorporating secular studies into a yeshiva curriculum has been a source of contention for centuries. In many circles, the study of the sciences and philosophy are frowned upon. They may adversely affect the student's *emunah* and/or may distract the student from his Torah studies. They are a *bittul zman*, possessing no intrinsic value. The rationale for permitting a limited number of secular subjects is that they are either required by government regulations or for economic reasons, that is, for the sake of *parnasah*, to earn a living.

The Rav, on the other hand, maintained that secular subjects, whether they be the pure sciences or the humanities, should be incorporated into the yeshiva curriculum. The Rav himself boldly and resolutely entered the arena of general culture and, with firm conviction, led the way to the integration into the modern world. Some of his writings like *Halakhic Man* and *The Halakhic Mind* demonstrate the breadth of his secular knowledge and his admiration for its wisdom. In his innumerable talks on biblical themes or philosophic topics, he drew upon the literature of philosophy and general culture for illustration or for analysis. Recently, I heard a tape recording of a talk he delivered during the fifties, wherein he espoused his philosophy of education. For him, secular studies possess a positive intrinsic value that enhance the understanding of *yahadus*, thus enriching our *hashkafah*. He valued Yeshiva University for providing its students with the opportunity to study secular subjects under the same roof with Torah studies. For a long period of time, his teaching schedule included Jewish philosophy courses in the Bernard Revel Graduate School. As indicated previously, his works reflect an extraordinary knowledge of secular subjects. His classic essay, *The Lonely Man of Faith* and his essay "Confrontation" could not have been written were he not conversant with a wide range of philosophical, religious and psychological literature. Furthermore, his cultural breadth included music, art and general literature. For him it was not "*Eit la'asot la'Hashem, hefaru toratekha*," a concession to the times. The truths and wisdom of the secular world were not to be dismissed.

Now to the third legacy. When he established the Maimonides School, he pioneered a revolutionary concept in girls' education. Girls were granted the privilege of studying Talmud alongside boys. They were encouraged to pursue studies in *Torah shebe'al peh* in the fullest sense, and it was he, himself, who inaugurated the first Talmud *shiur* for women at Yeshiva University's Stern College for Women.

In history there were individual women who acquired expertise in *Torah shebe'al peh,* and there were occasional echoes from authorities who interpreted Rabbi Eliezer's statement in a way that would not be construed as an absolute prohibition for them to do so. But these were isolated cases. The Rav, however, took the revolutionary step. Talmud should be included in the curriculum for women as well as for men. I once heard him declare that since women are obligated to study *mitzvos* which are incumbent upon them, then much of the Talmud is required for study. Subsequently, the Rav's policy has fueled the intellectual ambition of educated women, and today there are centers for higher Jewish studies for women that include Talmud as a major component of their program.

A fourth legacy was the Rav's religious philosophic advocacy of Religious Zionism. The Rav demonstrated unusual commitment to this ideology. Initially, he was a member of Agudat Israel. He even delivered a *hesped* in memory of Rabbi Chaim Ozer at one of its conferences. The Rav was a child of the Brisker world. His devotion to Rabbi Hayyim Brisker's methodology was absolute. He treasured the *chiddushei Torah* and cherished the *minhagim* and traditions. Thus, his disassociation with Agudah represented a rejection of family tradition. His loyalty did not deter him from breaking with the past. The shift from Agudah to Mizrachi was akin to an act of defiance. The penetrating essay, "*Kol Dodi Dofek*," originally presented as a public address, is a moving discourse about the obligation of every Jew to respond to the divine knock on the door of Israel's destiny. History records that the chasm between Agudah and Mizrachi was unbridgeable. Most *gedolim* opposed joining forces with secular Zionists. They, therefore, formed the Agudah to counteract what appeared to them the compromising policy of Mizrachi. The Rav's membership in the Mizrachi movement added prestige, and his stirring addresses fueled the hearts, souls and minds of its devotees. He was not averse, however, to criticizing the policies of the Mizrachi or of the government of *Medinat Yisrael* if he believed they violated fundamental moral principles.

A fifth legacy is in regard to the Orthodox relationship with non-Orthodox lay and rabbinic leadership. For many years, he lent his support to our involvement with the Synagogue Council of America. To fully appreciate his approach, one must take note of two matters. First, the Synagogue Council was a composite of three rabbinic and three lay synagogue associations, representing three different communities, namely, the Orthodox, Conservative and Reform movements. This body spoke as one voice in non-halakhic matters vis-a-vis non-Jewish religious groups and it also addressed broad American moral concerns. Each agency had veto power. No policy could have been formulated and no statement issued unless there was unanimous agreement. A standing policy was that no theological dialogue with either the Catholics or the Protestants may take place. This policy was an instruction given to the Orthodox groups by the Rav, who was generally opposed to theological dialogues with the non-Jewish groups.

The Rav also insisted that we must always preserve a line of demarcation between Torah *Yahadus* and the divergent movements. *Halakhah* must never be modified nor compromised.

An example of his firm attitude on this issue is his classic *pesak* on whether an individual may attend services in a non-Orthodox synagogue on Rosh Hashanah in order to hear the sounding of the *shofar*. His response was negative, even if there would not be any other possibility to observe this *mitzvah*.

However, the Rav did believe that as long as *halakhah* is not compromised, we are not precluded from having a working relationship and dialogue, even with groups who are guilty of flagrant violations of the *halakhah*.

The Rav's position on engendering dialogue with divergent movements, within the guidelines of *halakhah*, was disputed in the form of an *issur* promulgated by eight *Rashei Yeshiva*, amongst whom were included Harav Aharon Kotler and Harav Moshe Feinstein. The battle lines were drawn, but the Rav refused to budge. There are attempts to reread the Rav's intention, but the truth can not be dismissed. The Histadrut Harabbonim

(Rabbinical Council of America) constantly turned to him for guidance and advice in these matters, and he continued to consent to the RCA's membership in the Synagogue Council of America. The Rav's message was unequivocal: A firm uncompromising commitment to halakhic *Yahadus* permits one to cooperate with the non-halakhic Jew for the well-being of *Klal Yisroel.* In this far-reaching *pesak*, he saw the necessity of strengthening the unity of Israel.

The *Avot deRabbi Natan* (25:3) records a moving account of the impact of Rabbi Eliezer's passing on his disciples.

> לאחר שבת בא ר״ע ומצאו באריסרט׳ שבא מקסרי ללוד מיד קרע את בגדיו ותלש בשערו והיה דמו שותת ונופל לארץ והיה צועק ובוכה ואומר אללי רבי אליך אללי רבי אליך מרי שהנחת כל הדור יתום. פתח עליו בשורה ואמר אבי אבי רכב ישראל ופרשיו מעות יש לך עלי ואין לי שולחני לרצותן.

Upon hearing of his master's death, Rabbi Akiva cried out: "Woe is me, my teacher! Woe is me, my teacher! My master, who has left the entire generation orphaned!" So, we too weep and cry out. We, too, are orphaned.

The Rav's intellect encompassed the totality of our *mesorah* which incorporated both *Toras Hashem* and the breadth of human intellectual achievement. He was both a rebbe and a rav for our generation. He was the unique rebbe in Torah and, as the Rav, he guided us in our encounter with the world. He was "the halakhic mind," the strict intellectual, the "*ish ha-halakhah*," the halakhic architect, *"The Lonely Man of Faith,"* the religious soul in quest, "*uvikashtem misham*," the passionate seeker of Hashem, the "*shiur lezekher abba*," the Torah personality. He was the logician and the poet, the philosopher and the romanticist, the man of culture and the genius of *lomdus*.

Our Torah generation is now impoverished because we are bereft of the Rav *zt"l* who was the *gaon* of generations. But we must wipe our tears and look forward to the future with his legacy. We must not only keep it alive, but we must maintain the integrity of that legacy. May the Rav be a *melitz yosher* for *Klal Yisrael.*

FAITH AND INTELLECT: THE IMPACT OF THE RAV

RABBI MATIS GREENBLATT

Sometime in the latter part of the nineteenth century, Rabbi Yosef Dov Soloveitchik, the Brisker Rav, and great-grandfather of the Rav, showed samples of his son Hayyim's "Torah" (original interpretations) to Reb Yisrael Salanter. Reb Yisrael commented that in the future, this type of Torah would save the Torah world from the inroads of the *Haskalah*. The ninteenth century was a time when the truth and eternity of Torah were being undermined and challenged from many directions. Not the least challenge came from the scientific and technological revolution, and in the words of Matthew Arnold, "The Sea of Faith was once, too, at the full.... But now I only hear its melancholy, long withdrawing roar...."

To some within the Jewish world, the glorious tradition of Torah learning seemed to lose its luster as compared to the precision and supposed certainties of science and the scientific method. Reb Hayyim Soloveitchik's penetrating mind demonstrated that, in fact, undergirding the mass of Talmudic law was a profound, conceptual foundation. He showed that halakhic thought is "no less intellectually creative, brilliantly analytical, subtly abstract than the most abstract and exact sciences. On the contrary it exceeds them" (*U'Vikashtem Misham*, p. 49). His new method gained respect for Torah and attracted some of the best young minds to Torah learning.

The Rav imbibed his grandfather's method from early youth and developed that method to new heights of creativity. But the Rav did something else which Reb Hayyim did not do and perhaps was not necessary for his generation: The Rav confronted the predicament of modern man. His mastery of many areas of knowledge is not as important as the fact that he learned and experienced what it meant to live in the contemporary world.

It is frequently assumed that his awareness and knowledge of modernity reflected his approval or legitimation. In fact, as Chief Rabbi Jonathan

Sacks has shown, he actually recoiled from many of the values of Western life and civilization. But for those involved in contemporary life, he was a mentor and a guide. Many young men who might have been lost to the Conservative movement remained within Orthodoxy because of his example. How could one call Orthodoxy "old-fashioned" when this thoroughly modern giant was Orthodox and much more intelligent and knowledgeable than they in almost any field? Furthermore, contradictions and conflicts did not affect his unshakeable faith and *yirat shamayim.* The fact that he spent his time immersed in Talmudic studies not as an academic exercise, but as a living and dynamic truth, reflected his profound faith in the divine source of the Oral Law. This faith was communicated to his thousands of disciples who, in turn, established fresh links in the chain of *masorah.* And his internalized, instinctual *yirat shamayim* is touchingly illustrated in the story of his bursting into tears upon realizing that he had accidentally switched on a light on Shabbat.

The Rav's deep faith in the truth of Torah did not impede his search for, and appreciation of, general truth, and as a disciple of the Rambam he welcomed knowledge from whatever the source. He never feared truth even if he had unanswered questions. His anxieties and existential tensions arose from conflicts between the goals and values of society at large as opposed to the goals and values of Torah, or any perceived threats to his faith.

In his search for truth, he was unsparing of himself, as well as of others, and his approach was one of complete intellectual openness:

The Rav was scheduled to give two consecutive *shiurim.* During the first *shiur*, a young man offered an interpretation which did not please the Rav. He proceeded to upbraid the student for his lack of understanding. After the *shiur*, the second class entered the room, but the Rav remained silent, obviously deep in thought. The class was puzzled. Suddenly, he arose and hurried out of the room with the entire class close behind. He strode out of the building and entered a luncheonette where the young man was eating. The young man looked up appalled, and cringed as the Rav drew near, pointing his finger at him. But instead of additional rebuke, the Rav called out to him, "You were right and I was wrong! Tomorrow morning, I will explain!"

His thought was fresh and dynamic. A student once pointed out that he had contradicted something he himself had said earlier. He replied, "So what, I am not a *Mishnah* or a *Tana*."

He saw his role as teacher of all segments of the community, not only of advanced yeshiva students. His Saturday night Chumash classes and Sunday morning Talmud classes in Brookline were legendary, as were his heavily attended weekly Talmud *shiurim* in Congregation Moriah in New York. Dr. Yitzchak Twersky has pointed out that in view of the Rav's awesome knowledge, his teaching frequently required a major effort of *tsimtsum* or contraction, in order to make it appropriate for his particular audience.

The Rav wrote that "prayer is the continuation of prophecy, the difference is while within the prophetic community God takes the initiative – He speaks and man listens – in prayer the initiative belongs to man: he does the speaking and God the listening" (*The Lonely Man of Faith,* p. 57). One may ask what vehicle served to replace prophecy's role as communicator of the divine voice to man?

The Ramban teaches us that after the period of prophecy, the prophetic spirit lived on in the *chachamim* (scholars) "who know the truth through the divine spirit within them" (Ramban to *Baba Batra* 12a). The Rav's life reflected his belief that God spoke to man through his immersion in Torah. Torah is an interactive, creative process between God and man. The Rogotchaver Gaon, Rabbi Yosef Rosen, once said that when he prayed, he spoke to God; but when he learned, God spoke to him. In the last analysis, our main contact with divinity is via the divine word expressed through Torah. Halakhic man's preoccupation with theoretical *halakhah* in contrast to practical *halakhah* reflects his longing for transcendence. According to the *Zohar* (3:80), our faith is derived from contact and immersion in Torah. And through Torah, covenantal man spans the generations; he finds redemption from his insecurity and transcends narrow historical theories by living in the historical continuum of the *masorah* community (Op. cit. p. 72).

The Rav passed through earth like a meteor, leaving us a radiant body of thought and life constituting a mighty demonstration of his faith in Orthodox Judaism and in the divinity of Torah. His unquestionable greatness touched and elevated the lives of his thousands of students as well as all those who were fortunate enough to have known him. But perhaps, most of all, he was an indispensable link in the preservation of Torah in an era of unprecedented challenges.

THE RAV AS DARSHAN

RABBI KENNETH HAIN

At this moment of reflection, I recall the first time I heard the Rav *zt"l*. It was over thirty years ago in the Nathan Lamport Auditorium of Yeshiva University. For three and a half hours I, as a young teenager, sat mesmerized as this powerful lion of a man delivered a dazzling lecture to a standing room only crowd of two thousand Jews of all ages and backgrounds.

That experience, and dozens of others like it, was both exhausting and exhilarating at the same time. I have tried on many occasions to relive them by studying the published versions of the Rav's lectures. But while the written word does capture, somewhat, the intellectual brilliance of the Rav – his world view, his value system, his unique integration of the worlds of *halakhah* and *drush* – it cannot replicate the Rav's singular genius as an orator.

Much has and will be written analyzing the Rav's Torah and philosophy. However, his style and method as a *darshan*, a generally overlooked dimension of his creativity, also deserves careful attention and study. Of course, the originality and brilliance of his ideas were the primary factors of his greatness, but I have come to realize that it would be a mistake to ignore the significant and deliberate efforts the Rav made in determining how to convey his ideas. I believe that the way in which he delivered and articulated his message accounts for much of the reason why he had so much of an impact on our generation. To borrow the familiar analogy: a *drashah* of the Rav was more than the *cheftza* of his ideas; it was propelled by the *gavra* of his personal presentation.

Briefly stated, the Rav's uniqueness as a public speaker, both in the *shiur* room as well as in the public lecture hall, was his remarkable ability to overcome all barriers between himself and his audience, and between his audience and his subject matter. The listener was transformed into an active participant in the encounter, riding alongside the Rav on an often unforgettable journey.

What were some of the features of the Rav's oratorical persona that enabled him to be so effective as a *darshan*? How, indeed, did the Rav penetrate and essentially eliminate the wall between himself and his audience?

The first key element was the Rav's remarkable preparation. The Rav crafted every presentation with precision and never spoke off the cuff. The ever-present pile of rustling papers on his lecture table eminently attested to this fact. Rabbi Dovid Shapiro of the Maimonides School in Boston told me a story that demonstrated the Rav's insistence on preparation. While he was once speaking to a class at the school, Rabbi Shapiro noticed that the Rav was clasping some notes in his hand for the talk. Notes for a day-school class!

Amazingly, this extensive preparation, which often entailed scripting the entire *drashah* or *shiur*, did not stifle the Rav. On the contrary, the second key element of his success is that this preparation liberated him, allowing him the freedom to engage his audience in the creative process. In spite of the copious notes before him, the Rav's presentation was spontaneous in the sense that it was fresh and always attentive to the verbal and non-verbal cues of the listener. He sometimes may have referred to the same themes in his lectures – like the nature of *itzumo shel yom* of Yom Kippur, the dual covenantal obligations of *Knesses Yisrael*, and the miraculous quality of the Jewish renaissance in the State of Israel – but his presentation was different each time because of his sensitivity to the variety of interests and different levels of knowledge of his audience.

This essential component of the Rav's effectiveness was best reflected in his choices of language and formulations. In one setting he would refer to "Scriptures" and in another he would speak of *"Taireh"* with his memorable Litvish intonation. The Rav aimed to reach each of his audiences by adapting what he determined to be its requisite linguistic idiom, never compromising with a one-size-fits-all style of speaking.

The same was true of his content. The Rav exerted much intellectual energy in ensuring that his audience understood his ideas. His *Yahrzeit Shiurim* were almost exclusively devoted to *Seder Moed* in an effort to reach the broader audience that was in attendance. Yet, he never spoke down to them. He addressed them at a level that was just one notch above them, challenging without overwhelming them. His listeners knew and appreciated his effort to engage them and they responded in kind.

A third key element of the Rav's oratorical skill was his courage. He took risks in almost every *drashah*. Sometimes the risk was in the subject matter. For example, I can recall frequent forays into controversial, politically incorrect topics such as criticizing American presidents, secular Zionists, anti-Zionists, and the Catholic Church. He did not mince his words, once referring to the judge in the infamous Rosenberg trial as a "murderer." On other occasions, there would just be a moment, often in a side comment, when the Rav would express a striking view or display a raw emotion. When once describing the restrictive nature of the laws of *niddah*, the Rav dared to say that "the *halakhah* seemed vicious." This fearlessness and unpredictability made the Rav continually compelling.

On occasion, the Rav also successfully achieved high drama and even humor. Once, during a particularly long discourse on *Megillat Esther*, he portrayed the difficulty of Mordechai's request of Esther to see King Achashverosh. The Rav paused, poised for his next dramatic sentence, and then proceeded to describe this task as "a mission… mission… mission… *impossible!*" The audience exploded in laughter. Flashing his memorable grin, the Rav sat back knowing that, with this unexpected reference to the contemporary popular culture, he had captured the moment and our minds.

Finally, the most courageous, and perhaps the most distinguishing, feature of the Rav as a *darshan* was his willingness and ability to reveal himself. His striking self-disclosures about family, childhood and personal crises were warm and poignant, enabling his listener to better understand the point he was making and to feel a personal connection with him. These intimate personal revelations were never exhibitionistic but were always appropriate and dignified.

In a particularly memorable presentation at the Rabbinical Council of America's Convention in 1974, the Rav first connected the various stories of *Parshat Beha'alotekha* through a brilliant analysis of Moshe's frustrations with his role of leading the Jewish People. He then did something I will never forget. He changed his tone, cadence and facial expression and began opening up his heart. He detailed how his own life experience had mirrored that of Moshe. He revealed that he too had to cope with disappointment and disillusionment, both as a leader as well as in his personal life. The comparison was so real, the self-disclosure so powerful and emotionally charged that the experiences of Moshe Rabbenu and those of the Rav had become ours as well.

As a practicing rabbi who has tried to teach the Rav's Torah, my greatest challenge has been to convey his ideas with all of their power and impact. The Rav's thoughts will, hopefully, continue to be proliferated in both the written and oral form. But with his passing, his ideas in their most pristine and effective form – his presentation and style – we can only attempt to recapture.

It was my great *zechut* to have had the opportunity to hear and learn from our late beloved *rebbe zt"l.* He taught, inspired, moved and changed me. My life, like that of so many others, has been profoundly affected by his personality and his Torah. His approach and style has become a part of me even in subtle ways that I can only now begin to appreciate. May his words and voice continue to be heard.

DEFINING GREATNESS – WHAT IS A *GADOL?*

RABBI SHLOMO HOCHBERG

The Rav, HaRav Yosef Dov Halevi Soloveitchik, *zekher tzaddik livrachah,* in a lecture delivered at Maimonides School in Brookline on Motzei Shabbat HaGadol 5736, focused on a small section of the Haggadah, including the *passuk* in *Devarim* (26:5), "*Vayehi sham legoy gadol atsum verav.*" The *Sifrei* there interprets "*Vayehi sham legoy. Melamed shehayu metsuyanim sham,*" and then proceeds to interpret the next phrase, "*gadol ve'atsum.*" The Rambam's text of the Haggadah, however, divides the *passuk* differently; the Rambam places the word *Gadol* together with the preceding phrase: "*Vayehi sham legoy gadol,*" "there, he became a great nation."

What is the need for the word "*sham*"? The *Zohar* explains that specifically, there, in Egypt, he became a *goy gadol* – a great nation, but had the tragedy of Yosef never taken place, Jacob never would have become a *goy gadol.* Like the rose which grows beautifully amidst thorns, so Israel grows abundantly among enemies. The Jews as a people learned something from their experience as slaves among their oppressors which enabled them to become a *goy gadol.*

The Gaon of Vilna, in investigating the etymology of the word *goy,* proposes that it derives from the same root as *goyah* – the human body, each form of which is different from all others. In Tanach, the word *goy* applies also to a single individual – as in *Hagoy gam tzaddik taharog,* "will you kill even a righteous individual?" (*Bereishit* 20:4). A person is an individual because he differs from others not only physically, but also with regard to a specific individual way of life, with a unique ethic and code of behavior. That is the meaning of *goy* here – to be distinct, unique and singular. The Jews were *metzuyanim sham* – they stood out; the Jew can be identified and recognized by the gentile, despite his efforts to conceal his identity.

Why, then, is the word *gadol* necessary? What does it add to *metzuyanim sham*? Apparently, the noun *goy* alone isn't enough; only together with the adjective *metzuyanim sham* is the description complete; *goy* alone could be understood either in a positive or a negative sense (e.g. Germany in the

1930s and 1940s was certainly distinct, but for the worse). *Goy* alone can be either creative or destructive. So even if I know that the Jew in Egypt was distinct, I still must discover whether he stands out as an individual commanding respect, or the reverse? The adjective *gadol* erases that doubt. The community was a *great* one, which commanded respect! What does *gadol* mean? Two *pesukim* in *Devarim* (4:7–8) will help us understand.

> *Ki mi goy gadol asher Elokim kerovim eylav ke'Hashem Elokeynu bekhol kor'eynu eylav...U'mi goy gadol asher lo chukim umishpatim tzaddikim.*

A *gadol* is defined here by two characteristic traits. First, a *goy gadol* distinguishes itself in righteousness, in *mitzvot bein adam lechavero.* If the community as such, as well as the single individual, develops a fine sensitivity for justice, and hates discriminatory practice and chicanery, then it can claim to be a *goy gadol.* If a nation doesn't stop injustice, science and technology will not make it a *goy gadol.* Fairness and spontaneous indignation at hypocrisy are essential in order for a people to be considered a *goy gadol.* (The Rav noted that the United Nations lacks all this and is therefore a *goy katan.*) Modern man doesn't discriminate between righteousness and cruelty, whereas, a great nation is described as *asher lo chukim mishpatim tzaddikim.* In order to act morally and righteously, one must develop an instinct for righteousness. Modern man lacks this instinct, whereas the Talmud mentions simple *amei ha'aretz,* who were endowed with this instinct (the Rav added that the goal of the *mehanekh* should be to develop this instinct in the students). And secondly, *asher Elokim eylav... bekhol kor'eynu eylav* – a nation or individual who knows how to pray is a *goy gadol.* Avraham Avinu, the Patriarch of the *goy gadol* was the inventor of prayer, which has two prerequisites:

1. Humility – self-negation, a complete sense of dependence on *Hakadosh Barukh Hu – Ke'eynei shifchah el-yad gevirtah kein eyneynu el Hashem Elokeynu* (*Tehillim* 123:2). Modern man isn't capable of giving up independence when it's time to pray. Nations (or individuals) which practice atheism and agnosticism are the most arrogant and insolent – nations like the former Soviet Union. The Western world is at least sometimes ashamed to tell a lie. A nation permeated by faith is by nature much more humble than a nation pervaded by agnosticism.

2. Involvement in the stress and pain of others. Prayer must encompass not only oneself, but also others. Our standard *tefillot*, for that reason, are formulated in the plural. Prayers for the ill or of consolation always include others *betokh sha'ar.* If my prayer is limited to myself, then it's worthless. When Moshe tried to pray for himself in *Va'etchanan* (*Devarim* 3), he was immediately silenced by Hashem – *al tosaf davar elai.* A great nation, or individual, must have compassion for others; a prayerful community, where the community suffers for the individual, and the individual suffers with the community. Even the term *am* (nation) is related to the word *im* (with) as in *imo anochi betsarah* (*Tehillim* 91:15) – this is the banner of *am.* Solidarity is what keeps the nation together.

The Rav, *zekher tzaddik livrakhah*, was surely the *Gadol B'Torah*, as the master *ba'al masbir* and *melamed* of *halakhah* and *aggadah*, *kabbalah* and *machshavah* for our generations. He was supremely expert in every academic discipline with the unique ability to integrate every fragment of knowledge of the mysteries of Hashem's universe into a coherent whole. He was the consummate teacher, brilliantly elucidating to students of all backgrounds the most difficult concepts with clarity, simplicity and elegance.

Yet, in my view, above all this, was the Rav's greatest *gadlus*, even as he defined the word *gadol* above. The Rav displayed profound compassion and empathy for the oppressed, and was intolerant only of injustice or falsehood. He could be depended upon to give freely of his time and energy to respond to anyone in need. He was a true *anav* (how many people remember trying to get to the door first, before the Rav quickly opened it for others to pass through before him?). Those who witnessed him immersed in *tefillah* on Yom Kippur or Tisha B'Av or a "regular weekday" or at the Pesach Seder, could not help but feel the power of *tefillah*, and feel the Rav's humility, majesty, and permeating *kedushah*.

Rabbonim called upon the Rav for halakhic expertise, laymen turned to him for personal advice, and world leaders turned to him for his wise counsel and incisive understanding of global issues, not only because of his brilliance, but also because they recognized in him these defining attributes of true *"gadlus."*

Permit me, if I may, to include a personal, simple anecdote – one among many which display the Rav's greatness (and for which I wish to express my *hakarot hatov*). Nearly twenty years ago, shortly after I had become a Rav in Lowell, Massachusetts, some twenty five miles north of Brookline, I encountered several halakhic questions which I deemed too difficult to resolve without consultation. I requested an appointment with the Rav in his daughter's home (where he was then living) in Brookline, and was quickly granted one in the evening. Even then, the Rav was not well, but to accommodate me, he had added another appointment at the end of a long grueling day, delaying a well-earned and most needed rest. Upon my arrival, Dr. Atarah Twersky welcomed me into the living room, and as I waited patiently to meet with the Rav, it was apparent that phone calls were coming in from around the world, seeking the Rav's sagacious counsel. As the calls subsided, the Rav turned his attention to my questions, penetrating quickly to the core of each issue, furnishing answers to each query, and cogently elucidating the halakhic reasoning behind each response. This took but a few minutes. And then, for nearly an hour, the Rav proceeded to ask about my family, about my late father in law, *alav hashalom* (including the treatments which were then being pursued for his illness, and possible alternatives), about the *Shul* and day school in Lowell, about many people in the community whom he knew personally, about my welfare and that of my wife, about our feelings about *rabbanus* and *chinuch*, and on and on.

As I arose to leave, and to thank the Rav for his time and his help, he profusely thanked me for coming, and asked me to stay in touch. I had not wanted to bother him; he made me feel that I had done him a tremendous favor. From the Rav's perspective as a true *gadol,* perhaps I had.

"VEZEH LEKHA HA'OT KI ANOCHI SHLACHTICHA"

RABBI YAIR KAHN

I am not really fit for the task that has been thrust upon me. I was in the Rav's *shiur* for only a brief period late in the Rav's career. During that time I was not the best *talmid* nor the closest in personal terms to the Rav. I lack both the exposure and the understanding to evaluate who and what the Rav was. Therefore, I decided to address a different issue for which I am better suited: namely, what was the Rav to me. Then, hoping that my experience was somewhat representative, I broadened the topic to what was the Rav to us.

One of the Rambam's principles of faith states as follows: "*Ani ma'amin be'emunah shleimah shezot haTorah lo tehei muchlefet.*"

Torah is *dvar Hashem*, the eternal words of an infinite God. It is objective truth transcending time and space. It is not a function of history. It is ahistorical, meta-historical. In fact, *Chazal* claim that Torah preceded the creation of the world, before man, before history.

That a point in history can arise in which Torah loses its significance and relevance is absurd. That Torah can become merely a relic of some ancient civilization is impossible. Torah, by its definition as *dvar Hashem*, remains timeless and relevant within every historical context, be it the generation of Moshe Rabbeinu or the modern era.

However, *lo nitnei Torah lema'alachei hasharet. Yahadus* does not deny the human context. History is in a constant flux, society forever changing. Consequently, the human response, whether legal or moral, cannot remain static.

Ki be'or panekha natata lanu Torat chayim.

Torat chayim. A living and dynamic Torah was given us by the grace of God. *Natata lanu* refers to *Torah shebe'al peh.* The Torah given to *Am Yisrael,* interpreted by the *Chahmei haMesorah* throughout Jewish history, constantly confronting the new challenges inherent in a changing world. The chain of the *mesorah* links the response of *Torah shebe'al peh* to the external words of Sinai.

Divrei Elokim Chaim – The words of the Living God refers to a dynamic *Torah shebe'al peh* based on the authority of the timeless words of a living God. Somehow, infinite transcendent *Torah shebikhtav* merges with living, breathing *Torah shebe'al peh.*

Historical development is generally a gradual evolution, and can be perceived only from a distance. Under normal conditions, the continuity of *Torah shebe'al peh* is a natural process barely noticeable. However, at times, historical change is so dramatic, so abrupt, that the natural process mentioned above is impossible. Such a situation existed in the post-Holocaust era with the total destruction of European Jewry. Although the Jewish people physically survived the Shoah, Jewish life was transformed beyond recognition. Individuals survived while communities and their traditions perished. Jews were suddenly thrust into a totally new context, unprepared both socially and religiously for the enormous challenge they were about to confront. Traditional Judaism was faced with a crisis. Could *Yahadut* be applied in its new context while remaining faithful to tradition? Could a bridge be built over the chasm separating two such diverse cultures? Could the chain of the *mesorah* somehow link the new world with the old?

After the Shoah, Jewish life was transferred to two major centers: Israel and America. In Israel, while physical survival remained a concern, spiritual continuity posed less of a problem. The existing Israeli society into which the European refugees were absorbed was essentially a Jewish society, itself a product of European Jewish culture. Furthermore, since the refugees comprised a large percentage of Israeli society, newcomers felt less of a need to assimilate the culture and values of the existing society. Instead, it was necessary to begin to rebuild the wreckage of European Jewish culture along the shores of the Mediterranean. This process lent itself to a degree of continuity, despite the sharpness of change.

In America, the situation was far more critical. There, the Jewish refugee found himself in an already defined environment, foreign and alien to his previous experience. The Jew from the *shtetl*, his old world destroyed, found little comfort of familiarity in the land of opportunity. From a religious perspective, he found little value awarded to piety and devotion. Whatever religion existed was little more than empty ritual. Science and technology were revered, power and money worshiped. Historic and natural causality replaced *hashkafah* (a religious value system). The non-empirical belief that God actually plays a role in worldly events was viewed askance as primitive superstition, childish and silly from the enlightened perspective of modern man. It was difficult to imagine how the *shtetl yid* could manage to fit into American culture while remaining faithful to his tradition. It was difficult to imagine how the second generation, raised in America, could possibly relate to, and identify with, the "primitive" heritage of his non-American parents!

Today, to a certain extent, Orthodox Judaism thrives within the American context. The *mesorah* mysteriously managed to survive the devastation of the Shoah. Jewish tradition persevered despite the overwhelming odds. How? The answer is quite simple. *Yad Hashem.*

> *Vehayah ki timtse'enah oto ra'ot rabot vetsarot ve'antah hashirah hazot le'ad ki lo tishkach mipi zar'o.*

This *passuk,* referring to the suffering and tragedies which will befall the Jewish people, also contains a divine promise. Jewish tradition will always survive. Rashi comments: "*harei zu havtachah leyisroel ein Torah mishtachechet mizar'ah legamrei.*"

How was this promise implemented? Who was chosen to be this critical link in the *Mesorah*? Who was the "the messenger of the voice," the messenger elected by God, given the monumental task of furthering Jewish destiny at *this* critical juncture? One of the major *shlichim* was no doubt Moreynu veRabbeinu haRav Yosef Ber Soloveitchik *zt"l.*

The Rav was more than a *tzaddik*, *gadol hador*, *gaon*, and philosopher. A fuller appreciation of the Rav's significance and contribution requires the recognition that the Rav was instrumental in the realization and actualization of Jewish destiny. The Rav was largely responsible for the transfer of devotion to Torah and *halakhah* to an otherwise religiously complacent American scene. I would like to enumerate various arteries through which the Rav's message flowed. To claim that I can give a full account of the Rav's impact would be ridiculously arrogant.

Efes ketzeihu tireh vekulo lo tireh.

Although the Rav was multi-faceted, he was essentially a Brisker *lamdan.* Son of Reb Moshe *zt"l*, grandson of Hagaon Reb Hayyim, he was nurtured in the tradition of Brisk. At an early age, he was already recognized as an *iluy.* When he was only eleven, his father sent his notebook to Reb Hayyim. Upon reading the *chidushim*, Reb Hayyim ran coatless in the middle of a Brisk winter to show Reb Simcha Zelig, the *dayan* in Brisk, the *chidushim* of his grandchild. Reb Hayyim predicted that the Rav was destined for greatness.

Many of the Rav's *chidushim* now being published were written in his late teens and early twenties. Rev Velvel claimed that no one in America came close to the Rav in learning. When Rav Shmuel Rasovsky, then Rosh Yeshiva at Ponevitch, arrived in Boston for medical treatment, the Rav visited him in the hospital where they talked in learning. Rav Shmuel was so impressed that upon his return to Israel he said that there was no one to talk to on the level of the Rav. His style in learning combined rigorous conceptual analysis along with *koach hachidush,* novel and original ideas. It was this unique combination that made the Rav not only a great *lamdan* but a great *melamed* as well. His *shiurim* were unpredictable, dynamic and electrifying, while seeming so basic and obvious in retrospect. The number of *talmidim* affected by these *shiurim* reached the thousands.

Aside from being universally recognized as a *gadol b'Torah*, the Rav was also famous as a religious philosopher. His contribution to the world of philosophy affected a more limited audience, a select few who have both the philosophic knowledge and halakhic background to fully appreciate the Rav's works. And how many, even among the select, are capable of integrating the Rav's various ideas into a cohesive philosophic system?

Although I am not one of the select, the Rav as a philosopher had a major impact on me, and many like me, in terms of making Judaism relevant in the modern world, a recurrent theme in the Rav's writings. *Ish ha-Halakhah* defines the typological Brisker *lamdan* from a philosophical perspective. *The Lonely Man of Faith* grapples with the dilemma which the man of faith confronts in the twentieth century. *Halakhic Mind* reevaluates religious philosophy within the context of the recent divergence of science and philosophy. In his introduction to a philosophy lecture series in 1959, the Rav stated:

> My training was basically not in the philosophy of religion but in the philosophy of science, Kantian, neo-Kantian philosophy. So, perhaps, I have a strange approach to the philosophy of religion.... However, since I've been, so to say, cast in, or thrust in to a certain environment where the philosophy of religion was considered important, I try to interpret...Jewish religious concepts in philosophical terms. All I'll say to you is just my own subjective thoughts and feelings about Judaism. I have tried to interpret Judaism in modern terms.... For the Jew and his encounter with the modern world I have tried very hard.

The Rav dealt with many topics directly. Moreover, he created a frame of reference which enables us to grapple with various other issues not explicitly discussed. However, perhaps more important, is that the Rav, by virtue of his tremendous stature and the authority of his opinion, established for an entire community that Judaism is relevant in the modern world. He single-handedly removed from the agenda any notion that *Yahadut* was archaic and primitive.

The Rav fused *halakhah* and philosophy. Many *sugyot* form the framework for his philosophic ideas, and many of his *chidushim* have a philosophic basis. Parenthetically, I would like to note here that the Rav's major contribution to the world of Torah was in *Orach Chaim, Nashim,* and *Nezikin* were common turf of the *Achronim.* The concepts of *Kodshim, Zera'im*, and *Taharot* were discovered and developed by Reb Hayyim and Reb Velvel. In all these fields, the Rav was fluent and creative. However, in *Orach Chaim*, he was a pioneer, exploring new territory, discovering new concepts. Moreover, as I stated, his conceptual analysis in these areas merged with his world view. His conceptualization of *Hilkhot Tefillah*, *Hilkhot Shabbat* and *Hilkhot Yom Tov* is consistent with his philosophical approach. His analysis of *Hilkhot Aveilut* and *Hilkhot Teshuvah* is based on his psychological insights. He successfully integrated his world view with his Brisker analysis of *havayot de Abayei veRava.*

Both Torah and philosophy, *lehavdil*, are areas which the Rav studied and mastered, and in which he created. His level of accomplishment in each separately is impressive, while the combination mind-boggling. In both we are dealing with expressions of the Rav's genius, his amazing grasp of the subject matter and the brilliance of his ingenuity. There are other seemingly unrelated areas in which the Rav also excelled.

The Rav's talent as an orator was best demonstrated during his public lectures. He would talk for hours to thousands of people about complex and difficult issues. Nonetheless, the entire audience the whole time would be completely engrossed by the lecture. I have never encountered anything even remotely similar. He had a complete mastery of language. His descriptions were colorful and vivid. Characters came to life. When he spoke, there was an aura, a feeling that something was happening, something exciting and profound. The audience was riveted to every word, fascinated and absorbed. Astonishingly, the Rav accomplished this in English as well as his native Yiddish. The Rav's oratorical skills were complemented by quality of content. A wide range of materials were woven together by his skilled hands, from *Gemara* to *piyut*, from *Tanach* to *Chasidut*. All this was used to create a precious blend of *lamdanut*, *darshanut*, and *hashkafah*.

Furthermore, the Rav was inspiring as a *darshan*. Familiar stories of *Tanach* were reexamined from a deeper, more meaningful perspective. Attention was placed on detail, nuances were treated with delicate sensitivity. A story would spring to life of profound insight and relevant impact.

However, the Rav was more than a brilliant orator and an insightful *darshan*. As *mori ve-rabi* Rav Lichtenstein mentioned, the Rav was a poet as well. This, of course, does not mean that the Rav wrote verse or rhyme. Nor does it mean that he spoke with rhythmic beat. Wordsworth in his *"Preface to Lyrical Ballads"* wrote:

> What is a poet?... He is a man speaking to men, a man endowed with more lively sensibility, more enthusiasm and tenderness, who has a greater knowledge of human nature and a more comprehensive soul than are supposed to be common among

> mankind…. He has acquired greater readiness and power in expressing what he thinks and feels….

John Stuart Mill wrote:

> The object of poetry is confessedly to act upon the emotions; and therein is poetry sufficiently distinguished from what Wordsworth affirms to be its logical opposite, namely not prose but…science. The one addresses itself to the belief, the other to the feelings. The one does its work by convincing or persuading, the other by moving…. The truth of poetry is to paint the human soul truly…. What (great poets) know has come by observation of themselves. They have found within them one highly delicate and sensitive specimen of human nature on which the laws of emotion are written in large characters such as can be read off without much study.

Put simply, the poet has a greater perception of his own nature, and therefore, of human nature. This is coupled with the gift of expression, so that through the descriptions of the poet, the reader or audience becomes attuned to his or their own inward reality and experiences.

The Rav had the ability of describing religious and human feelings so expressively that the audience could relate, and to a certain extent, join, in the experience. The infinite remoteness of a transcendent God, the majestic triumph of humanistic creativity, the profound loss of the mourner, the overwhelming self-hate of the sinner, the loving caress of a caring God, are just a few experiences the Rav brought to life. People in the lecture were genuinely moved. They had heard more than a *shiur*, participated in more than a lecture; they had undergone a religious experience.

Allow me to attempt to express my childhood memories of the Rav. I can still vividly recall my father taking me to my first lecture over 20 years ago. Before the *shiur* there was a tremendous excitement; the air was pregnant with expectancy. There was no time to socialize. Everyone was driven by a sense of urgency and tension waiting for the Rav to begin. For me, a young child, it was like being brought to the *beis hamikdash* for the first time. Seeing the Rav was like catching a glimpse of the *kohein gadol.*

After the *shiur*, with problems solved and new insights attained, there was an elevated mood. People slowly began to filter out, many absorbed in discussion, some just chatting good-naturedly with friends. The atmosphere emitted a warm satisfaction, a special glow generated by holiness and sanctity.

Through his lectures, the Rav directly affected thousands. There is no possible way to estimate the number of people he indirectly influenced. His towering presence and unquestionable authority affected an entire community. He was more than a *rebbe*, he was a *manhig*. His bold stand on *Medinat Yisrael*, his outspoken opinions regarding secular studies, turned an entire community towards him for leadership and direction. Through him, the entire movement was given legitimacy; in him, they found security.

Chol haMoed, Erev Shabbat, "the day it was heard," I was overcome by an emotion that surprised me. I had not seen the Rav for over ten years and even when I was in his *shiur*, my contact with him was not on a personal level. I cannot say that I was surprised. Nevertheless, I was overcome by a sense of total lack of direction and leadership. *"Yosef einenah ve'ani ana ani ba."* I felt insecure, vulnerable. I had no idea what to do. I did not know how to continue. We had lost our beloved *manhig*, *gadol beTorah*, philosopher, orator, *darshan*, poet and leader, all fused into a single individual. The scope of the Rav's skills, the diversity of his brilliance, stuns the mind. Why was one individual so blessed by God?

If, for a moment, you pardon my audacity in attempting to analyze "the ways of the Lord," let me suggest that it was in order that the Rav should have the capabilities to succeed in the monumental task designated to him by the Creator of the Universe, namely, the continuation of the *mesorah* in post-Holocaust America. The Rav was a "messenger of the voice," a messenger sent by God at a point of crisis in Jewish history. His role was to further Jewish destiny. As such he was endowed with the talents and qualities necessary to fulfill that role. The Rav helped create a community devoted to Torah values and committed to halakhic norms. He established respect for, and kindled interest in, Talmud Torah. He picked up the gauntlet thrown to Judaism by modernity, and dueled brilliantly and valiantly so that today we can live comfortably as Orthodox Jews in the modern world. For this he had to be both *lamdan* and philosopher. He had to develop a message, and he needed the equipment to transmit that message to the masses. The Rav was a "messenger of the voice," and the strong messenger fulfills his duty.

In conclusion, I would like to quote selectively from a lecture the Rav delivered in 1973 in which he discussed the concept of "Messengers of the Voice" in the specific context of Mordechai and Esther.

> Who actually are these "messengers of the voice," those individuals whom God has chosen to implement His will and to act as his representative?.... Who are they?... Who are these charismatic personna elected by God to be history-makers, and with whom is Jewish history made possible? From Abraham to Moses, from Moses to Isaiah, from Isaiah to Rabbi Akiva, from Rabbi Akiva to Maimonides, and from Maimonides to the Ari, and from the Ari to the Ba'al Shem Tov, etc., etc.
>
> Who were these mysterious, cryptic figures who played the role so well with determination and self-effacement, humbly and yet consistently? These figures have always intrigued me, always stimulated my curiosity.

At this point, the Rav began an analysis of the *Megillah* to establish that a unity and identity existed between Mordechai and *Am Yisroel.* He continued:

> I'm afraid to say it: Mordechai is not just an individual, Oh no, not just a single person, Oh no, he is more than that. So what was he? What is he? He was not an individual. He was the people, a nation. Isn't this almost crazy? Isn't it sheer nonsense, absurd? Can an individual turn into a people? A single person into a nation? One man into a community...? I don't know. All I know is that Judaism held the view that it is not absurd. It is possible. Not only possible, it happened many times.... Let us take a look at Moses. God tells Moses to take the Jews out of Egypt.... The Almighty stated distinctly that he was concerned with the people.... And yet, after the episode of the Golden Calf, He told Moses: *Psal lekha shnei lukhot avonim karishonim.* He addressed

himself only to Moses. The second revelation, in contrast to the first revelation, was a strictly private affair, a private rendezvous between God and Moses." "Let no man ascend the Mountain with you."

Ve'ish lo ya'aleh imkha vegam ish al yera'eh bekhol hahar. In short, the second tablets were given to Moses, not the people. How did the people receive the Torah?.... (The answer is that) Moses personified 600,000 Jews. The individual turned into a people, into a nation. Of course it is a strange metamorphosis. Of course it is a frightening equation, an individual equals a people. But it is a talmudic equation: *shakul keneged.* It is a mysterious identity, and yet *Yahadut* believes in such a possibility.... The individual becomes the abode of the millions. Individual hyphen people, single person hyphen many, lonely man hyphen community. Abraham, Isaac, Jacob, Moses, Aaron, David. They were not just individuals.... Interesting is that our sages said, "David King of Israel lives, Moses did not die, Yaacov did not die." All these individuals in whom the multitude abides, all those individuals who merged with the community will not die....

THE UNIQUENESS OF *TORAT HARAV*

RABBI SIMCHA KRAUSS

The Gemara in Bava Batra (91b) states: "On the day which *Avraham Avinu* died, all leaders of the world stood up in a row and exclaimed, 'Woe to the world that lost its leader and woe to the world that lost its captain.'"

Just a few days ago, the Jewish community experienced the loss of its leader, its captain, its *rebbe.* We knew that the Rav was sick. For the past few years he was absent from public affairs. Still, the fact that he was with us, that he lived in our world, gave us some comfort and strength, Now, alas, "the Ark of God was captured" (*Ketubot* 104a). The world without the *Rav* – like the *beit hamikdash* devoid of the ark and its tablets – is a world with less light, a world where the sun's rays do not warm us as before, a world where the sun's clarity has dimmed.

The *Gemara* quoted above states that at Avraham's funeral, "The leaders of the world stood up in a row" and eulogized Avraham Avinu. Why does the *Gemara* stress that the leaders "stood up in a row" as they lamented the death of Avraham? Does the posture in which they eulogized Avraham, sitting or standing, make a difference?

The *Gemara* in *Sanhedrin* (37a) describes the seating order in a Jewish court. Judges sat in rows of semi-circles. Further, they sat in order of seniority. The most senior judge sitting in the first seat, followed by the others. When, for example, the senior judge died, the second judge moved into his seat, followed by the others. The newest appointee would then take the last seat. In other words, when a member of *Sanhedrin* died, there was always someone who filled his place.

When Avraham Avinu died, his position of leadership, his seat, became vacant. The leaders of the world stood up and wanted to move up, with the senior leader now taking Avraham's seat. But, insists the *Gemara,* "they stood up" and remained there. They were frozen in their position and could not move forward. The realization dawned on them that nobody could take Avraham's place. Nobody could sit in Avraham's seat. Avraham's seat had to remain empty.

The sadness and gloom that permeates our consciousness is twofold. First, we have lost our *rebbe*. Second, the emptiness and the vacuum that we experience as a result of the Rav's death cannot be filled. We now must live in a world without the ark and the tablets. We must continue to live rudderless and leaderless. Because nobody can take the Rav's place. His seat, remains, alas, vacant.

It is impossible, within this context, to describe the Rav's greatness. I just want to mention, at this moment, when grief is still so painful, how the Rav influenced me personally and how his teachings shaped my life.

I grew up in the late fifties and early sixties. The American experience, unlike the European climate with which I was more familiar, was not hostile to the practice of religion. Religious affiliation, the justification of "belonging" to a particular creed, was widespread. Philosophies about the utilitarian benefits of religious beliefs were forcefully articulated by Jewish and Christian spokesmen. This popularization of religion resulted in a "civil religion," an easy-going affirmation of universal religious values that did not demand total commitment. The rigorous demands of *Yahadut*, the exactness and precision of the halakhic gesture were foreign to this relaxed atmosphere, Submission to the halakhic norm was not equated with a genuine expression of Jewish living.

Other factors in American life augured against a total commitment to a life of s*hmirat mitzvot* and *Talmud Torah*. The "melting pot" concept was a dominant cultural value in America. Orthodoxy, with its insistence on some form of *havdalah bein Yisrael le'amim*, found it difficult to articulate its message in such an atmosphere. The development of day schools (*yeshivot ketanot*), for example, so crucial for Orthodox growth, was perceived by many as "un-American."

Additionally the erstwhile *ben Torah* had to contend with the lure of America as the great land of opportunity. For someone like myself, who arrived to these shores after the Shoah, and having lived first under the brutality of a Fascist Regime and then under the tyranny of a Communist dictatorship, the freedom was exhilarating. The knowledge that one can dream of entering any university and pursue any goal was intoxicating. This, coupled with the materialism of the times, made one think very hard before committing to a life of *Talmud Torah*. The choice of Torah as a vocation was not the ideal goal for a "nice Jewish boy."

The rewards of a materialistic life were not the only competition facing a person considering *Talmud Torah* as a vocation. Religion had begun to be challenged. The scientific revolution that began with Sputnik left its mark on the intellectual discourse of the times. While Gagarin's foolish boast that he did not meet God in space was not fully accepted, Americans did become enthralled by science and technology as a result of this breakthrough.

It was in this milieu that I had the good fortune of meeting the Rav. The first time I met him was not in person. My father *zt"l* gave me a copy of *Ish ha-Halakhah* and told me that while I "may not understand this essay now" it is worthwhile and I should at least attempt to understand it. I began reading and immersing myself in this work. Although my father *zt"l* was correct about not understanding it fully, I did emerge with certain vital impressions and messages.

First, I was dazzled by the Rav's mastery of *kol haTorah kulah* as well as *kol hachokhmot kulan*. I also formed the distinct impression that my premise about the irreconcilable chasm between a *"frum"* world view and a "modern" one was wrong. Through the Rav's essay, I learned that modernity and the Jewish tradition do share a common cultural language, that they can engage in dialogue and that they can co-exist on the same page. I surmised that if these seemingly contradictory systems can be reconciled intellectually, they can also be integrated in real life. I came to the conclusion that the effort to create a bridge between these two worlds is a worthwhile endeavor, that it is an expression of authentic *Yahadus*. The very tension of straddling both worlds can lead to a richer, fuller Jewish life.

Around that time, our family moved to Washington Heights (in Upper Manhattan) and, although I never was formally a student at Yeshiva University, I began attending some of the Rav's *shiurim*.

The first *Yahrtzeit Shiur* that I attended is still vivid in my memory. The Rav was overwhelming. The breadth and depth exhibited by the Rav was dazzling. I had a feeling that the background to the *shiur* was *kol haTorah kulah*; his encyclopedic mind drew from every possible source of our vast Torah archives. Then, after two and a half hours, the Rav continued his aggadic and hashkafic philosophical interpretation of the concept and theme of the *halakhah* he had discussed earlier. I never experienced such a tour-de force in the area of learning.

The overwhelming awe of the Rav did not diminish even after I began attending his regular weekly *shiurim* at Yeshiva, as well as the *shiurim* in Moriah Synagogue. Indeed, I became exposed to the manifold, multichromatic and complex personality of the Rav. I began to feel that the study of Torah is not reserved for *batlanim* (full-time Torah scholars). I began to experience the joy of Torah, the sheer elegance of a *sevarah*, the light emanating from the Rav's methodology as he reread a Rambam. The perception came to me, slowly but surely, that I need not be apologetic for devoting myself to Torah study. The Rav made me proud of being a *ben Torah*. The words in our morning prayers, "how good is our portion, how pleasant our lot, and how beautiful our heritage" were not pietistic phrases. They expressed my profoundest emotions.

The Rambam, in the introduction to *Mishneh Torah*, says that before his death, Moshe Rabbeinu wrote thirteen *sifrei Torah*. Each of the twelve tribes received one *Sefer Torah*. The thirteenth *Sefer Torah*, guarded by the *Levi'im,* was placed in the ark for eternity. The *Sefer Torah* in the ark served as a model. When questions of authenticity arose regarding a particular *Sefer Torah*, the one in the ark, guarded by the *Levi'im,* was the standard by which every other *Sefer Torah* was measured. The Rav's *shiurim* made us feel that he was the authentic *Sefer Torah* in the ark by which all Torah learning should be measured.

As a scion of the *Beit Halevi*, one had the clear impression that this *shiur* was a *mesorah* of genuine, authentic Torah. This expressed itself in two ways, both in substance and methodology. The Rav, a great *mechadesh* himself, generally built on his father's and grandfather's foundations. The Torah of Rav Moshe Soloveitchik and Rav Hayyim of Brisk were the lodestars by which the Rav navigated. The Rav insisted that the methodology whereby *halakhah* is interpreted should not be falsified. He insisted on "the purity of the *halakhah* both in its study and understanding." He fought against those who wanted to steer and reinterpret the *halakhah* in totally new ways "unanticipated by the *talmidei chachamim* of the past." The

Rav said these words when he eulogized his uncle, the Brisker Rav *zt"l*. They perfectly described his position as well.

The Rav *zt"l* is physically not with us. Alas, "the ark of the law was captured." We are, however, somewhat consoled by the fact that a lot of his Torah is being prepared for publication. We are fortunate that his *talmidim* will continue to uncover and spread his Torah and his *hashkafah*. Thus, the *Torat haRav* will continue to brighten our ways, and that of future generations, until we will merit the coming of *Mashiach*.

HESPED MAR: A EULOGY FOR THE RAV

RABBI DR. NORMAN LAMM

"A great prince in Israel has fallen today" – II Samuel 3:38

Surely, such a prince and such a giant, who became a legend in his own lifetime, deserves an appropriate eulogy.

I therefore begin with a confession: I feel uncomfortable and totally inadequate in the role of one delivering a eulogy for my rebbe, the Rav. Only one person could possibly have done justice to this task, and that is – the Rav himself; everyone and anyone else remains a *maspid she'lo kehalakhah* – "one who eulogizes without authorization." Nevertheless, we owe it to him to try our best. And so I ask your – and his – forgiveness at the very outset.

The Rav departed from us on the exact same day that, 17 years ago, we lost Dr. Samuel Belkin *z"l*, the late President of Yeshiva University, and the Rav eulogized him from this very podium on the day that he himself would be interred, erev the last days of Pesach. He referred to him then with the words of the Hagadah, as *arami oved,* a "wandering Aramean," and paraphrased that as a "wandering Litvak," who as a youngster was forced from his native town and took the wanderer's staff to these shores all by himself.

Unlike Dr. Belkin, the Rav was not a wandering Aramean. He was not orphaned at an early age. On the contrary, he had the advantage of a stable, aristocratic home, of encouraging and even doting parents. He was heir, at birth, to a distinguished lineage – the *bet haRav,* that of R. Moshe, R. Hayyim Brisker, the *Bet Halevi,* the Netziv, back to R. Hayyim Volozhiner.

His genius was recognized while he was still in the crib. At age 6, his father had hired a melamed to come to the house to teach him. The tutor was a Lubavitcher Hasid who taught him *Tanya* without asking leave of his parents. He learned it so well, that his father was shocked and fired the *melamid.* (His affection for Habad, however, would remain with him to the end.) He then became a disciple of his own father – demanding, challenging, and critical, yet approving and proud.

At the age of 10 he presented his father with his written Torah *hiddushim.* His father was so impressed that he showed it to *his* father, R. Hayyim Brisker, who was so impressed that he sent it to his dayyan, R Simcha Zelig. And, of course, he prophesied greatness for his precocious grandson.

The Rav's development continued unimpeded, and fulfilled and exceeded the hopes of father and grandfather.

The former Chief Rabbi of Israel, Rabbi Avraham Shapira *shlita,* told me the following story to which he was a personal witness.

When the Rav came to visit Israel, the one and only time during his life, in 1935, it was the last year of the life of the elder Rav Kook. The Rav spoke at several places – at Mercaz Harav, at the Harry Fischel Institute, and at several other yeshivot. At every *sheur* that he gave, Rav Kook's son, R. Zvi Yehuda, attended and listened attentively.

When Rabbi Shapira asked R. Zvi Yehuda why he was doing so, he answered as follows: His father received Rabbi Soloveitchik and they "talked in learning." When Rabbi Soloveitchik left, the elder Rav Kook told his son that the experience of speaking with Reb Yoshe Ber Soloveitchik reminded him of his earliest years when he was a student at the Yeshiva of Volozhin, during the time that Rabbi Soloveitchik's grandfather, Reb Hayyim Soloveitchik, first started to give *sheurim.* I believe, Rav Kook said, that the power of genius of the grandfather now resides with the grandson – and therefore, he said to his son, you should not miss a single *sheur* by Reb Yoshe Ber Soloveitchik.

But if, unlike Dr. Belkin, the Rav was not a wandering Aramean, then we may say of him that he embodied another passage in the Hagadah: "Know full well that your seed shall be a stranger in a land not their own," (Gen.15:13) that Avraham's children will be strangers in another land. He was not a "wandering Aramean" but a "lonely Abrahamite," a lonely Litvak, and this loneliness was one of the most painful and enduring characteristics of his inner life. This giant who was at home in every discipline, a master of an astounding variety of branches of wisdom, familiar with almost every significant area of human intellectual creativity, felt, ultimately, like a stranger dwelling in another's land. He somehow did not fit into any of the conventional categories. His genius was such that the loneliness attendant upon it could not be avoided – a fact which caused him no end of emotional anguish, yet gave us the gift of his phenomenal, creative originality. He was both destined and condemned to greatness and its consequences.

This sense of loneliness, isolation, and differentness had a number of different sources, all of which reinforced each other. One of them was emotional and began quite early in his life. The Rav poignantly describes (in his *U'vikashtem Misham)* his early experiences of fear of the world, of social detachment, his feelings of being mocked and rejected and friendless. The only friend he had was the Rambam and, as he grew older, all the other giants of the Talmudic tradition whom he encountered in his learning. The Rav identifies this as more than imagination and fantasy but as a profound experience – the experience of the tradition of the Oral Law. Yet, the sense of social loneliness and emotional solitude was not dissipated.

Indeed, that was the way he was brought up: he was taught to hide his emotions. He was never kissed by his father. He had no real friends in his childhood or youth and no truly intimate comrades in his adulthood.

This sense of alienation was not only a psychological and social factor in the various roles the Rav played in life; it was also central to his whole conception of life. His most characteristic form of analysis in his philosophic essays and oral discourses was the setting up of typological conflicts, of theoretical antitheses: Adam I and Adam II; *Ish haHalakhah and Ish haElohim;* the covenant of fate and the covenant of destiny; majesty and humility... And, ultimately, conflict and dissonance make for alienation and loneliness.

This philosophical approach stems from two sources. One was his attempt, probably developed in his days in Berlin, to defend Judaism from the encroachments of a self-confident and aggressive natural science and equally arrogant then-modern philosophy. To counter them, he adopted the Neo-Kantian view in which there is a distinct chasm that separates the natural order of objectivity, quantification, and determinism (at least on a macro scale), from the internal human realm of the subjective, qualitative, and passionate where freedom reigns.

The second source is, I believe, the *hashkafah* of his Mitnagdic forbear, R. Hayyim Volozhiner, who saw the world and all existence as multilayered and plural, as reflected in the *Halakhah* with its multiple judgments as in the Mishnah of Ten Degrees of Sanctity, as against the Hasidic view of a monistic and unified world, one which blurred distinctions and sought to overcome contraries.

Thus, for instance, Rav Kook, strongly influenced by the Hasidic side of his lineage, saw underlying unity beyond all phenomena of fragmentation and opposition, while the Rav's view was anything but harmonistic. He saw not wholeness but conflict, chaos, and confrontation in the very warp and woof of life. Man was constantly beset by a torn soul and a shattered spirit, by painful paradoxes, bedeviled by dualities, and each day was forced to make choices, often fateful ones, in the confrontation of savage contraries, of the jarring clash of claims and counter-claims in both conception and conduct.

Both these sources – the neo-Kantian and the thought of R. Hayyim Volozhiner – see fundamental disunity and a fractionation of experience in the world.

Such a vision of contradiction and incongruity leads inexorably to anxiety and tension and restlessness, to a denial of existential comfort and spiritual security. It results in *loneliness* – the Rav truly was "The lonely man of faith" – and this philosophically articulated loneliness with its depth crises becomes enduring and especially poignant when superimposed on a natural tendency to solitude and feelings of being a stranger in a foreign land.

Yet, paradoxically, in practice he made strenuous efforts to overcome these dichotomies, to heal the wounds of the sundering of experience and even of existence itself, to achieve the unity of man with himself, with nature, with society, and with the divine Master of the Universe – even though he knew that such attempts were ultimately doomed to frustration. Hence, his efforts to bridge the worlds of emotion and reason, of *Halakhah* and *Aggadah*, of Hasidism and Mitnagdism. Perhaps the very attempt to achieve unity and wholeness reflected his penchant for peace – a goal he valued and cherished – although he knew that in reality disharmony and the pain of inexorable conflict and contradiction controlled.

Thus, for instance, in the area of Jewish thought, where his fertile mind reigned supreme, he was a stranger amongst those who worked in Jewish philosophy. For he came to it from another world-one of greatness in Torah and mastery of *Halakhah* as well as the classics of both general and Jewish philosophy; and his assumptions and aspirations and insights were derived from the *Halakhah*, rather than seeing *Halakhah* as irrelevant to Jewish philosophy. Thus, for example, the Rav's reconciliation of the differing viewpoints of Maimonides and Nahmanides as regards the obligation to pray, whether its source was rabbinic or in Torah law, became the source of his teaching on the "depth crisis" of everyday life. Amongst such Jewish thinkers, he remained a *ger*, a stranger and alien in a foreign land. The Rav was a lonely Litvak.

Similarly, he was a master *darshan* endowed with a richness of homiletic ingenuity combined with charismatic rhetorical prowess and stellar oratory – undoubtedly the greatest *darshan* of our, or even several, generations. Yet he had no peer, no companion, no friend in this area too. The kind of *derush* that even the best of them practiced was not his home, not his way. He could be as ingenious – and more so – than the cleverest of them, with a sense of timing and drama that was astounding, but his uniqueness lay in his synthesis of both *Halakhah* and Jewish thought in homiletic guise rather than the conventional *derush*. Here too he was *a ger*, and the world of the other *baalei derush* was for him "a land not their own." It was not his home.

Even in *Halakhah*, where he was our generation's undisputed master, he still was a stranger in a foreign land. Other great scholars were also gifted thinkers capable of incisive insights, but he alone – in addition to his cognitive supremacy, his dazzling halakhic definitions, and his brilliant formulations – had a broader scope by virtue of his wider knowledge and his exposure to other modes of reasoning, which helped him in his halakhic creativity, so that he was singular amongst the giants of *Halakhah* of our time. Thus, his quality as a "lonely Litvak" expressed itself as well in his defiance of convention in dress and demeanor. He simply refused to conform to standards imposed from without, whether intellectually or in the form of stylistic niceties.

How did the Rav as a "lonely man of faith" overcome these bouts of loneliness, given his conception of dialectic and conflict as inscribed in human nature and existence itself?

First of all, his early emotional and social loneliness became bearable when he found fulfillment in his domestic life. Anyone who was privileged to visit with him and the late Rebbitzen in their home in Roxbury could tell immediately that for the Rav, his home was a haven – and a heaven. Do we not recall the bitter tears he shed at his eulogy for her?

The second way, in response to his existential loneliness, was spiritual. This man whose goal was never mere peace or happiness but truth, was able to assuage his feelings of being a stranger in a foreign land by his deep and unshakable faith. The "lonely Abrahamite" knew not only the anguish of alienation inflicted upon Abraham's children, but he also knew the secret of our ancient forefather – that of "You found his heart faithful to You" (Neh. 9:8): a faithful heart, a heart of faith.

How does faith overcome the loneliness of the stranger, the alien, the *ger?* Perhaps by understanding that none is more lonely, so to speak, than the One Who Is Without Peer Himself! Man's loneliness and Israel's loneliness as "a nation which dwells alone" (Nu. 23:9) are both reflections of the divine loneliness. Even as He is One, the unsurpassably and ineffably One, so is He incomparably alone – He has no peer (Dt. 4:35); and does not such absolute and transcendent *aloneness* imply, from a human perspective, unparalleled and unimaginable *loneliness?*

The Almighty reaches out to His human creatures, seeking, as it were, the spiritual companionship of humans: the commandment of loving God can be understood by the talmudic dictum that "the Holy One, blessed be He, desires the prayers of the righteous"; and man eases his own pitiful terrestrial solitude by linking his loneliness to the majestic loneliness of the Divine. So does loneliness join loneliness, and out of this encounter is born the divine-human companionship, nourished by divine grace and human faith. Bonds of friendship are created, as man gratefully acknowledges God as "my Beloved," and God regards the lonely Abrahamite as "Abraham My Friend."

Such exultation came to the Rav during prayer. During these precious moments and hours, suffused with the purest faith, the Rav found both the truth and the peace to which he devoted his life, as his driven soul was healed and unified. Recall his moving description, in his article "Majesty and Humility" (in *Tradition,* Vol. 17 [1978], p. 33), of his experience of prayer when his late wife, o.b.m, lay dying in the hospital. Reread so many other of his famous essays where he bares his soul and reveals the depths and heights of his pure faith as expressed in prayer and the companionship of the Master of the Universe.

Here did the Rav, in his most intimate and private moments, reveal the true dimensions of his spiritual *Gestalt* by dint of his profound faith. He was no longer a stranger, no longer an alien, no longer the lonely Litvak.

Finally, he was able to abolish or at least moderate both forms of his loneliness intellectually – and that, in a paradoxical manner: He found peace and tranquility – on the battlefield of *Halakhah* during his *sheurim* here at Yeshiva! Often, the Sages speak of halakhic debate as the "give and take" of *Halakhah*, *massa umattan,* which is also the term for business. It is a negotiation in the coin of ideas. But often they speak of a rougher kind of dialogue, as halakhic contention, *esek ba-Halakhah,* which refers not to a commercial analogy, but to strife, battles, as in Gen. 26:20, "they contended with him," referring to a struggle over the wells. *That* was the Rav's kind of *sheur!* That is what I think of when I recite the daily blessing, *la'asok be'divrei Torah,* "to *engage* in the study of Torah...." Engaged in a war of wits with his own students, parrying ideas and interpretations, entering the fray between Rashi and Tosafot, between Rambam and Ramban – and Ramban with the Baal Hamaor – and trying to resolve their differences in a manner typical of the Brisker *derekh* which he inherited and then modified and perfected, he found his peace and his companionship.

Permit me to relate a story that throws light on other aspects of the Rav's character. It was my second year in his *sheur,* and I was intimidated and in awe of him as was every other *talmid* – that is, *almost* everyone else. There was one student, the youngest and one of the brightest, who was clearly the least frightened or awed. The Rav had been developing one line of thought for two or three weeks, when this talmid casually said, "But Rebbe, the *Hiddushei HaRan* says such-and-such which contradicts your whole argument." The Rav was stunned, held his head in his hands for three agonizingly long minutes while all of us were silent, then pulled out a sheaf of papers from his breast pocket, crossed out page after page, said that we should forget everything he had said, and announced that the *sheur* was over and he would see us the next day.

I learned two things from this remarkable episode. First, we were overwhelmed by his astounding intellectual honesty. With his mind, he could easily have wormed his way out of the dilemma, manipulated a text here and an argument there, maybe insulted an obstreperous student, and rescued his theory and his ego. *But the Rav did nothing of the sort!* He taught, by example, the overarching goal of all Torah study as the search for Truth. That search for Truth was of the essence of his activity in Torah, and we witnessed it in action. He encouraged independent thinking by his pupils as a way to ensure his own search for the truth of Torah. The Rav was authoritative, but not authoritarian. No "*musar shmuess*" – no lecture in ethics – could have so successfully inculcated in us respect for the truth at all costs.

The second lesson came with the anti-climax to the story. The very next day, it was a Wednesday, the Rav walked into class with a broad, happy grin on his face, held out his copy of the *Hiddushei HaRan*, and said to the talmid, "Here – now read it *correctly*!" The Rav had been right all along….

What we learned was a secret of his greatness and success as a teacher, namely, his attention to preparation. I always thought that there was a vast difference between his formal, public *derashot* and his *sheurim* in class. The former were finished, polished, conceptually and oratorically complete products, a joy to behold, each of them a marvel of architectonics. The *sheurim* he gave in class were of an altogether different genre. They were dynamic and stormy, as he formulated ideas, experimenting with a variety of arguments, testing, advocating and discarding, proving and disproving, as he brought us into his circle of creativity and forced us to think as he thinks and thus learn his methodology in practice. A *sheur* by the Rav was always a no-holds-barred contest, a halakhic free-for-all, an open-ended process instead of a predetermined lecture.

Well, this incident proved otherwise. The Rav actually pulled out of his breast pocket his hand-written notes for this *sheur!* We were confounded: It was all prepared in advance! Yet his greatness was that, on the one hand he prepared assiduously for every *sheur,* leaving as little as possible to chance. On the other hand, despite this thorough preparation, the *sheur* indeed was open-ended, because he listened carefully to any serious challenge by even the youngest of his students and was ready to concede an error. *And all through this, so successful was he in engaging us in the act of creation, that we never realized that he had thought it all out ahead of time!* Attending his class, I always felt, was like being present at the moment of genesis, like witnessing the act of Creation in all its raw and primordial drama, as conceptual galaxies emerged from the chaos of objections and difficulties, as mountains collided and separated, "as He uprooted mountains and crushed them together" (as the Talmudic phrase has it), until, finally, a clear and pellucid light shone upon us, bringing forth new and exciting worlds. He combined preparation and openness, determination and freedom, the fixed and the fluid. What a master pedagogue!

So awesome was his performance as both a thinker and teacher, that emerging from an encounter with the Rav, whether publicly or privately, in a class or in an article, in *Halakhah* or in Jewish thought, it was impossible to avoid feelings of grave inadequacy, a vast inferiority. Each of us would think: How could I ever attain such depths, such heights of content or style, of thought or language? In students, that usually resulted in hero-worship; in colleagues and contemporaries – it often eventuated in envy and even enmity.

It is a measure of the Rav's character that he was not spoiled by our adulation, and he ignored the slurs against him; never, publicly or privately, did he mention them. Giants pay no attention to such slings and arrows.

Whenever I think back to the Rav as a *maggid sheur* I recall the fascinating tale recorded in *Pirkei de'R. Eliezer (chap.* 2):

R. Eliezer comes to Jerusalem where he meets his *rebbe*, R. Yohanan b. Zakkai. The latter invites his pupil to "say Torah," and he declines, explaining that he has derived all his Torah from R. Yohanan b. Zakkai and therefore has nothing to tell *him.* But, replies R. Yohanan b. Zakkai, you can do so; indeed, you can produce new Torah thoughts, such as were beyond what was received at Sinai! Sensitive to the fact that R. Eliezer is shy about displaying originality in the presence of his teacher, R. Yohanan b. Zakkai stands outside the study hall:

> R. Eliezer sat and expounded, his face as bright as the sun, with rays of light shining forth as they had from Moses' face [after God had appeared to him]; no one knew whether it was day or night. [Finally,] R. Yohanan came up behind him and kissed him

> on his head, saying to him: "Happy are you, Abraham, Isaac, and Jacob, that such a one as this one has issued from your loins." Said Horkenos, R. Eliezer's father: "He ought not have said that, but rather: 'Happy am I that such a one has issued from my loins.'"

Similarly, the Rav's Torah was a revelation of Torah in its own right. There was something radiant about him, his vigor, his dynamism, as the original analyses and pursuit of truth and creative gestures poured forth from him in such triumphant excitement. Moreover, as a *rebbe* or teacher, he was simply unsurpassed. His gift for explanation, for elucidating a difficult concept or controversy or text, was that of sheer genius; who could compare to him? Happy are the Patriarchs of our people, happy are his father and grandfather *zikhronam liverakhah* – and happiest of all are we, we who had the good fortune to study under him. How sad I am for our younger students who did not and will never be so privileged; at best they can get only a reflection of his greatness at second hand.

What kind of person was the Rav? Despite his no-nonsense attitude while teaching he was a man of sensitivity and graciousness. It would not be a mistake to say that he was, in the best sense of the word, a gentleman. He might have been a terror in the classroom, but he was attentive and polite and accepting and warm outside the *sheur.* Above all, he possessed great kindness and he was a *baal tzedakah,* a charitable person.

He was also very vigorous. In the days of his strength, his *yemei ha'aliyah,* he never walked; he ran. It is almost as if his body was rushing to keep up with the flow of his ideas. Vigor, dynamism, vibrancy dominated his being, from his "*lomdus*" to his gait.

Above all, the Rav was a man of independence. He was a true heir of his great-great-grandfather, R. Hayyim Volozhiner, who held that in Torah study you must go after the truth no matter who stands in your way; respect no person and accept no authority but your own healthy reason. So, the Rav was his own man, and often went against the grain of accepted truths and conventional opinion. Once, after a particularly original *sheur,* a stranger who was not used to such unusual independent creativity, asked him, "But Rabbi Soloveitchik, what is your source?" He answered, "a clear and logical mind."

He was an independent thinker not only in his *Halakhah* and his philosophy but also in his communal leadership. He had great respect for some of his peers – eminent *Rabbanim and Rashei Yeshivot* of the generation – but he did not allow that respect to intimidate him. He rejected fanaticism or zealotry as well as small-mindedness, even as he deplored lack of faith. He was not afraid to be in the minority, and refused to be cowed by pressure of the majority. He was horrified by extremism and over zealousness as well as superficiality and phoniness in communal policy-making almost as much as he contemptuously dismissed them in "learning." And if he sometimes seemed to waver in setting policy or rendering a decision in communal matters, it was because he saw all sides of an argument and was loathe to offend or hurt even ideological opponents.

Thus, for instance, almost alone amongst contemporary *Gedolei Torah* (talmudic authorities), he viewed the emergence of the State of Israel as evidence of divine grace; he saw its appearance as opening a new chapter in Jewish history, one in which we enter the world stage once again. He was not afraid – despite the opinions of the majority of *Rashei Yeshiva* and his own distinguished family members – to identify with the goals and aspirations of Religious Zionism.

Perhaps the most significant area where he diverged from other Gedolim and followed an independent way was with regard to secular studies, to *Torah Umadda*. The Rav was an intellectual Colossus astride the various continents of human intellectual achievement and all forms of Jewish thought. Culturally and psychologically as well as intellectually, this made him a loner amongst the halakhic authorities of this century. How many preeminent Halakhists in the world, after all, have read Greek philosophy in Greek, and German philosophy in German, and the Vatican's document on the Jews in Latin? A Ph.D. from the University of Berlin in mathematics and especially philosophy, he took these disciplines seriously, not as an inconsequential academic flirtation or a superficial cultural ornamentation, or as a way of impressing benighted and naive American Jewish students who did not know better. There is no doubt where his priorities lay – obviously, in Torah – but he did not regard *madda* as a *de facto* compromise. The Rav believed that the great thinkers of mankind had truths to teach to all of us, truths which were not necessarily invalid or unimportant because they derived from non-sacred sources. Moreover, the language of philosophy was for him the way that the ideas and ideals of Torah can best be communicated to cultured people, it is Torah expressed universally; and he held as well that his philosophic studies helped him enormously in the formulation of halakhic ideas.

The Rav had no use for the currently popular transcendent parochialism that considers whole areas of human knowledge and creativity as outside the pale. We must guard, therefore, against any revisionism, any attempts to misinterpret the Rav's work in both worlds, akin to the distortion that has been perpetrated on the ideas of R. Samson Raphael Hirsch. The Rav was not a *lamdan* who *happened* to have and use a smattering of general culture, and he was certainly not a philosopher who *happened* to be a *talmid hakham,* a Torah scholar. He was who he was, and he was not a simple man. We must accept him on his terms, as a highly complicated, profound, and broad-minded personality, and we must be thankful for him. Certain burgeoning revisionisms may well attempt to disguise and distort the Rav's uniqueness by trivializing one or the other aspect of his rich personality and work, but they must be confronted at once. When the late R. Yehezkel Abramsky eulogized R. Hayyim Brisker, he quoted the Talmudic eulogy, "if a fire has blazed up among the cedars, what shall the hyssop do," and interpreted that as: after the giants have been taken from us, who knows what the dwarfs who follow them will do to their teachings...

The Rav was exceedingly loyal to our Yeshiva. Thus, when some 14–15 years ago we faced the threat of bankruptcy, I asked him to help rescue the Yeshiva, and he immediately accepted. At a meeting in the late Herbert Tenzer's office in 1978 he appeared at a critical meeting of our leaders and read to them his confession of gratitude to Yeshiva University. He spoke of how much Yeshiva meant to him, how it afforded him a platform, how critical it was in whatever he had attained in his life, how much it meant to his family.

It was he who gave *semikhah* to some 2,000 rabbis and thus influenced hundreds of thousands of Jews in America and throughout the world. And he graciously allowed us to name the *Semikhah* Program the Rabbi Joseph

B. Soloveitchik Center for Rabbinic Studies, because he knew it would help the Yeshiva. He was, indeed, the *ruah hayyim* of the Yeshiva.

Additionally, the Rav refused to isolate himself in an ivory tower. He sought contact with ordinary Jews – whom he *never* disdained. This practical turn of mind and interest served him well. Thus, the Rav functioned not only as a *rosh yeshiva* but also as a *rav,* as a Rabbi for ordinary Boston *baalebatim.* As such, he was in contact with the realities of American Jewish life, and as a result his halakhic decisions and communal policies were leavened by an intimate awareness of their lives and loves, their needs and limitations and aspirations their strengths and their weaknesses. His *rabbanut* in Boston was the perfect counterpoint for his life as *rosh yeshiva* in Manhattan, and protected him from making decisions that were appropriate, perhaps, for the high ideals of a yeshiva but not for *amkha,* for ordinary laymen. He dominated the ivory tower; it did not dominate him.

The Rav was deeply devoted to his family. Just as his father was *his* teacher, so did he teach his three children – and he treated his daughters the same as his son. He was fortunate to have brilliant children, illustrious sons-in-law, and gifted grandchildren; all are involved, in one way or another, in the world of Torah, many of them educated at Yeshiva and some teaching here.

But most important to us – his students and their students and the thousands who came under his or his students' influence – is what he meant to us as our *rebbe.*

Despite the austere majesty and the irrepressible dynamism of his *sheurim,* and despite the fear of coming to a class of the Rav unprepared, we intuitively knew that we had a friend – a father, an older brother – in him. We invited him to our weddings, and later to our children's weddings; and he came. We consulted him on our personal as well as rabbinic problems; and he listened and advised. We presented our halakhic inquiries; and he taught us "the way in which they shall follow," as God said to Abraham regarding his descendants.

He exerted a powerful emotional pull on his students: I know so many, each of whom secretly (and sometimes not so secretly) *knows* that he was the Rav's favorite disciple! Who knows? Perhaps all were and, then again, perhaps none were. He so profoundly affected the lives of so many of us – in the thousands – and yet he remains somewhat remote, because hardly a one *fully* encompasses all of his diverse areas of expertise, let alone the acuity of his intellect. Those who were his *talmidim* in *Halakhah* generally were not fully informed or sensitive to his thought, and those who considered themselves his disciples in philosophy hardly appreciated his genius in *Halakhah*. So, he had many students and no students.... But cannot the same be said of the Rambam – some of whose students followed his *Halakhah*, and some his philosophy, and very few, if any at all, both?

The Rav never blurred the distinctions between the roles of *Rosh Yeshiva* and *Hasidic Rebbe*. He aspired to have *talmidim,* not *Hasidim* – challenging, questioning, independent minded disciples, not fawning, accepting, unquestioning acolytes. That is why at the same time that he forced us into systematic thinking and molded our *derekh,* our methodology, he also gave us "space," insisting that we think and decide certain halakhic questions on our own. He lived his interpretation of the injunction in *Pirkei Avot* to proliferate students – literally, "set up many students" – as, "make a great effort to have your students *stand* on their own" and not be permanently tied to your apron-strings. But so great was his personal charisma that many of us ended up as both *talmidim* and *Hasidim*....

In II Kings 1 we read of the last moments in the life of the prophet Elijah as he is accompanied by his disciple Elisha. Elijah has been told that he must prepare to be swept up to Heaven in a whirlwind, and so he wishes to take leave of his talmid But three times Elisha refuses to leave his *rebbe*. Elijah casually splits the waters of the Jordan, and teacher and pupil cross the river. Elijah and Elisha continue their conversation – an important one, but not relevant to my point – and then we read: "And it came to pass as they were walking, *walking and talking,* that there appeared a chariot of fire and horses of fire which separated the two men, whereupon Elijah was swept up by a whirlwind to heaven."

I have often wondered about that last, fateful, conversation as the two walked, each to his own destiny, "walking and talking." What did they talk about, that *rebbe* and his *talmid,* during that somber but very brief period of time? How I would have wanted to be privy to that incredible conversation!

Further, I was always troubled by the peripatetic nature of that conversation, *walking and talking,* why a *walking* discussion, why not seated or standing?

In response, I put myself in Elisha's position vis-a-vis my own *rebbe*, and wonder: if I were granted but ten minutes with the Rav, both of us certain that this was the last chance to talk before the winds bore him away, what words would pass between us? I would not presume to suggest what he would say to me; but what would I say to him? What last message, last impression, would I want to leave with him?

Two things: First, I would walk with him rather than sit or stand because when walking you do not look at each other; I would be too embarrassed to do that. For I would say to him: *Rebbe*, forgive us for taking you for granted. You were so much a part of our lives, so permanent a fixture of our intellectual and spiritual experience, that we too often failed to tell you how much you meant to us, as children often neglect to let their parents know how much they love them. We were so engrossed in our own growth that we ignored your feelings. I leave you with a feeling of shame.

Second, we thank you. Our hearts overflow with gratitude to you, our master in Torah and in life itself.

There is not one of us who does not owe you an undying debt of gratitude. You inspired us; we bathed in admiration of your genius, fought to be accepted as *talmidim* in your *sheur,* and were actually proud when you took note of us – even to be singled out for rebuke for a "*krumer sevoroh*," for our intellectual sloth or slovenliness. You were our ideal, our role model, even though we all knew that our natural limitations prevented us from ever reaching your level. We thrilled at the sheer virtuosity of your creativity and the brilliance of your originality in your *sheurim* in which you forced us to join you in bold experiments to dissect *a sugyah,* understand a *makhloket Rishonim* (a halakhic dispute among early authorities), propose a solution to a puzzling Ramban, and – to be critical of you! You gave shape and direction to our lives. We knew we were in the presence of greatness, that our *rebbe* was a unique historical phenomenon. And deep down we were secretly frightened at the prospect that some day we would no longer have you with us.

What consolation can make up for our enormous loss? For now that greatness is gone, hijacked from us by history. No more for us the exquisite intellectual delight of his incomparable *sheurim,* the esthetic pleasure of discerning the artistic architectonics of his masterful *Yahrzeit derashot,* the edification of his eulogies, the wise counsel we sought from him on matters private or public.

The years of his decline have drained us of most of our tears. But with the finality of his passing, we utter a collective sigh to the very heavens, a composite sigh composed of one part of disconsolate *avelut* of an endless and bottomless sadness; one part of pity for the world, "*rachmones*" for a world now denied the privilege of the presence of the master of Torah of this generation; and one part of a promise to him that neither he nor his *derekh* nor his *hashkafah* will leave our midst or ever be forgot. And that is why I would *walk* with him, walk and talk, because sitting or standing imply an end, no future, stagnation, whereas walking implies something unfinished, a destination still beckoning, a sense of ongoing continuity. Our loyalty to the Rav and his teachings will live as long as we do, as long as our *talmidim* do, as long as this yeshiva exists; it will go on and on. Here, in this yeshiva where he presided as *rosh yeshiva* for half a century, his presence will always be palpable, his teachings will endure, and the memory of our master the Gaon, Rabbi Joseph Ber Halevi Soloveitchik, "will not cease from among us and our children forever," in the words of the book of Esther.

And finally, the sigh contains one part of love. Yes – to this scion of Litvaks for generations, those of emotional restraint who abjured any display of affection as unbecoming ostentation, to this commanding and self disciplined intellect, we express openly and unabashedly our affection and our love. And so I would conclude my "walk and talk" session with him by saying, "We loved you, *rebbe*, and if we felt inhibited and embarrassed to say it to your face, we profess it to you now. We feared you, we admired you, but we loved you as well."

How appropriate it would have been for the Rav, that living dynamo, to leave this world as Elijah did, carried off to heaven in a whirlwind.... But alas, that was not granted to him.

When R. Avraham Shapira came here a few years ago to give a *sheur* and he met the Rav for the first time, he kissed him publicly, and whispered to me, as an aside, "It's a *mitzvah* to kiss a *sefer Torah.*"

Nothing lasts forever. Even a Torah scroll does not endure forever. Sometimes, we know of a Torah scroll which was burnt, such as the one consumed together with the martyred R. Hanina ben Teradyon. At other times, a Torah scroll does not have the fortune of such a dramatic end whereupon the parchment burns but the letters fly away to their Source; in stead, it is a Torah scroll which wears out, it suffers, withering away slowly, as letter by letter is painfully wrenched away from it, until it is no more. That, because of our sins, was the bitter end to the life of our very own Torah scroll. It was the very thing he feared most, and it happened to him. In the words of Job, "that which I feared has come to pass." Alas!

But we know that even if the Torah *scroll* is gone, the Torah *teaching* of the Rav will always live on with us. I recently heard of something that happened some years ago at the Brisker Yeshiva in Jerusalem, led by Rabbi Dovid Soloveitchik, son of R. Velvele Soloveitchik *zt"l.* The details may be fuzzy, but the essential story, I am told, is true.

A very, very old, bent-over man wandered into the yeshiva one day, and sat down and began to learn by himself. Reb Dovid came over and greeted him. The old man asked, "Is this the Hebron Yeshiva?" No, answered Reb Dovid, this is the Brisker Yeshiva. At which the old man opened his eyes wide and, in disbelief, asked, *"Reb Hayyim lebt noch,* is then Reb Hayyim still alive?"

It transpired that the old man had studied in Brisk when Reb Hayyim was still alive, and left in 1913. Caught up in the Russian Communist Revolution, he was exiled to a remote area in Georgia, completely cut off from any contact with fellow Jews, especially those from Lithuania. He continued his studies for some 75 years all by himself until the great Soviet emigrations to Israel began. He had just arrived, and that is why, upon encountering the Brisker Yeshiva, he thought that Reb Hayyim was still alive....

And, indeed, Reb Hayyim still lives....

And we are here to testify and promise that *"moreinu verabbenu R. Yoshe Ber lebt noch,"* our *Rebbe* still lives, and always will, in our midst!

I read someplace that the Gaon of Vilna said that in the World of Truth they await the coming of a *talmid hakham,* who is accompanied to the Heavenly study hall in *Gan Eden,* so that he can deliver a *sheur* and expound his best *hiddushim.* He is given 180 days to prepare this public *derashah.*

Farewell, *Rebbe!* You always prepared for us, well and meticulously, and you no doubt will do the same now. And when you give your *sheur, your derashah,* before the Heavenly Court, with all the great *Gedolei Torah* of the ages in attendance, those who were your closest companions and comrades during the years of your lonely sojourn, remember us – Your family and your *talmidim* – even as we shall always remember you; and may your merit and the merit of your Torah and your *hiddushim* protect us and grant health of body and mind and soul, peace – peace above all! – in every way, and love of God, love of Torah, love of the people of Israel, love of others and their love of us, to all of us – your family, your disciples and their disciples, and all of this Yeshiva to which you came half a century ago, which you graced with your greatness of mind and heart, and which was your home and our home together – and in which your presence will always be palpable and from which your memory will never fade.

For you were a blessing to us in your life-time. And *zekher tzaddikim liverakhah,* your memory will be a blessing to us forever, until the coming of the Messiah, may he come speedily in our time.

THE RAV'S HUMAN QUALITIES INVOKE INDELIBLE MEMORIES

ABRAHAM LEVOVITZ

By now you may have heard any number of *hespedim* for the Rav, *zekher tzaddik livrachah.* Certainly he has been eulogized on four continents. And so it was with great reluctance that I accepted your rabbi's invitation today. But, in a way, he was right in wishing to provide you, his congregation, with a slightly different perspective than the usual accolades the Rav has received in the past *hespedim.*

For that is precisely what I intend to do here tonight. Since you already know what a giant he was in learning and in leadership, what caliber a *talmid hakham* he was, the scion of the *beit haRav*, et cetera, et cetera, I have come to give you what some may be surprised to hear: to tell you about the man, the Rav as a man among men. And I am sure you will be surprised.

In 1968, the Rav delivered a *shiur* on the first *yahrzeit* of his mother. Before he started the *shiur*, he gave a few introductory remarks that I think would be appropriate tonight:

There is a verse in *Eichah,* the book of Lamentations: "Jerusalem remembers, in the days of affliction and her anguish, all her treasures that she had from the days of old." Remember? How can she forget? Of course she remembers! Yet the Rav explained that the term *zakhor* has many semantic levels of meaning. *Zakhor Yerushalayim* here means not only to remember, but to appreciate. Jerusalem only now appreciates what she had...all her magnificent treasures which she had but failed to appreciate. After all was lost she looked back nostalgically at the *beit hamikdash*, the *kedushah*, her independence, all of which she took for granted, and felt no indebtedness. Too complacent she felt, as if God owed it to her. Only now does she appreciate what she had.

And so it is similar with human nature. The tragic feature of man is that he does not appreciate the basic values around him. Only when they are gone, in retrospect does he reflect on the loss. In a mood of nostalgia, he yearns for the irrevocable experiences of the past, which cannot be recaptured.

Chazal felt that not only Jerusalem fell into that tragic category, but that the loss of a father, mother and *rebbe* came under the same category. These are people not fully appreciated in their lifetimes, and only after their deaths do we realize their worth and the irrevocable loss we must face. Now, immersed in grief, we remember the significance and precious nature of the departed.

The *Gemara* in *Brachos* tells us that after the great Tana Rav's death, thousands of his *talmidim* were returning from his funeral and sat by the banks of a river to eat. They suddenly bewailed the fact of their loss when they came upon an elementary *she'elah* in *halakhah,* that of *zimun,* which had to be solved. They weren't able to solve the simplest of questions, and only at that point did they realize their loss. "Rav is dead and we failed to learn from him even the basic rules of *zimun*."

The Rav felt that the *Gemara* was trying to express *Chazal*'s notion of a lost opportunity. These *talmidim* were suddenly plunged into a painful realization of the loss of their teacher, not being able to learn to have him immediately there to answer any question, to be close at hand.

Whether it be a father, a mother or a teacher, *Yahadut* equates them all as being in the same category. *Chazal* felt that with Rav's *talmidim*, the example of the lost opportunity was so poignantly expressed, to be able to learn from their *rebbe* as much as possible while they were still alive. This was a human frailty, a tragedy, the nostalgic moment of painful realization, a distressing, excruciating feeling mixed with guilt, a longing for the object of love that cannot be retrieved, gone forever.

To speak of the Rav for me is a highly personal matter. It is to speak at once of a friend, a confidant, a mentor, a *rebbe*, a teacher, an advisor, a father and an instructor.

For many, the Rav's inherent shyness was interpreted as conveying a demeanor that was inaccessible, cold, remote, in a world of his own, a professor, a *rosh yeshiva.* Yet those who made the effort, putting aside their own aloofness, who tried to become close to him without ulterior motive, were rewarded with a warmth that was as surprising as it was genuine.

If a man can be measured by the legacy he leaves, and not necessarily monetarily, then surely Rabbi Joseph Soloveitchik, *zekher tzaddik livrachah,* my *rebbe*, was a giant among giants. Not only was his largesse in the form of knowledge – which he shared generously with his students and the general public – it was also a lesson in how one is to behave and live within the context of *Yahadut* and *hesed.* Compassion, gratitude and the ability to forgive are always important attributes. But to the Rav they were always primary concerns when dealing with people.

Compassion for Those in Need

Being privileged to live in Brookline, in close proximity to the Rav, allowed me to be a witness to the essence of his humanity – his unique *hesed.* His compassion for those in need superseded any other obligation or priority on his agenda. One example concerns a young man, stricken with cancer, who was in the Rav's *shiur* at Yeshiva University. One day, at the end of *shiur*, he advised the Rav that he would be leaving early each day for the following six weeks so that he could be on time for his chemotherapy treatments. Since the young man's illness was confidential, no one in the class ever guessed why the *shiur* ended early each day for the following six weeks, then, after that period, it resumed, exceeding the time allowed for that class, as was generally expected. Until this young man's life ended, the Rav continued to be a source of great comfort not only to him but to his family as well.

The Rav loved children. Every Simchat Torah night he would personally pick the children to be called up for an *aliyah.* On the day of Simchat Torah he would stand at the *bimah* and listen to every child who read the Torah and give him a personal *yasher koach.*

There was a ritual at the Maimonides *minyan.* Every Shabbos between *Minchah* and *Ma'ariv* the Rav would sit on his chair and the congregation would stand next to him, asking questions about the *sedrah* of the week. On Shabbos, while he was holding court, my grandson, who was about six years old at the time, was standing next to me and asked if he could ask the Rav a question. I replied, "Of course, go up to him and ask." Little Elie pushed his way up to the front and stood there. The Rav noticed Elie and asked him if he wanted something. Elie answered, "I would like to ask you a question." The Rav motioned to him to come closer. Elie walked over and asked, "Why does the Torah start with the letter *beis*? It should have, started with the letter *aleph*." The Rav smiled. "I will tell you," he said. "The Ten Commandments were given to the *aleph* and it starts with *anochi*, and the Torah was given to the *beis*, and it starts with *bereishis*." The Rav looked at Elie and asked him, "Do you like that answer?" Elie smiled and said, "Yes, thank you," and ran back to me, beaming, "Did you hear what the Rav said?"

To be grateful for an act of benevolence is as important as the act itself. This was a distinctive quality never lost on the Rav.

Each year, a few days after Yom Kippur, I received a letter written in the Rav's hand, thanking me for my contribution to the success of the *Yom Tov* davening at Maimonides. In his inimitable style, he signed them "Joseph Soloveitchik." No title before or after; not even a letterhead on the stationery.

Nobility and Humility

I always will cherish these notes as an example of his nobility and humility, which the Rav developed into an art form. His simplicity in dress and his aversion to all acts of reverence on his behalf were characteristic of his need to be considered as only a *melamed*, a teacher, the title he was most proud of.

To forgive an offense usually calls upon the deepest humane resources one has, because it is so difficult to understand all the components that led to the act itself, and to realize that we are all vulnerable. Many years ago, a young Jewish attorney was sentenced by a Boston judge to do community service, and a friend of his asked if he might serve in some way as a volunteer at Maimonides School rather than spend time in jail. Everyone was aghast at the suggestion except the Rav, who, without hesitation, explained that we must help this man rehabilitate himself And so he did, with the help of the student body, and the entire incident proved to be a learning experience for us all.

Forgiveness and Generosity

To forgive a stranger for an act against society is not easy, but even more perplexing is forgiving someone who has caused you personal grief.

Over the years, the Rav was treated unkindly by an individual in the Boston area who perceived him as a threat and did what he could, by word and deed, to cause him considerable anguish. This person eventually found himself in conflict with the law and discovered that the Rav, the man he tormented, was the only one in a position to help him. Setting aside any vindictive feelings that may have surfaced, the Rav proceeded to rescue him.

The Rav was, above all, a generous man, a giving person, in the financial sense of the word. On being called up to the Torah, never did he pledge a *nedavah*. He always stated the exact amount of the commitment. And he was the first to give to charitable causes that promoted Israel and *yeshivot* there.

While visiting the Rav once, I remember seeing a *meshulach* from the *Eidah haCharedis* at his door, who flashed a check at me, signed by the Rav, as if to say, "Mr. Levovitz, see, the Rav gave even more than you." This was quite true, since I was aware of this organization's activities against the appointment of Dr. Meir *zt"l* to head the Shaarei Zedek Hospital, and consequently was reluctant to donate to the *Eidah haChareidis*. I went inside and confronted the Rav. "*Rebbe*, do you know who that was?" I asked. "Yes, I'm fully aware," he replied. "*Rebbe*, do you realize that, were you to set foot on Israeli soil, he would lead a bunch of his followers with posters and yelling on the tarmac of Ben Gurion airport, 'Go home, Rabbi Soloveitchik?'" He looked at me and smiled. "Yes," he replied, "but he promised not to use the money I gave him for the posters."

The Rav saw the need to help the poor irrespective of their politics or their associations. All he could see was their need, despite possible personal ramifications.

Some of the most meaningful memories, however, were those intimate moments, when after *shul* on *motza'ei Shabbos*, while the Rav waited the extra *zman* to be able to ride home, you could catch him and ask him anything. He was relaxed, the Shabbat was over, and the burden of the week ahead was not yet hovering over him. During those wonderful, cherished moments, he would often open up, express his innermost thoughts, desires, yearnings, wishes, failures, disappointments, and you had the feeling that he was letting you into his *sanctum sanctorum*, the innermost reaches of his being, a place reserved for the select few. It was a special place where he was very exposed, tender and vulnerable. At these times, we came to love him as one would a friend, and realized his incredible aloneness in the world, and the burden he carried. At these moments, we felt privileged, just to be in his presence, to be in the aura of such honesty, greatness and humility. Once you have beheld such charisma, you realize that this is the genuine article; this is *gadlus*, there is no substitute. He was able to sit and talk to you at your level without ever making you feel small, insignificant or unimportant.

Listening and Sharing

The Rav listened, a lost art today, and I was always surprised by his responses. Never were they the stock-in-trade, perfunctory, cliched answers, but, especially on those intimate evenings, they were full of understanding, sympathy and the feeling that he, too, often experienced the same doubts, fears and anxiety we were talking about. To know that he not only listened but actually shared in the experience was comfort enough for me.

The final testimony to the Rav's legacy was the funeral itself, held at Maimonides School, on a day that could not have been more inconvenient for all concerned. It was *Chol haMoed* Pesach. Many local people were away. Many families had guests. It was *Erev Yom Tov*, a day after Shabbos. Planning to travel was nervewracking. Alternate arrangements for spending the last days of Pesach were the order of the day.

Yet with all the obstacles and fears of being stranded, thousands somehow managed to come from Florida, California, many more states, and Israel. The entire school was used. Video and sound systems were relayed into every room, the gymnasium and the library. When one area was filled, people were directed into another, in an extremely orderly manner. There was no pushing, no shoving. Common courtesy was evident everywhere. The only sounds audible besides prayers were sobs of grief. Respect was shown to those charged with organizing this massive congregation. Directions were followed without complaint or criticism. The people who came were there to show their respect and love to this man who taught them how to behave with sensitivity, civility and dignity in a world that has lost the ability to appreciate these qualities....

I have lost the most important man in my life. He really knew me and I loved him. He was everything to me: *rebbe,* teacher, mentor, advisor, and above all, yes, a friend.

Pursuit of the Truth

If I have been able to paint a slightly different picture of this man among men, of his humanity, his love, his forgiving nature, his nobility, his aristocracy, his charity, and above all, his human frailty, then I would have been successful in portraying a man whose character, insight and vision were a constant and persistent force in the challenge and pursuit of the truth.

May his life be an inspiration to us all, in a world in which the traits he held to be so dear have almost vanished. May his lesson, his true lesson, his very life, not be lost on us all.

Zekher tzadik livracha. May his memory be a blessing forever.

OUR REBBE: A SERMON OF TRIBUTE TO RABBI JOSEPH B. SOLOVEITCHIK

Rabbi Dr. Haskel Lookstein

According to the Talmud (*Niddah* 30 b) we are all under oath. The oath was administered to us prenatally. Commenting on a verse in Isaiah (45:23), "For before me every knee must bend and every tongue must pledge," the Talmud says that just a moment before birth an angel administers the following oath to each of us: "Be righteous and do not be wicked. And even if the whole world tells you that you are righteous you should consider yourself to be wicked in your own eyes."

This oath does not predestine us for a particular kind of life. Rather, according to our revered teacher, Rabbi Joseph B. Soloveitchik, of blessed memory, it gives us a double mission: first, to be righteous and not wicked; and second, never to feel that we are righteous.

The Rav, in a book of essays published in translation in 1987 (*Yemei Zikaron*), states that this oath, administered to the fetus just before birth, renders all of us as *sh'lichim* – agents of God. We all have a task to perform in this world. Just as Moshe Rabbeinu was given a mission – to take the Jews out of Egypt – so each of us has a mission. Each of us is a *shaliach* of God in the carrying on of our lives.

That is why we were born now. God knows our *sh'lichut* (our mission), our ability to carry it out, and the conditions necessary for its fulfillment. He waited until the time and circumstances were just right before allowing us to be born. Now is our time.

The sainted Chief Rabbi of Palestine, the late Rabbi Abraham Isaac HaKohain Kook, used this idea to explain a little understood prayer which we say five times on Yom Kippur at the conclusion of each *amidah*. "O God: Before I was born I wasn't worthy [i.e., I wasn't ready to fulfill my mission] but now that I have been born it is as if I hadn't been born yet [i.e., I have not fulfilled the mission assigned to me]."

Rabbi Soloveitchik goes on to explain that a *sh'lichut* from God, as opposed to a mission assigned to a person by another human being, is never fully understood. We never quite know what our mission is in life and, therefore, we have to do the very best we can in every situation assuming that there is a connection between each situation and the mission that God has assigned for us.

Despite the essentially unknowable character of our mission, we might nevertheless ask what was the *sh'lichut* that God assigned to Rabbi Soloveitchik? Perhaps the best indication of what it might be is contained in a question and answer that the Rav used to like to pose: "You ask me what I am? *Ich bin a melamed* – I am a *melamed,* a teacher." I learn and I teach students, all kinds of students: adults and children, men and women, family, community, *yeshiva talmidim*, and all kinds of people. That is the way the Rav saw himself. Even when be lectured in *halakhah* and in *aggadah* for four to five hours to a Lamport Auditorium in Yeshiva University packed with more than 2,000 listeners, he was essentially a *melamed*: an extraordinarily gifted, learned, talented, eloquent, powerful, charismatic *melamed.*

II

Where did this *shali'ach* come from? He came from the House of Brisk (Brest Litovsk). His father was Rabbi Moshe Soloveitchik; his grandfather, Rabbi Hayyim Brisker Soloveitchik; his great-grandfather, the *Bais HaLevi* – whose name the Rav bore – and the scion of the family was Reb Chaim Volozhiner, the peerless student of the Gaon Eliyahu of Vilna.

From this extraordinary matrix of great scholars, Rabbi Soloveitchik inherited a tradition of brilliant, precise, meticulous scholarship in Torah. He was his father's student, learning day and night with Reb Moshe. He never went to school except for a very brief period at a very young age. After a matter of months, his parents pulled him out of the school because they were dissatisfied with it. His father then set about giving the young Rabbi Joseph Dov everything that he had in him, the entire Torah of the House of Brisk. In 1932, when the Rav was about to come to America, Reb Moshe boasted about his son to my father and to others in the following words: "My son can learn ten thousand times better than I – but I was his *rebbe.*"

From his father, Rabbi Soloveitchik received something other than great Torah scholarship; he gained a tolerance for the views of others and a love for Zionism. Reb Moshe Soloveitchik taught in the Tachkamoni School in Warsaw, a school that was modern by the standards of that day and in which secular education was also provided to the students, something which would have been anathema to Reb Moshe's brother, Reb Velvel Soloveitchik, the Brisker Rav.

Some of the tolerance and modernity came to the Rav (and perhaps also to the Rav's father) from the Rebbetzin Pesha Soloveitchik. She was the daughter of Rabbi Elya Pruzhiner, who was a great *talmid hakham* but who also gave his daughters a broad education, informal though that education might have been. The Rav's mother was extraordinarily pious, punctilious about the observance of *halakhah*, careful even about such esoteric laws as *chadash*. But she was also a widely-read person in world literature. When asked once by a grandson if she had read one of Tolstoy's novels, she looked at him with a combination of disbelief and insult at the thought that her grandson might have entertained a doubt about her having read a Tolstoy novel.

When the Rav was twenty-two, his mother and father sent him to his first school to receive the only formal academic degree he ever earned. The school was the University of Berlin and the degree was a Ph.D in philosophy, specializing in the Neo-Kantian school with a dissertation on epistemology and metaphysics. The elder Soloveitchiks provided the Rav with tutors to prepare him to enter the University. During his tenure of approximately seven years in Berlin, the Rav and his father wrote constantly back and forth in intricate discussions of Torah [Ed.: see the recently published *Igrot HaGrid*].

With an understanding of his background, and the intellectual and educational context in which the Rav was formed, we can now attempt to understand his *sh'lichut* as a *melamed* – a teacher and a *rebbe*. We should understand, however, that his mission as a teacher began not with students in general, but with his own family for which he was not only the father but also the Rav. His children and his children-in-law were his prime students just as he himself was the prize student of his father.

Atarah and Yitzchak Twersky, Tovah and Aharon Lichtenstein, and Haym Soloveitchik all learned at the foot of a loving but demanding father and father-in-law. To see the two sons-in-law sitting *shiv'ah* with their jackets ripped on the left side was to gain a glimpse of the role of the Rav as father and *rebbe* to all of his children and, for that matter, to his grandchildren and his nieces and nephews. Moreover, it must be emphasized that the Rav's education was given equally to the women of the family as well as to the men. If Atarah Twersky is today teaching Talmud in a Boston institute of Jewish study for women, she is carrying on a tradition in which her father fervently believed: the same education for men and women, the same high standards and the same high expectations for both sexes.

What did the Rav teach his family and all of his other students? In short, what were the elements of his *sh'lichut* as a *melamed*?

III

He taught us all rigor and organization, depth and breadth in all fields of knowledge. His mind was well organized as it was breathtakingly deep and broad. He used to end every *shiur* with the same question: "*Vos haben mir g'lerent* – what have we learned today?" "He would then cite the major principles of a two-hour *shiur* – "We have learned one, two, and three." His students would sit there, having been overwhelmed by the erudition and analysis of this man, and having stenographically copied down every word they could in the hopes of being able to understand it fully, only to later realize at the end of the *shiur* that there were actually three or four major points that were made. Suddenly the mass of information and analytic thought was clear and obvious even to the average student.

Moreover, the Rav used to do this no matter how long the lesson was. In a *yahrzeit shiur*, conducted annually on the anniversary of his father's death, when the lecture could last anywhere from four to five hours, he would always begin with a series of questions. He would raise the first question and then review it. He would then raise the second question and review questions one and two. He would then develop a third question and then review questions one, two and three. By the time he was finished with the questions he might have six or seven questions and he would have reviewed every single one of them in a summary at the end of the development of each. He would then go on to develop one principle which would answer the seven questions and the process would then repeat itself. He would look out at the listeners and say: "What did we ask? We asked, first (and then he would proceed to show how his principle answered the first question), and then we asked, second," and so on until the conclusion of the analysis.

He was not beyond being a bit playful in his summarizing of a lesson. Often he would look at the perplexed students before him and ask at the conclusion of a *shiur*: "You understand me well?" and we would of course all nod affirmatively. He would then turn to a student and with a smile on his face, he would say: "Repeat it!" while the student would look for the nearest trap door through which to disappear. The student was not alone; he was just the Rav's playful victim.

IV

In addition to rigor, organization, depth and breadth, the Rav illustrated the principle that everyone was entitled to the best education in all fields. This education was to be provided to both genders and it was to be found not only in Torah but also in the major disciplines of western civilization. When the Rav founded the Maimonides School in Boston in 1937, he established it as a co-educational institution which it remains to this very day. He gave the best education in all spheres. The school is sometimes thought of as a prep school for Harvard. When a graduate of Ramaz, 32 years ago, was contemplating a choice of college, having been accepted in every fine school of higher learning from Columbia to Yeshiva University, and including Harvard, his grandfather suggested that he consult with the Rav. The Rav looked at the young man and said: 'What's the question? I sent Haym to Harvard." The best for everybody.

He expected his students at Yeshiva University to be steeped in Torah and comfortable in existentialist thought. He wanted them to be at home with Rudolph Otto's *"The Idea of the Holy"* as well as with the concept of *kedushah* in Nachmanides; to be comfortable with Immanuel Kant's categorical imperative and with the principle of *mitzvah* as defined by Maimonides; to be familiar with both *E-l nistater* and with *Deus absconditus, E-l nigleh* and *Deus revalatus.*

The Rav was a great intellectual, with an abiding respect for all knowledge and with a commitment to the principle set forth by Maimonides in his commentary on the Mishnah: *kabbeil et ha'emet mimi she'amarah* – accept the truth from whomever it comes. He was even known to be an avid reader of the most worthwhile books on The New York Times' bestseller list, perusing them while on the train to and from Boston in the years before shuttle flights made the trip much shorter.

We have, then, two principles of his *shlichut:* 1) rigor and organization, depth and breadth of knowledge; 2) the best education for everybody. This brings us to the third principle which he not only taught but which he modeled magnificently: absolute integrity in the presentation of knowledge. An oft-repeated story provides one illustration of this quality. Many years ago he came into the *shiur* on Wednesday, after having presented a very involved analysis the day before, and asked his students: "Did you understand yesterday's *shiur*? Did it all make sense?" When they all nodded their heads, he is supposed to have said: "I could fool all of you all of the time. The analysis was all flawed. It was wrong. I only realized it later when I got home. Let us relearn the entire subject."

That was hearsay for me, though it was in character with the man. There is another example, however, which I saw with my own eyes at least three times in four years of *shiurim*; on one occasion I was even personally involved. The Rav built up a magnificent analytic structure in explaining a subject in the Talmud and commentaries. Toward the end of the analysis a student noticed a discrepancy, a conflict between what the Rav was teaching and what we had learned several months earlier. The student gently raised the question by asking: "*Rebbe*, how does this fit with the analysis that we developed some months ago on a similar subject?" The Rav's eyes opened widely and he said to the embarrassed student: "You are right, I am wrong. Do you hear students? He is correct; I am incorrect. I'll have to go home and relearn the entire subject and present it again tomorrow."

Nobody who witnessed this kind of absolute integrity will ever forget it. It would have been so easy for this master of Talmudic learning to have shouted down an inexperienced student. It would have been easy, but it wouldn't have been Rav Soloveitchik. His standards of honesty were uncompromising and he did not find it difficult to admit error in the face of an intellectual challenge by a student a generation removed from him and eons behind him in intellectual gifts.

V

Rigor and organization, the best education for everybody, absolute integrity, and now to a fourth quality – his humanity.

Most of the Rav's students did not quite appreciate the warm and loveable human being he was. He was not easy to get close to, but that was not his doing; it was ours. He appeared to us as so great, brilliant and learned that he was intimidating; but if one made the first move, the Rav was there, gentle, concerned, very accessible, and in a way, loving. He was almost happy to be approached. In his own way, I believe he was shy, but he responded very warmly.

He used to write Rosh Hashanah notes by hand to all of his children and grandchildren. He didn't simply send a card with a signature. Until he was not able to hold the pen anymore, he wrote personal notes. He was extraordinarily attached to his family and made time for them. This included generations of nieces and nephews and their children. In turn, he was not only respected but greatly loved. As his brother, Rabbi Ahron Soloveichik, declared at the funeral service, he was heroically cared for by his daughter Atarah and his son-in-law Rabbi Yitzchak Twersky.

He gave us – his students – signals of his humanity in some of his playful words and expressions. Not too many years ago, when a former student of his was driving him home from a wedding, and doing what all of us used to do when we would get the Rav in a car – ask him all kinds of questions – the Rav listened patiently to a series of questions which were all begun with the words "What does the Rav think about...." Finally, with a playful smile, he responded: "I'll tell you what the Rav thinks; the Rav thinks you should keep both of your eyes on the road."

Perhaps more revealing of his human side was something which happened at a *shiur* almost 40 years ago. Mr. Joseph Ellenberg opened the door in the middle of the Rav's *shiur* and popped his head in. The Rav turned in the direction of the door and Mr. Ellenberg, said: "There is no reservation for you (it was his responsibility to check on the Rav's plane reservations back to Boston). The Rav asked "What name did you ask for?" Mr. Ellenberg responded, "I asked for Rabbi Joseph B. Soloveitchik." The Rav laughed and said "I never make reservations in that name. Nobody knows how to spell it. Just ask them if there is a reservation for Joe Solo!" Whereupon the class erupted in laughter, with the Rav leading the way, and we all saw a human side to this extraordinary great man and scholar.

Another aspect of the Rav's humanity was his compassion and *hesed.* He was a *ba'al tzedakah*, personally generous to a variety of causes and individuals. He was generous with his time to people who needed him, giving advice in times of crisis and comfort in times of tragedy. He gave himself fully to the sustenance and enhancement of the Maimonides School without benefiting personally in any way.

An example of his *hesed* was illustrated in the case of a graduating senior in the early years of the school, who was accepted into Radcliffe. She came from a home of very modest means in which the expectation was that when she would be graduated from high school she would go to work to support herself and help support the family.

When the Rav heard of this he called in the parents and told them, kindly but firmly, that she must go to college; she must go to Radcliffe and he would make sure that this choice was available to her, and it was.

His approach to *p'sak* – decision making in matters of Jewish Law – further demonstrated his kindness and compassion. He told us when we studied *Yorah Dayeh* with him that it was not a Rav's job when presented with a question in *kashrut* to declare *treif*, throw out the dishes, or something of that nature. He told us that our role as students of Jewish Law was to search for opinions which we could somehow combine in order to come out with a decision which would spare people losses and hardship.

On one occasion I heard a lecture from a prominent *rosh yeshiva* who *paskened* that a pregnant woman whose amniocentesis showed that the fetus was afflicted with Tay Sachs was not permitted an abortion. The scholar was so emphatic about it that he felt that testing for Tay Sachs was not even indicated because if found, there was nothing which could be done anyway. I happened to be having dinner with the Rav in the home of a member of his family that evening and asked his opinion. He answered immediately: "A Tay Sachs fetus can be aborted up to the sixth month." I must have raised my eyebrows evincing some surprise. The Rav said very calmly to me: "Have you ever seen a Tay Sachs baby?" I replied that I had not. He said: "I have. We have a Tay Sachs baby in Boston. I tell you that an abortion is permitted through the sixth month." It was quite clear to me that human values informed this decision of the Rav. (A similar halakhic judgement is found in the writings of the *Tzitz Eliezer*.)

VI

Finally, in addition to teaching us rigor and organization, the value of the best education for all, the importance of absolute integrity and the qualities of humanity and compassion, Rav Soloveitchik's *sh'lichut* manifested itself in his ideological and practical centrism. He was the antithesis of extremism in religion and in politics.

The Rav was tolerant of those with whom he did not agree. He had friends in other movements of Judaism. One such friend was a Conservative Rabbi in Boston, Rabbi Shubow.

He had many *minhagim* and *piskei halakhah* in which he fervently believed, but which he did not force upon his students. On the contrary, he zealously guarded the student's *minhag*. I recall when we discussed *kiddush* on Friday night, and it was clear from the Rav's analysis that after the conclusion of the first paragraph, and beginning with the blessing over the wine, one should sit for *kiddush*. Innocently, I asked, "So, what should we do? Should we sit for *kiddush*?" He looked at me with astonishment and answered: "You should do what your father does!" This was part of his understanding of a wide range of religious possibilities and expressions.

On another occasion he was even more pointed in his avoidance of extremism. Thirty-five years ago, I had heard him explain in his *shiur* that the lenient *p'sak* of the Rama applied to elevators on the Sabbath: the prohibition is a rabbinic one; above the fifth floor it is considered *I efshar be'ofen acher* (unreasonable to do it by climbing stairs); and if the purpose is to perform one of the *mitzvot* of *Shabbat* (eating, sleeping, studying, visiting the sick, etc.) then asking a non-Jew to operate the elevator would be permissible *ab initio.* About ten years ago, I came to him to ask whether he still held the view with regard to modern, self-operating elevators. He looked at me quizzically and said: "Chatzkel, what did your father do?" I answered that my father asked a non-Jew to push the button so that he could go up to the eleventh floor. He responded to me with astonishment: "So why should you be more religious than your father?" I, of course, protested that I was not trying to do that at all but that I merely wanted to know whether his view had remained the same after thirty-five years. He assured me that his *p'sak* on the elevator did not change. But the lesson was one which I can never forget.

It may have been in that same conversation that he asked me as our meeting was ending, "Chatzkel, how is Ramaz doing?" I said, "fine, thank God." He asked – as only the founder of a school who cared about it himself would – "How is your enrollment? Do you have more applicants than you have spaces?" I answered that thank God we did. He said: "That's because you haven't changed." I asked him: "*Rebbe*, what do you mean?" He replied: "You haven't pulled to the right. Don't let them pull you to the right."

The Rav's centrism and moderation were evident also in his politics. He was passionate about the State of Israel but extremely concerned about the tendency to make political decisions on the basis of messianic expectations. He saw the State of Israel as an opportunity to be seized and appreciated, as he wrote most eloquently in *Kol Dodi Dofek*. Many of us, however, recall his *t'shuvah shiur* at the YMHA in New York in September of 1967, when he cautioned us about the euphoria which followed the Six Day War, and the tendency of *rabbanim* of all stripes to give halakhic opinions on the prohibition or permissibility of returning any land to the Arabs. The Rav, in a striking aside, assured the thousands who packed the Y Auditorium that he knew very well what *kedushat eretz Yisrael* was and understood clearly the differences between the *kedushah* which the land had intrinsically from the time of Abraham, and what was gained in the time of Joshua and the later period of Ezra. He said, however, that there is a *kedushah* which is higher than the *kedushah* of the Land of Israel and that is the *kedushah* of the People of Israel. He firmly recommended that the decision on returning or not returning land should be based essentially on what will safeguard the lives of the 2.5 million Jews who were living in Israel at that time.

Rabbi Soloveitchik was prepared to deal with the world and to meet the varied challenges of life. One of his most illustrious students describes his saying once that there really ought to be a Fourteenth Article of Faith, "I believe that the Torah is applicable to all ages and to all people."

VII

These are some of the salient elements in the *shlichut* of Rabbi Joseph B. Soloveitchik, of blessed memory. They are among the most profound lessons which the Rav taught as a messenger of God to his family, to his students, and to this generation which was blessed by his presence.

He taught powerfully by words, but equally magnificently by example. He was a majestic *melamed* – riveting, mesmerizing, almost hypnotic in his presentations. One could sit and listen to him for hours and barely realize the passing of time. And to have the privilege of watching him in informal moments, or to sit with him at a dinner table in a family home, was to absorb lessons in humanity, compassion, integrity and, yes, nobility that are beyond measurement.

In his essay on *sh'lichut*, the Rav wrote that *sh'lichut* from God is endless and while the *sh'lichut* would like to go on and continue indefinitely this is not possible for a human being. Moshe Rabbeinu pleaded with God to be allowed to continue and God answered him: "I tell you.... Generations will accept your mission upon themselves and they will fulfill the tradition until the end of time. Now, Moshe, your request: 'May I cross (the Jordan) and see the Land' has no significance whatsoever. You see full well that a human being can never completely fulfill his mission in this world and, therefore, it is incumbent upon you to give up your soul immediately...." "And Moshe died there, the servant of God, by the mouth of God."

Our Rebbe's life as a *shali'ach* ended on the fourth night of Pesach. It is our task to take upon ourselves his *shlichut* and fulfill his tradition until the *yom acharon* – the end of time.

MEMORIES OF A SPIRITUAL GIANT

RABBI DR. ISRAEL MILLER *z"l*

On Friday morning, April 9, the second day of *Chol haMoed* Pesach, I stood in the room in Brookline, Massachusetts where the soul of the Rav *zt"l* had been called On High, and recited *Tehillim* beside his *tallit*-shrouded body. "But his delight is in God's Torah and in this Torah doth he meditate day and night." My mind wandered back 52 years to the Friday night, when I sat beside the tearful Rav in the Soloveitchik apartment on Fort Washington Avenue in Washington Heights at the *aron* of his father, our *rebbe*, R. Moshe *zt"l*, and chanted those self-same applicable words of the Psalmist. I was one of the yeshiva students who volunteered for *shmirah* then, as the Rav's students and admirers volunteered to fill the hours before our *rebbe*, R. Yoshe Ber, was laid to rest beside his beloved life companion.

Fifty years of consecrated memories of a spiritual giant, who influenced the course of Jewish life through his philosophy, his genius, his insights, his learning, his teachings, and above all, through his students. He prided himself upon being a *melamed*. "But what is so bad about being a *melamed*?" he asked, "We speak of God as being a *melamed* when each morning we recite the *brachah*, *Baruch atah Hashem, hamelamed Torah le'amo Yisroel.*"

And what a *melamed* he was! His *drashot* were not only memorable and stimulating because of his gifted oratory, or masterly use of language, or originality of message. They were profound and inspiring learning experiences for the hundreds who crowded into Lamport Auditorium to hear him. He could explain the most difficult thoughts so that even a neophyte could grasp their meaning.

In addition to my other duties, Dr. Belkin *zt"l* asked me to administer the Yeshiva program for half a year before Rabbi Charlop was chosen as dean. I recall trying to place a newly-arrived young student in a proper first year *shiur* and the student's words of protest. He insisted on being in the Rav's *shiur*, saying that he had heard the Rav and could follow his train of thought and understand him. I responded that he could aspire to enter the

Rav's *shiur* someday in the future, and he would then appreciate the analysis and intricacies of what he now considered simple concepts. When that day came, the young man expressed his gratitude.

The Rav's memory and recall were fabulous. In the sixties, I escorted him to a personal meeting with Rav Unterman *zt"l* who was visiting New York after being chosen as Israel's Ashkenazi Chief Rabbi. As we entered the room, the Rav told Rav Unterman that they had met before when Rav Unterman had come to Brisk to see Rav Hayyim *zt"l*, the Rav's grandfather. The Rav proceeded to repeat, to the Chief Rabbi's amazement, the *dvar Torah* which Rav Unterman had spoken to Rav Hayyim more than 50 years ago. But even with his uncanny memory, he meticulously wrote his lengthy major *drashot* – a lesson in itself for each of us.

He took pride in his role at Yeshiva, and in the school he and his Rebbetzin had created in Boston. For though he was internationally prominent, he was most at home in the atmosphere of learning and study. Aware of his insistence upon excellence, I hesitatingly accepted the Rebbitzin's invitation many years ago to deliver the High School Commencement Address at Maimonides in Brookline. I asked the Rav whether there was any message he wanted me to stress. He smiled and said, "I rely upon you for the message, but I will give you two 'do nots': do not speak to me and do not speak about me." I hope I am not disobeying him when I speak now and say, "Thank you *rebbe* – for everything. Please forgive us if we speak about you; it helps us bear our grief."

THE RAV IN PERSPECTIVE

Rabbi Yisroel Miller

We say of a Jew who passed away that he was *niftar*, which means "he left, went off." That word is short for the expression *niftar l'olamo*, "He went off, to his world." He left this world, which does not belong to us, we cannot take it with us; and he went off to his world, the heavenly world, the world the righteous possess, forever.

A few weeks ago, when Rav Yosef Soloveitchik *zt"l* left us, he was *niftar l'olamo,* he went off, to his world, a world that is his in a way we do not begin to comprehend. When we study Torah and we quote Rashi, for example, we do not say "Rashi wrote," or "Rashi said," in the past tense, but rather "Rashi writes, Rashi says," right now, because Rashi continues to live.

Rav Soloveitchik himself used to say how he opens the *Gemara*, and Rambam enters the room. Rambam and Rashi and Tosfos, and later commentators including Rav Soloveitchik's famous grandfather Rav Hayyim; they are all around the table, spiritual giants exploring together the depth of God's Torah; Rav Soloveitchik himself, and all of us, are privileged to listen in, and perhaps even to add a word to two of our own.

It is not for us midgets to measure which Torah giant is tallest. But everyone knows that in his mastery of *Gemara* and rabbinic literature, Rav Soloveitchik was among the very, very, top. As a master teacher, the author of brilliant *shiurim* analyzing profound ideas, with outstanding clarity and astonishing insight, many considered Rav Soloveitchik THE master, almost in a class of his own.

I have a certain view of Rav Soloveitchik, a vantage point which very few people share, and that is: If you ask, "How many students were in Rav Soloveitchik's yeshiva?" People will answer, "Over the years, there were thousands." But that is not quite correct. Because, Yeshiva University, where Rav Soloveitchik taught since the early 1940s, strictly speaking, was, not Rav Soloveitchik's yeshiva; by which I mean, he was not the boss.

The *rosh yeshiva*, the dean who set policy and actually ran the Yeshiva, was Rabbi Dr. Samuel Belkin. Even after Dr. Belkin died, and Rabbi Dr. Norman Lamm took over, Rav Soloveitchik's official position was "Professor of Talmud." And though Rav Soloveitchik towered over everyone around him, he did not push himself into areas that belonged to Drs. Belkin and Lamm.

So, how many students were there in Rav Soloveitchik's yeshiva? The answer is about fifteen. In 1940, Rav Soloveitchik founded a yeshiva for advanced students in Boston, MA. There were no secular studies, no outside distractions, just pure Torah. One of those fifteen students was a young man from Baltimore, who had just returned from the yeshiva in Slabodka, Lithuania. He moved to Boston to study under Rav Soloveitchik, and was one of the few students to remain in Boston after Rav Soloveitchik moved to New York and the yeshiva closed.

That student, who was among the very first to receive *smichah* from Rav Soloveitchik, was my father. I, growing up in Boston, in my father's home, and attending the day school founded by Rav Soloveitchik, have a certain perspective which might be worth sharing.

Rav Soloveitchik was a very private person. To speak of the man he was is to intrude on that privacy, and that is not for me to do. He was also a man of considerable controversy. That controversy is worth studying. However, as in most Torah controversies, the general rule is: Those who know the truth about it, don't talk, and those who talk about it, don't know.

What I do wish to examine is the following question: 49 years from now (whether or not *Moshiach* arrives by then), for what will Rav Soloveitchik be most remembered? Besides his greatness in Torah knowledge, and being known as a *mensch*, what was his unique contribution to *Klal Yisroel*, a contribution for which our children and grandchildren remain in debt? No one knows the future. But my guess is that in the long run, Rav Soloveitchik will be seen to have made two contributions which are unique.

The first, and most important, is that he created the awareness that one can be a Jew in the modern world. I don't mean merely that an observant Jew can be a doctor or a businessman. I mean: 150 years ago in Eastern Europe, it was widely presumed that anyone who received an intensive secular education would abandon *Yiddishkeit*. The rabbis said it was because the universities taught heresy. But many people began to suspect that the universities were teaching ideas, and that Judaism could not withstand intellectual challenge.

There is a widespread misconception some people still have. That philosophy has somehow disproved religion and that modern science surely disproves religion. It was believed that a truly educated, enlightened person, cannot have passionate faith, and surely will not observe old-fashioned rituals like *kashrus* and *mikvah*.

People today cannot imagine the ridicule of religion in educated circles two generations ago. Philosophers from Nietzche to Bertrand Russell, and most of the followers of Freud and Darwin and Marx, the one thing they agreed upon is that religious ritual, i.e., *halakhah*, is primitive. Even among rabbinical students, faith was weakened, which is why so many yeshiva boys ended up in non-Orthodox seminaries. Others felt confused or theologically insecure, and faith was a subject one avoided discussing.

Along came Rav Soloveitchik, armed with his vast Torah knowledge, and armed also with his doctorate of philosophy from a German university. An Orthodox rabbi, a *talmid chakham*, who was not only conversant with modern philosophers, but who joined their ranks with his own writings, writings which most educated readers can't even follow.

The impact was electrifying. Not that he answered questions of faith, but just by being there, Rav Soloveitchik gave people faith that there *are* answers. Is ritual observance for simpletons? Anyone who reads Rav Soloveitchik's essay, *"Ish ha-Halakhah,"* knows that this is not so. Is religious faith outmoded? Any reader of Rav Soloveitchik's essay, "*The Lonely Man of Faith*," knows that faith is more a necessity now than ever before.

But even people who did not read the essays, and who never met Rav Soloveitchik, and even some in Orthodox circles who opposed them – even for them, the fact that he existed validated a whole generation of observant Jews, and was a vital link to the continuity of Torah in the modern world.

This is no small matter. The Jewish people can debate falsehood, but you cannot debate ridicule. Over a lifetime, Rav Soloveitchik gave the emotional security to see that the Torah system is intellectually sound, spiritually inspiring, and stands proudly in the modern world, second to none. What Rav Hirsch did in Germany, Rav Soloveitchik did in the United States; and that is a *zechus*, a merit, forever.

Rav Soloveitchik's second unique contribution was that he presented Torah wisdom in a manner that could be appreciated by non-Torah people. That is unique and extremely important.

An expert in mathematics or biology or automobile repair is not necessarily an expert in human relations, or happiness, or anything outside his or her field. But Torah is different. Torah is the word of God, and someone great in Torah becomes the possessor of something we call "wisdom." I will not try to define what wisdom is, but it surely includes some understanding of the meaning of life. Do Torah giants possess wisdom? Certainly. Is some of that wisdom found in their writings? Certainly. Is that wisdom discernable to someone without a yeshiva background? Unfortunately, usually not.

A brilliant essay in a scientific journal may not be appreciated by a layman at all. And so, too, in Torah, the famous *Mirrer mashgiach* was an ethical Einstein whose writings are awesomely impressive, if you are trained in the Eastern European style of Torah ethical research.

But Rav Soloveitchik was different. He managed to adapt Torah thought to contemporary Western style so that Torah ideas could be appreciated, to some extent, by anyone. Even gentiles can read Rav Soloveitchik's essays and recognize: there's something there. And this is such a *kiddush Hashem*, and such a vital need, for gentiles, secular Jews and observant Jews, that as years pass we will come to see Rav Soloveitchik as the trailblazer, unique in his time; and will remain a unique accomplishment for many years to come.

These two contributions certainly do not sum up the man or his work, and I make no attempt to do so. But I must add one point, which I learned from my father. Rav Soloveitchik hated dishonesty. He despised fraud of any kind. Whether it was dishonesty in financial matters, or the kind of fraud involved in the search for status and power, this behavior was abhorrent to him. He did not like to criticize, and he seldom spoke out in public; and therefore, there are many who call themselves his disciples, who take that title in vain.

THE GRANDFATHER FIGURE

Rabbi Elazar Muskin

How can one eulogize the departed? What can we say that will give both comfort and inspiration? As I begin a eulogy for the Rav, the following words fill my mind:

> The Talmud in *Berachot* (6b) remarks: "*Agra dehespeida daluye.*" The merit of a funeral oration is in raising the voice. Tonight, perhaps more than ever before, we are here to cry, not to sit in silent indifference, but to cry.
>
> The eulogy, however, must not only engage our emotions; it also must address our minds. We must tell a story, the story of the one to whom we bid farewell forever. Yet it is strange that until the last day on earth we remain a sealed book even to those who knew us best. Anonymity is an integral part of human destiny. As *Kohelet* wrote, "*Sof davar hakol nishma.*" At the end of the matter all is heard. Only at the conclusion of the *davar*, the human career, only at the end of a life story, do we inquire, "Who was he?" Only then, *hakol nishma*, all kinds of questions are asked.
>
> A while ago, people simply didn't care. Now they are concerned; now they care. Yesterday the question could have been answered easily. It could have been addressed directly. Today we know not where to inquire, we know not who can answer our question. Nevertheless, the *halakhah* insists that the question be raised.

These reflections on the meaning of a eulogy are not my own. Instead, as on so many other occasions, the ideas and words I employ originated with the Rav. He personally utilized these very words when he eulogized others, and certainly they describe what he should mean to us.

The Rav, as everyone knows, challenged us intellectually. But, as many do not know, he also challenged us emotionally.

My first encounter with the Rav came when I was still a youngster studying at the Hebrew Academy in Cleveland. My father's family in Boston had close ties with the Rav, and he spoke at the *bar mitzvah* of one of my cousins. I'll never forget hearing the Rav when he spoke at that *bar mitzvah*. I thought he spoke for a long time, but the adults wanted more. I was amazed how he mesmerized the audience and how when he concluded his talk everyone discussed what he said. I had never seen such a reaction before, and it remains an indelible memory.

When I returned to Cleveland and shared this experience with my teachers, they responded with derision. My rabbis had no respect for the Rav because he didn't share their more insulated view and philosophy. They couldn't understand how a Torah scholar could have a Ph.D. in philosophy and endorse secular studies. My father, of blessed memory, however, knew that the Rav was the greatest Torah scholar of our generation, and he always encouraged me not to listen to the negative remarks.

I entered the Rav's *shiur* when I began the *Semichah* Program at Yeshiva University in the fall of 1978. Although I couldn't wait for the opportunity, I entered the class with great trepidation and fear. I worried, "Would the Rav call on me to read the *Gemara*? Would I be prepared and able to answer his questions?"

The best way to describe such trepidation is found in the account of Reb Izele, Rabbi Chaim Volozhin's son, of his father's visit to his teacher, the Vilna Gaon. Reb Itzele recalled, "As the wagon drew closer to Vilna, father's face became pale. By the time we came to Vilna, it was difficult to recognize him. Again he turned to me and inquired trembling, 'You too want to go to the Rabbi?' I gathered myself together and said, 'Yes.' As we were standing at the door of the chamber of the Gaon, his knees actually quaked out of awe for his teacher" (quoted in Norman Lamm, *Torah for Torah's Sake,* pp. 5–6).

Eventually, of course, the Rav did call on me to read the *Gemara.* It was Wednesday, January 10, 1979, when it happened. I was literally trembling. My voice cracked and my hands shook from fear. We were learning *Perek haZahav* in *Bava Metzia*, and I had prepared for weeks for my inevitable fate. But, by the time I was his student, the Rav no longer was a young man. In fact, he already was a grandfather and had acquired a grandfather's patience and compassion. Instead of encountering the fiery and demanding teaching style that had been his trademark, I found benevolent humor and encouragement. Before I began to read the Talmud, the Rav stopped me and said, "Read carefully. Don't worry. I won't eat you for lunch!"

The Rav had become the very grandfather figure that he loved talking about in his description of the biblical Jacob. The Rav noted that only Jacob, not Abraham, Isaac, or for that matter Moses, endowed our people with our name. We are called either *Bnei Yisrael* or *Beit Yaakov*, both Jacob's names. Furthermore, in the midrash, only Jacob is called *"zaken,"* the elder, even though he didn't live as long as his father or grandfather. What was it that earned Jacob this right and privilege? The Rav noted that Jacob was the only patriarch who established a line of communication with his grandchildren. It was Jacob who said that his grandchildren, Ephraim and Menashe, were to him like his sons, Reuven and Shimon.

When a grandfather hands over the *mesorah*, the traditions of our faith, to his grandchildren, then and only then do we have the secret of eternity. The Rav once wrote, "It was Jacob the elder who listened to their problems, conversed and worked closely with them, played and planned with them. Jacob knew the secret language of '*mispar hadorot,*' uniting the generations."

The Rav, like Jacob of old, listened to our problems and helped us resolve them with great understanding. I vividly recall visiting the Rav in his apartment at Yeshiva University when I was at my first pulpit in New York. My wife, mother-in-law, and grandmother-in-law joined me. The Rav was well acquainted with my wife's family because her late maternal grandfather, Mendel Siegman, was the founder and president of the Moriah Shul on Manhattan's West Side where the Rav served as rabbi.

During our meeting, my mother-in-law asked the Rav if women were allowed to dance with a *Sefer Torah* on Simchat Torah. The Rav responded with an emphatic no, but then added "not because of the laws of *niddah*. This has nothing to do with *niddah*." I then asked the Rav why he was so opposed to having women dance with a Torah. He responded, *"minhag beit haknesset."* Not knowing how to explain this to laymen, I asked for a clarification. The Rav replied, "Explain by telling them it is a question of synagogue etiquette. This is the way our mothers and grandmothers did it, and that is why we must continue this tradition. We are not more pious today than our mothers and grandmothers, and they didn't dance with a *Sefer Torah.* So, too, we must not allow for a new etiquette to be created."

In just a few words, the Rav articulated the entire concept of *mesorah*, tradition. With a grandfather's disposition, he bridged the gap between generations. He spoke our language and taught us to love the entire gamut of Torah knowledge. He created a dialogue for all of us with the great rabbis of old, and yet, at the same time, he was conversant with all literature, philosophy, and science of the modern age. No knowledge was rejected; rather it was all used together with *halakhah* so that a new line of communication would be formulated.

Although we called him "The Rav," I believe we can add *"zaken"* as well. He was the one who mastered the ability to engage all generations in a dialogue with the *mesorah. "Ve'hu haketz,"* this is the secret that will lead us into the messianic age, and for that we are eternally grateful to the Rav who was our *"zaken"* as well.

May his memory be a source of blessing for all of us.

REMEMBERING THE RAV

RABBI DR. BERNARD A. POUPKO

At the historic dedication of the US Holocaust Memorial Museum in Washington, President Clinton stated that "a head without a heart is not humanity."

To us, the students and disciples of Rabbi Soloveitchik, the "Rav" spoke with a passion about the plate worn by the High Priest upon his forehead and the Breast Plate of Judgment upon his heart. Covering the Priest's forehead, the *tzitz*, the plate, symbolized unadulterated knowledge and pure reason.

The *choshen,* which covered the High Priest's heart, symbolized love, magnanimity, compassion and genuine sensitivity. It embraced all the names of the Tribes of Israel. The *tzitz*, the Rav said, represented the authoritative verdict of *halakhah* and the *choshen* resolved questions of national magnitude involving peace and war and other national concerns.

The majesty of Judaism is emphasized when there is a synthesis of the heart and the mind. And when there is no heart to support the decisions of the mind, you have a culture which can produce on the one hand, Beethoven, Goethe, Brahms and on the other hand, Hitler, Himmler and Eichman.

In his essay "The Typological Theology of Rabbi Joseph B. Soloveitchik," Dr. Eugene Borowitz, a Reform Judaism theologian, writes: "He [the Rav] is more sophisticated than Kaplan, more erudite than Buber, more rationalistic than Heschel."

Novelist Mark Mirsky says that Soloveitchik is "the greatest storyteller I have ever heard." And Reform theologian, Arnold Woff, predicts that people will still be reading Soloveitchik in a thousand years. Universally recognized as the outstanding Talmudic dialectician of the century, the Rav is regarded as the intellectual mentor and leading Torah authority in modern Jewish history.

His countless lectures, unique in their astonishing depth and originality, were not confined to a mere analysis of the biblical, talmudic or

Maimonidian text. Invariably, he would always relate his observations and conclusions to the contemporary challenges and problems confronting Jews and the world at large. Thus, he spoke with prophetic vision and emotions about the emergence of the State of Israel which he considered among the singular greatest miracles in the history of our people.

He would say: "In the darkest night of *churban* and extermination, and of pain, there was the Divine knock on the door of *Knesset Yisroel* from the hand of Providence. *Kol Dodi Dofeik*. It was a moment of grace and compassion which fortunately we Jews did not ignore. We recognized the historic opportunity of that summons from the Divine. This was one of the rare and precious opportunities which were not wasted by our people.

"It was in the middle of the dark night, lyar, 5708, when the horror of Auschwitz and Treblinka, Majdanek and Buchenwald touched the consciousness of a part of humanity. The revelations of the gruesome savagery perpetrated by doctors and academicians of Berlin and Heidelberg Universities with the complicity of the native population of Eastern Europe brought about a mood of resignation, doubt and hopelessness within the Covenental Community. Jews confronted a divided world, one part from which they were expelled and the other part which would not admit them."

At this painful moment in our history, the Rav said the miracle happened when the US and the USSR for the first time found themselves in the same camp at the UN and voted in favor of the establishment of the Jewish homeland.

And the Rav concluded with a remark that the UN resolution did not give us the State of Israel. It rather made it possible for us to bring it into being.

The establishment of the State of Israel, according to the Rav, not only restored Jewish dignity and national self-esteem, but it has also emphatically refuted the dogma of the Church about the "punishment of the wandering Jew for the crime of deicide – the irreversible expulsion from his homeland."

The emergence of the State of Israel is a total rejection of this cynical assertion, according to the Rav, which in no small measure was responsible for the suffering and humiliation of our people throughout the ages.

He, the preeminent Talmudist, halakhist, theologian and philosopher, was sensitive to, and aware of, the complex problems and challenges confronting our people in the diaspora and in Israel. His teachings and his statesmanship consistently reflected the grandeur and the nobility of the Torah sages of the Pharisaic tradition. His great legacy of scholarship and leadership will be felt throughout the future centuries.

MY REBBE, THE RAV

RABBI DR. SHLOMO RISKIN

"I heard so many eulogies, and each one gave a radically different picture of the Rav." This sentence was expressed by many in the aftermath of the loss of the Torah giant of our generation, HaRav Yosef B. Soloveitchik *zt"l.* I can only respond by recounting my graduation from the Makhon Haim Greenberg Teachers' Seminary in Jerusalem 1961. At a special dinner arranged by our Professor of Modern Israeli literature, Dr. Tuchner, three of us were asked to read aloud the papers we had written on Shai Agnon's rather ambiguous short story masterpiece, "The Orchestra." As you might very well imagine, the three of us presented three totally different interpretations: for me, the story dealt with the tension between religion and art, with the former emerging victorious. The graduate who followed me attempted to prove that art was the victor, and the third in line insisted that the tale was a synthesis between Kafka and Nietzche, concluding that indeed God was dead. Shai Agnon was in the audience. Professor Tuchner smilingly asked him to adjudicate between the three interpretations. The venerated writer rose, insisted that he would not relate to the preceding papers, but that he would only agree to recount the following story:

In a small town in Europe, where the inhabitants lived in such primitive conditions that they had never seen a mirror, a householder went to a far-away village and purchased a mirror at the local fair. He made this acquisition because it was cheap, without really knowing the function of the article he had bought. No sooner did he bring it into his house than his wife began to rant and rave: "You old foolish hypocrite, you've brought another woman into my own home!" The householder himself seemed even more perturbed: "I have to come home, only to find another man living in my abode!" Their argument became increasingly heated until they summoned the Rabbi to render his judgement. "I don't understand," said the Rabbi. "I see neither a strange man nor a strange woman. I see only a wise old Jew with a beard." Shai Agnon sat down.

Many have been the eulogies – both in oral and in written form – that have attempted to distill the essence of the Rav's teaching. Rarely have they been repetitious, and frequently they appeared to clash. The Rav was, after all, a most complex and profound personality. Each of his students saw within him and emphasized that aspect of his thoughts and personality which we ourselves yearned to develop – and turn into. Hence the differences – which, as the varied hues of the diamond, merge and blend into a brilliant and dazzling light. Hence with great fear and trepidation – and emotions of unworthiness – I herewith add my own reflections and recollections of my experience with greatness.

The intellectual legacy of Rav Soloveitchik – the uniqueness of his thought as a halakhist, philosopher and theologian of Judaism – can be summarized in seven areas:

1. *Halakhah*, Jewish ritual law, not only provides a philosophical construct as complete and all-encompassing as that of Kant and Hegel, but also speaks to the most profound questions and dilemmas of the human predicament. Reflected in the details of the sounds of the Rosh Hashanah *shofar* is the basic human need to cry out to a Higher Force with a request to live, and to break out of a world of limitation, uncertainty and tragedy into a life of eternity and redemption. The laws of repentance express human freedom and our ability to recreate ourselves and the world around us. Every detail of *halakhah* is our attempt to bring the Divine into the world around us, to make form and perfection out of matter and chaos. The Song of Songs expresses the human search for God, the cosmic hide-and-seek of a world in which the Almighty and His creatures are constantly searching out and eluding each other. Halakhic detail mirrors the universal within the particular, and our religio-legal framework gives us the ability to rise above our physical limitations and instincts to enable us to experience the dimension of eternity.

2. The human being is both limited and limitless, bestial and God-like, aggressive and passive, extroverted and introspective. Man stands apart from the universe in his desire and ability to scientifically subdue and technologically transform, and, at the same time, yearns to be a part of the

universe, to relate to its rhythms, to be at one with its tempo, to serve and to maintain. The same individual who establishes partnerships, who builds organizations and successful businesses, requires a sensitive and caring family soulmate and should participate in covenantal communities devoted to prayer and study. The inner life and value system of our traditional laws and mores must reflect our desire for redemption as well as for re-creation, our ability to sacrifice as well as to succeed, in-reach as well as out-reach, communion with the Divine as well as competition with our peers. This more inner directed life of the covenant is the true message of the Sabbath, the most authentic function of the synagogue community. And if an observant lifestyle does not reflect the inner message of sustained spirituality, we have succumbed to Western materialism and forfeited the birthright of our faith.

3. Rav Soloveitchik believed profoundly in the Oral Law as transmitted by our Sages (*emunat hakhamim*), and even interpreted the Yom Kippur *Avodah* and the Passover Seder Haggadah explication as reflecting our faith in the truth of this tradition. But Rav Soloveitchik did not believe in the infallibility of any particular sage, in the cult of the *rebbe* or *rosh yeshiva.* He imbued his students with the ability and the obligation to study the sources for themselves, to respect the views of those authorities who preceded us but to reserve the right to interpret in accordance with our own understanding and to strive to discover new insights and revelations. I remember coming to the Rav in the early 60s with a burning question of the day: Should we stage demonstrations on behalf of Soviet Jewry as urged by a number of then youthful activists (Yaakov Birnbaum, for example), or is it preferable to follow the policy of "quiet diplomacy" urged by establishment *Gedolei Torah*? "Why do you ask me?" queried the Rav sincerely. "This is a question for leading Sovietologists!" And when a Professor of Soviet History of Columbia University spoke out in favor of activism, Rav Soloveitchik supported our demonstrations.

4. Rav Soloveitchik believed in the study of the Oral Law, as well as the Written Law, as the most direct manner of achieving closeness with the Divine. Torah study was therefore a form of Divine Service, and was the

best way of discerning what it was He desired of us. It is inconceivable that women be denied this fundamental privilege, opportunity and obligation. He taught Torah to his daughters, encouraged his students to teach women, and gave a traditional *shiur* in *Gemara* and *Rishonim* at the inauguration of the Belt Midrash at Stern College for Women. A number of times, he paraphrased for me: "In our generation, when women attend University and study physics, philosophy and literature, anyone who does *not* teach his daughter Torah is teaching her immorality."

5. The Rav believed in the truth of Torah, and in God as the Ultimate Source of truth. He was therefore fearless in his pursuit of truth, confident that the knowledge of true science, philosophy, mathematics, literature and psychology could only enhance our understanding of Torah and our relationship to the Divine. Even more that that: the Torah commands us to conquer and subdue the world. Clearly this is only possible if we are armed with the most advanced understanding of science and technology, of philosophy and psychology. Torah dare not remain isolated in the corner, insular and apart from the world at large. This was Rebecca's message to Jacob ("Go out to the fields, my son"), this is the Divine mandate to Israel to sanctify the world and be a light unto the nations. I remember well my initial agitation when, as a young *rebbe* in the James Stern School at Yeshiva University in 1964, I heard that the Belfer Graduate School in Science was being moved to the main complex together with the Rabbi Isaac Elchanan Theological Seminary. I feared lest the Yeshiva be overwhelmed, and I led a delegation of "Young Torah-ists" to complain to the Rav. "Don't be an *againstnik*, and don't be afraid," he counseled. "Torah will not only survive, it will prevail."

6. It was Rav Soloveitchik who established an unequivocal distinction between Orthodoxy and Conservatism when he ruled that it is preferable to pray at home on Rosh Hashanah without a *shofar* than to participate in a synagogue service where men and women sit together. For the Rav, the *mechitzah* reflected the great divide between a religion of commitment and a religion of convenience, between a covenantal community which creates a synagogue in accordance with the design of tradition and *halakhah*, and a

nostalgic community which creates a synagogue in accordance with the design of Western social mores and contemporary standards of behavior. And for the Rav, the public declaration involved in sanctioning a synagogue which contravened our legal traditions could not be permitted as a legitimate halakhic alternative.

7. The Rav had the courage to stand alone, to suffer for his convictions – in the sense of his commitment to Torah learning, the most profound commitment of his life – even if it meant his isolation from that community with which he had the most in common. This *gadol baTorah* was unappreciated by the world of *rashei yeshiva*; the *lamdan hador* (Torah scholar par excellence) was excluded from the highest society of *lamdanim*. He even broke from his revered and beloved grandfather, Reb Hayyim Brisker, with regard to two cardinal issues, which were apparently for him non-negotiable: 1) his wholehearted acceptance of secular university learning, which enabled him to proudly serve as the *Rosh Yeshiva* Primus of Yeshiva University, and 2) his enthusiastic endorsement of religious Zionism, expressed in his essay "*Kol Dodi Dofek*," a magnificent paean to the State of Israel as the confirmation of our covenant with God and the dawn of our redemption as a nation. He also served as President of the Mizrachi Movement in the United States for many decades. Indeed, our contemporary Joseph was resented and hated by his "brothers," because he dared to dream the dream of change and relocation from Europe, because he dared to envision a universal Judaism whose message could influence the entire cosmos. The Torah world outside of Yeshiva University exacted from him the bitter price of loneliness and isolation – in life as well as in death – because of these convictions, but he had the courage to stand alone, seemingly secure in the knowledge that to be alone with God is to be with a majority of one.

Having said all of this, the aspect of the Rav which was most palpable for us as students was the Rav as *rebbe* and *melamed*, the Rav as *masmid* and *mechadesh* (developer of new insights) in Torah. His abilities as a teacher of Torah par excellence were certainly expressed in the *Yahrzeit derashot* for his father Rav Moshe *zt"l,* when he would brilliantly expound on the halakhic profundity of a Talmudic passage for two hours, and would then stirringly develop its theological, ethical and existential ramifications for the next two hours. And in his *teshuvah shiur* for the Rabbinical Council of America between Rosh Hashanah and Yom Kippur, which would invariably begin with a *halakhah* in the Rambam but would then continue to dynamically transform not only our intellectual understanding, but also our emotional and psychological outlooks. The Rav could hold an audience of thousands spellbound, revealing the depths of Torah as well as of his own soul, enabling every one in the audience to feel that he was addressing only him. But perhaps the most consistent expression of his genius was every single classroom *shiur*, which was truly an experience in itself. We knew that the *shiur* was prepared, because the Rav had all of the material at his fingertips; but he was also always creatively developing the material and we were privileged to be witnessing, and even participating, in the development.

But on an even deeper level, the Rav was involved in an intimate dialogue with Rava and Abaye, Ravina and Rav Ashi, the Rambam and the Ravad, the Vilna Gaon and Rav Hayyim. They were his companions in learning, his *havrutai*; they lived for and with him, and he made them alive for us as well. The everyday world was shut out, and these great personalities were brought in. They came to life before our very eyes, their ideas were brilliantly illuminated, and their debate became the most important focus of our lives.

For me, however, the truly significant dimension of the *shiur* was the clear message that the Rav was engaged in a search for truth; there was no truth greater than that passage in the Talmud, and there was no pursuit worthier than its proper interpretation. A difficult passage in the Rambam had to be understood – and we felt the Rav's pain if he felt his explanation was inadequate as well as his joy when he believed that he had discovered the true *p'shat*. He once told us how, as a child, he would fall asleep listening to Rav Moshe, his father, teaching a *haburah*, a select or choice group of disciples. His father would ask question after question on a passage in the Rambam, and when his explanation caused the questions to disappear like the rain clouds in the wake of dazzling sunshine, the young Yoshe Ber would exultantly jump out of bed and run into the kitchen falling into his mother's arms shouting, "The Rambam won, the Rambam won!" But if his father would conclude with, "The passage of the Rambam still requires illumination, the young Yoshe Ber would cry himself to sleep. "To have, grown up in my home and not to have become a *lamdan* would have required me to truly have been a *gaon*," the Rav once smilingly said. "After all, the Rambam and the Ravad were daily dinner guests. And Heaven forfend if I interpreted a passage incorrectly – even informally over the dinner table."

The Rav had been trained from earliest childhood to labor in Torah – and to logically and textually prove everything he said. He once recounted that, as a small child of four or five, he came to his father crying bitterly: "Shmulik [his brother] wanted to hit me." Rav Moshe amusedly asked: "How do you know he wanted to hit you?" "Because he hit me," said the young Yoshe Ber. "So why didn't you complain that he hit you?" Persisted Rav Moshe. "Well, I always hear you ask your students to prove whatever they say. Had I said that Shmulik hit me, I wouldn't have been able to prove it, since there were no witnesses. But if I said that Shmulik wanted to hit me, I could prove that; after all, he did hit me…."

This was the kind of precise training he attempted to give us. We were expected to labor in Torah, to prove our every contention, to be textually and logically precise – and, above all, to learn how to properly conceptualize the text. I'll never forget the first day I was admitted to Rav Soloveitchik's *shiur*. When I left my house dressed with a jacket and tie, my younger sister looked at me sadly and said: "Didn't you like the shirt I gave you for your birthday?" I changed into her present of a green shirt, trying not to be cognizant of the fact that it clashed horribly with my blue jacket. I entered the Rav's classrom as a freshman in college, intimidated by the vast number of students generally much older than I, awestruck at the privilege of studying with the *gadol hador*, and frightened by stories of the "crouching lion" sharply critical of his students' mistakes. Nevertheless, I chose a front row center seat; apparently my desire not to miss a word or a gesture proved stronger than my fear. The Rav strode in, the class rose to attention; the Rav sat down followed by the class, and I remember being struck by the square black beard, the piercing concentrating eyes. He opened his *Gemara*, scanned the room and said: "You, with the green shirt, read the *Mishnah*." We were studying the Tractate *Sanhedrin*, and I confidently began to read, thinking I had adequately prepared the text. "What does the *Tosfot* say?" asked the Rav. I told him, in effect reciting in Yiddish the question and the answer of this classic Talmudic commentary. "You think I don't know you can translate? What does *Tosfot* say? What is the concept behind his question?" The Rav hammered his questions into me, and I was at a loss for the answers. I had not as yet learned his method. I didn't know what he expected. Mercifully, when he went around the class, no one else gave the proper response. He dismissed all of us, admonishing the class to study the first 10 pages of the Talmud by heart, and said he would resume class after Rosh Hashanah and begin with an oral exam: only those who passed would remain in *shiur*.

I'll never forget that Rosh Hashanah. I hardly prayed at all, masking a Tractate *Sanhedrin* underneath my *machzor* and studying at every cantorial repetition. I returned to class only to find half the students already gone, frightened by the specter of an oral exam. And as time went on, I learned the Brisker methodology, got used to the "paper-chase" atmosphere of the classroom and felt that I was benefiting immensely from Rav Soloveitchik, the great *lamdan*, as well as Rav Soloveitchik the master pedagogue. And then I learned the most important lesson of my academic career.

We were learning *Masechet P'sachim*. Yeshiva College had two divisions during those years, the Yeshiva – for those with extensive *Gemara* backgrounds who had generally studied in Yiddish – and the Teachers' Institute, for those less interested in *Gemara*, where the classes were conducted in Hebrew. There was a student in Teachers' Institute with an excellent head for Talmud study whom I adopted as a "project;" I studied with him every evening, encouraging him to switch into the Yeshiva division. I was quite proud when he was admitted to the Rav's *shiur*, but he was frightened to sit anywhere but in the last row behind a column. As time went on, and due to my constant prodding, he moved up a row each week – until he was finally seated just one row behind me. The *sugya* was "nine stores," a difficult topic which dealt with presumptions of majority and its halakhic ramifications. The Rav had been dwelling on this passage for a number of weeks, and, after raising many objections to all the usual interpretations, was just concluding an original and creative construct which removed all contradictions. My "project" whispered a question, which I believed was excellent – and devastating. "Ask the Rav," I prodded. He did – and an explosion ensued. "How did you get into my class?" raged the Rav. "You belong back in Teachers' Institute." Mercifully the class ended, but I saw all my work going down the drain.

The Talmud class emptied out, and the second shift – the *Yoreh Deah* Rabbinical students – came in. In those days the Rav gave two classes back-to-back and a few of us remained for the second class as well. Generally, the Rav would immediately close the *Psachim* and open the *Yoreh Deah.* This time his *P'sachim* remained open, and he placed his head in his hands in intense concentration. After almost twenty minutes, during which time no one breathed a word he looked up at me. "Who asked the question at the end of the *shiur?* Friedberg? Take me to him." The class remained seated, perplexed. The Rav strode out with me at his heels, and I led him to the *Tov Me'od* Dairy restaurant, otherwise known as "Greasy Spoon," across Amsterdam Ave. Everyone was shocked when the Rav entered the restaurant, immediately out of respect jumping to their feet. From the corner of my eye I caught Friedberg, eating an omelette. His color had finally returned to his cheeks. His recovery was short-lived, however. The Rav immediately saw him. "Friedberg." The hapless student began to tremble. The Rav continued: "You were right and I was wrong. Because of your question, I'll have to learn the passage all over again and completely rethink my interpretation. Thank you."

The Rav returned to the class and opened the *Yoreh Deah* as if nothing had occurred. But I had learned a far more important lesson than anything which could have been said for the remainder of the class. It was eminently clear to me that for Rav Soloveitchik, pursuit of truth was of paramount concern. And he was training us, hopefully the leaders of the next generation, to properly pursue that truth in the pages of the Talmud and its commentators.

When I was ordained, I asked the Rav for advice. He said four things: "First of all go to *minyan* every morning. You'll be up late, you'll want to learn into the night after the telephone stops ringing – but congregants, as well as the Almighty, properly expect the Rabbi to be at *minyan* every morning. Secondly, pursue your doctoral studies – your education is not complete without a Ph.D. Thirdly give *tzedakah* and do *chesed.* Rabbis ask their congregants to give *tzedakah* – but it's important that the Rabbis themselves give *tzedakah.* And always remember that the primary function of a Rav is to be responsible for the *chesed* within his community. And finally, but most importantly, say a *Gemara shiur* to students every day. You must remain heavily involved in study, and teaching *Gemara* is the best way to guarantee that." It was the best advice I ever received, and I still try to be faithful to his sage directives.

At our *Semichah* Convocation, the Rav interpreted the passage in the Tractate *Sanhedrin* that describes how in earlier times the master would convey his ordination by placing his hands on his disciples' head. The literal meaning of *"semichah"* is "reliance," or a "leaning on," and the usual interpretation is that the student relies on or leans on, the *rebbe*-teacher for the Tradition, for his knowledge and ability to interpret and decide the law. "However," said the Rav, "it certainly goes both ways. Indeed, when one sees an older man with his hands on a younger companion, one usually assumes that it is the elder who is leaning on the younger for support. So I believe it is the same with ordination. We, the older generation must lean upon you, the younger generation, for our future, for our eternity. If you don't carry on our teachings, we are consigned to oblivion. If you convey our traditions, we live through you, into succeeding generations, as "part of eternal Torah…."

The Rav's voice has been stilled, and at a time when we need him most. A world in which Torah has become narrow and repetitive is in desperate need of his breadth and creativity; a world in which Torah has become insular and computerized is in desperate need of his universalism and sensitivity. I fear that the heads and shoulders of us, his students, are too frail for the weight and depth of the traditions he tried to bestow upon us. I pray that we find the strength of soul and the breadth of spirit. I pray that we grant him his well-deserved eternity.

THE RAV AS COMMUNAL LEADER

Rabbi Dr. Bernard Rosensweig

There is a providential principle in Jewish History.[1] As religious Jews, we believe that God never abandons the Jewish people and that in a time of crisis, He always provides us with new hope and new leadership. This has been true throughout Jewish history, and the American experience is no exception. When the Rav, Rabbi Joseph B. Soloveitchik, came to the United States in 1932, the Torah community was at a terrifying crossroads. To read the literature of the twenties, thirties and forties is to wade through countless eulogies over the impending demise of the Orthodox community. We were consigned to the limbo of obsolescence, and we were assured that a Torah-true Jewish life could not strike roots in the pragmatic soil of America.

There were good grounds for these assessments and predictions; everything pointed in that direction. Only a guiding, providential hand could change the course of history; only a towering spiritual and intellectual figure could, by dint of his teachings and his personality, reverse the process of religious self-destruction and open a new era of Jewish creativity on the American continent. That man was the Rav.

The Rav was the architect of our approach to Torah Judaism. He was not the creator of what some now call Modern or Centrist Orthodoxy; that preceded his coming to the shores of America. Men like Rabbi Dr. Bernard Revel were the original visionaries of *Torah u'Madda*, but it was the Rav who was destined to give it direction, substance and meaning. Through his *shiurim*, lectures and essays, his *Weltanschauung* was impressed on the minds and hearts of two generations. Thousands hung on his every word, and his comments and statements became guides for action.

The status of the Rabbinical Council of America as an authentic Orthodox rabbinic body was legitimated by the presence of the Rav in our midst. His universally recognized Talmudic erudition, coupled with his vast secular knowledge, made him the undisputed guide and teacher for the

[1] Cf. *Midrash Rabbah, Kohelet* 1:5.

Modern Orthodox rabbinate and its lay constituency. And given his identification with the RCA, the Agudas haRabbanim could no longer trifle with the RCA and its decisions.

The Rav, in his capacity as the Chairman of the RCA Halakhah Commission, revealed another aspect of his prodigious personality: the Rav as *posek*, as halakhic decisor. The Jewish world revered the Rav as creative teacher, as halakhist par excellence, and as the seminal Jewish thinker. Few had the opportunity to experience him as a first-class authority in practical areas of Jewish Law and the author of responsa on religious and social issues, which reflected his masterful scholarship, his brilliant insight into the American Jewish community and his ability to communicate his decisions in a manner which made them binding on broad sections of the community.[2]

It was in this capacity as *posek* that the Rav took his stand, for example, against mixed pews. In the forties and fifties, the problem of mixed pews became a very serious matter for the Orthodox rabbinate. Orthodox synagogue after Orthodox synagogue was falling to the Conservative movement over this issue. Finally, the struggle was joined in the secular courts when two famous cases were brought, one involving a synagogue in New Orleans and the other a congregation in Mt. Clemens in Michigan. In this struggle, the RCA and the Union of Orthodox Jewish Congregations of America, which played a key role in this legal confrontation, were buttressed by the strong position which the Rav enunciated and which was used in these cases.

In unusually strong terms, the Rav denounced those Orthodox rabbis who were lax, timid or indifferent to the principle of separation – reflecting the depth of his feeling on this issue. In clear and decisive language, he declared that a "synagogue with mixed seating arrangements forfeits its sanctity and is unfit for prayer…."[3] It was in keeping with this unequivocal opposition to mixed pews that he directed a young man, who lived in a neighborhood where the only synagogue was a mixed-pew congregation, to

---

[2] Cf. L. Bernstein, *Challenge and Mission* (New York, 1982), 51–64.

[3] Cf. B. Litvin, *The Sanctity of the Synagogue* (1987), 110.

remain at home on Rosh Hashanah and not hear the blowing of the *shofar* "rather than to enter a synagogue whose sanctity has been profaned."[4]

The Rav rejected any attempt to justify mixed pews on the basis that it was being practiced by increasing numbers of congregations. In his view, it was completely irrelevant whether five percent or fifty percent of the pulpits of Orthodox rabbis were mixed. The violation of a religious or ethical principle does not affect its validity and cogency even when a large segment of the community is guilty of that violation. Dramatically, the Rav posed the rhetorical question: "Was the commandment against murder declared null and void while Nazi hordes were practicing genocide?"[5]

The Rav's statement here, as well as in other areas, had a powerful impact. The number of mixed pew positions serviced by Orthodox rabbis has been sharply reduced and has become a rare phenomenon. The Rav's decision fortified the Orthodox rabbinate not only because of its substance, but also because of the manner in which the Rav succeeded in intellectualizing the traditional opposition to innovations in the synagogue. He not only spelled out the *halakhah* in a language which educated American laymen could understand, he also advanced a cogent rationale for the *halakhah* which could not be readily dismissed by those who sought to impose reason rather than religious authority as the arbiter of religious law in the synagogue.

The Rav's relationships and influence moved across a wide spectrum and embraced the greater part of American and world Jewry. The people who related to him and sought his guidance and advice covered the gamut of the Jewish community, including the late giants of the previous generation. Rav Moshe Feinstein was his cousin and his friend; his relationship to Rav Hutner went back to their days in Berlin, as did his relationship with the Lubavitcher Rebbe. I remember accompanying the Rav to three meetings with Rav Aharon Kotler in 1949. Witnessing the mutual respect and the genuine friendship which flowed between these two spiritual giants is an experience which remains indelibly imprinted on my mind.

---

[4] Ibid., p. 115.

[5] Ibid., p. 141.

Thirty years later, in 1979, I accompanied the Rav to a meeting with the leadership of the Joint Distribution Committee. The Va'ad Hayeshivos had asked the Rav and me (in my capacity as president of the Rabbinical Council of America) to intercede on their behalf for a much-needed grant for their institutions. When we walked into the conference room, the top leadership of the Joint was present. Not one of them was an Orthodox Jew, but when the Rav walked in, instinctively, they stood up as a sign of their respect for a great man.

The Rav spoke to them for thirty minutes – and they were mesmerized. He developed the concept of *hakarat hatov*, of gratitude, and he thanked them for what the Joint had done for his family in the aftermath of the First World War. I can still see that wonderful smile which lit up his face as he told them that he could still feel the taste of the chocolate in his mouth. He then proceeded to apply this principle to the need to support Torah and Torah institutions. When he was through, the president of the Joint responded that because the Rav had appeared before them and had spoken to them, the grant would be forthcoming.

The Rav provided Orthodoxy with respect, dignity and stature by articulating its basic philosophical premises. It was within the framework of the Rav's thinking and approach that the RCA involved itself in an internal struggle over relationships with non-Orthodox rabbinic bodies and non-Jewish religious groups. The Rav's role in determining these directions was crucial and definitive.

The RCA, as a rabbinic body, had maintained ongoing relationships with the Conservative and the Reform movements – and we did so on the basis of ground rules which our halakhic authority had set down for us. For many years, the RCA and the UOJCA were members of the Synagogue Council of America, which housed representatives of the Conservative and Reform movements as well as our own.

In 1956, our relationship to non-Orthodox bodies was challenged when eleven *roshei yeshiva* signed an *issur* prohibiting Orthodox rabbis from belonging to the Synagogue Council of America. The RCA then turned to its Halakhah Commission for direction. The truth is that a definitive decision was never handed down. The Commission and its chairman, our beloved Rav, were criticized for equivocation and for not taking a stand.

But the Rav's approach was the only wise course to take. The Rav felt that the atmosphere was too highly charged emotionally for a public response. He had not been consulted by the signers; indeed, they had asked him to join in the *issur* only after the fact – and one can easily speculate as to the reasons. Nonetheless, they were colleagues in the larger sense and men of scholarly distinction. The Halakhah Commission would not disagree publicly now that they had ruled, and neither the Rav nor the RCA were prepared to sever all relationships with these eminent men and their world. In such a circumstance, "no decision was also a decision."

The Rav set down for us his famous guidelines of *kelapei chuts* and *kelapei penim.*[6] In an interview with a Yiddish newspaper, he made this historic distinction (which he had previously made at an earlier RCA conference). Underlying his approach was the unity of the Jewish people. When the representation of Jews and Jewish interests vis-a-vis the non-Jewish world – *kelapei chuts* – are involved, all groups and movements must be united. There can be no divisiveness in this area, for any division in the Jewish camp can endanger its entirety.

"In the crematoria, the ashes of Hasidim and *anshei ma'aseh* [pious Jews] were mixed with the ashes of radicals and freethinkers. We must fight against an enemy who does not recognize the difference between one who worships and one who does not." However, in internal matters – *kelapei penim* – such as education, synagogues, rabbinic organizations and halakhic decisions, "when unity must be manifested in a spiritual-ideological meaning as a Torah community, it seems to me that the Orthodox cannot, and should not, join with other such groups that deny the foundations of our *Weltanschauung.*"

Within this framework, the Rav strongly opposed joint religious services with the Conservative and Reform movements; he also urged the RCA never to sign proclamations with other national rabbinic bodies, "particularly if it should manifest a religious character." These guidelines enabled the RCA to cooperate with other groups in external matters

---

[6] *The Jewish Day,* November 19, 1954.

without compromising or blurring the lines which separate the Torah community from those who do not have a similar halakhic commitment.[7]

In a similar vein, the Rav provided direction for the Torah community on how to address non-Jewish religious manifestations. In "Confrontation," the first essay of the Rav's to appear in English,[8] the Rav developed the ground rules for that very delicate and potentially dangerous relationship. We need not re-articulate those positions here, but it was in keeping with those principles that the Rav took a strong stand on Vatican II. In 1960, at the time of Vatican II, the Jewish community was asked to send representatives to the Council as observers. Then, like today, there was a strong inclination in certain circles not just to go to the Vatican, but to run. The Rav was unalterably opposed to sending Jewish observers to participate in Vatican II, which was, in his view, strictly a Christian matter. Indeed, no official observers were sent. The minute the Rav opposed it, Dr. Nachum Goldman (Chairman of the World Zionist organization), who was anxious to participate, withdrew rather than oppose the Rav and jeopardize the unity of the Jewish community.[9]

In 1962, the Rav had a secret meeting with Cardinal Willebrands, a Church liberal who was very friendly to Jews and very active on Vatican II, at Willebrands' request. The purpose was to discuss the possibility of a religious dialogue between Jews and Christians. The Rav rejected this notion totally, using the basic arguments which he had developed in "Confrontation." He understood the missionary character of Christianity and its commitment to both demonstrate its truth and persuade individuals and groups to accept salvation through a Christian affirmation of faith.[10]

The RCA remained loyal to the guidelines which the Rav had set down, and distinguished between theological discussions and ethical-secular concerns, which have universal validity. Every program involving either Catholic or Protestant churches in which we participated was carefully scrutinized and analyzed – we literally would go over it with a fine-tooth

---

[7] Cf. L. Bernstein, *Challenge and Mission*, p. 56, where Bernstein quotes a letter from the Rav to Rabbi Theodore Adams *z"l*, on August 11, 1953.

[8] *Tradition,* Vol. 6, pp. 5–29.

[9] Cf. L. Bernstein, *Challenge and Mission*, p. 206, for the background.

[10] Based on an article written by Dr. Hillel Seidman in the *Morning Journal* at the time.

comb. Every topic which had possible theological nuances or implications was vetoed, and only when the Rav pronounced it to be satisfactory did we proceed to the dialogue.

Few people realize the kind of influence the Rav wielded in Israeli affairs. When I was President of the RCA, I received a call from the then-Prime Minister Begin's office asking me to receive his personal advisor on Russian affairs, who was coming to America with a special mission in which we could play a key role. The emissary arrived, and he, I, and Rabbi Israel Klavan met in the offices of the RCA. At that meeting, the emissary laid out the Israeli concern on Russian Jewish emigration, in which approximately ninety percent of the immigrants were opting for America. The Israelis felt that only those Jews who agreed to go directly to Israel should be allowed to emigrate, and all others should be actively discouraged. He asked us to intervene with the Rav and solicit from him a statement supporting that position. He felt that with the Rav's religious and moral authority, they would be able to sell their position to world Jewry.

I had personal reservations, but I agreed to speak to the Rav. I flew up to Boston and met with him in his study. He rejected the notion out of hand and related to me that his father, Rav Moshe, had told him during the 1920s and 30s that to get a Jew out of Russia was in the category of *pidyon shevuyim* (redeeming captives) and should be undertaken at all costs. At that point, the Israeli government dropped its plan, only to revive it a number of years later.

During the Lebanon War, the Rav was terribly agitated by the situation. He felt that the Israelis had gone too far, particularly in the last phase of their operation, which involved the Christian invasion of the Palestinian camps of Sabra and Shatilla. When the question of a special commission to investigate what had happened in Sabra and Shatilla was brought before the Israeli cabinet at that time, the swing votes were in the hands of the National Religious Party; it was the Rav's insistence that the Commission be established, which played a major role in the decision of the Mafdal to opt for the creation of a Commission and the results which then followed.

The Rav's position on the future of Judea and Samaria was solicited by spiritual and political leaders of every shade and description. It is true that the Rav consistently rejected the notion that the obligation to hold onto

Judea and Samaria at any cost is a religious or halakhic imperative; at the same time, the Rav never said that Israel should give back all of Judea and Samaria. He insisted that the future of the territories should be determined by those who are its properly constituted authorities, in terms of the best long-term interests of the Jewish people, with the least danger to human life. Only those who are politically and militarily informed, and whose lives depend upon that decision, have the right to make that decision.

The Rav clearly had a great love for the land of Israel and a great affection for the State of Israel. He saw the State as a means to an end, as meaningful only insofar as it helps fulfill the historic destiny of what he called "the covenant of the committed." The State of Israel, dedicated to God, aware of its unique historical and political position, is an indispensable instrument of national religious fulfillment.

The Rav, in one of his addresses to the Mizrachi movement, said:

> You may ask, what is the attitude of Orthodoxy to the State of Israel? Certainly our attitude is positive, can it possibly be otherwise? Which faithful Jew can be against Israel?.... But the State is but one bank of the river.... We admire the State with all our heart, we pray for her welfare, we send her our sons and stand united to defend her. But it is not the highest good. Our highest ideal is our faith; the basic foundation of our existence is that which is "beyond the river," which symbolizes the people in confrontation with God and its unique way of life. If the question is put to us – what do you choose, a secular State of Israel or the God of Israel? – then it must be clearly understood that all of us, with one voice, will choose the God of Israel.[11]

The Rav himself was a card-carrying member of Agudath Israel. In 1935, he traveled to Israel, for the first and only time in his life, to try out for the position of Chief Rabbi of Tel Aviv. He made a brilliant impression with his *shiurim* and lectures, but he was not elected. The reason that was given was that he was too young. The real reason was that his great-uncle, Rav Meir Berlin, vetoed him because of his Agudah credentials.

---

[11] *The Rav Speaks*, pp. 116–17.

The Rav was the star of Agudah conventions, and people flocked to hear him. For example, when Rav Chaim Ozer Grodzensky died, it was the Rav who delivered a masterful eulogy over Rav Chaim Ozer at the Agudah convention. At that time, no one questioned the Rav's credentials, and his Berlin doctorate was not a detriment to his honored position in the Agudath Israel hierarchy. However, in the forties, the Rav underwent a slow transformation, and by the fifties, he was a committed Religious Zionist. The Rav admits that his "links with Mizrachi grew gradually," that he had his "doubts and reservations about the validity of the Mizrachi approach," and that his decision ran counter to his family tradition.[12] But the Rav made his decision firmly on behalf of the Mizrachi movement. He was impressed by its achievements. He was convinced that "from the point of view of history, Religious Zionism had saved the honor of religious Jews." It had created "a network of schools in which *Bnei Akiva Yeshivot* and *Hesder Yeshivot* are the crown; it has insured the unity of the Jewish people by making matters of personal status answerable to the Rabbinate and excluding civil marriage." The Rav recognized this and affirmed that without the pioneering efforts of the Mizrachi movement, the "yeshiva world" could not have transplanted itself to the land of Israel in the aftermath of the Holocaust.[13]

However, to our great sorrow, while the Tribes of God thousands of years ago finally admitted Joseph's righteousness and begged his forgiveness today, a segment of our brethren still lack the capacity to see reality as it is and possess the courage to admit their error. Even today, after Treblenka and Auschwitz – as assimilation putrefies a great portion of Diaspora Jewry and the State of Israel is occupied in protecting the Jewish settlement from the Arab Amalek – they hold fast against their brother Joseph (Religious Zionists) "and they viewed him from a distance."

It goes without saying that the Rav did not always agree with positions and actions taken by the Mafdal;[14] nor was he above leveling his criticisms when they were warranted, in his opinion. Nonetheless, the Rav supported Religious Zionism with great consistency, reaffirmed his faith in its

---

[12] Ibid., pp. 34–36.

[13] Ibid., p. 32.

[14] Ibid., pp. 9 and 185–6.

historical validity, hailed its enduring achievements on behalf of religious Jewry and, to the end, never wavered in his commitment to the movement.

The Rav's multi-faceted personality, unfortunately, lends itself to distortion and revisionism. The process has already begun, and many of those who presume to speak in his name sometimes do him a great disservice. The Rav was, throughout his lifetime, the teacher of Torah par excellence, and all of his involvements were simply reflections of that commitment. At the same time, he was, like other *gedolei Yisrael,* no recluse, and his impact was felt in many directions. To picture him in any other light is to distort reality. Never, then, has it been more important to place the Rav, his life and his contributions in historical perspective. This is a humble but sincere attempt in that direction.

PERSONAL REFLECTIONS OF THE RAV

RABBI JACOB S. RUBENSTEIN

A myriad of tales will be told of this multi-faceted man who, like a prism, radiated variegated hues of colored light to a host of viewers.

I was not Rav Soloveitchik's student. I did not sit at his feet and hear his *shiurim*. But I drank thirstily from his nurturing well and as such was a disciple. I have no striking anecdote or sagacious insight which he conveyed to me. I have only what I witnessed. Only recently, upon his death, did I reveal the incident to a small group of congregants. I was in the middle of a *Gemara shiur* to ninth graders at the Maimonides School in Brookline, Massachusetts, when the Rav quietly walked in unannounced to observe the class. Now I had studied with internationally renowned professors, I had heard *shiurim* and visited with *gedolim*. But when the Rav walked into my classroom I froze with awe and fear. My students knew that my demeanor had been radically transformed, but did not display any notice of my being overcome. Intimidated beyond description, I was unable to continue the *shiur*. Having lost the ability to speak coherently, I haltingly told the students that it was time to meet with their *chavrusas* for *chazarah* (review). Within seconds, desks were rearranged and the classroom became a mini *beit midrash*.

All along, the Rav stood at the back of the room observing the atmosphere of learning. The pride in my charges did not, however, relax my personal tension in having the Rav observe me as much as the class.

Three students came over to ask me a question. They wanted a more clearly-defined explanation of *kavod hatzibbur*. A thought occurred to me. I told them that with the Rav in the class they had an unusual opportunity to ask a *gadol*. Assuring them that it was appropriate, I boldly, without prior permission, announced to the class that the Rav would take questions. Hearing no reluctance on his part, the students walked over to the Rav with *Gemaras* in hand. For ten minutes the students engaged the Rav in learning, demonstrating the skill and knowledge my teachings had imparted. One by one, other students gravitated around the Rav, who patiently and warmly embraced them with a polite and measured tone and slow, deliberate speech, and offered perspectives to young minds on Talmudic history, halakhic principles and protocol. Dialogue ensued, more explanations followed. Their eyes were fixed on the Rav. Enraptured, the students absorbed every word and gesture. No one would have imagined a more poignant scenario.

The students emerged from the encounter elevated and invigorated. Their faces radiant with affection and veneration. Ennobled by the Rav's gentleness and generosity, they emmoted gratitude for the precious moment they had with the Rav. He had come to observe them, but it was he who was observed. It left an indelible impression on me, and especially the young women who sought his explanations.

A HESPED IN HONOR OF RAV YOSEF SOLOVEITCHIK

RABBI DR. JONATHAN SACKS

The Talmud states in the name of R. Yirmeyah bar Abba: *"Al yippater adam mechavero ella mitokh devar halakhah* – when one comes to take leave of a friend one should do so by communicating to him a *halakhah, shemitokh kakh zokhrehu"* – because through that *halakhah* which you have taught him, the friend will always remember you.

What exactly did Rav Yirmeyah bar Abba mean? Our lives are constructed out of relationships. We live amongst friends and above all amongst teachers. But every human relationship is fragile: people part, they move on, they separate. How then do we construct permanence out of these relationships? The answer, of course, is through memory. People leave but we remember them, they stay in our hearts. But memory too is impermanent. After *yud-bet chodesh,* even according to *halakhah,* after a gap of twelve months a person fades into oblivion.

What then is the only permanent form of memory. The answer is a *devar halakhah.* Because a *halakhah* is not just something, that we remember. A *halakhah* is something that we live. When somebody has taught us a *halakhah,* he has taught us something that changes our lives: we know that this we must do or this we must not do, and we know it because of him. Part of us has changed and therefore something of that person lives permanently in us. *Halakhah* is the one bond, which is permanent, and the one memory that endures. HaRav, Hagaon Rav Yosef Ber Soloveitchik has taken his leave of us and of this world, and we, whether we met him or not, whether we knew him or not, are bereaved because we are not merely his *chaverim,* his friends, but we are also called living – and he will always live in our minds.

It is impossible to do any kind of justice to his teaching and I will not even try. I have written about his work and there is much more, of course, still to be said. But I just want to say two things this evening, a *kelal* and a *perat,* a general and a specific point.

Let me begin with the *perat* and with two personal memories. I had the privilege of meeting the Rav twice. The second occasion was exactly ten years ago when I was invited to be the Rav of what was a shul in his own area, the Young Israel in Brookline. Interestingly enough the burning issue in Brookline was making an *eruv* and the success of any Rav depended upon his ability to construct an *eruv*. As a result I had to be taken to meet the Rabbanim in Boston to see if they had faith that I could make an *eruv*.

I went to see the Bostoner Rebbe, the Talner Rebbe (Rav Soloveitchik's son-in-law, Reb Yitzchok Twersky), and of course I was taken to see the Rav himself. He was then already over 80 and had been unwell for some time. In fact those who were present at that gathering told me it was one of the last occasions on which he recovered his full vigour.

It was as if he could hardly believe what had happened. Forty years ago when he came to Boston, America was a *treifeneh medinah* and yet in forty years exactly it had become a *mekom Torah,* a place of learning. In fact he said to me, "the *hatmadah,"* the devotion to learning of young American Jews, is greater than it was in the great days of my late grandfather *zt"l*, Reb Hayyim of Brisk. "The quality," he said, "I won't talk about. But the quantity is greater."

And I came away understanding what *Chazal* meant when they said "*Nittenah Torah bishloshah devarim: beesh, bemayim uvemidbar,* the Torah was given with three things, with fire, with water and in the wilderness." In the 1940s, America was truly a Jewish wilderness. But the Rav proved that if you give Torah with *esh*, with fire, and with *mayim*, with a thirst and a thirst quenching capacity, then even in a *midbar* you could create Torah. But of course I realised something that he in his *anavah,* his self-effacing humility, would not even have thought, let alone articulated. The transformation of a country in forty years from a *midbar* to a *mekom Torah* was largely due to one person, to him. There are very few leaders in the history of *Am Yisrael,* very few *gedolim* to whom it was given to change the contours, the very character of an entire Jewish community, an entire country – but Rav Soloveitchik did it. He did it for the United States, the largest Jewish community in the world. There were others undoubtedly who played a part in that development, who built schools and *yeshivot* but mainly within a limited circle of their own *talmidim.* Rav Soloveitchik did it across the country, in depth, at the grass roots. That was the second time I met him.

But it was the first time I met him that I discovered the basis for what he achieved. The first meeting took place fifteen years earlier, twenty-five years ago, in 1968 when I was a student. It took place in the corridors of Yeshiva University. The Rav was accustomed to sit and prepare his *Gemara shiur* or sit in with his *talmidim* as they prepared the *Gemara shiur.* And he said, "For you, I will come outside." I remember sitting on the bench with him just outside the room, in the corridor, for two hours, and in those two hours he taught me about *halakhah.*

In order to realise what Rav Soloveitchik taught a whole generation about *halakhah* we have to understand what *halakhah* was before Rav Soloveitchik, before he succeeded in being *machazir haTorah leyoshnah,* in restoring its former glory.

For generations of Jews *halakhah* was *hamaaseh asher yaasun:* it was Jewish law, the do's and don'ts, the *arbaah chelkei Shulchan Arukh, lamed-tet melachot* of Shabbat, *issur vehetter,* it was the *Shakh,* the *Taz,* the *Magen Avraham.* And for generations of Jews that was enough. It was more than enough. That was the *"ahavat olam beit Yisrael ammekha ahavta,"* that was the everlasting love through which *Hakadosh Barukh Hu* give us *Torah umitzvot chukkim umishpatim otanu limmadita* – and taught us all these law. And therefore *venismach bedivrei toratekha uvemitzvotekha leolam va'ed* – we rejoyced in them – *ki hem chayyeinu ve'orekh yameinu* – because in those laws were our lives and the length of our days.

But, in fact, for at least a century before Rav Soloveitchik *halakhah* was *munachat bekeren zavit, halakhah* was dethroned in one community after the other. It did not speak of the spirit of the age. For a century Jews outside a very narrow circle of *shomerei mitzvot* were not interested in the *Shulchan Arukh.* They were interested in ethical monotheism, universal brotherhood, in tolerance, in peace. They loved the words of the prophets, at most they read *Pirkei Avot.* The late Gershom Scholem once pointed out that Martin Buber wrote two volumes called *The Tales of the Chasidim,* and that you can read through the entire work without ever discovering that Chasidim kept *halakhah!* That was an elevated intellectual level, the level that you and I remember from the generation of our parents. It was very simple – God does not mind if you carry on Shabbat, so long as you are a good human being. That was *halakhah.* A *davar gadol* was *maaseh bereshit,* the great things were the philosophical ideas. The *davar katan* was talmudic study. The *Gemara* was a relatively small thing, overlooked. *Halakhah* was legalistic, casuistic, concerned with minutiae. If you read the books and sermons published in English between 1840 and 1940 you will note how rarely the word *halakhah* occurs or indeed any particular *halakhah.* They are almost totally absent. What Rav Soloveitchik did was therefore remarkable and unique. He transformed the thinking of a whole generation. Today, my publisher in America tells me that if you want to sell a book in America, it has to have the word *halakhah* in the title. There are hundreds of books and periodicals on *halakhah.* Even the people who do not believe in *halakhah* have *halakhah!* There is Conservative *halakhah*, even Reform *halakhah.* Rav Soloveitchik was not only the *ish halakhah* the *halakhah* personality *par excellence,* but he restored *devar halakhah,* the word of *halakhah* to the language of Jewish thought.

How did he do it? He explained this to me, in the corridor of Yeshiva University 25 years ago. When I first saw Rav Soloveitchik there. I understood better the passage in the Torah where it refers to Moshe Rabbenu when he descended from Mount Sinai: *velo yada Mosheh ki karan or panav* that his face was shining – *vayyireu migeshet elav* – and the people were scared to approach him. I was terrified of Rav Soloveitchik. I was terrified to approach him. He had burning eyes. He was obliviously a "lonely man of faith" – and yet when we started talking about *halakhah*, he started *shokeling,* he became animated, he put his arm around me, he was what Elie Wiesel calls "a soul on fire."

And what he said was very simple and fundamental. Yet it had never been said before. He said, "In the past, Jewish philosophy – *machashevet Yisrael* – and *halakhah* were two different things. They were disconnected." "In truth," he said, "they are only one thing and that one thing is – *halakhah.*" The only way you can think Jewishly and construct a Jewish philosophy, is out of *halakhah.* He gave me one example. He said, "You have read Professor A.J. Heschel's book called *The Sabbath?"* I said, "Yes." He said, "It's a beautiful book, isn't it?" I said, "Yes." And he said, "What does he call Shabbat? – a sanctuary in time. This is an idea of a poet, it's a lovely idea. But what is Shabbat? Shabbat," he said, "is *lamed-tet melakhot*, it is the thirty-nine categories of work and their *toladot,* and it is out of that *halakhah* and not of poetry that you have to construct a theory of Shabbat." That was his example.

I think that he may have felt constrained from giving what he regarded as the prime example, as is very clear from his writings. The prime example was Rambam. There were in a sense two Rambams. There was Rambam who was the *ish halakhah*, the greatest halakhist of the Middle Ages, who wrote the *Mishneh Torah.* And there was Rambam the great philosopher, the author of the *Moreh Nevukhim,* of the *Guide of the Perplexed.* They are two different Rambams. They speak a different language. Indeed, there is argument amongst scholars as to which is the real Rambam.

The Rav was critical of the philosophical Rambam. He writes in *The Halakhic Mind* that Rambam's philosophy was influenced by the ancient Greeks, by the medieval Arabic thinkers, the Islamic neo-Aristotelians, none of whom were Jewish. When Rav Soloveitchik philosophised, *shivviti lenegdi tamid*, the man he put in front of him eternally was the Rambam, but never the Rambam of the *Moreh Nevukhim, always the* Rambam of *halakhah*, of the *Mishneh Torah.* What was the difference, the paradigm shift that the Rav brought, which is truly revolutionary in the history of Jewish thought? The easiest way I can explain it is simply this. The phrase *taamei hamitzvot*, has two connotations. It means the reason for commandments and reasons are external to a *mitzvah.* With things that happen before the *mitzvah* or after the *mitzvah.* The Rambam in the *Guide,* as a philosopher, deals with the *mitzvot* and he explains their historical background. (what went on before) and their consequence (what happens after their performance). Thus for Rambam, the *taamei hamitzvot* are external to the *mitzvah.*

However, the phrase *taamei hamitzvot* could mean something completely different. *Taam* not only means a reason, it means, a taste. *Taamu ureu ki tov* – the taste of the *mitzvot.* What does the *mitzvah* feel like, not externally but internally, not before and after, but *bishat maaseh,* while you are performing it?

The Rav actually believed and proved in all his works that when you carried out *mitzvot* you entered a world of thought that was quite distinctive – the world of Jewish philosophy. The *Sefer Hachinnukh* says

"Acharei hapeulot nimshekhu hatevavot" – how you act affects what you feel. The Rav said in effect, *acharei hapeulot nimshekhu hamochot, hasikhliyyot* – what you do affects how you think. *Halakhah* is not merely a way of acting, it is a way of seeing the world. In one obvious sense, we see things in *halakhah* that do not exist in physical space. In relation to a *sukkah*, for example, the *halakhah* recognizes certain imaginary constructions – *gud assik, gud achit, dophan akumah,* which count as walls, *mechitzot,* as far as the laws of *sukkah* are concerned, but which are not physical walls. They exist in *halakhah.* But they do not exist in the world of the senses. A casual observer who knew nothing of *halakhah* could not see such walls. But to the person who knows the law, they are as real as constructions of brick or stone. The *ish halakhah* the person whose mind is shaped by the *halakhah* – sees things in a different way.

Rav Soloveitchik profoundly meditated on this, in the most general and systematic way. Some of his deepest reflections relate to *Hilkhot Teshuvah,* the section of Rambam's Code in which he deals with the laws of repentance. Here the Rav discovered the *halakhah*'s deepest insights into the human personality. By being an *ish teshuvah*, a person of *teshuvah*, your whole personality and way of thinking about yourself changed. A person of *teshuvah* was constantly bringing about personal renewal. The Rav loved *chiddush,*and believed that the greatest *chiddush* was in the self. Thus when you study carefully Rambam's *Hilkhot Teshuvah,* you understand that the *mitzvah* of *teshuvah* to be *mechaddesh et atzmo,* to renew yourself.

So we can now understand what the Rav did for a generation who thought that *halakhah* was dull and detailed and dry. He made it vivid, made it vast. *"Miyom shecharev beit hamikdash ein lo leHakadosh Barukh Hu be'olamo ella daled amot shel halakhah bilvad,"* said Chazal – from the day the Temple was destroyed the Holy One Blessed be only has in His world the four cubits of *halakhah.* Rav Soloveitchik turned it around and in effect said that it is within the four cubits of *halakhah* that you find the infinity of *Hakadosh Barukh Hu.* It was as if the Rav had found *halakhah "afar min haadamah,"* dry dust, *"vayyippach be'appav nishmat chayyim"* – and he breathed into it the breath of life – *"vattehi halakhah lenefesh chayyah"* – and he made *halakhah* come alive. So when the Rav left us a *devar halakhah* he left us the *devar halakhah,* a renewal of our whole understanding of *halakhah.* That is the *kelal.*

Having said this, I want to add one of detail. It is very striking that from his earliest published writings in the 1940s, the Rav was preoccupied with death. Time and again he returns to it in his writings. In *Ish haHalakhah*, at various points he keeps coming back to it. He explains how *ish halakhah,* the halakhic personality, is calm, serene, detached, like a mathematician, unfazed by anything because he comes to the world with his *a priori* categories, he has things mapped out in advance. But there is one thing that troubles the *ish Halakhah,* the fear of death. He tells stories several times about his late grandfather, Reb Hayyim of Brisk who was terrified of death. He relates in the name of his father, Reb Mosheh, that when fear of death would seize hold of Reb Hayyim, he would immerse himself in the study of the laws of *avelut* and the laws of *tumah* and those laws of death and defilement would somehow or other cause his terror to subside. I lose count of the number of times he refers to it in *Ish haHalakhah.*

If you look through his published writings, many of his most powerful statements are given in the form of *hespedim.* His great lectures on *teshuvah* were given on *yahrtzeits,* always in memory of someone who had died. Again and again he comes back to concepts of *aninut and avelut.* I know of no other Jewish writer who speaks of death so often – and in very strange ways.

For instance, he gives several examples about the Vilna Gaon; I quote only one. In *Ish haHalakhah* he states that when the Vilna Gaon's brother died, upon learning about this on Shabbat, the Vilna Gaon showed no emotion at all. On Shabbat you cannot mourn. As soon as Shabbat was out and they had made *Havdalah,* the Vilna Gaon burst into tears. And this for the Rav was the zenith of *ish halakhah,* that you could control your grief.

Nonetheless, each time I read these passages, and there are several in the book, I have been troubled. But, "*lo nittenah Torah lemalakhei hasharet*" – the Torah was not given to angels. Human beings have emotions. Unlike angles we are moved by sadness, exhilaration, fear and joy. Even Mosheh Rabbenu, as the Rambam points out, gave way on one occasion, to anger. Perhaps the deepest of all human emotions is grief – the devastating sense of loss when someone close to us is taken from us. How then could the

Rav believe that it was the task of the *halakhah* to make us immune to grief? Not only does this verge on the impossible. It comes close to being inhuman. Precisely now, as we struggle to come to terms with our grief at the loss of the Rav, we ask this question of the Rav himself. Why was he so obsessed with death?

The answer, I suggest, is this: the Rav lived through the Shoah. His great works, *The Halakhic Personality* and *The Halakhic Mind* were written while the Holocaust was taking place. And we have to understand that for the Rav the Shoah was not only the massacre of six million Jews. It was the massacre of the Torah itself, *kivyakhol.* The entire world of Torah from which the Rav stemmed, from which Torah derived, of Brisk, of Volozyhn, of Eastern Europe, had gone up in flames. It is very striking that in neither work that he wrote while the Shoah was happening, although he knew that it was happening, does he mention the Shoah. The Shoah figures very little in his writings. And yet I believe the impact of the Holocaust on the Rav was immense. He was a person terrified and traumatized by death, let alone by this unprecedented destruction. Not only did the Shoah test his faith to its limits, but it left him in a real sense not just a survivor, but the survivor. He was the one link with the world of Brisk, he was the one on whom the mantle rested. He was one on his own. And he was one on his own in a land, in America of the 1940s, that was utterly insensitive and unreceptive to the values of the world. They had never heard of Brisk. The Rav frequently refers to his biblical namesake, Yosef. Like Yosef, he was a lonely man of faith, separated from a world that he had lost, on his own, in the highly technocratic hedonistic cosmopolitan world of Egypt, which was for the Rav the ancient equivalent of the USA.

The Rav's first words in print, the introduction to *Ish Halakhah,* are a quotation from the *Gemara* in *Sotah* (36b) which refers to Yosef in Potiphar's house and how he might have sinned had not the image of his father appeared before him at the crucial moment. Rav Yosef Soloveitchik felt all the time that he carried with him the image of that vanished generation. It was his source of life. When a person has lived through such an absolute tragedy, what they most want to do is forget. We know this because almost no one wrote about the Shoah for twenty years after it happened. We know this because Noach, *ish tzaddik* having lived through a

Shoah, through the *mabbul* wanted to get drunk and forget everything. We know this from *Yosef Hatzaddik* himself who, having lived through the trauma of being separated from the world of his parents, also wished to forget. He called his firstborn Menasheh – *"ki nashani Elokim et kol amali ve'et kol beit avi"* – for God has made me forget all my sufferings and my father's house. That is the natural human reaction – to want to deny and forget.

However, Rav Soloveitchik could not forget because locked up in his soul and in his memory, was all that was left of that world and only his memory could keep it alive. So throughout his life's work we sense a profound meditation on the relationship between *halakhah* and death at three different levels. Firstly, there was the psychological level which he learnt from Rabbi Eliyahu Pruzhiner and from the Vilna Gaon that when you are terrified of the chaos, the abyss, you study order and that composes the mind. That was the first and least important level.

There was a second level. Rav Soloveitchik held that the *halakhah* actually changes our perception of time. We believe that what is past is past, what is present is here and what is future has not yet been. The Rav felt that the *ish halakhah* operates in a completely different framework of time. He says the consciousness of *ish halakhah* embraces the entire company of *chakhmei hamasorah,* the sages of our tradition. He lives in their midst, discusses and argues questions of *halakhah* with them, delves into and analyses principles in their company. All of them merge into one time experience. He walks alongside Maimonides, he listens to Rabbi Akiva, he senses the presence of Abbaye and Rava.

I know this was something his *talmidim* felt – that he lived in the presence of the past generations of the sages. Thus he explains assertions such as *"David Melekh Yisrael chai vekayyam"* (King David is alive) or *"Yaakov avinu lo met"* (the patriarch Jacob did not die), to mean that the great sages of our past never died. There can be no death among the company of the sages of tradition. If you study *halakhah* you bring people who have died back to life again and by studying the *halakhot* of Brisk and that destroyed, murdered world he brought it back to life again. That was the second level.

But there was a third and deeper level still. In *Kol Dodi Dofek* he says something very profound. He says there are two responses to suffering. There is the ordinary human response and there is the halakhic response. The ordinary human response is to see yourself as an object. Why is this happening to me? It is happening to me, and I am an object. The halakhic response is to see it as a subject and the *ish halakhah* does not ask why is this happening to me, but what shall I do? And the Rav knew what he had to do. *"He'emidu talmidim harbeh"* raise up a new generation of disciples that would replace those who were murdered in Eastern Europe.

The Rav constantly bore in mind the statement of Rambam in *Hilkhot Avel* that avelut is part of *teshuvah*, that mourning is part of the process of repentance and return. The Rav never forgot this. His mourning for a whole murdered generation took the form of bringing the next generation to *teshuvah,* to return to the *halakhah* which had been so devastated.

But even more profoundly still, the word *teshuvah* does not merely mean to return. *Lashuv* means to come back. But *lehashiv* means to bring back, to restore. Somehow, mystically, mysteriously, in that generation of disciples who had never before existed in America, the souls of those who had died were being restored, reborn. We touch here on a subject none of us can fathom, but which we sense, obscurely. I believe that Rav Soloveitchik was engaged in nothing less than *techiyyat hametim,* bringing a dead world back to life.

I believe that between the lines of our conversation ten years ago, he hinted at something vast and mysterious. Towards the end of his life he was in effect able to say that *Brisk had been reborn in America. Halakhah* had triumphed over death. The world of the *yeshivot,* that had been so cruelly destroyed, lived again.

If it did so, it was because of him. Rav Soloveitchik stood *bein hametim uvein hachayyim,* between the dead and the living, as the sole link between a generation that had died and one that had not yet been born. He was the "branch plucked from the burning." And he replanted it so that it became again a tree of life.

Few people in Judaism's history achieved so much. The Rav did not give way to pride. He knew, more than most, the force of Rabban Yochanan ben Zakkai's statement: "If you have learned much Torah, do not claim credit for yourself, since it was for this that you were created." But he lived through a tragic and epic time. Like Rabbi Chanina ben Taradyon he had seen the *Sefer Torah* set on fire: not just the Torah scroll, but community after community of saints and sages who were in themselves living Torah scrolls. Like Rabbi Chanina he saw "the parchments burning, but the letters flying upwards." The physical parchment could be destroyed. But the letters could never be destroyed. It was Rav Soloveitchik's greatness that he brought the letters down to earth again, reassembled them into sentences and chapters that could be understood by the next generation and reinscribed them on their hearts.

"Al yippater adam mechavero ella mitokh devar halakhah shemitokh kakh zokhrehu." Rav Soloveitchik taught us in the most dramatic way possible that *halakhah* keeps memory alive and by keeping memory alive it keeps the Jewish people alive even when they have been overshadowed by death. We are overshadowed and overwhelmed by his death but because he taught us not just a *halakhah,* but *the halakhah.* We shall never forget him and he will live because he changed our lives.

"Ein osim nefashot latzaddikim – divreihem hem zikhronam." We make no monuments to the righteous other than this, that we take their words as their memory. *Yehi zikhro barukh leolam va'ed.* May his memory be blessed forever.

THOUGHTS ON *PARSHAT SHEMINI*: IN MEMORY OF RABBI JOSEPH B. SOLOVEITCHIK *zt"l*

RABBI DR. JACOB J. SCHACTER

Together with so many Jews across the world, I am still overcome with a great deal of sadness over the very recent passing of Rabbi Joseph B. Soloveitchik *zt"l*, one of the greatest leaders, teachers and *talmidei chachamim* of the twentieth century.

Rather than attempt a full analysis of his extraordinary contribution to modern Jewish life on so many levels, I want to let the Rav speak for himself, and share with you a *dvar Torah* I heard from him eighteen years ago this week.

On Sunday morning, April 13, 1975, the Rav delivered a talk at the annual breakfast sponsored by the Chevrah Shas of Boston. Normally the Rav would deliver a *shiur* on Sunday mornings, but this morning was different. He was to deliver not a *Gemara shiur* but an analysis of aspects relating to the *parshat hashavua*, *Parshat Shemini*. It was a talk delivered on an ordinary Sunday morning before an audience of maybe fifty people.

At that time, the Rav *zt"l* was interested in the connection between the *parshah* and the *haftorah*. As is well known, the assumption is that there always is some thematic or conceptual connection between the two. The *haftorah* is taken from II Samuel, Chapters 6–7, and describes how King David was moving the ark of God to what would become the city of Jerusalem. It was placed on a new cart and everybody was happy, full of joy: *"Vedavid vekhol beit Yisrael misachakim lifnei Hashem bekhol atsei veroshim u'vekhinorot u'vinevalim u'vetupim u'vimna'anim u'vetseltselim"* (6:5). All of a sudden, the oxen stumbled and the ark was in danger of falling. Uzzah, son of Avinadav, one of the leaders, was standing right there. He reached out to catch it, to hold on to it, to make sure it would not fall. And then, the *pasuk* informs us: *"Vayichar af Hashem be'Uzzah vayakeihu sham Ha'elokim al hasha'al veyamat sham im aron Ha'elokim"* (6:7).

On the face of it, the link of this incredible story to the *parshah* is obvious. The *parshah* describes the death of Aharon's two sons who died making an offering to God that was inappropriate – neither required nor requested. Yes, their intention was *leshem Shamayim*, but it was a mistake. Similarly, in the *haftorah* story, Uzzah, too, meant *leshem Shamayim*, but he, too, made a mistake.

But the Rav *zt"l* went further than this and suggested that the similarity is much deeper. What follows is copied from my notes, almost word for word, to provide a sense of the style and thinking of the Rav *zt"l:*

> Both stories are indicative of the human tragedy, of any man – no matter if he be a king or a private citizen, an illiterate or great philosopher. The tragedy of mortal man consists not only in the fact that he is mortal, that it is impossible for him to escape death, but also in the fact that when death strikes, it scoffs at man, it strikes at the most inappropriate and unsuitable time. Death is a tragedy whenever it happens, there is a special sarcasm in death, striking particularly at a moment of great joy. Death scoffs at man – at his hopes and victories, at his festivals and holidays. Not only does it want to destroy man, but it spoils his rare moments of joy and happiness. When he celebrates the most cherished victory for which he worked so hard and suffered so much, when he is ready to harvest the fruits of his painstaking efforts, then death attacks ruthlessly and cynically.
>
> *Vayehi bayom hashemini,* on the eighth day of the ceremony to consecrate the *mishkan*, Aharon haKohen was the happiest man. *Chazal* (*Yalkut Shimoni, Vayikra*, #520) tell us that he was awarded ten crowns on that day. All his hopes and aspirations came true on that day. His joy was so great that it overcame the entire community. *"Vayar kol ha'am vayaronu vayiplu al peneihem."* Everyone broke out in singing and ecstatic shouting and rapturously fell on their faces. And, suddenly, Nadav and Avihu make a mistake and: *"Vateitzei esh milifnei Hashem vatochal otam vayamutu lifnei Hashem"* (*Vayikra* 10:2).
>
> The same occurred in the *haftorah* story. The ark was being moved to *ir David*, the entire Jewish people was happy, playing musical instruments, and suddenly the marshal of the procession

was smitten by God. The joyous assembly suddenly turned into a mourning community; death struck at a most inappropriate time. This is one aspect of the similarity – complete surprise and deep sadness overtaking the Jewish people on their happiest day.

And then, there is a second aspect. What is most mysterious about both stories is not the punishment, *per se*; not that death befell them (Nadav/Avihu and Uzzah), but that death befell them so quickly. It is the swiftness of the retribution and the magnitude of the punishment that is strange. Yes, they made a mistake, but, after all, their intention was good; they were carried away by overpowering ecstasy and, to express their joy, in the case of Nadav and Avihu, they took the incense to bring as an offering to God. So, asks the Midrash, why did God punish them immediately, without a chance to repent, without a chance to pray, to do *teshuvah?* Why does God display such patience to the really wicked and did not do so to them! After all, *ve'ad yom moto techakeh lo.*

And the same question intrigues us in the case of Uzzah as well. He acted the way he did in order to protect the ark! The oxen had stumbled and he was afraid it would fall to the ground. True, an error was made. It should have been carried on the shoulders of the *kohanim* and not moved by oxen. But this is only a *mitzvas aseh,* and *Chazal* say (*Yoma* 86a): *"Avar al aseh veshav eino zaz misham ad shemochalin lo."* He should have been given a chance, but he died immediately, *"Vayamat sham im aron HaElokim"* (*Vayikra* 6:7). Why?

Both narratives tell us one basic truth very relevant to us. For we live today, at best, in complicated times. When Jews, either as individuals or a community, reach the stage of *giluy Shechinah*, when the Jewish historical existence is determined not by the natural nexus of cause and effect, but by God Himself directly watching over the Jewish people, then any violation is punished immediately and severely. When it is obvious for all to see that the Jewish people are under the special, unnatural care of God, living in a state of *hashgachah nisis*; when there is a special close proximity between God and man, then God demands complete obedience and, if it is not forthcoming, he punishes immediately, without allowing for a chance to repent. At such a time, the virtue

> of *erech apayim* is not practiced by God; the emphasis is not on *rav chesed* but on *rav emes.*
>
> It is only when historical destiny is tied up with natural elements, when pure historical-causality guides man, then – and only then – is God patient; then and only then is punishment slow in coming. But when Jews enjoy the favor of God, punishment is swift in coming.

This is just the first section of a six-part lecture delivered by the Rav *zt"l* that Sunday morning in Brookline. The first part is eerily relevant when thinking about the *petirah* of the Rav himself, for was he not taken from us precisely on *yom tov,* on our "festival and holiday," in our "moment of joy and happiness?" It was then that death attacked, "ruthlessly and cynically." But the relevance of the second part is harder to understand. I wonder what the Rav *zt"l* meant when he said: "We live today, at best, in complicated times." Did he mean in post-Holocaust times? For surely the question that disturbs us about Nadav/Avihu and Uzzah hounds us with regard to the Holocaust. And even the question that apparently did not disturb the Rav *zt"l* about Nadav/Avihu and Uzzah confounds us deeply with regard to the Holocaust, i.e., not only "the swiftness of the retribution and the magnitude of the punishment" but the death itself. Retribution for what? Punishment for what? Those words ring hollow, and their application woefully inadequate. There is no explanation, and we follow the model of Aharon in *Parshsat Shemini* (10:3) who was silent in the face of the terrible tragedy which struck him.

I do not believe that the Rav *zt"l* was addressing the Holocaust that spring morning in Brookline, but he did address it on another occasion, a number of years earlier. I heard about it from my father, Rabbi Herschel Schacter, who was particularly struck with how the Rav *zt"l* ended his talk – and the way he ended then is the way I want to end here.

In the moment of the greatest sorrow one can imagine, when a child stands at the freshly dug grave of a parent, our tradition bids us to recite a special *kaddish.* Torn with grief, bursting with pain, we do not cry out to God in angry rebellion, but we declare the greatness and sanctity of the Divine name:

יתגדל ויתקדש שמיה רבא. בעלמא די הוא עתיד לאתחדתא, ולאחיא מתיא ולאסקא לחיי עלמא.
ולמבני קרתא די ירושלים, ולשכלל היכלה בגוה, ולמעקר פלחנא נכראה מן ארעא, ולאתבא פלחנא די שמיא לאתרא, וימליך קודשא בריך הוא במלכותה ויקרה.
בחייכון וביומיכון ובחיי דכל בית ישראל בעגלא ובזמן קריב ואמרו אמן.

May God's great name be glorified and sanctified in a world which He will recreate anew, make renewed and reborn. [May He] rebuild the city of Jerusalem and erect His Temple therein, to uproot all evil and idolatry from the world and to restore the true worship of Heaven to its proper place. And the Holy One, blessed be He, will reign in His royalty and His glory in your lifetime and in your days and in the lifetime of the entire household of Israel without delay, speedily, and soon, and let us say Amen.

ABOUT THE RAV: THESE THINGS I REMEMBER

Dr. Alvin I. Schiff

Rabbi Joseph Ber Soloveitchik *zt"l* was a towering intellect with unparalleled mastery of Judaic sources, particularly Talmud and Jewish philosophy; he had an encyclopedic knowledge of secular subjects and general culture; and, in addition to Hebrew, Aramaic, Yiddish and English, had an intimate comprehension of Greek, Latin, German, Russian and Scandinavian languages and literature. He was a brilliant, exciting teacher, and an inspiring, captivating, fearless public orator and charismatic communicator.

The Rav, as he was lovingly known, was aptly referred to as a *gadol.* Indeed, he was a *gadol hador*, the scion of *gedolei hado*r (see *Brachot* 63a). More than that, he was a *gadol olam*, as were his forebears. To be sure, he was a titan among giants whose persona embraced much more than the public qualities which made him a legend in his lifetime. He called himself a "*melamed*," yet he was beyond a shadow of a doubt the outstanding *rosh hayeshiva* of our times. The Rav was a Gaon who possessed an array of personal attributes – some well known, others less discernable. These qualities and notions will now be made public, as people who knew him will begin to ascribe to him those unique characteristics and concepts with which they are familiar. In this light, it is my privilege to… share some of my personal remembrances of the Rav.

I first saw Rabbi Soloveitchik when he came to Boston as Rav in 1932 and, as a child of six, I remember the excitement associated with his arrival. Two years later, I remember his visit to the Beth El Hebrew School, the Talmud Torah of the Beth El synagogue, one of the large congregations that he served as Rav. There were no Jewish day schools in Boston at that time. The Beth El Hebrew School was an intensive, high-standard supplementary Jewish educational institution where students studied for a minimum of ten hours per week, exclusive of mandated junior congregation on Shabbat and special programs throughout the year. As an eight-year-old, I vividly recall his visit to my class, when an excited teacher, accompanied by the principal, Mr. Tumaroff, introduced him to the students, after which the Rav engaged us in conversation for a very long time. I remember coming home that evening and telling my parents about the "big" rabbi who visited our class and made us feel so very good about *limudei kodesh*. Moreover, he spoke to the pupils in clear, understandable English, unlike the older rabbanim in the community. In addition to visiting classes, one of the reasons the Rav would come to our school was to encourage the children in the graduating class to continue their Jewish education after they completed elementary school. Towards this end, the Rav organized a Hebrew High School at Beth El which was eventually incorporated into the Prozdor of the Hebrew Teachers College in Roxbury. Years later, I learned from Mr. Sidney Hillson, principal in the late 1930s, that Rabbi Soloveitchik would visit Beth El in order to discuss ways of enhancing the curriculum.

Despite the scope and intensity of the Beth El Hebrew School program, the Rav realized the need for an all day Jewish school environment and an even more intensive Judaic Studies program for Jewish children in the Boston area. And, after overcoming the apathy and opposition of communal leaders and parents (the antagonism and resistance were severe), the Rav succeeded in 1937, as a young man of 34, five years after coming to Boston, to establish the co-ed Maimonides School in Roxbury. With the exception of the Hebrew Parochial School founded in Baltimore in 1917 (renamed Yeshiva Hafetz Hayim in 1933 in memory of the famed scholar Rabbi Israel Meir Hakohen of Radin, Lithuania, and now popularly known by the name Talmudic Academy), the Maimonides School was the first modern yeshiva in the United States established outside New York City. It took no small amount of perspicacity, courage, leadership, perseverance and the investment of much time and energy to launch Maimonides, now a major Jewish day elementary and high school.

The Rav took special interest in his new educational institution which he visited regularly during the first three decades of its existence. The board of education of Maimonides was chaired diligently by his wife, Tonya, until her untimely demise in 1967, and, since that time, by his daughter Atarah Twersky. The Rav's visits to Maimonides were moments he cherished. He was very proud of the school. Yet, he realized that its achievements were due largely to the efforts of the principal and teachers. He once told Rabbi Moses Cohn, the long-time principal, "I get all the credit for all the work you do."

In founding Maimonides, the Rav made it crystal clear that girls would be given equal educational opportunity. This decision was based upon his strongly held opinion that the *akeret habayit* was ever so crucial in raising the Jewish child, particularly in the Western society. As such, every Jewish girl had to have a sound Judaic background. His feeling about the influential role of the mother (spouse) regarding the educational progress of children is supported by a variety of contemporary research studies in education.

The Rav felt deeply about developing intelligent, educated Jewish laity, both male and female. He believed that women were no less endowed intellectually than men were. Consequently, it behooved the Jewish community to provide girls with as excellent a Jewish education as possible.

Moreover, the Rav stressed that Jewish education for women was halakhically appropriate and desirable. For these reasons, he enthusiastically supported the founding of Stern College for Women and its Beit Midrash program, and gave the opening *shiur* in the Beit Midrash in 1977.

Rabbi Soloveitchik's charismatic, oratorical artistry was beyond compare. He was able – via his vast command of Judaic-Hebraic literature coupled with his incredible grasp of philosophy, mathematics, and other secular subjects, and his penetrating insight into contemporary affairs and his perspicuity – to reach all levels of his audiences. As Rav in Boston, his base of operation was divided among a variety of synagogues in Roxbury, Dorchester, and Mattapan – contiguous communities populated by some 80,000 Jews. As a child, I often heard this area referred to as *Yerushalayim d'America.* One of Rabbi Soloveitchik's main functions was giving *shiurim* before *Minchah* on special Sabbaths, alternating among the various synagogues. Several friends and I in the Hashomer Hadati (now known as Bnei Akiva) would religiously follow him from *shul* to *shul*, sitting attentively for two and three hours at a time. While we did not understand all that the Rav was saying (even though we were conversant in Yiddish) and, more often than not, understood very little, we were mesmerized by his *koach hahasbarah* – his remarkable ability to communicate, to elucidate and interpret – and we relished the fact that we were in the presence of a *gadol.*

The synagogues were all large – some with seating capacities for as many as 2,000 people. Many hundreds walked distances to attend the Rav's *shiurim*. He was able, without a microphone, to keep their rapt attention for the length of his lectures. On the podium, at each of his discourses, was a large stack of *seforim* to which he often referred. For the opening of one of his *shiurim*, which he always prepared diligently, he had copies of *The New York Times* and several local newspapers. To us, it seemed like a special happening. We were to be treated to an analysis of current events. To be sure, the Rav used this opportunity, in 1940, to address his remarks to the United States government about the Nazi intentions and activity in Europe. His fiery words made such an incredible impression upon us. For months on end, during our weekly Hashomer Hadati *sichot*, we discussed anti-Semitism and the need for a Jewish homeland. Moreover, we organized a letter-writing campaign to the White House, which like other Jewish efforts, was to no avail at that time.

The Rav was committed to *kashrut* in the Jewish community of Boston. He was the *rav hamachshir* for Morrison and Schiff, the delicatessen factory founded by my grandfather. From my uncle and cousin, who headed Morrison and Schiff, I heard many stories of the Rav's strict application of *kashrut* laws.

When the Rav was invited to be the Rav of the Boston Jewish community, the *Va'ad Ha'ir* requested Morrison and Schiff to engage him as *rav hamachshir* to supplement his salary. As long as my grandfather was alive, Morrison and Schiff did not need a *mashgiach*. After he died in a tragic accident, the *Va'ad Ha'ir* and Morrison and Schiff decided that *kashrut* supervision would be in order. This happened at the time the Rav arrived in Boston.

Many years later, during the Rav's long tenure, from 1932 to 1980, as *rav hamachshir,* some of his friends thought he should give up the *hashgachah* at Morrison and Schiff since, they said, it was beneath his dignity. He refused because he didn't want people to think that there was something wrong with the *kashrut* of Morrison and Schiff. Moreover, he was grateful to Morrison and Schiff for hiring him when he needed the supplemental income and he enjoyed his relationship with the company.

In addition to the Rav, Morrison and Schiff engaged a *mashgiach temidi* to oversee the *shechitah* and the manufacture of the delicatessen. The Rav spoke regularly to the *mashgiach* who appreciated his guidance and prompt responses to questions he had.

Once a month, my cousin, Joseph, who was an officer of Morrison and Schiff, and later its president, would drive the Rav to a Manchester, New Hampshire, slaughter house where bull meat was prepared. During the one and one half hour trips, the Rav knowingly discussed an unusually wide variety of topics mostly in Yiddish with my cousin.

Generally, when Joseph came to pick up the Rav for the drive to Manchester, he would wait for the Rav to finish his daily fast reading of four or five newspapers. My cousin told me that very often there were "urgent" phone calls from all over the world, particularly from Israel and England and from rabbis in North America.

One morning, the Rav entered my cousin's car and said excitedly: "*vos zogst du vegen di Red Sox*," noting that he was amazed at the Red Sox performance that week.

One story, above all others, that my cousin related to me demonstrates the Rav's deep knowledge of the secular world and science and his amazing ability to grasp new scientific information.

The Rav knew that before joining Morrison and Schiff in an executive capacity, Joseph served as chemical engineer in Oakridge, Tennessee, where research and experimentation with atomic energy took place in preparation for the atomic bomb. About seven years after World War II, during one of their trips to Manchester, the Rav asked Joseph to tell him about the procedure of creating atomic energy. Joseph was amazed at the Rav's knowledge and ability to grasp new scientific concepts. The Rav seemed most interested in the processing of raw uranium 234–235 which was the only fissionable uranium, and readily engaged in conversation about the two processes of obtaining atomic energy – the electromagnetic method and the gaseous diffusion method. According to Joseph, the Rav demonstrated great eagerness to learn more about the production of atomic energy.

One morning in 1978, when my cousin came to pick up the Rav for their visit to Manchester, he noticed a limousine with diplomatic flags parked near the Rav's home in Brookline, Massachusetts and several police cars surrounding the limousine. The police on guard refused to let my cousin come near the Rav's house. After a fifteen-minute wait, from the distance he saw an elderly gentleman and three younger men leave and enter the limousine. On route that day to Manchester, the Rav told Joseph that Menachem Begin had come to see him and asked him to become Chief Rabbi of Israel. The Rav was not eager to discuss the reasons for his refusal, but mentioned that he had many challenges to address in the United States.

Another story about the Rav reveals the depth of his concern and compassion for people, particularly for former students. One day Joseph received an urgent telephone call from the Rav who was in New York for his weekly *shiurim* at the Rabbi Isaac Elchanan Theological Seminary. "Mr. Schiff, I understand that Morrison and Schiff used milk powder last month in the manufacture of cocktail frankfurters," he said rather heatedly in English. The Rav's information came from a former student, who, it appears, wanted "to score points" with the Rav. This former student worked at the Department of Agriculture and made a chemical analysis of Morrison and Schiff's delicatessen products. It turned out that his analysis was faulty and he was promptly fired by the Department of Agriculture for making a serious erroneous judgement and for communicating his findings to the public, which was against Department of Agriculture's policy. After hearing about the former student's termination, the Rav called my cousin and, in Yiddish, asked him to do the Rav a favor. Could Joseph help the former student to regain his job at the Department of Agriculture. After all, the Rav said, he meant well and should be forgiven for his unfortunate error. "I have *rachamanus* on him. This will destroy his professional status and earning power," the Rav explained.

One final observation about my cousin's intimate view of the Rav. The Rav was always immaculately dressed and groomed at a time when most *rabbanim* my cousin knew did not pay much attention to their attire and appearance.

I recall two incidents when I was a young child in the late 1930s involving the Rav in *kashrut* matters. I remember the Rav talking animatedly with my father, who supervised *hashgachah* for the *Va'ad Ha'ir*, about the fee levied on the kosher butcher shops for *kashrut* supervision. The Rav was complaining about the increasing difficulty to collect the annual fee from the thirty or so kosher establishments in Greater Boston. He wanted fervently to guarantee the continuation of *kashrut* supervision in Boston and wanted my father's help in this matter.

I remember, too, the Rav leading a demonstration against a butcher shop in the Grove Hall section of Roxbury, a densely populated Jewish area. I recall the Rav standing on a truck, speaking out against the shop that claimed to be kosher but would not submit to *kashrut* supervision. The Rav told my father that he was personally involved because he wanted to insure that no other butcher shops would think of dropping communal *hashgachah*.

My brother recently told me a story about the Rav which speaks volumes about his sensitivity towards his wife Tonya. It involved a cousin of my brother's daughter-in-law who served for some time as the Rav's helper.

When the Rav grew older, during the days he would give *shiurim* in the Rabbi Isaac Elchanan Theological Seminary and stayed overnight in the YU dormitory, a yeshiva student would usually room with him as a helper. One evening, the Rav noticed that his helper got all dressed up. When the Rav inquired as to the reason, the yeshiva student told him that he was going out on a date. While they talked, the Rav noticed that the socks of the helper, who was seated during their conversation, were torn. The Rav suggested that he go to the Rav's dresser and use a pair of the Rav's socks. The helper did as the Rav recommended, returned to the Rav and told him that all the socks were white. The Rav smiled, acknowledged the fact that all his socks were white and told the yeshiva student that his wife had difficulty with colors and found it hard to pair his socks. In order to spare her the problem of sorting and pairing his socks, he decided to wear white socks only.

When I was director of Graduate Jewish education and coordinator of undergraduate education programs at Yeshiva University in the 1960s, I would often discuss matters relating to Jewish educator training with the Rav. One thing stands out in my mind regarding these conversations. He emphasized the need for "excellent pedagogic preparation" for yeshiva and day school teachers on the primary, elementary and secondary school levels. He was equally emphatic about the importance of training qualified supervisors for Jewish schools. The Rav frequently said, given the sophisticated Western society in which Jewish schooling takes place and the kind of professional preparation teachers and principals of secular education receive, it is imperative for teachers and principals in Jewish schools to be trained according to the best principles and practices of education. He strongly advocated for the professionalization of Jewish educators.

In one of my long discussions with the Rav in 1976, at the request of Dr. Norman Lamm at the beginning of his presidency, about the Rav's feelings regarding proposals made by the President's commission appointed by Dr. Lamm, regarding the future of Yeshiva University, the Rav made many comments that revealed how avidly he felt about the modern Orthodox Zionist way of life. The Rav was always much more at ease in his home. The first of our two discussions took place in Brookline. At the end of our meeting, the Rav said, pointedly, "You didn't ask me what gave me the most *agmat nefesh*." I then asked this question. In his response, he spoke emotionally about the dissonance sometimes created by the post-high school Yeshiva experience of students in Israel. The Rav was very disheartened by the tension created by some of the children of his former students who, after returning from a year or two of study in Israel, rejected their family's religious views and practices. After all, he noted that these former *semicha* students were observant, modern Orthodox Jews and did not deserve such treatment from their progeny.

Besides being the epitome of Isaachar (the Biblical-Talmudic personification of Torah learning and teaching), the Rav experienced the vantage point of Zevulun (the personal depiction of the support of Torah learning). He was a member of the initial Professional Advisory Committee of The Program Development Fund for Jewish Education (PDF), a cooperative enterprise sponsored by Joseph Gruss and The Federation of Jewish Philanthropies of New York, which I was privileged to chair. Other members of the committee included Dr. Gerson Cohen, Chancellor of the Jewish Theological Seminary; Dr. Eugene Borowitz, Professor of Jewish Philosophy, Hebrew Union College-Jewish Institute of Religion; Dr. Isadore Twersky (the Rav's son-in-law), Nathan Littauer Professor of

Hebrew Literature and Philosophy, Harvard University; Dr. Emanuel Rackman, Rabbi of the Fifth Avenue Synagogue and co-chair of The Program Development Fund; Sanford Solender, Executive Vice President, Federation of Jewish Philanthropies; Sol Litt, PDF chair; and Joseph Gruss, PDF benefactor. The committee met every six weeks in my office at the Board of Jewish Education of Greater New York for five years, from 1973 to 1978.

The Rav came punctually and regularly to the meetings, participated actively in our deliberations and helped guide the development of the Fund for Jewish Education in Greater New York. His input was crucial in establishing allocation guidelines which eventually led to the distribution of ninety percent of the funds to *yeshivot* and day schools in Greater New York. This was no mean accomplishment. The PDF and its successor organization, The Fund for Jewish Education (FJE), have distributed well over $200 million in support for Jewish education in Greater New York. (Author's note: By 2001, over 400 million dollars has been distributed to schools in Greater New York.)

Overwhelmingly, the money was contributed by Mr. Gruss (via the Carolyn and Joseph Gruss Monument Fund), whose admiration for the Rav knew no bounds.

Two years prior to the official founding of PDF in 1973, Joseph Gruss challenged Federation to match a $100,000 contribution towards building repairs for yeshivot. After a group of Federation lay leaders responded to the challenge, which I presented to them on behalf of Mr. Gruss, the question, "How can we best allocate $200,000, a relatively small sum, to so many yeshivot crying for the support?" The Rav, Dr. Emanuel Rackman, and I met several times to develop criteria of eligibility and guidelines for the distribution of the funds. The success of the building repair program led to the establishment of PDF, and later the FJE.

During one of our visits with the Rav in Boston, Dr. Rackman and I were witness to his genius. The Rav realized that if the PDF program succeeded, there would be more support forthcoming to yeshivot from the same funding source. How right he was! A judgement he rendered was vital in determining how the funds would be spent. Only a mind and heart such as his could make such a recommendation. In discussing the physical facility needs of yeshivot, we determined that, in order of priority, grants should be awarded for removing hazardous conditions and Fire Department violations. In the first category, the Rav suggested that buses for the *yeshivot* in Brooklyn be included since they could be considered a *dirah ara'it* and, therefore, qualify for a building grant. Travelling through unsafe streets in a rickety bus is a hazardous condition. The Rav knew full well that the beneficiaries of this recommendation would be Hassidic and right-wing yeshivot whose leadership and rank and file did not support him and publicly opposed his views of Jewish life, especially his ardent support of Zionism and the State of Israel. Nevertheless, the Rav ruled that buses are a priority condition for building repair funding. Since that decision, made in 1971, millions of dollars have been expended on new buses for *yeshivot*.

Concerning the Rav's Zionist orientation, like the Netziv who supported *Hibat Zion* from the beginning (in the last two decades of the nineteenth century) and was a member of its executive, and like his great uncle Rabbi Meir Bar Ilan, a forceful leader of Mizrachi during the first half of the twentieth century, the Rav was personally involved in religious Zionism and served since 1946 as Honorary President of The Religious Zionists of America, and, since 1968, as Honorary President of Mizrachi Hapoel Mizrachi World Organization. As an ardent supporter of the State of Israel, he demonstrated his sympathies for, and strong support of, the State by receiving Israeli Prime Ministers, Presidents and Chief Rabbis who paid their homage to him in Boston.

On a personal level, I vividly recall the Rav's visits for *nihum aveilim* to my brother's home in Brookline, Massachusetts, where we sat *shivah* for our parents. Each time the Rav would visit, he would enter silently, take a seat near us and sit in absolute silence for a long period of time epitomizing *va'yidom Aharon*, the silence of Aharon after the deaths of his sons, Nadav and Avihu. During each *shivah* visit, which he made in late afternoon, the Rav would sit silently and stare into space until it was time for the *Minchah* service in which he participated intensively.

One final observation about the Rav is in order. In my discussions with him about Yeshiva University's role in the American Jewish education scene, it was so apparent that he was fiercely loyal to YU, particularly since it embodied his philosophy of Judaism and was the only school of higher Jewish learning that guaranteed the implementation of his ideas regarding *Torah U'Madda.*

Rabbi Joseph Ber Soloveitchik *zt"l* was the master artist and YU was his canvas. He was the master architect and YU was his blueprint. *Yehei zichro baruch!*

THE RAV'S PHILOSOPHICAL LEGACY

Rabbi Dr. David Shatz

For his thousands of *talmidim*, the most vivid and faithful characterization of the Rav *zt"l* will always be that of a *gadol hador*. His main vehicle of communication was the *shiur*; his natural idiom, the *shakla vetarya* of a *sugya* and the complexities of a Rambam or *Milchamos*, his dominant intellectual pedigree. Brisk and not Berlin. Efforts to portray the Rav as a philosopher first and foremost, or as wavering between two allegiances and two worlds, will inevitably ring false to those who experienced him directly. Certainly in terms of sheer impact, the number of *musmakhim* and *lamdanim* whom the Rav produced utterly dwarfs the number of students who sought to mine and expand his thought along more straightforwardly philosophical lines.

Even so, while the need to keep this perspective is essential, no tribute to the Rav can ignore his place as a *ba'al machshavah* and as – in a perfectly pure sense of the term – a major Jewish philosopher. That one person was both a towering *gadol* and a preeminent thinker, who commanded respect far outside the *yeshiva*'s walls, is remarkable.[1] Most theologians, after all, belong to academic departments. They dedicate their full professional lives to philosophizing, and so productivity and high quality are entirely expected of them. By contrast, the Rav seemed to do it all as an avocation, to be pursued in scant left-over time. Moreover, it is not just that we fail to appreciate his genius if we blind ourselves to its full scope; no less unfairly, we miss the breadth of his spirituality and sensitivity. Only by seeing the Rav as a whole can we fully grasp the implications of our loss.

Two questions are therefore apt: What has the Rav bequeathed to Orthodox Jewish philosophy in the modern world? And what can Orthodox thinkers do to carry on his legacy?

---

[1] A prominent philosopher who several decades ago was in the Rav's *shiur* made a remark to me that is impossible to forget. This philosopher had made controversial, but truly original, contributions to his field of specialization. Although at the time of our conversation he was only marginally involved in Orthodoxy, he explained to me why he had felt so free to pursue original and sure-to-be-contested paths. "It's because I had Rav Soloveitchik," he explained. "You see, after encountering him, I could not be intimidated by anyone else's intellect. Everyone else fell short."

Time and again in his writings, the Rav highlights conflict, tension, discord, dialectic and paradox.[2] Yet beyond the puzzles and anomalies that he himself so brilliantly delineates, we ourselves confront anomalies when we reflect upon his pursuit of philosophy and when we assess the impact of his ideas on Jewish life.

First, as to his pursuit of philosophy. The Rav sets out a wide array of personality types: Adam the First and Adam the second, *Ish hada'at* and *Ish hadat*, *Ish Hahalakhah*, *Ish Rosh Chodesh*, and more. Yet it is a challenge to locate in this panoply the exact fusion of *geonut* in Talmud with genius in philosophy that he – and he alone – embodied.[3] Halakhic man, for example, would not have written the essay *Ish Hahalakhah*. The whole point of that essay, after all, is that halakhic man finds the world of *halakhah* entirely sufficient for his spirituality, discovering therein his freedom and his creativity. An *Ish Hahalakhah*, so described, would see no point indulging in a psychological or philosophical reconstruction of a halakhic personality, let alone one cast in neokantian categories. But that is exactly what the essay is.[4]

Turning next to "The Lonely Man of Faith" (*Tradition* 7, 1965), the categories of Adam the First and Adam the Second fall short of representing the Rav with precision. The "man of faith" does not combine philosophical and literary reflection with Talmudic greatness, but rather

---

[2] As others have remarked, the stress he places on antitheses and dialectical swings is distinctive and represents a turn in Jewish thought. Cf. Rabbi Jonathan Sacks' essay, "Alienation and Faith," *Tradition* 13-14 (Spring–Summer 1973): 137–62.

[3] As Matis Greenblatt noted to me, the force of this point depends on the familiar question of whether the ideal types which the Rav depicts have an instantiation in real life. If they are "pure" types only, and are not necessarily exemplified in reality, then in actual life particular individuals – like the Rav – might combine various types, but the union would not itself be represented as a separate type in the Rav's panoply. In *Ish Hahalakhah*, the Rav on the one hand affirms that the types are abstractions, but on the other hand refers to real-life "halakhic men," leaving us unsure of his position. But in any case, the Rav never explains in *Ish Hahalakhah* why a phenomenological treatment of a halakhic personality, such as that he undertakes, might be of value; he refers only to other sorts of non-halakhic inquiries. In other words, there is no type which engages in exactly the sort of investigation he undertakes in the essay, so the paradox stands. As I indicate below, *U'Bikashtem miSham* might provide materials for a solution.

[4] See also Rabbi Jonathan Sacks, "Rabbi J. B Soloveitchik's Early Epislemology: A Review of *The Halakhic Mind*," *Tradition* 23:3 (Spring 1988): 86, note 10.

scientific and technological activity with covenantal existence. As Professor Gerald Blidstein frames the paradox:

> "Majestic" first Adam realizes his potential and fulfills a godly mandate by subduing the physical world and perfecting it. But the positive appropriation of this major characteristic of Western civilization is not accompanied by a corresponding imperative to appropriate Western culture, its philosophical or literary achievements. This assertion seems improbable, or at least paradoxical, with regard to the Rav, whose major writings are suffused with modern Western philosophy and literature, and whose very intellectual world is constructed, in part at least, with materials provided by modern culture. Yet the paradox is fact; The Rav is a paradigm of the synthesis of Jewish and Western culture, but he nowhere prescribes this move or urges its legitimacy. The Rav constructs his thought within the categories of Western culture, but nowhere explicitly assigns a specific role to this culture."[5]

Not only do we fail to grasp how one individual could have so integrated the worlds of *halakhah* and *aggadah* on the one hand with the world of general culture on the other, but the why eludes us as well.

One might argue that these paradoxes are mitigated by the essay, "*U'Bikashtem Misham*";[6] for there the Rav portrays the religious odyssey of a personality that seems closer to his own, thereby also perhaps providing a justification for his own pursuits.[7] Even if this is so, our sense of paradox

---

[5] Gerald Blidstein, "On the Jewish People in the Writings of Rabbi Joseph B. Soloveitchik," *Tradition* 23:4 (Spring 1989):14. A contrast to Rav Kook springs to mind. Rav Kook spoke in exalted terms of the value of general culture in a total religious life, and developed a broad framework within which to motivate such a warm embrace of culture. But Rav Kook was not himself an expert in any secular discipline. The Rav, on the other hand, mastered secular disciplines – science, literature and philosophy – but nowhere extolled their pursuit expressly.

[6] Published in *Hadorom* 47 (5739): 1-83, but apparently first drafted in the 1940s.

[7] Other responses are possible. For example, the achievements of Adam the First might be read broadly, as including all cultural productivity ("Lonely Man of Faith," 14); Blidstein goes on to advance an interesting resolution of his own.

grows when we look next at the influence and impact of the Rav's philosophy.

The Rav was most revered by the community of "Modern Orthodoxy," a community that he built, and for over half a century has ceaselessly inspired. Yet his philosophical thought is curiously removed from some of the chief concerns and positions of that constituency. For instance, as we have already seen, the protagonist of *Ish Hahalakhah* is not a "modern" Jew, albeit he finds (in *halakhah*) the freedom and creativity which the "modern" Jew craves. More significantly, the early pages of "Lonely Man of Faith" make the boundaries of the Rav's inquiry there sharp and clear:

> I have never been seriously troubled by the problem of the Biblical doctrine of creation vis-a-vis the scientific story of evolution nor have I been perturbed by the confrontation of the mechanistic interpretation of the human mind with the Biblical spiritual concept of man. I have not been perplexed by the impossibility of fitting the mystery of revelation into the framework of historical empiricism. Moreover, I have not even been troubled by the theories of Biblical criticism. However, while theoretical oppositions and dichotomies have never tormented my thoughts, I could not shake off the disquieting feeling that the practical role of the man of faith within modern society is a very difficult, indeed, a paradoxical one.
> ("Lonely Man of Faith," 9).

Almost consistently in his writings, the great cognitive conflicts of our day – evolution and creation, history and Bible, history and *halakhah,* philosophy and religion – are dismissed entirely.[8] In fact, the Rav maintains that "[faith] does not lend itself completely to the act of cultural translation. There are simply no cognitive categories in which the total commitment of

---

[8] This point is also made by Rabbi Jonathan Sacks in *Tradition in an Untraditional Age.* One should note (as Shalom Carmy has pointed out) that "Lonely Man of Faith" implicitly contains a powerful response to a problem seized upon by biblical criticism, viz., the ostensible conflict between the "two" accounts of creation. Of course, this *"da' mah shetashiv"* is an incidental by-product of the Rav's theorizing; he is occupied with a whole other set of problems.

the man of faith could be spelled out" ("Lonely Man of Faith," 60).[9] This emphasis on the unrationalized dimension of faith gives rise to another paradox. The Rav is often seen as a contemporary exemplar of the Rambam's orientation. Yet the synthesis of faith and reason so avidly sought by the Rambam is no part of the Rav's objectives. "It is not the plan of this paper," reads the opening line of "Lonely Man of Faith," "to discuss the millennium-old problem of faith and reason." What Rambam and Saadya labored strenuously to produce – a set of cognitive claims about the nature of God and the world that would stand up to scientific and philosophical scrutiny – is given short shrift in his analysis. In fact, the closing pages of *The Halakhic Mind* constitute a frontal assault on the entire program of medieval Jewish philosophy. And yet what is the most popular model for Modern Orthodox thought if not the Maimonidean synthesis?[10]

The Rav's justification for involvement in the secular world is also crucially different from both the Rambam's and that which is commonly championed today. He does not contend that such involvement will generate a richer, more accurate body of philosophical, historical and scientific claims and hence a more sophisticated and durable faith. Nor does he base his position on the idea that exposure to secular disciplines produces a refinement of spiritual sensibilities. Rather, his endorsement of culture is founded on a principle rooted in *sefer Bereshit* – one we might describe as moral. Human beings fulfill their divine charge and actualize their divinely ordained nature only by aggressively striving to improve human existence in concrete, material ways. They must "harness the elemental forces of nature" to conquer disease and to subdue the threats that nature poses to human life and security. Only by doing so do they imitate God's creativity, fulfill the responsibilities imposed by the mandate "*milu et ha'aretz vekivshuhah*," and attain dignity. Remarkably, this powerful and visceral argument, that secular disciplines make *yishuv olam* possible, has relatively little resonance in Orthodox writing on the subject of secular studies.

---

9 *The Halakhic Mind* offers a rather different perspective, however. Compare also "*U'Bikashtem miSham*."

10 See also David Singer and Moshe Sokol, "Joseph Soloveitchik, Lonely Man of Faith," *Modern Judaism* 2 (1982): 227–72, p. 249.

Likewise, the Rav offered a trenchant critique of Western culture, but one finds little of that in recent "modern" Jewish theology. His repeated claim that the only authentic source of Jewish philosophical teaching is the *halakha* is much in need of explication,[11] but this vision of a *halakha*-based Jewish philosophy has not been significantly extended by others beyond paradigm cases like *teshuvah* and *tefillah* – much less elevated to a methodological principle.

If on some issues, the Rav's positions were more restrained and "conservative" than those of his constituency, in other respects, some of his constituency seems narrow and parochial by comparison to him. In "Confrontation," the Rav put forth an eloquent, philosophically-based opposition to theological dialogue. His stance exerted tremendous impact. Yet in that same essay, he spoke of the need for Jews to join and cooperate with non-Jews in redressing social ills and creating a better society: "we stand with civilized society shoulder to shoulder against an order which defies us all."[12] Few have expanded on that theme, and it has not found a translation into our communal life. Often, the universal thrust of the Rav's writing is lost or underappreciated. When Doubleday Press chose to issue "Lonely Man of Faith" as a book, it did so because the essay was perceived as what it in fact is: a profound characterization of the place of religion in the modern world, an articulation of a predicament felt universally, a portrait of a condition belonging to what the Rav persistently calls "man." Thus it is not a work of import to Jews alone.[13] Yet strangely, even some of the Rav's admirers are uncomfortable with the suggestion that "religion" is here an operative category. It is as if we adulterate his message to us if we concede that it speaks to others as well.[14]

---

[11] Lest it be thought that the imperative of *"vekivshuhah"* is a but a narrow one confined to the development of medicine and technology, we should note that economics and politics, for example, no less than science, can play a vital role in the transformation of human life. The Rav himself describes the achievements of Adam the First broadly ("Lonely Man of Faith," 14).

[12] On the importance and centrality of this claim, see Marvin Fox, "The Unity and Structure of Rabbi Joseph B. Soloveitchik's Thought," *Tradition* 24:2 (Winter 1989): 44–65.

[13] "Confrontation," *Tradition* 6:2 (Spring–Summer 1964): 5–29, p. 17.

[14] Note that, whereas the text of "Lonely Man of Faith" draws frequently on the Bible, the Rav confines sources from *halakhah*, *aggadah* and *parshanut* almost totally to the

The Rav's philosophy, then, as distinct from "the Rav's Torah," is less in evidence on the Orthodox landscape than one would expect. Why is this so?

Several explanations suggest themselves. Surely in some cases we are dealing with respectful, reasoned and informed disagreement (though not necessarily made explicit). After all, disciples may emulate the Rav without submissively accepting all that he says on haskhkafic matters. They emulate him by replicating the process of creative thought – this in consonance with the Rav's well-known mandate to *talmidim* to think for themselves.[15]

There is another reason that people might invoke for not following the Rav's philosophy, namely, uncertainty about exactly what views to attribute to him. The Rav's ideas diverge from work to work; based on this, one might contend that his philosophical disquisitions were tailored to specific audiences, social contexts, and personal circumstances. Because of the acutely personal and highly contextual character of the philosophical writings, readers – however greatly inspired and affected – may yet hesitate to build a definite, abiding outlook upon what the Rav says in particular places.[16]

While in some cases, reasoned disagreement and methodological caution may account for why the Rav's philosophical work has not had more influence, we need to consider another hypothesis: neglect.

This should not necessarily be said with a critical edge. Whereas yeshiva training makes halakhic discourse familiar (if never easy!), philosophical writings are daunting and difficult in the absence of a comparable educational background. The Rav in particular utilizes a vocabulary and

---

footnotes, creating, to some degree, a separate track of discussion. The first eighty-one pages of *The Halakhic Mind* are also almost exclusively universal in thrust, but those universal reflections ultimately lead to a "particularist" conclusion in the final section.

[15] Dr. Norman Lamm relates a story from his days in the Rav's *shiur*. The Rav asked him to explain a *Tosafos* that had been covered the day before. Dr. Lamm replied obligingly by repeating exactly what the Rav had said in the previous day's *shiur*. "Your problem is," chided the Rav, "that you come in here with your *yetzer hatov*, and you leave your *yetzer hara* at the door."

[16] Another, admittedly speculative, explanation of divergences is the following. Just as in *shiurim* and *derashot*, the Rav on different occasions might construct varying approaches to a single text, problem or position, so too in philosophy he furnished a multiplicity of perspectives on particular problems. In other words, the Rav may have approached each philosophical "assignment" as a self-contained unit; the inquiry would begin afresh.

thought structure which have to be explained in terms of a vast cultural context and which, at many points, show a dated quality. For *talmidim*, there is a real question whether the time investment needed to gain the background is worth the potential loss of growth in *lomdus*. Aggravating the problem of comprehension, the Rav's extraordinary powers of oral pedagogy and *hasbarah* – which navigated *talmidim* through the most demanding of *sugyot* – were not often available as a means of clarifying and disseminating his philosophical ideas publicly. Also, because the Rav seldom referred to the philosophic writings in *shiur*, and it was plain that they occupied a relatively small portion of his time, it became easy to assume that they were not essential to his outlook and spiritual quest. As more and more of the Rav's *chiddushei Torah* appear in written form, the philosophic works will face a still stiffer competition for attention, and some people may quite legitimately argue that they ought to be made secondary in the hierarchy. Our lives are not long enough, nor minds capacious and quick enough, to absorb even a significant fraction of what the Rav's mind had both absorbed and created by early middle age; so we must make choices.

To these more understandable reasons, for neglect of the philosophical writings, I feel compelled to add a less honorable one. Some people perhaps harbored a fear that the concerns, contents, and methods of those writings were sensitive – and should therefore be shut out.

Whatever the reasons for neglect, whether benign or otherwise, in all likelihood the Rav would have been driven to greater levels of philosophical expression had he found a regular forum for discussing theology with others of a similar bent and expertise. Question and criticism in the context of a larger community inevitably force a thinker, particularly a great one, to sharpen his formulations, fill in lacunae, and expand his agenda. It is striking that a classic like "Lonely Man of Faith" was invited by a group other than the Rav's base constituency.

I am not in a position to say how deeply the Rav sensed that his broader concerns were not being widely discussed and assimilated, nor to comment directly on whether, if so, that disappointed him.

Anecdotal evidence from reliable sources suggests he *did* know it and *was* disappointed.[17] Be that as it may, we must beware the potential cost of perpetuating such neglect. The Rav's thought would be appropriated, analyzed and disseminated by individuals who may not be in a position to place the philosophical dimension of the Rav in the context of his total persona. Admirers of the Rav need to preserve and protect that total persona, and accordingly ought to construct their own informed representations of his philosophy and its context.

In closing, I would suggest one final hypothesis to account for the phenomenon I have dealt with. The explanation, basically, is that to accept the Rav's philosophy, a breadth and depth of spirit and commitment is required, that lies far beyond the reach of most people. Let me elaborate.[18]

When I was first exposed to "Lonely Man of Faith" as a college student, I, with others, was deeply disappointed by the paragraph quoted earlier in which the Rav dismissed the problem of synthesizing secular disciplines and religion. Isn't he sidestepping the real problem, we asked? Yet over the years, I, like many who spend their careers in academia, have come to realize the immaturity of that criticism. The more I studied philosophy – and others will say much the same thing – the more I came to realize the limits of the contemporary stress on "rigor," the poverty of intellectual gymnastics. Philosophical problems are first and foremost *human* problems. The ones that really matter are those that engage the soul in its entirety, and the solutions that really last in the minds of people are those that anchor themselves in emotion. As Yehudah Halevi would have asked, how often does an elaborate proof of God's existence create religious fervor?[19] How often does an "intellectual" solution to the problem of evil really do anything for humans who confront evil's stark reality? Significantly, the problem that the Rav chose to deal with in "Lonely Man of Faith" – the

---

[17] Rav Aharon Lichtenstein touched on this question in an inspiring address to the OU at its 1992 convention; he noted both private and published remarks by the Rav.

[18] With regard to the theme I will now broach, I also refer the reader to Shalom Carmy's moving and perceptive essay, "Of Eagle's Flight and Snail's Pace," written for the Orthodox Forum in March 1993 and published in *Tradition* 29:1 (Fall 1994).

[19] Cf. "Lonely Man of Faith," 32: "The trouble with all rational demonstrations of the existence of God consists in their being…abstract logical demonstrations divorced from the living primal experiences in which these demonstrations are rooted."

sense of loneliness and alienation – is psychological; it issues from the whole being and not from cognition alone. Correspondingly, he opted for visceral resolutions, those that could take hold in the deepest recesses of personality, while eschewing philosophical *pilpul*.[20] But to hold on to the visceral resolutions is extraordinarily hard – even for those who, soured on "rationalist" approaches, realize that this is where the true resolution is to be found. The Rav had the needed spiritual depth. We as a rule do not.[21]

Thus it is that in "Kol Dodi Dofek," the Rav denigrates the value of theoretical solutions to the problems of evil, supplanting the quest for understanding God's ways with an emphasis on concrete empathy and initiative, a response that calls for powers of spirit and not mind alone. In this connection, we should recall the unusually intimate bond between autobiography and philosophy in the Rav's thought, which further testifies to the remarkable interaction between personality and intellect. This nexus is plain as day in *Ish Hahalakhah* – in the prefatory citation about Yosef seeing his father's visage, in the explicit reminiscences, in the overall subject and purpose. We meet it as well in the intensely personal statement that opens "Lonely Man of Faith":

> What I am going to say here has been derived not from philosophical dialectics, abstract speculation, or detached impersonal reflections, but from actual situations and experiences with which I have been confronted. [The lecture] is a tale of a personal dilemma.

Personal elements are also detectable in the rousing, often poetic, drama of *U'Bikashtem miSham*, the galvanizing Zionist passion of "*Kol Dodi Dofek*," and much more.

The Rav, then, placed his intellectual quest in an emotional frame and his emotional existence in an intellectual one. If we will never fully

---

20 "This commitment is rooted not in one dimension, such as the rational one, but in the whole personality of the man of faith." ("Lonely Man of Faith," 60).

21 Medieval Jewish thinkers undoubtedly had the same depth of spirit, but the religious character of their intellectual environment made it unnecessary for them to actualize that potential fully. The Rav, by contrast, lived in a climate that forced him to make the potential actual.

understand how he integrated the worlds of *halakhah* and philosophy, still less will we understand how he was able to deal with the deepest and most affecting feelings of human life, both private feelings and universal ones, in intellectual categories; categories which, for all their rigor and high level of abstraction, never robbed the emotions of their richness and authenticity.

Some of the Rav's most stunning intellectual explorations were conceived as *hespedim*. *Hespedim* can go to two extremes – cold, dry intellectualism on the one hand; gushes of inchoate, unstructured, and hence ultimately uncommunicated, feeling on the other. Armed with a perfect *makor* and a breathtaking conceptual apparatus, the Rav took hold of emotions, shaped them, ordered them, structured them; thereby he made them shareable, communicable, comprehensible. Recall, too, that much of the Rav's *halakhah* and *hashkafah* were prepared to mark occasions, from *yahrzeits* to *siyumim*. For the community, the intellectual rhythm of the year was set by personal occasions in the Rav's life. Likewise, much was delivered at especially evocative times such as *Aseres Yemei Teshuvah* and Tisha B'Av.

Halakhah objectifies emotions, according to the Rav, and so too can a halakhic or philosophical discourse enable Jews to deal with highly charged moments. The act of learning produces a *"kiyyum hamitzvah"* – of remembering, of mourning, of rejoicing, or whatever the occasion called for.

To return now to our puzzle: why hasn't the Rav's philosophy taken full hold? We must appreciate the gulf between the Rav's personal spiritual powers and our own. His idea that faith is untranslatable and unrationalizable is not easily internalized. Resigning oneself to incessantly moving between opposing poles – from aggressiveness to submissiveness and back – is an arduous task, and we also have trouble handling the "defeat" inherent in submissiveness, of which the Rav often speaks. We find it demanding to see ourselves as charged with responsibility as both "majestic" and "covenantal" beings, and we have difficulties integrating membership in a particular community with membership in the human community as a whole. A "man of faith" achieves these states; but he is lonely indeed.

I suggest that we think of the challenge ahead, of appropriating the Rav's philosophy, not as the intellectual mastery of ideas *per se*, but as the summoning of spiritual reserves; not as the task of learning from a text but rather that of being inspired by a model. The Rav taught us by example that it is no intellectual embarrassment to be a person of faith in the contemporary world, to affirm belief in the face of powerful cultural challenge. What we require to follow his lead is not more intellectual insight alone but more emotional and spiritual depth. To adapt the final words of "Lonely Man of Faith," are we "entitled to a more privileged position and a less exacting and sacrificial role"?

THE RAV WAS A TEACHER, PAR EXCELLENCE

RABBI DR. NISSON E. SHULMAN

I cannot describe to you how much his students grieve at the loss of this great man. The cry of Elisha, when his master Eliyahu Hanavi was taken to heaven in a chariot of fire, was *"Avi avi, rechev Yisrael u'farashav,"* "Father, O my father, O charioteer of Israel!" So we feel and cry out at the loss of our Master, whom we, his students, called simply and affectionately, the Rav.

He has ordained more than 2,000 rabbis who lead our people throughout the world, amongst them Dr. Norman Lamm, President of Yeshiva University, his son-in-law Rabbi Aharon Lichtenstein, *Rosh Yeshiva* of Yeshivat Har Etzion, and many more. In turn, each influences thousands more in his spirit. No one in this generation has offered greater inspiration and created a greater love for learning and a respect for the intellectual quest.

He was a shy man. He loved his students, but the students had to make the effort to approach him. He was firm, fiery, anguished physically and emotionally. To whatever he turned he showed amazing brilliance. Every area of science, mathematics, physics and philosophy was open to him. Empirical observation was .absolutely necessary. He would not decide a question concerning an electric appliance on Yom Tov or *chametz* on Pesach or household heating or plumbing, until he analyzed its intricacies himself. Even geography and geopolitics was an open book to him. A younger contemporary of his remembers an unusual practice of his, which developed during the Second World War years in Boston where he was rabbi. After Shabbat, rabbis and lay leaders would gather in the Rav's house. He would place a globe in the middle of the living room and would give his analysis of the war campaigns of the week in the various far-flung theaters of war against Hitler and Japan. He often predicted campaigns to come, such as MacArthur's in the Pacific.

He came from a long line of sages: his grandfather, Rabbi Hayyim of Brisk, the Volozhin *Rosh Yeshiva*, his great-grandfather, also in that position, his father Rav Moshe. Each Soloveitchik took immense pride in his son. The Rav used to tell of his grandfather, Rabbi Hayyim, that he would rise out of respect for his son "Rav Velvel" (the Rav's uncle) whenever he would pass his study. Rabbi Velvel then began to enter the house by crawling through the rear window in order not to pass his father's study, thus to avoid causing the father to rise before his son. The same was true of the relationship between the Rav and his father Rabbi Moshe. My father knew them both and was close to them. "The only time," said my father, "Rabbi Moshe Soloveitchik, the Rav's father, was angry with me was when I tried to tell him that he himself was no less a sage than his son."

Rabbi Soloveitchik, the Rav, was a teacher, par excellence. He had a marvellous clarity of exposition, called *hasbarah*. But above all, he was a man of truth. I remember one moment in *shiur* when he exploded into anger. A particularly abstract and difficult passage took two days to analyze, and we left marvelling at his brilliance. The next day, however, with two precise questions, he destroyed the whole edifice he had carefully constructed. He then grew angry that no one else had asked him these questions, saying, "I can't understand how you could let me get away with this! Apparently I could sell you the moon!" And all of us thought that with his power of explanation and exposition, indeed he could. He then proceeded, for the next two days, to reconstruct the passage till it made perfect sense from every vantage point. Another person might have been satisfied with the first attempt. Not he. If it is not true, it cannot be allowed to stand. Truth is to be pursued above all else.

To him, the Talmud was a mathematical system, endowed with even more precision than mathematics or theoretical physics. He was therefore constantly looking for unifying themes in its pages, searching for underlying principles that would run through a tractate, a chapter, a section of Jewish law. "What does this Mishna really say? What does Rabba want? What lies behind his words?" These were his catchphrases, which he would repeat again and again.

There is a family tradition among the Soloveitchiks not to publish in their lifetime. A few essays of the Rav were published as books, but his students overcame this by publishing some of his lectures indicating they were the ideas of the Master. Actually, mountains of material remain. For four years I recorded two hours a week of special lectures to a very learned Congregation Moriah in New York. He took back the only tape, when in those days tape recorders were huge machines. Those reels are only a tiny fraction of what remains. For years he gave an annual major *yahrtzeit drashah*, which drew overflow crowds, standing room only.

This *drashah* in memory of his paternal and maternal grandparents as well as his father lasted five hours without stop. Two hours of *halakhah*, two hours of Jewish thought, and usually he went overtime thirty minutes in each section. No one else could match it. There were teachers who were deep as the sea. There were preachers who were charismatic and thrilling. But none had the combination of both talents. To these lectures came thousands people thronging the great auditorium of Yeshiva University, many standing for the entire time all around the hall, and others using every inch of space in the great study hall in an overflow room fed by a public address system.

His students loved him, despite his reserve. He was the *posek*, decider of Jewish law for the Rabbinical Council of America, the largest rabbinic organization in the world outside of Israel, even though he did not like to decide questions of *halakhah*. He was the head of the Rabbinical Council's Halakhah Commission, and there was no question in politics, medicine, interrelationships of groups, etc. with which he did not deal. Rabbis would call him from around the world with questions. He really cared. He came to my own aid innumerable times. In every response, his compassion shone through. And he also had a sense of humor and of the ridiculous.

I remember once that a commanding officer in the United States Navy demanded I call my "Pope" in order to get a dispensation for shaving on the third day of a Yom Tov Shabbat combination. I said, "We have no Pope." He said, "I can't believe you have no one who isn't like the Pope, and I can't believe you can't get a dispensation so that you can shave in order to appear in the proper military dress code at the great gathering where you are ordered to deliver the invocation. This is a direct order to call your Pope!" I called Rabbi Soloveitchik and remember opening the conversation with "*Rebbi*, will you visit me in the *chad gadya*?" – a slang term for jail or brig. I told him that I know the answer but was commanded to call him, because he is the closest I could find to a "Jewish Pope," and I have a direct order which I am going to disobey about shaving. "At least," I said, "this gives me a chance to hear your voice, in itself an inspiration." He laughed and said, "Well, I hope you pass the test." I did pass the test, did not shave, and even so, he did not have to visit me in jail.

When we had no *mohel* on the base – even though I could train an observant Jewish doctor to be the *mohel* (but there were certain problems with this) – it was his guidance that saved the day.

I remember a particularly touchy question where a synagogue would have liked a strict interpretation which he felt would be out of order since it would be hurtful to someone, and his command was: "Do this resolutely. You must endorse this and allow no other power to influence your decision."

In the Fifth Avenue Synagogue we had the opportunity to make Shabbatons for university students in the area, for we were close to New York University, City University, Columbia University, Barnard and Yeshiva University. We did so successfully a number of times. There were a few powerful synagogue leaders who objected, saying, "They are not our children. Their parents belong to other congregations." Rabbi Soloveitchik told me then that making weekends for college students was *yeihareg ve'al ya'avor*, a matter of life and death. "You must continue to do this," he said, "and must give up the position if they persist in their objection. Because if one Jewish boy and girl would marry who might otherwise have intermarried, you have won your share in the world to come."

The Rav was an ardent Zionist. In his words, "The Mizrachi movement saved Orthodox Judaism from being forgotten in history as far as the restoration of *Eretz Yisrael* is concerned. I might sometimes be critical of certain methods which may be employed by the Mizrachi leadership in *Eretz Yisrael*." "Nevertheless," he said, "*Al mishkavi baleylot*, in my sleepless bed at night, when I see my life in retrospect and reminisce about events and experiences, I recollect certain incidents through which I begin to realize how basic the Mizrachi philosophy was. *Hashgachah*, the Providence of the Almighty, has confirmed the truth of the Mizrachi outlook on the world. We could have been condemned by history to absolute anonymity. Mizrachi wrote a glorious chapter in the rebuilding of our land." Rabbi Soloveitchik therefore would appear at Mizrachi conventions, and offer an annual lecture to them.

To the Rav, philosophy and theology, indeed all thought, was to be based on *halakhah*. We, his students, could therefore never consider him a philosopher or a theologian or a *darshan*, but an interpreter of *halakhah* on every level: *peshat*, the clear explanation; the meaning behind the *peshat*, the symbolic meaning, on the level of *aggadah*, philosophy, and even Kabbalah. Rambam was his friend. He said that when he studies, Rambam is on his right, Rashi before him, Rabbenu Tam and the Rosh on his left.

It is true that the Rav was so sick for the last six or seven years that he could not be reached nor could anyone hold a conversation with him. But at least he was there, and we were reassured by his presence on this earth. Now he is gone. And when I heard the sad news, that the last of the great sages of that generation has left us, I could think of only one phrase of all the passages in the Talmud he taught us: "When Rabbi Elazer lay dying and Rabbi Yohanan came to visit, they both began to weep. The Master asked, 'Why are you weeping?' The student answered, 'I weep for this beauty that will pass from this earth.' And the Master said, 'For this I too weep.'" They did not refer to physical beauty, of course. They meant the beauty of rav and student, spiritual father and son, walking together, in the spirit and the learning of Torah. "For this we must surely weep" (*Berachot* 5b).

HESPED OF THE RAV

Rabbi Yaakov Weinberg *zt"l*

I am not going to attempt to do that which a *hesped* ought to do, that is to characterize and to give over a definition of the meaning of the one whose loss we have come to memorialize. I will, instead, try to be *menachem* or console ourselves, somehow or other to give ourselves strength, to find some way to assuage the feeling of pain, the feeling of loss, that his leaving us has caused.

This is far too difficult a task for me to undertake. I would prefer, perhaps, only to speak in some sense not of the man, but rather of some of the impact he has had; not to describe who he was, but rather to describe some of the effects that his teachings, his presence, his being, have had upon the rest of us, those who he has left behind.

The *pasuk* says, "*Ve'im bechukosai teileichu.*" We all know the *Chazal* that Rashi brings, "*shetihiyu ameilim baTorah.*" The *pasuk* makes it very clear that it is not sufficient to be a great *talmid chacham*; it is not enough to know all of Torah; it is not enough to be a man of *gemilus chasadim*; it is not enough to be a man of gigantic intellect; it is not enough to be a man who fulfills totally all the dictates, the teachings, of the Torah itself. The Torah requires that if you are to be a follower of Hashem, one who keeps the ways of our Creator, you must be *amel baTorah*; you must work with diligence to undertake the burdens in the learning of Torah. Only with *ameilus* in Torah, only with the back-breaking undertaking in your learning, can you be considered and designated as a *bechukosai teileichu*, one who follows the path, the teachings of our Torah.

Strange enough, at first appearances, it would seem to be an astonishing requirement. Is it not enough to keep all of the *mitzvos*? Is it insufficient to be a gigantic *talmid chacham*? Is it so necessary to be one who breaks his back in the study of Torah? Why? Of course, upon reflection, it becomes so clear and so true. Indeed it is not sufficient to do the *mitzvos*. It is not sufficient to learn the Torah. It must be precious to us. The Torah is the reality of the relationship between ourselves and He who gave it to us. It is a *bris kerusah* between ourselves and the One who has taken us to be His children. And if there were not this feeling of this unique preciousness, of that which is special, so meaningful, so joyful, so extraordinary in the Torah, then the Torah does not have that effect upon our existence which, alone, can make us truly those who go the path of the *chukei Hashem Yisbarach.* If the Torah has this meaning; if it does provide us with the understanding of its unique preciousness; if we do, in fact, become aware of that which is unique and special and different about the Torah, then we will necessarily break our heads and our backs and our minds to elucidate, to clarify, to understand, to delve, to know, the truth that Torah gives us. It is only when we are prepared to be *ameilim baTorah* that we truly understand the meaning of *chukei Hashem* and we are truly prepared to go in the path which He has outlined for us.

It is *ameilus baTorah* that designates, that defines, the life of the Jew. Of all the other aspects of our lives, *this* is the source of our continuity, of our survival, of our ability to know and to teach, to give over, and to live by that which we received from the mouth *kaviyachol* and hands *kaviyachol* of *Hashem Yisborach* Himself.

I think back to this giant who has left us, of the incredible breadth, the unbelievable depth of his erudition, the enormity of that which he knew and was at his fingertips at all times, to be brought up and to be a source of teaching and giving over, not just to his students but to all of *Klal Yisrael.* He was a genius; his mind was an incredible mind. Torah took to him like water going downhill. He looked and he understood, he read a page and it was his. He saw a *Ktzos* and he knew from where it came and where it would lead. Where was that *ameilus*? That for which the rest of us have to sit and sweat through earnestly, he took in his stride and it was his because of a mind that was supremely great. He had the ability to speak, to give over, to inspire, to lift up an audience, so that they transcended their mundane lives. They entered, at least for the moment in which they were *zocheh* to hear from him, into a world that was totally different from the normal one, in which they became acquainted with the incredible depth and breadth of our Torah, in which they were lifted beyond their normal capacity by the clarity of his words, by his ability to present Torah in a way that all minds would be able to focus, understand and follow. It was a gift given to him by the Creator Himself. It was not the result as with so many orators who sit and work and practice in front of mirrors. It was a gift given to him by *Hashem Yisborach*. It was his by virtue of a *matanah*. This was no *ameilus* in his coming to be able to do that.

The unbelievable *ahavas haTorah* that this man had, the *ahavah* that he had for a *sevarah*, the love that he had for a *bachur* who sat and learned, the affection that came out of him for the one who asked a meaningful *kashah*, the joy that he expressed when he heard a scintillating *teretz*, the *ahavas haTorah* that was impossible to miss when standing in his presence, when talking to him. The *kavod haTorah!* I was present and saw myself how this giant, recognized and seen by all as being a giant in Torah, stood up *bimelo komah* to pay homage to a young *rosh yeshiva* who walked into the room, who did not reach *karsulav* (his ankles). What *kavod haTorah!* What *ahavas haTorah*!

He learned on his father's knees, he drank it with the milk from his mother's breasts. His father and his mother were *ohavei Torah* and *mekhabdei Torah*. They had no other sense of existence but Torah. It is no wonder that this man grew up an *ohev Torah*, a *mechabed Torah*, one whose life was built and centered upon the greatness of Torah, the learning of Torah, and the joy of Torah. It was from his infancy that this is what he lived on, this is what he grew up with, the joy and the pleasure of a *kashah* and a *teretz*, of a *chakirah* and a *hesber*, of an ability to see beyond the surface. What greater pleasure, what greater joy, did this man have, does *anyone* have, who has been exposed to, and felt and tasted, that extraordinary pleasure that can be had in Torah and in Torah alone, unmatched by any other experience that this world offers anyone? Is it any wonder that he grew up with this *ahavas haTorah*, and with this *kavod haTorah*? It was a birthright that he had and it was this extraordinary facility that made him unique among *gedolai haTorah*.

He was great, clearly, in erudition, in depth, in profundity. There were others of that stature that we were *zokheh* to have in our generation. We were *zokheh* to giants who were as great and gigantic as him, but there was one aspect in which he was unique, in which he was not matched, and that is *hasbarah*. He had the ability to so give over a *sevarah*, to so explain the inner meaning of a passage, of a concept, that his language itself became a part of the learning. This *koach* of *hasbarah*, in placing the words in such a way that the very words described what it was that he was talking about and become a part of the whole concept itself. This use of language, to be able to open up that which otherwise would be hidden, this use of the words of Torah to make it possible to see clearly why it was that one presentation was the truth and the other was not. It is in this extraordinary facility of *hasbarah* that he was unique. In this, he had that which no one else could have. Yes, the Brisker method itself is built on this facility and this ability of presentation. But his *hasbarah* was in a class and in a situation of its own. In this, he was truly unique. But this, too, was a development from a *masoras avos* that he had, from a *zeideh* and a father and an uncle who brought it out of him, who trained him, who gave him the ability and the background with which to be able to develop this and bring this forth. All of this is greatness which means so much to us and which we appreciate so greatly.

We have to be grateful for, and recognize, the Torah that he taught, that we drank, the Torah that he expounded that was a part of our growth, the Torah that he was *marbitz* and brought to hundreds and thousands, the Torah that he gave new insights and concepts that otherwise we would not have been exposed to, or that we would not have come to see and understand. From our point of view, that is sufficient. What more can we ask, what more can we desire from a teacher and a *rebbe* and a *gadol baTorah*, but that he expound and teach and explain and make available to us that which otherwise we could never get? From our point of view, and from that which we have to speak of or be grateful for, there is nothing more that we can ask for or desire.

If we are to understand what he truly contributed, we have to go back to that *ameilus baTorah*. The hallmark of a true *talmid chacham* is *ameilus baTorah*. Where did his *ameilus baTorah* show itself? In what did it express itself? *Rabbosai*, I will tell you that which not many know, because not many could have seen and appreciated it. This man, this *gadol*, this *mechadesh chiddushim*, this man from whom there flowed in a torrent of new insights, new concepts and new understandings, a constant flow of original thoughts, a *ma'ayan hamisgaber*, would sit up nights and be unable to sleep or rest or sit when there was a hard Rashi, a *shevere* Rashi, that he could not reconcile; a Rashba that seemed not to make sense. He could not live with it. He could not exist until somehow or other, he had broken through and resolved the *shverikeit*, the *kashah*. He could not eat. He would not sleep. He would sit, hour after hour after hour. This man would work because that Rashba had to be resolved. There is truth there. There is *emes* there, an *emes* that is hidden, an *emes* that he had not been able to find. And he couldn't live with it. It was impossible for him to bear until he broke his mind and his back working to clarify it, to try to explain it. And then, the *simchah*, the joy, when the resolution came and he saw this is the *pashat* that Rashba is saying. He caught the meaning of the Rashba; he had conquered the world! You couldn't give him millions of dollars and have him react with that sense of joy, of *simchah*, that the resolution of the *shevere* Rashi meant to him. This is *ameilus baTorah*, breaking a back and breaking a mind to understand, to elucidate, to clarify, to come to know the meaning of an *emes* in Torah. Never mind the Rambam. A Rashi, a Rashba! To him, it was an impossible thing to be able to go away and leave a Rashi *shver*, a Rashba unanswered. It was this *ameilus baTorah* that made all the rest possible. It was this *ameilus baTorah* that opened up the extent and the reach of his mind. This *ameilus baTorah* gave and fertilized, grew and was able to absorb and give over, to learn and to teach. It was a vitality, a force, to move the rest of his learning. This *ameilus baTorah* made it real, made it *chashuv*. He knew what Torah was.

The *kavod* and the *ahavah* that he had for Torah did not come just from *masoras avos*, but it was renewed daily by his own commitment to the work, the need to find the *emes* in Torah, to bring forth that which otherwise would be hidden, to reveal the deepest aspects or reaches of that which a *Rishon* or perhaps even an *Acharon* had to say, never mind a *Gemara*, and to give it to us. And, more than anything else, it is this commitment to the other, giving of oneself without stint, without restraint, without qualifications, to give totally and completely, absolutely every last ounce of one's being, through the revealing of the *emes* of Torah, that made him the force that enabled so many to drink with thirst at his feet, and which constitutes the depth of our loss when this man was taken away from us. That vitality of Torah, that *ameilus*, that utter and total commitment to the *emes* of Torah. The rest, perhaps, we will be able to find in his writings; the rest, perhaps, we will be able to find in the continuity of his teachings, through his *talmidim*. The rest, perhaps, we will be able to have remnants of by all those whose lives were touched by his being. But this *ameilus* that he stood for, this totality of commitment, this absolute acceptance of Torah as being truly supreme, the ultimate justification of life itself, the fullness of the meaning of existence itself, is a loss that will not be able to be replaced. This strength that gave all those who came in contact with him some inkling as to what Torah is to us Jews, as to what Torah is to the existence of mankind, and to what Torah is in God's creation will be missing. His presence and his presence alone gave us that, and with the loss of that presence, this we cannot duplicate. It is, perhaps, for those who have been touched by him, to try to carry on his commitment to Torah and to *emes*, to understanding and bringing forth that which is hidden and to reveal the depths, and to do that with a sense that so much of it came from him. With that, perhaps, we will be *zocheh* to a continuity, to an ongoingness of his presence in our midst, and with that we will have to find some measure of *nechamah*.

IN MEMORY OF HARAV SOLOVEITCHIK *zt"l*

Rabbi Tzvi Hersh Weinreb

The Rav was a complicated person. Not everyone appreciated him in his lifetime; not everyone appreciated him after his *petirah*. But I would like the word to go out to communities outside of Baltimore and to the world that this community appreciates, that *Am Yisrael*, *Klal Yisrael*, has lost a great *gadol* and a great *manhig*. Let the word go out that, at least in Baltimore, the *rashei yeshiva* of one of the major *yeshivot* of the United States and the world were all present at this *hesped* and participated actively. Let the word go out that the *rabbanim* of both branches of Agudas Yisrael were present and participated. Let the word go out that every Rav of every major *shul* in this community was here tonight. Let the word go out that at least in this one community there is an appreciation of the *gadlus* of Moreinu haRav Yosef Ber Soloveitchik *zt"l*.

One of the central concepts Rav Soloveitchik left us in his analyses of *halakhah* is the concept of a "*matir*." This concept has its roots in the *Gemara*, especially with reference to *kodshim*, Temple worship, where in order to be able to do a higher-level *mitzvah*, one first must perform various prerequisites; the prerequisites serve as *matirim*. The prerequisites allow one to elevate oneself to a greater height. Rav Soloveitchik taught that the prerequisite for *tefilla*, for saying the *Shemona Esrei*, for daring to pray to God, is *pesukei dezimrah,* saying *shevach vehoda'ah*, praising God, and thereby knocking on His door requesting permission. Rav Soloveitchik taught us that the *birchos haTorah* that we recite every morning are *matirim* for the privilege of studying the holy words of His Torah. He taught that *teshuvah*, repentance, is a *matir* for *tekias shofar*. One has to have permission to do great things, and the Torah gives us ways of achieving that permission.

I seek now permission to offer words of *hesped* in memory of Rav Soloveitchik. I know not what the *matirim* are, what can grant me this permission, except for my humble awareness that I am inadequate to the task. Indeed, anyone would be inadequate to the task of being *maspid* Rav Soloveitchik except for, of course, Rav Soloveitchik himself.

And so I will draw upon two sources: (1) my own inner experience, the depth of my personal experience and (2) the words of the Rav himself.

I remember as an adolescent boy, studying at a yeshiva, a great yeshiva, and studying with my own *zaide*, *alav hashalom*, many many hours a day, one particular year of my youth. At the end of a certain course of study, of several months of *hasmadah*, I felt a bit overwhelmed by it all. How could I make sense of all the *blatt Gemara*, all the details, all the *shakla vetarya*, all the *kushyos* and *terutzim*? It was hard for me to get a handle on it all. I was looking, I later realized, for the *oznayim laTorah*, the handles by which to grasp the mass of information I was beginning to acquire. One day, a friend of mine invited me to one of the Rav's *shiurim* on *Gemara*. He was learning the same *masechta* I had been learning at that time. And, in one *shiur*, I heard him say, "Well, there are two *dinim*, there are two ways of looking at this whole topic. There's this way and there's that way. There's the *ma'aseh hamitzvah* and the *kiyum hamitzvah*. There's the *cheftza* and the *gavra*. There's the *chalos* and there's the *sibah*." And he began to speak in a terminology that for me then was new, but was not new to him although he charged it with a sense of newness. And then I realized that this man had the handles. If I could somehow learn the organizing principles that he knew, I would have a way in which to take all of this information and begin to categorize it, and make sense of it, organize it, remember it; to work with it, to build on it. This was a gift for which I will forever be thankful to him.

A little later, I struggled, as did so many young men of my age, my time, and my place, with what seemed to be contradictions between the Torah that I learned from my grandparents, my parents and yeshiva, and the secular knowledge that I was delving into formally and informally, reading, studying and attending university. It cannot be denied that any thinking person struggles with these conflicts. Some sweep them under the rug, some deny them, some are plagued by them throughout their lives. Others find ways of somehow subordinating the secular knowledge to the supremacy of the Torah, giving the Torah an extra spice and giving the secular knowledge a meaning and a place and a perspective. Most of those who were able to do so learned it from the Rav *zt"l* who was able to be a master of secular philosophy but not to be contaminated by it, who was able to elevate secular knowledge to a higher purpose, who was able to be *mevatel* that which indeed needed *bitul*, and to elevate that part that was able to ennoble and to give meaning and relevance to people of a certain time and place who needed that secular knowledge. The Rav was able to do so; he modeled that for me and I thank him for that gift.

Earlier this evening, Rav Yaakov Weinberg mentioned one of the unique characteristics of the Rav, and that was his *koach hahasbarah*, his ability to explain. There is something else about the Rav that was unique. The Rav was able to speak about his personal emotions. Most *gedolei Torah* that I have heard from a distance, who were great in Torah, surely had deep feelings but never spoke very much about their personal lives, about their personal feelings, about their hopes, their disappointments, the road that they traveled in order to get to where they were, their dreams, their hallucinations, their frustrations. If they would ever speak about it, it was limited to a very private audience. The Rav made his personal innermost feelings the material of his *drashos*, the material of his books. "Lonely Man of Faith" is not just the title of one of his most famous essays; the lonely man of faith is a self-description of Rav Soloveitchik. *Ish haHalakhah* is not merely a title of a work; *Ish ha-Halakhah* is a description of himself. "*Kol Dodi Dofek*," that *kol dod*, the voice of the lover, was beating, knocking on the doors of his own heart. He could speak of his frustrations, he could speak of his loneliness, he could speak of the death of his wife. He could mourn for his wife in public. He could speak of nearly going mad with grief during the year of his triple *avelus*, the year he lost his wife, his mother and his brother. He could speak of these openly, and use his own personal experience to inspire people to greater heights. And the secret of how he was able to deal with all the feelings within him was the Torah, the *nechamah* he found in the Torah.

The Rav published his first major work during the war years and it was called, *Ish haHalakhah*, *Halakhic Man*. It was republished along with some other essays of his, and the publisher wanted to give a title for the book as a whole. He had various titles in mind and came to Rav Soloveitchik just before he was so infirm that he would be able to communicate with him no longer, and asked him what title he suggested. The Rav suggested the following title: *Ish haHalakhah: Galui veNistar*, *The Man of Halakhah: Revealed and Hidden*." It's interesting that with those two words, "*galui venistar*," the

Rav was giving us something that came from deep within him. He was telling us that there are two *dinim*, two aspects, to the world; there are two aspects to man; there are two aspects to God, and there are two aspects to HaRav Soloveitchik. They are the aspect that was *galui*, open, revealed and public, and the aspect that was *nistar*, hidden, secret.

The Rav was a master at giving *hespedim*. He gave a *hesped* for the Brisker Rav, his uncle Rav Velvel *zt"l*, Rav Chaim Heller *zt"l*, and numerous other individuals. On *vav Nisan*, 5717, 1957, he gave a *hesped* for Rav Ze'ev Gold *zt"l*. In that *hesped*, he distinguished between two types of *yamim tovim*: a *yom tov* that has a *kedushah geluyah*, an open sanctity, and a *yom tov* that has a *kedushah nisteres*, a hidden sanctity. Pesach, Shavuos, Sukkos, Rosh Hashanah, Yom Kippur, all have a *kedushah geluyah*. Their *kedushah* is palpable, tangible. One can come into the *beis haknesses* on a Rosh Hashanah, a Pesach, a Shavuos and see. There are *bigdei yom tov*, the *tefillos* are different, the mood is different, the food is different. That's *kedushah geluyah*. But there's one *yom tov* whose *kedushah* is hidden and that's *Rosh Chodesh*. The first day of every month is also a *yom tov*. But we dress normally, we go to work, there's no *issur melachah*, there are no special meals, at least not in a significant sense. *Rosh Chodesh* is a very quiet *yom tov*; its *kedushah* is inward. We say *Hallel*; in the *beis hamikdash* there were *nesachim*, special *korbanos*, but it's a very modest, inner, almost secret type of *kedushah*.

Whenever Rav Soloveitchik would develop a point homiletically, he would not draw from the resources of *drush*, but rather he would draw from the resources of *halakhah*. He would say, "Take a look at *Rosh Chodesh*. *Rosh Chodesh* is very paradoxical indeed. Although out in the street in Baltimore or in Tsfas, *Rosh Chodesh* has very little special *kedushah*, in the *Mikdash*, *Rosh Chodesh* had full *kedushah*. The same *parshah* in *Parshat Pinchas*, which tells us about the *korbonos musaf* for Pesach, Shavuos, and Sukkos, tells us about the *korbon musaf* for *Rosh Chodesh* without any discrimination. When the woman Shunamis is asked why she is going to the *navi*, she is asked, "*Madu'a at holeches elav, lo Chodesh velo Shabbos*?" *Rosh Chodesh* is on an equal plane to Shabbos. And we do not mention *Rosh Chodesh* in *tefillas* Rosh Hashanah, the *Gemara* says, because the same *zikaron* that applies to Rosh Hashanah applies to *Rosh Chodesh*.

Indeed, the Rav wrote that he once heard from his father Rav Moshe *zt"l*, and then later found its *yesod* in the *Hasagas haRamban* on the *Sefer haMitzvos*, that in the *mikdash* there was a *mitzvah* of *simchah* on *Rosh Chodesh* like there was a *mitzvah* of *simchah* on *yom tov*. Explains the *Gemara*, yes, there may be a *din* of *simchah* on *Rosh Chodesh*, but the *din* of *simchah* on *Rosh Chodesh* is different from the *simchah* on *yom tov*. On *yom tov*, the *shalosh regalim*, the *mitzvah* of *simchah* is fulfilled through *achilas kodshim,* while on *Rosh Chodesh* the *mitzvah* of *simchah* is expressed only through *shir vehoda'ah.* But there is a *mitzvah* of *simchah* in both! How paradoxical it is, he writes, that the *kedushah* of *Rosh Chodesh* does not penetrate into the secular world. In the secular world, *Rosh Chodesh* is an ordinary day like any other. However, in the *beis hamikdash*, the weekday *begadim* of *Rosh Chodesh* are not seen but rather we see more deeply than the weekday clothing; the underlying *kedushah* reveals itself in the *mikdash.*

Rav Soloveitchik was a person who lived in both worlds and functioned in both worlds. He functioned in the ordinary weekday world and there all we saw was a *Rosh Chodeshdicke Yid.* We saw a man who wore an ordinary hat and a short jacket and it wasn't black. And you saw a person who had no airs about himself, who spoke perfect English. You saw a person who had much of the accoutrements of the secular world, a person who had a degree, a philosopher who could speak to philosophers – and did. You saw a secular person, you didn't realize that underneath he was saying *Hallel* all the time.

Then you would come into the *mikdash.* You would come into the classroom and there you would see that *Rosh Chodesh* was no different from Pesach, Shavuos, and Sukkos, no different than Rosh Hashanah, perhaps even no different then Yom Kippur. Because, in the *mikdash*, everything else was shed. Gone was Kierkegaard and gone was Kant. Rising to supremacy was the Rambam and the Ravad. In the *mikdash* you saw that underlying *Rosh Chodesh.* On the surface you saw *Rosh Chodesh* as ordinary, but underneath, in the *mikdash*, you saw *Rosh Chodesh* as being *"Zichron echad,"* the same as Rosh Hashanah.

Rav Soloveitchik's name was Yosef, Yosef Dov, Yoshe Ber. He proudly carried the name of his "great" great-grandfather, the Beis Halevi. The Rav often spoke about Yosef and I would venture to say that he saw somehow his own struggle as resembling the struggles of *Yosef Hatzaddik*. *Yosef Hatzaddik* was also a person who wore *kesones pasim*, and Yosef was also a person who wore *bigdei malchus*, was *mishneh lamelech*, spoke many languages and understood them all. And *Yosef Hatzaddik* also had many trials because of the temptations of the world, and *Yosef Hatzaddik* also was misunderstood by his brothers.

I think the Rav saw a similarity between his inner experiences and that of *Yosef Hatzaddik*. He writes, "His brothers thought that personal holiness, a pure heart, a humble soul pouring out to Hashem, that all of these things are not consistent and are irreconcilable with the simple beauty of *olam hazeh*. And therefore his brothers looked upon him with some mistrust and some suspicion." To some extent, he writes, "it was his own fault. He curled his hair a little too much in his desire to impress others and to want others to approve of him. But the brothers' eyes could not discern that all the outer beauty with all of its shine and all of its grandeur was only a veil that covered the true form, the true essence, of this Yosef. His *kesones pasim*, his beautiful cloak, separated him from his brothers. They only saw him from a distance." It is from a distance, the ultimate distance, the unbridgeable distance, that we are seeing him now.

We must remember that just as Yosef was mainly concerned with three things, so too was Rav Soloveitchik. He wasn't concerned with existential philosophy and he wasn't concerned with neo-Kantism. He wasn't concerned with the culture of *Mitzrayim* and he wasn't concerned with the culture of Berlin. He had three concerns.

The first: *Ha'od avi chai*? Is my father still alive? The concern for the past, the tradition, the true *mesorah*.

The second: *ve'es achichem hakoton taviu elai*. Bring me your young children. Let me influence them. This is the message that he gave to the America of the 1940s and 1950s. Bring me your young children, your children who otherwise would be in Harvard and Yale, who otherwise would be in the University of Chicago and philosophy departments all over the country. Bring them to me, bring them to the *bais hamidrash* and I will teach them that, yes, *Od avi chai*.

And finally his third concern: *ve'es achai anochi avakesh*. He was always seeking his brothers. He was always seeking a link, a connection, and this was his bitter disappointment and this was his loneliness. The loneliness of the lonely man of faith. He could never quite find someone to fully appreciate him, to whom he could talk the languages that he knew. They saw him from afar and had all sorts of suspicious ideas because he was an "*ish Rosh Chodesh.*"

On Shavuos, we studied together one of the Rav's *shiurim*, a *shiur halakhah*, on the subject of *birchos haTorah*. It was a long *shiur*; it took me three and a half hours to get through it, for me to explain the background Gemaras, the Rambam, the Ramban, and the *Sefer haMitzvos* that was the *yesod* for his *chidush*. His *chidush* was this, very simply, very elegantly: *Tefillah* is a *kiyum* of *avodah shebalev*. Prayer is the way that a person achieves spirituality, the way that a person worships with his heart by sitting, standing, and taking out a *Siddur* and saying the words of the Siddur with *kavanah*, with tears, with fervency, with concentration. That's how a person achieves *le'avdo bechol levavchem*, worshipping God with all your heart. Rabbi Soloveitchik revealed a pearl and the hidden pearl is that there's another way also to be *mekayem avodah shebalev*. There's another way to serve God with your heart and that's *Talmud Torah*. *Talmud Torah* is not one whit less of a spiritual experience than is prayer. It's not that Torah is intellectual studies and *tefillah* is communicating with God. He based it upon the Rambam in the *Sefer HaMitzvos*, and he summarized the whole pilpul with these words: "The person who studies Torah serves God with all his heart and his soul. He also fulfills *avodah shebalev* and also fulfills *le'avdo bechol levavcha*." The Rambam *paskens* in *Hilchos Talmud Torah*, "Even though it's a *mitzvah* to study Torah day and night, most of one's *chochmah* one achieves at night. If a person wants to be privileged to achieve the crown of Torah, he should be careful with of all his nights and not waste a single night in sleeping and eating and drinking and idle conversation, only with Torah and *chochmah*. The song, the *rinah*, of Torah can only be sung at night as it says, 'Come, stand up, sing at night.' Whoever studies Torah at night, a special thread of grace will be stretched out for him by day."

Rabbi Soloveitchik used this Rambam to fortify his belief that there is an aspect of Torah that can better be studied at night and that aspect of Torah is communion with the *Ribbono Shel Olam*. By day, one studies for knowledge, by night one studies to unite with Hashem. Rabbi Soloveitchik develops this beautifully as you can easily see in the first *shiur* in the second volume of *shiurim* in memory of his father *zt"l*.

I would like to conclude with the words of this Rambam. For ninety years, we had a certain sun, a certain light on this world, a light that could come from Brisk, come from the Beis Halevi and Rav Hayyim. A light that could enlighten and illuminate the words of the *Gemara*, the words of Shas, the words of the Rambam, the words of the Ravad. And it would do so in a language that would reach people whom it would never have reached otherwise. The Rav shed light on dark corners that no other light could illuminate. There was that *yom*, that day. Now we've lost *gedolim*, many *gedolim*, and we see no *gedolim* on the horizon. The period that we're entering into now, sadly to say, tragically to say, is one of being *yesomim*, *ain ozer*. It's hard to see *gedolim* of the caliber that we're accustomed to, and he is among the last of them. And so we're entering into a period of night. And the Rambam is teaching us something very important. We need to realize that there is a *yom*, a *shemesh*, a sun. Yes, we may not have Rabbi Soloveitchik's intellect, but if we study this Torah, if we study the Torah he studied, then we can somehow piece it and create our own light in the night, in the darkness. That is our task, the task of this *dor*, the task of the present, of the future. The task is to recognize that we are in a *laylah*, we are in a state of night, we are bereft of a chain of *gedolei Torah*, the last of whom we've just seen pass away, Rav Yosef Dov Soloveitchik.

But while we are in a night, there's something about the night that's very, very hopeful. Because the night, and the recognition that it's night, brings a certain *anavah*, a certain humility, to all of us and that is the humility that ultimately leads to Torah. As thirsty people seek water, so too the Torah finds itself only among people who appreciate that we're in the night. Perhaps that's the meaning of the Rambam. It's a *mitzvah* to learn when there are great *roshei yeshiva* and great *magidei shiur* and great *gedolei Torah*, and also at night when you can't find great men any longer. Nevertheless, strangely enough, paradoxically enough, we have the hope that we can learn the Torah of the night. If a person wants to be *zokheh* to the crown of Torah, he must not feel defeated by the lack of leadership, by the lack of *gedolei Torah*, by the lack of models, by the lack of ideals here on earth, but rather should remember those *yamim*, those men who shone like days, to be inspired by them and not lose even one night. He should rather realize that if we will study Torah in this *laylah*, in this darkness that we now experience because of the loss of this great *gadol baTorah*, Hashem will reward us for our perseverance in spite of our frustrations, in spite of our feelings of inadequacy. And He will reward us with a special grace that we will have by day.

It's difficult, difficult indeed, to close a *hesped* for Rabbi Soloveitchik because one feels totally inadequate. What I've tried to do is give you some of my feelings, some of his language, some of his feelings, and a little bit of his teaching. And I hope it will whet your appetite so that during your nights you will taste some of his days and we will all be *zocheh* to the full fulfillment of that last pasuk "by day, *Hakadosh Baruch Hu* will command His grace toward us," because "by night his song, the Torah, was with us."

May his memory be blessed and his merit be upon us.

A PERSONAL TRIBUTE TO HAGAON RAV YOSEF DOV SOLOVEITCHIK *zt"l*

Rabbi Saul Weiss

After reading some of the half-hearted eulogies in memory of the Rav, written in various periodicals, I was reminded of the talmudic maxim, "We drink of their water but their names we do not mention" (*Horayot* 14a). Rav Soloveitchik, who was classified by Rabbi Moshe Tendler as "the greatest *rosh yeshiva* of our generation," has taught and inspired tens of thousands of Jews with his Torah and wisdom – indeed, "we drink of his water" but for some misguided and myopic reason, some refuse to mention his name in the Torah world and accord him the proper dignity and recognition among our Torah giants.

Unfortunately, I am not a *talmid* of the Rav. I never attended his *shiurim* in Talmud at Yeshiva Rabbeinu Yitzchak Elchanan, nor did I sit in awe of his presence in a classroom, trembling that his finger would point to me, indicating that I should say the *Gemara*. I did not have the *zechus* to hear his rebuke nor to be chastised by him for failing to properly comprehend the words of our sages. Nevertheless, the Rav was my beloved *rebbe* and spiritual mentor for the better part of my adult life.

I first saw the Rav when I was about 16 or 17 years old. I was then a *talmid* at Mesivta Torah Vodaath – and for some inexplicable reason, attended the Rav's annual *yahrzeit shiur* for his father Reb Moshe *zt"l* which was held at Yeshiva University. Needless to say, I was mesmerized by that first *shiur* which lasted well over four hours. When I returned to my yeshiva the next day, the *mashgiach* came over to me and said: *"Nu, vos hut Reb Yoshe Ber gezogt?"* (What did Rabbi Soloveitchik say?).

From then on, year after year, I was drawn by some metaphysical magnetism to these *yahrzeit shiurim* and I listened to the Rav as he engaged in an intimate dialogue with the Rambam, with Reb Akiva Eiger and with his grandfather Reb Hayyim. And each time the *mashgiach* would ask me: *"Nu, vos hut Reb Yoshe Ber gezogt?"* Everyone, even those who would not publicly acknowledge his greatness, wanted to know what Rav Soloveitchik said. Yes, so many of us "drink of his water, but his name we do not mention."

I wrote earlier that I am not a *talmid* of the Rav, but I did have the *zechus* of listening to his *motzei Shabbos shiurim* for over 15 years at the Maimonides School in Brookline – and it was a rare occasion indeed that a week would go by when I would not relate to others an insight gleaned from the Rav's *shiurim*. Yes, it is true that I never sat in awe of his presence in a classroom, but whenever I had to phone the Rav concerning some halakhic problem in the community, I didn't just pick up the phone – there was first a "*hinini muchan u'mezuman*." I paced the floor up and down. I had to rehearse exactly what I was going to say, so that I would phrase the question properly. My wife knew just by looking at me that I was about to call the Rav. And the Rav always answered the call! I will never forget the time the Rav kept me on the phone for over half an hour, analyzing in great detail an intricate halakhic question. To me, that was the ultimate manifestation of *ahavat chesed* as well as *ahavat Torah*.

A number of weeks ago, Rabbi Moshe Tendler, in commenting on the Rav's extraordinary pedagogical skills, remarked that during the *shiur* the Rav often said that he does not want to impose his interpretation of the *Gemara* on his students. "*Ober dos is nisht gevain emes*!" said Rabbi Tendler, "That wasn't true, for once the Rav gave his *peshat* in the *Gemara*, it was clear to all that there could be no other interpretation. Once the Rav clarified a difficult Rambam, it became so simple that we wondered *"vos is gevain azo'i shver"* (what was so difficult)?

The Rav was such a multi-faceted unique personality that (as has been said by others) no one could possibly eulogize him. There is a rabbinic expression pertaining to outstanding Torah giants – *"Torah u'gedulah bemakom echad"* (Torah profundity and communal influence in one individual). The Rav was unique in that he possessed *"Torah gedulah ve'chokhmah bemakom echad"* (Torah brilliance, communal influence and secular wisdom and philosophy in one individual). Perhaps it may be said that from the days of Moshe ben Maimon until the days of Yosef Dov ben Moshe, no person arose in Israel who possessed that unique spiritual combination.

With the passing of the Rav, who was designated by his son-in-law, Rabbi Yitzchak Twersky, as the *yachid shebador* – the unique one of our generation – we have become a *dor yatom*, an orphaned generation berefit of Torah leadership and spiritual guidance. We wonder if the glory of the Torah world as exemplified by the *gedolei hador* whom we have lost during this tragic decade will ever be reestablished. I believe that the Rav himself alludes to an inspiring message of communal consolation in his insightful interpretation of a perplexing midrash in *Bereishit Rabba* (3:1). The Midrash proclaims that the Almighty is "*borei olamot u'machrivan* – He creates worlds and destroys them." Rav Soloveitchik asks: "What is the purpose of multiple creations? Why did the Almighty build a new world after each destruction? It was to teach us a moral lesson – to build anew after each disaster! Our lives may be shattered and we become disillusioned. We are charged to arise, to imitate our Creator, to rebuild, to refashion a new world for ourselves."

Yes, we have lost the irreplaceable giants of our tradition during this past decade and we are indeed a *dor yatom*, an orphaned generation. We are, however, charged by the Almighty not to become disillusioned, but to recharge our spiritual batteries, to rebuild the Torah world that is crumbling about us, to refashion ourselves by emulating the meticulous moral striving and magnificent Torah obsession of Reb Moshe, Reb Yaakov and Reb Yoshe Ber – may the memories of the righteous be a source of blessing for all of us.

THE CHALLENGE OF THE RAV'S *zt"l* LEGACY

RABBI DR. WALTER WURZBURGER *z"l*

A number of years ago, a reporter who had interviewed the Rav *zt"l*, in preparation for an article on him, turned to me for background information. Before the journalist could address any questions to me, I asked him what impression he had formed of the Rav *zt"l*. He replied, "Never in my life did I encounter an individual for whom even the simplest things were so highly complicated and complex."

Unfortunately, we live in a world that prefers oversimplifications to complexity or profundity. This is one of the reasons why the Rav *zt"l* was so widely admired and so little understood. The Brisker method of Torah learning with its emphasis upon "two *halakhot*," *ma'aseh* vs. *kiyum*, *cheftza* vs. *gavra*, etc. was reflected not only in the dialectical tensions of his philosophy but was actually internalized in the core of his personality.

It is not surprising that there are so many different images that various individuals have of the Rav *zt"l*. According to the *Pesikta*, at Sinai every individual heard the voice of God in accordance with the individual's capacity. We, too, only caught partial glimpses of some aspects of the Rav's *zt"l* personality.

Some pictured the Rav *zt"l* simply as a giant of *halakhah*, a *rosh yeshiva*, who had acquired extensive knowledge of science and philosophy in order to win back American Jewry to Torah. But such revisionist biographies fail to take account of the fact that it was his intellectual and spiritual restlessness which prompted him, in the first place, to defy the family tradition of Brisk and to leave behind the sheltered environment of his youth to study in Berlin. As he once told me, "you have no idea how difficult it was for my generation to move from the traditional milieu and expose ourselves to the currents of modernity. Even my children cannot appreciate it, because they already found a paved road. But we had to pioneer a new approach."

Many individuals were so dazzled by the brilliance of his intellect that they failed to appreciate his religious passion. Because *Ish Hahalakhah*, his earliest published major article appeared decades before this *U'vikashtem Misham*, people confused what was intended only as a typological study with the exposition of the Rav's *zt"l* complete religious philosophy.

Witnessing how the Rav *zt"l* recited *Hallel* and *Nishmat Kol Chai* during the *Seder* left an indelible impression upon me. No one who has observed him on such an occasion could think of the Rav *zt"l* as a cold, detached, purely intellectual *talmid chakham*. Having been exposed to the intensity of his religious passion, I can appreciate why he always spoke in such glowing terms of the joy Yom Kippur brought to him, and why he saw in the Rambam's last chapter *of Hilkhot Teshuvah*, with its reference to the passionate love of God as well as the two concluding chapters of the *Guide* the very essence of the Rambam's religious ideal. Moreover, the Rav's *zt"l* analysis of prayer attests to the profundity of his religious experience.

Because of his uncompromising quest for truth, the Rav *zt"l* refused to sacrifice depth to neatness, complexity to spurious unity. For him, dialectical tension is an ontological necessity – not a disturbance to be resolved. As Jews, we are mandated to live in two worlds. As he put it in his "*Chamesh Derashot*," our goal is to encounter both *chessed and emet*. *Chessed* requires that we actively participate in the conquest of nature and involve ourselves in the effort to utilize our intelligence for the purpose of alleviating human needs and thus contribute to the building of civilization. But at the same time, we also must respond to *emet* – the truth that is contained in the divinely revealed Torah.

The Rav *zt"l* always insisted that the world of Torah be governed by its own autonomous methodology. Just as Kant had contended that the categories governing the phenomenal world cannot be employed outside of the realm of possible experience, so the Rav *zt"l* argued that to employ the methods of science or historic scholarship to the analysis of Torah is an illicit application of categories to a realm to which they are totally inappropriate.

The relentless pursuit of *chessed* and *emet* were to the Rav *zt"l* the very essence of piety. He always felt that ethical responsibility and intellectual honesty were mandated by the religious norm of *imitatio dei* (*vehalakhta bidrakhav*). For the Rav, *halakhah* was not merely a divine system of law to be obeyed, but the matrix of values and insights upon which Jewish philosophy must be based. There was no room for smugness and complacency in a religious orientation which demanded that human beings forever engage in a never-ending struggle to respond to the demands of *chessed and emet,* of Adam I and Adam II, of majesty and the "Covenantal Community." This constant wrestling is the hallmark of Jewish destiny.

Those of us who were privileged to be the Rav's *zt"l talmidim* realize that no amount of words can do justice to the impact of his personality. We shall study his writings in the hope that just as the Rav *zt"l* taught us that the ideas of Torah ultimately may lead to the encounter with the Divine Presence, so may the Rav's Torah result in his continuing presence among his *talmidim* and his *talmidim's talmidim. Gedolim tzaddikim bemitatam yoter mibechayyeihem.*

AFTERWORD

MEMORIALIZING THE RAV: TIME AND THE *MASORAH*

RABBI DR. DAVID SHATZ

The death of a great person often leads to hyperbolic expressions of his virtues and inflated assertions of irreplaceability. With time the sense of loss is lifted, as new leaders emerge to take the person's place. Yet looking back at the eulogies collected in this book with the benefit of a ten-year hindsight, what is striking is that if delivered today they would be expressed with the very same pathos and sense of irreplaceability as when they were first articulated.

Ten years after the Rav's death, our sense of loss is every bit as acute as it was then – maybe even more so. Orthodoxy in America, while in some respects stronger today than in the Rav's time, suffers every day from his absence. Issue after issue inflames passions and divides the community, while no voice speaks as a final authority for his constituency. Over the years, different people proclaim what the Rav did or did not stand for, drawing from various lessons for decisions confronting Orthodoxy today. There is thus an intense struggle to keep the Rav alive so he may continue to be our guide. I offer here some reflections on that struggle. Whereas the eulogies in the book are retrospective, focusing on what the Rav was, this essay is prospective, as it focuses on what the future holds.

Let me share in particular a worry that many devotees of the Rav harbor. To those who knew him or of him in his lifetime, the Rav, for all that he seemed larger than life, was a tangible, accessible and extraordinarily vivid presence. Memories of his voice, his dynamism, and the aura radiating from his *shiurim*, are seared into our consciousness. It is very natural for us to wish that the next generation of students and leaders will maintain the same level of reverence, affection and attentiveness to the Rav as we do. But the question that faces us is whether this is possible, when they lack the first-hand exposure that we had. That is the worry.

A very short time ago, to present someone as a twentieth-century figure was to confer an aura of contemporaneousness, of relevance, of vibrancy and vitality, even if (like Rav Kook) the thinker had died well before mid-century. But what happens in 2010 or 2050? At that point, saying that someone lived in the twentieth century will date him, freeze him in time, rendering him a figure of a bygone era. A person who was a vibrant force in the recent past may hold but marginal influence in the near future. In my generation, what the Rav said and did was news. For the next generation, it will be history. It will be a generation "*asher lo yada et Yosef* – who did not know Joseph" (Exodus 1:8) in the personal, experiential sense. They will not have a memory of the living presence we knew. Can we convey to another generation what the great figures of our generation represent?

This worry can only be exacerbated by the oft-heard claim that only those who knew the Rav on a personal level can understand what he stood for and how he thought. By stressing that the only way to understand him is through memories of his living presence, we imply that future generations cannot know him at all. Surely that is a depressing thought.

Such pessimism can and must be combated. To begin with a small point, audio, videotapes and vivid photographs will help future generations relate to the past, but there is something far more fundamental at stake here. In truth, making personal contact a condition for understanding, appreciating and relating to a great figure, flatly contradicts one of the foundations of the Rav's understanding of time and of the *masorah*.

The Rav distinguishes two ways a person can approach the past: One is to treat the past as dead and frozen, as no longer here. The other is to treat the past as something vital, flowing into the future, as a dimension that can come alive if we use it creatively. Time is not an insuperable barrier to knowing the sages of the tradition; with the right attitude, consciousness and sensibility, the past can be recovered.

The Rav often emphasized that despite the *halakhah*'s emphasis on precise measurements of time, as in, for example, constructing the calendar and setting *zemanei tefillah* (times for prayer), our concept of a *masorah* is of a legacy that bursts through barriers of time.

> The consciousness of halakhic man...embraces the entire company of the Sages of the *masorah*. He lives in their midst,

> discusses and argues questions of *Halakhah* with them, delves into and analyzes fundamental halakhic principles in their company. All of them merge into one time experience. He walks alongside Rambam, listens to R. Akiva, senses the presence of Abbayei and Rava…"*ein mitah u'geviyah behaburat hakhmei hakabbalah*, there can be no death and expiration among the company of the Sages of the tradition." Both past and future become, in such circumstances, ever present realities.[1]

Who cannot learn from the Rav's endearing memory of his days as a little boy, hearing his father give *shiur* in his home, when the Rambam would be surrounded by "enemies," *rishonim* wielding weapons of logic to refute him, but R. Moshe Soloveitchik would come to the rescue with a powerful *sevarah*, to the delight of Yosef Dov. "Father saved the Rambam!"[2] Look how alive Rambam was for him then and in all his later years. "Now too we are friends…. All the Sages of the *masorah* from Moses till today became my close friends." We know next to nothing of the Rambam's one-on-one conversations, but we live with him through his writings. How could we engage Hillel or R. Akiva or Ramban or Rashba or R. Akiva Eiger as we do, if first-hand physical acquaintance were a prerequisite? Which individual who learned in the Rav's *shiur* can forget how he brought *rishonim* and *aharonim* alive, so they were sitting right there, in that world unto itself, his classroom? The concept that temporal and spatial distances can be overcome lies at the heart of our *masorah*. The choice to leap across those distances, to bring the past into the present, to engage the writings of past masters so as to keep them alive – that choice is in our hands and those of our descendants.

Divreihem hen hen zikhronam – the words of the righteous are their memorial, says R. Shimon ben Gamliel (*Yerushalmi Shekalim* 2:5). If we keep the Rav's teachings alive, both his halakhic thought and his philosophy, we keep him alive for centuries to come. Disseminated with ardor, those teachings will keep him in the company of future generations. Realizing the

---

1 *Halakhic Man*, Lawrence J. Kaplan trans. (Philadelphia: JPS, 1983), 120.

2 See "*U'Vikkashtem Misham*," in *Ish ha-Halakhah: Galuy veNistar* (Jerusalem, 1979), 230–32.

nature of *masorah* as bursting through time can thus dissipate pessimism and lead to an energetic vitalization of the Rav in both *halakhah* and *mahashavah*.

The passage of time poses another challenge to those of us who want to see the Rav's legacy perpetuated. As I've already implied, the Rav has left us two legacies – his *halakhah* and his *mahashavah* (I hasten to add that these must not be separated), and he did more than anyone to bring them into a dynamic interaction. Talmudic and halakhic learning thrives today, but the world of *mahashavah*, Jewish thought, languishes, plagued by naivete and oversimplication. Already in his own time, the Rav felt that while his *halakhah* was pursued passionately, his philosophy was ignored. It is obvious from the treasure trove of manuscripts that the Rav left at his death that philosophical works are an immense part of his legacy, and to fail to perpetuate them is to leave out a product of his fecund mind that is of critical importance. Moreover, he cared deeply that his students appreciate religious experience through philosophy.[3]

Rabbi Yitzhak Twersky *z"l* has made the point that the Rav used philosophy as part of his intellectual capital, as an interpretive tool, and that the philosophy is a *tzurah*, a form, in which he couched his *chomer* (lit. matter), i.e., his ideas.[4] But the nature of this interpretive process is clarified in "The Lonely Man of Faith" in a way that might lead us to pessimism:

> When the man of faith interprets his transcendental awareness in cultural categories, he takes advantage of modern interpretive methods and is selective in picking his categories. The cultural message of faith changes, indeed constantly, with the flow of time, the shifting of the spiritual climate, the fluctuations of axiological moods, and the rise of social needs.[5]

The separation proclaimed in this passage between the faith commitment and its cultural translation gives rise to an unsettling thought. The Rav's philosophy plunges into intellectual controversies that raged

---

[3] See "Religious Immaturity," in Aaron Rakeffet-Rothkoff, *The Rav* (Hoboken, NJ: Ktav Publishing, 1999) 2:238–41.

[4] See Y. Twersky, "The Rov," *Tradition* 30:4 (Summer 1996): 28–33.

[5] "The Lonely Man of Faith," *Tradition* 7:2 (Summer 1965): 64.

during the nineteenth and early twentieth century, but thereafter quieted, and it alludes often to philosophical schools whose day has passed. Much of his philosophical vocabulary is no longer in vogue. In other words, precisely because the Rav's philosophy is an act of "cultural translation," precisely because it is so exquisitely sensitive to the spirit of his times, his more technical writings stand in danger of losing, over time, some of their vitality and relevance.

This is a paradox inherent in the genre of *Torah vehokhmah* or *Torah u'madda*. We want thinkers to speak the language of their age. Yet, the more a particular thinker's expressions of a Torah viewpoint are verbalized in terms of the idioms and assumptions of his age, the more he takes account of his generation's needs and circumstances, the more he presents a union of Torah and cutting edge *madda* – the greater the danger that these expressions will eventually become dated and their enduring message lost. Add to this the fact that the Rav himself occasionally stresses the personal, subjective nature of his thought, that he prefers phenomenology (the psychological description of religious consciousness) to logical argumentation on behalf of faith, and that he presents ostensibly contradictory viewpoints in different places – and the task of extracting stable and enduring lessons becomes intimidating indeed. It may be no accident that, more and more, literature on the Rav's thought consists of academic scholarship about the Rav and his context, and not of specific lessons to be extracted from his oeuvre. The genre in which he wrote does not make the extraction easy.

In response, let me point out, first, that the concern with obsolescence is about the Rav's more strictly philosophic works – *Halakhic Man*, *The Halakhic Mind*, "The Lonely Man of Faith" – and not about those works that are relatively free of technical philosophical vocabulary. The oft-quoted remark of a non-Orthodox admirer that "if I am not mistaken, people will still be reading him in a thousand years"[6] is true of works like *Al HaTeshuvah*, even if there is a fear that other works may seem dated because of their less accessible vocabulary. More importantly, some rabbinic figures of the nineteenth century flourished posthumously in the

[6] Rabbi Arnold Jacob Wolf in *Shema*, September 9, 1975.

twentieth, proving vibrant and influential, even though they too showed signs of their times. Rabbi Samson Raphael Hirsch's Romanticism and Hegelianism and time-bound theory of language and symbols did not prevent him from being appropriated throughout the twentieth century and into the 21st; nor in the twentieth century did Rabbi Abraham Isaac Kook's influence suffer after his death, though his thought is rooted in nineteenth-century progressivism as well as Kabbalah. Progressivism was shattered by the Holocaust, but that did not hinder Rav Kook's ascent in popularity. To be sure, part of the reason for the success of Rav Hirsch and Rav Kook is that they did not use the language of philosophy. Recall, however, that Rambam is the most enduring writer in Jewish history, yet *Guide of the Perplexed*, and even parts of *Sefer HaMadda* in the *Mishneh Torah*, are shot through with Aristotelian and neoPlatonic jargon and formulations.

If Rambam traversed the temporal gap, it is because people found in him elements that transcend the particular context in which he wrote, so that those elements could be applied creatively in later times. Just so, what we need to do to perpetuate the Rav's thought is to find its timeless messages. We must feel the duty to expound his works in the idiom of contemporary men and women. Such themes as the dialectical character of religious existence, the need to combine intellect with emotion, the ongoing battle against evil, and the *halakhah* as a source of Jewish philosophy – these and many more ideas can be framed in universal terms that give them ongoing relevance.

Historical studies of the Rav can also be of great importance, but we should develop such studies with an awareness of how a good history may address needs of the present. When R. Yitzhak Twersky *z"l* wrote history about Rambam or about law and spirituality in the sixteenth century in his capacity as a Harvard professor, he excelled at making the history contribute to an ongoing discussion. When a historian is skilled and thoughtful, he can make his subject relevant. It is to be hoped that enough histories of the Rav will not be written for history's sake alone, but with the larger objective of conveying his teachings and establishing their continuing relevance.

In emphasizing the need for spreading the Rav's teachings, I do not mean to minimize a very different way of memorializing him: through stories. He himself often used stories of personalities in the thick of his own philosophical explorations.[7] In the period after the Rav died, I was struck by how much of the eulogizing of the Rav took place through storytelling. There were wonderful anecdotes about his charming relationship with first-graders in Maimonides; his concern for one of his *shamashim* (aides) who was going out on a date but didn't have the proper socks; his *hesed* toward the Irish Catholic housekeeper who had fallen on bad times, and about his hosting a party for a chambermaid at Yeshiva University.

Why stories? The reason, I suspect, is twofold. First, the Rav was such a towering figure that we needed to remind ourselves of his deep humanity. Second, storytelling by its nature does not seek to display everything at once, a task that is simply undoable. Faced with the difficulty of articulating what this prodigious man stood for, we turned to glimpses. I would stress that the stories are valuable, not only because of what they say about the Rav's humility and R. Hayyim-like kindness (R. Hayyim Soloveitchik was known – as his *matzevah* attests – as *rav hesed*), but also because of the way they illustrate motifs of his philosophy. The story about his helping a first-grader who had been expelled from class because she didn't know the *humash* assignment illustrates beautifully, and concretizes, his words describing the Torah community: "the teaching community is centered around an adult, the teacher, and a bunch of young vivacious children, with whom he communicates and communes.... '*Yesh lanu av zaken veyeled zekunim katan*, We have an old father and a young child"' (Gen. 44:20).[8]

Similarly the many stories of his own *hesed* reflect a theme that is utterly central to his thought concerning the Jewish value system, from his writings on Zionism to his endorsement of technology to his analysis of the nature of teaching. *Hesed*, he stated in an address to the Maimonides school, is the password of the Jew. The stories bring out not only the person but the integrity, the unity, between the teacher and his teaching, *harav u'mishnato.* Storytelling and philosophizing are not mutually exclusive; as the Rav did,

---

[7] For an account of this trend, see Reuven Ziegler, "Hidden Man, Revealed Man: The Role of Personal Experience in Rav Soloveitchik's Philosophical Writings," *The Torah U'Madda Journal* 11 (2002).

[8] "The Community," *Tradition* 17:2 (Spring 1978): 23.

we must merge these genres together. Indeed, precisely by fusing personal reminiscences with learned exposition, the eulogies in this volume bring out the many dimensions of the Rav, and ultimately the wholeness of his thought and personality.

In summary, the challenge of perpetuating the Rav's legacy is great, but so is the opportunity to enrich the hearts and minds of generations to come. We need to engage his writings, extract the timeless message in the time-bound parts of his oeuvre, and relate his biography to motifs of his thought. In this way we may see illustrated yet again that great principle of *masorah*: "There is no death and expiration among the company of the Sages of the tradition."[9]

---

[9] I thank Dr. Joel Wolowelsky and Rabbi Reuven Ziegler for their comments.

IN SUPPORT OF MY SON'S CANDIDACY AS CHIEF RABBI OF TEL AVIV

RABBI MOSHE SOLOVEITCHIK *zt"l*

Below is a translation of the letter sent by Rabbi Moshe Soloveitchik on 19 Elul, 5695 (1935) to Jacob Joshua Bauminger, secretary of the Religious Council of Tel Aviv, whose committee was to select the next Chief Rabbi of Tel Aviv. The letter was published at the conclusion of *Sefer haYovel liKhvod Moreinu haGoan Rav Yosef Dov Soloveitchik* (Jerusalem: Mossad Harav Kook, 1984), Vol. 1, p. 620.

Rabbi Emanuel Pinchas Frankel prepared the translation for inclusion in this book.

Praise God, the 19th of Elul, 5695

For the Rav, the Torah genius, righteous and holy, repository of great wisdom and analytical skill, possessed of great breadth of mind and spirit, Rav Bauminger, may his lamp burn brightly.

Though I have not met you personally, I am familiar with your distinguished reputation, and this is what gives me confidence in turning to you. Inasmuch as my son, the true Torah genius, Rav Yoseph Ber HaLevi Soloveitchik, the Chief Rabbi of Greater Boston, here in America, traveled this past summer to *Eretz Yisrael*, and spent several months there, where he became an official candidate for the position of Chief Rabbi of Tel Aviv, the selection of whom is now pending. And it is regarding that matter that I come by this letter to address you.

He really has no need of titles, praises or commendations, for as I have seen in the Israeli press, his Torah and his wisdom have preceded him and declared his greatness, such that he is already established and well-known as one of the great Torah personalities of the generation. But in my opinion, even this description does not capture his full measure and significance, because a superficial familiarity cannot compare to a permanent connection. And who is in a better position than I to appreciate his nature, for I have witnessed his growth and development from the day of his birth until now.

Although it is true that the Torah does not allow for the testimony of a father concerning his son, this aspect of the Law does not apply to a phenomenon visible to all. Nor do I come as a witness, for the sun blazing in the sky does not require a witness to verify its presence. Rather I come only to offer some clarifying insight regarding him, that he is indeed one of a kind, whose uniqueness requires special contemplation, for he is truly a priceless ornament belonging to the people of Israel.

From his earliest childhood, he exhibited awesome intellectual ability, by no means whatsoever commonplace. My father and master, teacher and spiritual guide, the righteous Torah genius, spiritual guide of Israel, of righteous and blessed memory, prophesied regarding him that he was created for greatness, and that he was destined to become a mighty and overarching tree. And when once my father came across a notebook containing my son's original Torah insights, his wonderment was indescribable. He declared that the insights recorded were true Torah ideas. Afterwards, my son's development in Torah and wisdom proceeded in great and swift strides, to the point where he now stands as a Torah giant, in whom all of Israel takes pride.

In previous generations, it was considered a practical impossibility for Torah knowledge and general knowledge to be combined. However, in this generation, it is already possible to find Torah and general wisdom connected to each other symbiotically in certain great individuals. And this is the manner in which this phenomenon has occurred: the level of Torah knowledge attained by the greatest Torah scholar of the generation is transcendent, and comparable to the Torah knowledge of the greatest of earlier generations. While at the same time, his similar greatness in secular knowledge makes him absolutely unique.

There is no doubt that he is presently singular in this generation in his understanding of Torah. His level of understanding is such that it is the counterweight and his opinion is decisive in all the Laws of the Torah; the lighter ones, and the more stringent. Many years ago, the Torah genius, the head of the Religious Court of Kovno, wrote concerning him that the Law is in accordance with his opinion in all areas of the Torah (I am including with this correspondence an excerpt from his letter). And how much more so is that true now, for with regard to true Torah scholars, as they age, the deeper and more settled do their thoughts become.

He knows the entire Torah, from beginning to end, with a deep and clear knowledge. He has studied everything, matters that are still practiced in our time, as well as matters that are no longer practiced, e.g. *"Zeraim," "Kodshim," "Taharot,"* and the laws and procedures involved in the Sanctification of the New Moon. And he is indeed like a "cemented cistern that does not lose a drop" [a reference to the description of Rabbi Eliezer ben Hyrkanos by his teacher, Rabban Yochanan ben Zakkai, in *Pirkei Avot* 2:11 – trans.].

He is the solitary figure in the generation in innovation and insight into the conceptual structure of the Torah. He has prepared a manuscript on all the volumes of the *"Yad HaChazakah"* (the "Mighty Arm," the magnum opus) of the Rambam, soon to be published, and his words there enlighten the eyes, and gladden the heart, as on the day that the Torah was given at Sinai. By grasping his wonderful explanations, everyone feels that his words are true and certain. He is a flowing stream of pure, living water, and the welling forth is continuous, absorbing and exuding the wisdom of the Torah in words that are crafted of pearls.

He was a prodigy and a Torah genius in his youth, and now the entire Torah is inscribed upon his heart. He is therefore capable of teaching and rendering correct decisions in all practical problems and disputes arising with regard to all the Laws of the Torah, in the manner of the most outstanding members of the *Sanhedrin.* And he is a craftsman in more than one branch of Torah study; he acquired in great measure expertise in the "desserts of wisdom" [defined by Rabbi Eliezer ben Chisma as astronomy and Torah-related mathematics, in *Pirkei Avot* 3:23 – trans.], that crown him, so to speak, and give him special grace and beauty.

He obtained the doctoral degree in philosophy with highest honor at the University of Berlin, where the faculty was in awe of his great intellectual gifts, and the unprecedented breadth of his deep understanding. He is an original thinker in the area of philosophy as well, on the highest level of that discipline. He has published some philosophical material in the German language, and everything he has written is from the perspective of holiness.

His fear of Heaven is more important to him than his wisdom [as Rabbi Chanina ben Dosa recommends in *Pirkei Avot* 3:11 – trans.]. He is filled with reverence for Hashem in all his limbs, his tendons and his blood. He is righteous and full of loving-kindness in his behavior. He is literally a work of ethics, and he is capable of being a living example by his Torah, by his wisdom and by his fear and reverence for Hashem.

He is a leader among the leaders of Israel. He is active in public affairs, a person of powerful influence. His personality encompasses everything that is necessary for a leader of Israel. He possesses refined character traits. He practices courtesy at all times. He flees from honor and hates bribery. He greets all whom he encounters with a smiling face, and he holds the key to the understanding of all human personalities. Hashem has also blessed him with sublime oratorical ability, such that it is as if pearls come from his mouth. He speaks eloquently in public in several languages: Hebrew, Yiddish, German and English; and his influence upon his audiences is very great.

His tremendous knowledge of *Chochmat Yisroel* gives him abundant material, he expresses his thoughts precisely, and with an unusual ability to explain his ideas clearly, and by so doing, he captures the hearts of the people. And he receives from them in turn love and honor and respect.

And now I will come directly to the matter concerning which I wish to communicate with your distinguished Torah personage. A city such as Tel Aviv is a microcosm of the Jewish people; it therefore needs a leader of the whole people, one who can speak to the whole nation, and influence all of its varied communities. And now the eyes of all Israel look to Tel Aviv and focus on it. It is obvious that its Chief Rabbi must be the greatest of the generation, a truly outstanding individual, whose influence will extend also to the Diaspora.

My opinion and the opinion of all those who recognize the quality of my son, this great giant, is that he is the one and only individual capable of assuming this high office. He is the one capable of being the "central bolt" supporting the structure from side to side [a reference to the walls of the Sanctuary erected by the people of Israel in the desert of Sinai; each of its walls was strengthened by a "*beriach tichon*," a "central bolt" that traversed the entire length of the wall – trans.). And he will be the one who will be able to attract and hold onto all the divergent ideological camps within the Jewish people. And who, among all the great leaders of Israel, can compare to him, in being a shepherd to our Jewish brethren in Tel Aviv? He is indeed the great leader whose mind and personality encompass all worthwhile gifts. In the area of Torah, he is the greatest of the scholars; he is also a genius in general wisdom, one who has been granted truly unique intellectual and spiritual gifts within the people of Israel. With his tremendous ability to influence others, with all his fresh and youthful vigor, he is the one who can capture the Land in the spiritual sense, and also in the material. His home will be a "place of assembly of the wise" (see *Pirkei Avos* 1:4), and he will influence all the divergent intellectual camps. These will seek Torah from him, those will seek general wisdom, and still others will be bound to him and follow his direction, out of love, honor and respect, as experience has already shown.

I have heard that there are some who say that he is too young for the position. First of all, that is not the case. He is, praise God, may he live a long and healthy life, in his mid-thirties, an age at which in previous generations, intellectually and spiritually great leaders of the generation were accepted in the most prestigious positions, and they had great influence over the Jewish people, and their opinions were decisive in all matters affecting the Jewish religion. And those scholars who were older, cooperated with them in a spirit of love and brotherliness, and they gave honor one to the other. And indeed, the conclusion to be drawn from his relative youth is quite the opposite! It is that youth itself that demonstrates his greatness. For as a relatively young Torah scholar, he is already considered an equal among even the greatest of the more elderly scholars.

"Who is a true '*zaken*'? [literally, an 'elder']. The one who has acquired wisdom" (*Kiddushin* 32b). Rabbi Elazar ben Azariah was appointed "*Nasi*," "Prince" or "Leader," although at the time there were others who were older chronologically, and his appointment was due only to his great wisdom. And he said at that time "I am as if seventy years old" (see *Berachot*

27b–28a). And also, the fact that he was a tenth-generation direct descendant of Ezra proves that he was the appropriate choice, from the point of view of wisdom and from the point of view of distinguished lineage.

In every generation, wisdom is the first criterion for leadership. It possesses the line of authority, and it has built the Congregation of Israel. When Rabban Yochanan ben Zakkai had to make his fateful decision, he chose, instead of any material pleasure, and also instead of the Temple in its glory, "Give me Yavneh and its Torah scholars," for on the preservation of Torah is dependent the preservation of the people of Israel. And he [Rav Yoseph Ber HaLevi Soloveitchik – trans.] is the greatest of the wise, and all the laws of the Torah are measured and weighed in his mind with an accurate understanding, to their very depths.

Now I ask of your distinguished Torah personage himself, and also to exert your influence upon the other members of the Committee, that they evaluate the matter intelligently and correctly. Then they will surely be convinced that he is the only one who would surely succeed in Tel Aviv, in particular, and in all of *Eretz Yisrael* as well, and in the entire people of Israel, as a whole.

May his distinguished Torah personage be written and inscribed in the Book of the Righteous, with the immediate verdict of a pleasant and long life!

From one who respects and honors him,

Moshe HaLevi Soloveitchik

LIST OF SOURCES

Some of the *hespedim* printed here have already been published in a number of different venues. We are grateful to the following rabbis and publications for their permission to reprint their material:

Yisroel Miller, *B'nai B'rith Messinger* (May 14, 1993).

Shalom Carmy, Edward Davis and Israel Miller, *The Commentator,* Yeshiva College (April 28, 1993).

Walter Wurzburger, *Hamevaser,* Yeshiva College (May 1993).

Jacob J. Schacter, *Hamitzpeh: A Festschrift in Honor of Rabbi Milton H. Polin* (New York, 1998), 19–21.

Menachem Genack, Hillel Goldberg, Allen Goldstein, Matis Greenblatt, David Shatz, *Jewish Action,* Union of Orthodox Jewish Congregations, 53:3 (Summer 1993).

Louis Bernstein, Menachem Genack, Saul Weiss, *The Jewish Press* (April 16, 1993; October 8, 1993; September 9, 1993).

Hershel Billet, *Kotlaynu,* Yeshivat Hakotel (September 1993).

Haskel Lookstein, *Kehilath Jeshurun Bulletin* (April 17, 1993).

Jonathan Sacks, *L'Eylah,* (September 1993).

Abraham Levovitz, *Legacy,* The Maimonides School (October 1993).

Alvin I. Schiff, *The Observer,* Stern College for Women (May 1993).

Norman Lamm, *Seventy Faces: Articles of Faith,* Vol. 1 (Hoboken, NJ, 2002), 3–22.

Julius Berman, Emanuel Feldman, Aharon Lichtenstein, Mosheh Lichenstein, Bernard Rosensweig, *Tradition,* Rabbinical Council of America, 30:4 (Summer 1996).

Jeffrey Bienenfeld, Shlomo Hochberg, Jacob Rubinstein, *Viewpoint,* National Council of Young Israel, 35:3 (Fall 1993).

CONTRIBUTORS

Rabbi Julius Berman is a senior partner in the firm of Kaye, Scholer, Fieman, Hays and Handler, and past president of the Conference of Presidents of Major American Jewish Organizations.

Rabbi Louis Bernstein *z"l* was the rabbi of the Young Israel of Windsor Park and a past president of the Rabbinical Council of America and the Religious Zionists of America (Mizrachi).

Rabbi Jeffrey Bienenfeld is the rabbi of the Young Israel of St. Louis, MO.

Michael A. Bierman, editor of this book, is Supervisor of the Rockland County Adult Home, Pomona, NY, and Adjunct Professor of Jewish Studies at Fairleigh Dickinson University.

Rabbi Hershel Billet is the rabbi of the Young Israel of Woodmere, NY and president of the Rabbinical Council of America.

Rabbi Yosef Blau is the Mashgiach Ruchani of the Rabbi Isaac Elchanan Theological Seminary of Yeshiva University.

Rabbi Kenneth Brander is the rabbi of the Boca Raton Synagogue, FL.

Rabbi Abba Bronspigel is the *Rosh Yeshiva* of Beis Medrash L'Talmud, Queens, NY.

Rabbi Shalom Carmy teaches Jewish studies and Philosophy at Yeshiva University. He is editing the Rav's manuscripts on the philosophy of prayer for the series *Me-Otzar HoRav.*

Rabbi Zevulun Charlop is Dean of the Rabbi Isaac Elchanan Theological Seminary of Yeshiva University, and is the rabbi of the Young Israel of Mosholu Parkway, Bronx, NY.

Rabbi Edward Davis is the rabbi of the Young Israel of Hollywood-Ft. Lauderdale, FL.

Rabbi Emanuel Feldman is rabbi emeritus of Congregation Beth Jacob, Atlanta GA., and immediate past editor of *Tradition*.

Rabbi Menachem Genack is the rabbi of Congregation Shomrei Emunah, Englewood, NJ, and the Rabbinic Administrator of the Kashrut Division of the Orthodox Union.

Rabbi Dr. Hillel Goldberg is the Executive Editor of the Intermountain Jewish News, Denver, CO.

Dr. Allen Goldstein is a medical specialist in NY, and had served as the Rav's physician.

Rabbi Dr. Moshe Gorelik is rabbi emeritus of the Young Israel of North Bellmore, NY and a past president of the Rabbinical Council of America.

Rabbi Matis Greenblatt was the Literary Editor of *Jewish Action*.

Rabbi Kenneth Hain is the rabbi of Congregation Beth Sholom, Lawrence, NY, and a past president of the Rabbinical Council of America.

Rabbi Shlomo Hochberg is the rabbi of the Young Israel of Jamaica Estates, NY.

Rabbi Yair Kahn is a *ram* at Yeshivat Har Etzion, and editor of the Rav's *shiurim* for the series *Me-Otzar HoRav*.

Rabbi Simcha Krauss is the rabbi of the Young Israel of Hillcrest and president of the Religious Zionists of America (Mizrachi).

Rabbi Dr. Norman Lamm is President of Yeshiva University.

Abraham Levovitz is President of the Maimonides School in Brookline, MA.

Rabbi Dr. Aharon Lichtenstein is co-*Rosh Yeshiva* of Yeshivat Har Etzion.

Rabbi Moshe Lichtenstein is a *ram* at Yeshivat Har Etzion.

Rabbi Dr. Haskel Lookstein is the rabbi of Congregation Kehilath Jeshurun, NY and the Principal of the Ramaz School.

Rabbi Dr. Israel Miller *z"l* was Vice President Emeritus, Yeshiva University.

Rabbi Yisroel Miller is the rabbi of Congregation Poale Zedeck, Pittsburgh, PA.

Rabbi Elazar Muskin is the rabbi of the Young Israel of Century City, Los Angles, CA.

Rabbi Dr. Bernard Poupko was the founding rabbi of Congregation Shaare Torah of Pittsburgh, PA.

Rabbi Dr. Shlomo Riskin is the Chief Rabbi of Efrat and Chancellor of the Ohr Torah Stone Institutions.

Rabbi Bernard Rosensweig is rabbi emeritus of the Kew Gardens Adath Jeshurun Synagogue, Queens, NY and a past president of the Rabbinical Council of America.

Rabbi Jacob S. Rubenstein is rabbi of the Young Israel of Scarsdale, NY. and a past President of the Rabbinical Council of America.

Rabbi Dr. Jonathan Sacks is Chief Rabbi of the United Hebrew Congregation of the Commonwealth.

Rabbi Dr. Jacob J. Schacter is the Dean of the Rabbi Joseph B. Soloveitchik Institute, Brookline, MA, and series editor of The Rabbi Soloveitchik Library.

Rabbi Dr. David Shatz is Professor of Philosophy, Stern College for Women, Yeshiva University; editor, *The Torah u-Madda Journal*; and editor of the series *Me-Otzar HoRav: Selected Writings of Rabbi Joseph B. Soloveitchik.*

Dr. Alvin I. Schiff is the Irving I. Stone Distinguished Professor of Jewish Education, Azrieli Graduate School, Yeshiva University.

Rabbi Dr. Nisson Shulman was the rabbi of the St. John's Wood Synagogue, London, England.

Rabbi Ahron Soloveichik *zt"l* was a *Rosh Yeshiva* at the Rabbi Isaac Elchanan Theological Seminary, Yeshiva University, and founder of the Yeshivas Brisk of Chicago.

Rabbi Yaakov Weinberg *zt"l* was the *Rosh Yeshiva* of Yeshivas Ner Yisrael, Baltimore, MD.

Rabbi Zvi Hersh Weinreb is the Executive Vice President of the Union of Orthodox Jewish Congregations. He was formerly the rabbi of Congregation Shomrei Emunah, Baltimore, MD. His *hesped* was transcribed by Janet Suness.

Rabbi Saul Weiss was the rabbi of Congregation Agudath Achim, Brockton, MA.

Rabbi Dr. Walter Wurzburger *z"l* was rabbi emeritus of Congregation Shaaray Tefila, Lawrence, NY and Professor of Philosophy at Yeshiva University.